BRITAIN & JAPAN
BIOGRAPHICAL PORTRAITS
VOLUME III

BRITAIN & JAPAN

Biographical Portraits

VOLUME III

Edited by

J.E. HOARE

JAPAN
LIBRARY

BRITAIN & JAPAN: BIOGRAPHICAL PORTRAITS
Volume III
Edited by J.E. Hoare

First published 1999 by
JAPAN LIBRARY

Japan Library is an imprint of Curzon Press Ltd
15 The Quadrant, Richmond, Surrey TW9 1BP

© Japan Society Publications 1999

ISBN 1–873410–89–1 [Case]

British Library Cataloguing in Publication Data
A CIP entry for this book is available
from the British Library

Set in Bembo 11 on 11½ point
Typesetting by Bookman, Hayes, Middlesex
Printed and bound in Great Britain by Bookcraft, Midsomer Norton, Avon

Table of Contents

Japanese Names
Japanese names generally follow the Japanese convention, that is, family names come first. However, in a number of cases in where the subject became well-known in the European convention of given name followed by family name, that practice has been followed in the text.

List of Contributors

BEST, Anthony — Lecturer in International History at the London School of Economics. He is the author of *Britain, Japan and Pearl Harbour: Avoiding war in East Asia* (London: Routledge, 1995), and a number of articles on Anglo-Japanese relations in the interwar period.

CHECKLAND, Olive — Formerly of the University of Glasgow, she is now Associate Editor with special responsibility for East Asian entries of the forthcoming *New Dictionary of National Biography*.

COBBING, Andrew — Associate Professor of Japanese History, Kyushu University, and author (among other studies) of *The Japanese Discovery of Victorian Britain* (Richmond: Japan Library, 1998).

CORTAZZI, Hugh — British Ambassador to Japan 1980-84. He has written numerous books on Japan, and most recently published his memoir *Japan and Back, and places elsewhere* (Folkestone: Global Oriental), in 1998.

GALLIMORE, Daniel — Post-graduate student at Linacre College, Oxford, writing a D. Phil. thesis on Japanese translations of Shakespeare's *Midsummer Night's dream*.

GOW, Ian — Founding Director of the Scottish Centre for Japanese Studies, he is now Chairman of the School of East Asian Studies and senior Pro-Vice Chancellor, University of Sheffield. He has written extensively on Japanese military history, and civil-military relations.

HOARE, J.E. — Research Counsellor, Foreign and Commonwealth Office. Among his publications are *Embassies in the East: The Story of the British and their Embassies in China, Japan and Korea from 1859 to the present* (Richmond: Japan Library 1999), and (with Susan Pares), *Conflict in Korea: An Encyclopedia* (Santa Barbara, CA: ABC-CLIO 1999)

ION, Hamish — Professor of History, Royal Military College of Canada. He is the author of various studies including *The Cross and the Rising Sun* 3 vols. (Wilfred Laurier Press).

ITOH, Keiko   Granddaughter of Kano Hisaakira, she is a consultant on media matters with the World Bank London office, and concurrently a research student at the London School of Economics, working on the Japanese community in interwar Britain.

KORNICKI, Peter   Reader in Japanese History and Bibliography at the University of Cambridge. His recent publications include, *The Cambridge Encyclopedia of Japan* (with R. J. Bowring) (Cambridge: CUP, 1993), and *The Book in Japan: A Cultural History from the Beginnings to the Nineteenth Century* (Leiden: E. J. Brill, 1998).

KURAMATSU, Tadashi   Postgraduate student in the Department of International History, London School of Economics. He has published a number of articles on aspects of naval limitation and Anglo-Japanese-US relations in the interwar period.

MADELEY, Christopher   Lecturer at Chaucer College Canterbury. He is currently working on a study of links between the British and the Japanese motor vehicle industries.

NISH, Alison   Developed an interest in the subject of rugby in Japan during her JET placement at Fushimi Technical High School, Kyoto, where she began to collect the material that formed the basis of her Master's thesis at the University of Sheffield.

NISH, Ian   Emeritus Professor of International History, London School of Economics. He has most recently edited *The Iwakura Mission in America and Europe* (Richmond: Japan Library for the European Association for Japanese Studies, 1998)

KOYAMA, Noburu   Librarian in charge of the Japanese collection in the University of Cambridge Library. His study of international marriages in Meiji Japan, *Kokusai kekkon daiichigo* (Tokyo: Kodansha), appeared in 1995.

PEDLAR, Neil   Taught physics for many years in the International School in Tokyo, and published a regular column in the *Japan Times*. His most recent book is *The Imported Pioneers: Westerners who helped build Modern Japan* (Folkestone: Japan Library, 1990).

PURVIS, Phillida   Currently runs 'Links Japan', which

promotes non-profit sector exchanges between Britain and Japan. She is a former member of HM Diplomatic Service, and worked for several years for the Daiwa Foundation.

READ, Edna   Well-known for her promotion of the arts in Milton Keynes, and runs an art consultancy, Edna Read and Associates. She has just completed the text of a book about her parents.

TAMAKI, Norio   A professor in the Faculty of Business and Commerce, Keio University, Tokyo, and author of *Japanese Banking: a History, 1857–1957* (Cambridge: CUP, 1995)

THORNE, Ben   Life Vice-President of the Japan Society.

TOWLE, Philip   Philip Towle is a member of the Centre of International Studies, University of Cambridge.

TSUNEMATSU, Sammy   Director of the Soseki Museum in London. Among his publications at *The Story of Yoshino Markino* (1997), and the first English translation of Soseki's *Travels in Manchuria and Korea* (Folkestone: Global Books, 1999).

Preface

A Bonding Process

BEN THORNE CMG MBE

Life Vice-President, The Japan Society

EARLY IN 1968 I was sitting comfortably in Hong Kong as No 2 in the British Trade Commissioner's Office when I was 'invited' by my masters in the Dept. of Trade & Industry to transfer to Tokyo and assume the post of Director of the planned British Week Office. Although it offered a coveted promotion I was not all that keen. I had never set foot in Japan, spoke no Japanese, indeed had met only two Japanese in my whole life (as neighbours in England) and really had only wartime propaganda images to focus on. However, my wife, Sylvia, added her voice to the pressure from Whitehall and when I received assurance that I should be able to play cricket there I succumbed.

Within days of accepting I had packed a couple of bags and caught a flight to Haneda, leaving a long-suffering wife to sort out the remnants of our life in Hong Kong, ship everything and with our youngest take the boat to Yokohama where I would collect them in eight weeks' time.

Little did I imagine when I landed at Haneda that this was the beginning of a thirty-year relationship which lasts to this day. In fact it almost ended in a fortnight because I found myself pitched into what appeared to be a no-win scenario. I had a fair amount of experience in the trade promotion field including the successful Hong Kong British Week of 1966. Not another soul in Japan, including the staff being seconded to my office from the embassy, had the remotest idea what I was talking about when I tries to explain the technicalities of the project. The Tokyo retail scene offered almost none of the prime requirements for a successful promotion and the vast web of protection and controls in place was a daunting obstacle. When I explained to my new colleagues what had to be done in the next eighteen months, Bob Irving, my designated deputy told me I and the whole DTI were raving mad and resigned on the spot – well, nearly. I did manage to talk him round and we made a good team as well as becoming good friends.

I was under the banner of the British embassy and its leading denizens at that time included Sir John Pilcher as HM ambassador, Hugh Cortazzi (later Sir Hugh) as commercial counsellor and John Figgess (later Sir John) as information counsellor. Two of them are featured in this book and the third wrote those features. What a formidable and knowledgeable, even overpowering, triumvirate they seemed to me in my isolated position. Partly from pressure of work, but I suspect mainly from distaste for the project that I represented, it was two weeks before Sir John recognized my existence. He relented later partly because he was kind and good humoured by nature but also because he soon found that we had generous provisions for cultural events dear to his heart. The man who made me think I ought to give the project my best shot was Hugh Cortazzi. He was such a blazing enthusiast, had already done preliminary high-level sales pitches to bureaucrats, politicians, and businessmen and was prepared to move mountains daily. Most of all he helped me to get some basic ideas about how things worked in Tokyo.

Sufficient to say that somehow we drew all the threads together and the British Week in Tokyo, opened by HRH The Princess Margaret in September 1969, became the largest single British trade promotion ever mounted anywhere up to that time – perhaps it still is. More important, it was to be a catalyst marking the beginning of a burgeoning business relationship that has grown steadily and metamorphosed several times. From simple, uncomplicated roots largely in branded consumer goods sold through old established merchant houses, both British and Japanese, and retailed almost entirely by the great department stores of Japan, the relationship expanded during the early seventies into technical and industrial trade as well as the arts. Then, in the early eighties, Britain became almost a foster parent for the movement into Europe of Japanese production skills. The effects of the 'Big Bang' also meant an interlocking of financial relationships. All of these things brought rapid expansion of the numbers of British and Japanese living in one another's countries.

Far the greater expansion has been of Japanese living and working in Britain (though I do not underrate the powerful effects of the JET scheme that has allowed some thousands of quality young British graduates to live and work in Japan; the brain-child of a Briton it was picked up and funded by a Japanese government more enlightened than it is given credit for) and all this rubbing of shoulders had undoubtedly brought a level of familiarity, understanding and friendship that would have delighted those Victorian founders of this Society whose vision was to create just such an ambience though they could hardly have envisaged the explosive influence of air travel for the masses and the IT revolution.

Stemming from these and other changes in human affairs and encouraged by the so-called 'globalization' of economic affairs, the political interests of our two countries have become interwoven to a remarkable extent. There is cooperation if the field of international relations that was unimaginable when I was serving in Tokyo in the seventies. Even I never thought the day would come when the two governments would exchange officials of the FCO and Gaimusho and DTI and MITI at working levels. Indeed, in my day mutual suspicion and recrimination, albeit in the most polite terms, were the main part of the daily diet especially in commercial negotiations though there were, in hindsight, glimmers of light.

As for me, I became inextricably involved throughout the seventies in Britain's efforts to understand what was happening in Japan and benefit from the vast expansion of their economy. I served as commercial counsellor in the Embassy for six years, proud to be one of Hugh Cortazzi's successors, and left on retirement from the public service in 1979 just before his return as ambassador. That was not the end of the affair for me as I became and adviser and consultant to various British businesses and also got directly involved in some trading activities with Japanese friends. I joined the Society as soon as I returned to London because it offered a way of keeping in touch with old friends and Japanese affairs and have served in various capacities ever since.

That led me to participation in the early planning for the Japan Festival of 1991 which so magnificently marked the centenary of the Society. Being involved with the main committees I was able to watch from the inside the creation of that mammoth event, costing as it did about £20 million. I played a part in the decision of Midland Bank under its Chairman Sir Kit McMahon (who deserves the greatest credit) to donate £1 million without strings and become British founding sponsor. That led to the subsequent assumption of the equivalent Japanese role by Toyota and a positive avalanche of support. Looking through the official programme one finds several pages of lists that read like a Roll of Honour of British and Japanese corporates and other bodies who gave till it hurt, both money and time. Above all, dozens of individuals on both sides, led by Sir Peter Parker for Britain and Shoichi Saba for Japan, literally slaved to bring understanding and cohesion out of widely differing attitudes and methods of organization. Theirs may have been the largest contribution to mutual good relationships though of course the nationwide multitude of events were visited and seen by hundreds of thousands. Furthermore, the Festival spawned two successors: the Japan Festival Fund and the Japan Festival Educational Trust, in their respective fields, continue to provide rewards and incentives for those still engaged in the bonding process.

The last operational office I held in the Society was as Chairman of the Publications and Lectures Committee and that is how I became involved in the production of this volume. Third in the series, the book is about a further score or so of people who, over the years, have laboured to bring Japan and Britain closer together in many different ways. I doubt whether any of them thought they were doing something special: more likely that they were just doing a job they enjoyed. Yet each of them did achieve something of value in the field of human relations and it is right that we should record and commemorate their efforts.

The labour involved in bringing together all the contributors and contributions ready for publication falls squarely on the Editor. The Society has been lucky to have Jim Hoare to fill this entirely voluntary role. He is a busy man with a full-time job and many other interests. Yet he has been unflagging in keeping the rest of us up to scratch, always constructive and helpful as well as patient with the editorial committee. He deserves all the credit for meeting our deadlines. It almost goes without saying that the contributors were the key ingredient and on behalf of the Society I thank them all for their generous cooperation. Our publisher is another enthusiast for the cause of UK-Japan relations and Paul Norbury has gone beyond the call of duty in getting the book off the press and into out members' hands.

Last but certainly not least, I wish to acknowledge an immense debt to two fellow organizations in the field of UK-Japan relations. The Society is not rich and books of this kind are not capable of being self-financing. Without the generous financial support of the Daiwa Anglo-Japanese Foundation and the Great Britain Sasakawa Foundation we could not have undertaken the task.

Postscript

Reflecting, at the time of writing this message, on the visit to Britain in the Spring of 1998 by Their Imperial Majesties, The Emperor and Empress of Japan, I suspect that this visit may have sealed the bonding process between out two countries. For 50 years there has remained one tainted, unhealed blemish. I mean the issue of the treatment of British prisoners-of-war and especially those in Burma. I have a personal feeling that this boil may have been lanced during the visit and will now heal. Their Majesties were so plainly civilized and charming, so clearly concerned to express sorrow for the past within the constraints of their constitutional position; and the protagonists for the PoW lobby were able to engage the media, have their unfettered say and discover for themselves that time moves on, that the debate is virtually closed. Already the struggle for economic well-being occupies centre stage with Japan and Britain as leading players.

AUTUMN 1998

Introduction

SINCE 1991, the Japan Society has published a series of books aimed at bringing out the role of individuals in developing contacts between Britain and Japan. The first, under a different title, was edited by Sir Hugh Cortazzi and Dr Gordon Daniels, while Professor Ian Nish edited the next two, *Britain and Japan: Biographical Portraits* volumes one and two. I am most grateful to the Society for the invitation to edit this third volume in the *Portraits* series and hope that as a collection it is as useful as its predecessors, helping both to improve Anglo-Japanese relations and increase our mutual understanding.

This time, the period covered is somewhat longer than in the earlier volumes. It begins in the late eighteenth century, almost before one can speak of modern Anglo-Japanese relations, with one of the least known of the Royal Navy's great surveyor-explorers, William Broughton, whose accounts of the Ainu and of the Kurile islands in 1796 and 1797 are still of interest today, as is his account of his visit to Korea in 1797. It ends as up to date as you can get, with the living theatrical producer and interpreter of Shakespeare, Ninagawa Yukio, and with the continuing story of rugby in Japan. The latter essay not only increases our knowledge of a relatively neglected area, the study of the British contribution to Japanese sport, but also serves to bring a new member of the Nish family into the study of Anglo-Japanese relations.

On the way, some familiar and some not so familiar figures take their place, sometimes in roles very different from those which most of us know. The importance of Itō Hirobumi's short visit to London in 1863 is brought out in Dr Cobbing's essay. Sir Hugh Cortazzi's account of Thomas Blakiston, merchant, explorer, and something of a rough diamond, perhaps provides the link between the age of Broughton and the treaty port period. Fukuzawa Yukichi is shown in Dr Tamaki's essay to have been able to exploit his library acquired in London in the 1860s to lay the foundations of a not-inconsiderable fortune, while his role in the origins of the Yokohama Specie Bank provides a curious link to the essay by K. Itoh on the inter-war head of the same bank in London, Kano Hisaakira.

As might be expected, given the large number of Britons who served in that capacity, various employees of the Meiji government (*O-yatoi*) figure prominently. They include well-known figures such as Admiral Douglas and his naval mission, Frank Brinkley, sometime artillery instructor and later journalist and apologist, and engineers and scientists such as Henry Dyer and J.A. Ewing. There are lesser-known ones as well, such as the Rev. James Summers, at one time professor of Chinese at Kings College London, and a man with a talent for causing problems. Summers apart, the only other religious figures appear in Hamish Ion's account of Archdeacon Shaw and Bishop Bickersteth, and their role in the establishment of a Japanese Anglican Church.

One of those who benefited from *yatoi* training was Tanakadate Aikitsu, who features in an essay by Neil Pedlar. Apart from the Douglas mission, naval and military matters feature in Philip Towle's essay on British observers of the Russo-Japanese War of 1904-05, and in Kurumatsu Tadashi's account of Admiral Saitō Makato. Although employed by a private firm long after the classic *yatoi* years, the account of Arthur Penniall and his work in the fledging Japanese motor industry in the 1920s shows links more with the Meiji era treaty ports than it does with the dark days of the 1930s.

There are fewer diplomats than in the earlier volumes. On the Japanese side, Professor Nish restores a British dimension to the life of Aoki Shūzō, usually seen as part of the Gaimushō's German tradition, but a major player in treaty revision negotiations with Britain in the 1890s. Phillida Purvis's account of Aso Kazuko deals with somebody who was on the edge of diplomatic life, while Sir Hugh Cortazzi's sketch of Sir John Pilcher deals with a larger-than-life British diplomat, ambassador in Tokyo 1967-72, who could arouse strong emotions among his more junior colleagues. Sir Hugh also describes the life of Sir John Figgis, soldier, diplomat and connoisseur.

Figgis is not the only figure from the world of the arts, for in one way or another, artists and writers are well represented in this volume. There is Olive Checkland's account of the Meiji painter Kawanabe Kyōsai, Sammy Tsunematsu's interesting detective work on Natsume Sōseki and the pre-Raphaelite Millais, and Neil Pedlar's equally intriguing examination of the possible links between John Morris's pre-war Tokyo experiences, described in his book *Traveller from Tokyo*, and George Orwell's novel *1984*. Clearly, Orwell drew on a number of sources, but it would be hard to quarrel with the idea that Morris's pre-war Tokyo bears an uncanny resemblance to some aspects of *1984*.

In other ways, too, this set of *Portraits* shows a more sombre side to Anglo-Japanese relations. The tensions and human misery of the 1930s and 1940s come out in very different ways, from the essay by Anthony Best on the slightly shadowy figure of Arthur Edwardes, and in his somewhat ambiguous role as a paid supporter of Japan, and the more poignant account by Mrs E.R. Read of her father and his sufferings in detention even before the outbreak of the Pacific War, sufferings also echoed, but more distantly, in Kana Hisaakara's story.

The post-war period was one of rebuilding links. As well as Sir

Hugh Cortazzi's accounts of Figgess and Pilcher, who played important roles in that process, we also have his essay on Ariyoshi Yoshiya of the Nippon Yūsen Kaisha whose happy memories of pre-war London life played a part in his post-war efforts to encourage the re-establishment of good relations between the two countries. Aso Kazuko, daughter of Yoshida Shigeru, who together with his wife featured in an earlier volume, followed a similar path, putting the links and friendships made in pre-war London to good use in Tokyo after 1945.

★　★　★

During the various stages of this work, I have had the guidance of an *ad hoc* editorial committee set up by the Japan Society. It was that committee that suggested the original list of subjects and whose members undertook some of the effort of contacting possible authors. Such guidance was essential, especially since my own knowledge of suitable subjects was very limited. The final roster is inevitably somewhat different from that first suggested, since some of those approached were unable or unwilling to take on the task, while others, hearing of the proposed book, volunteered new subjects for consideration. The result is a book that is also slightly longer than originally intended, with twenty-seven entries.

I am grateful to all the authors for their cheerful cooperation, especially to those six whose texts went missing in the post, and who promptly and willingly provided replacements. I hope that none feels the editorial hand, or the editorial pen, has been wielded too firmly! Apart from the editorial committee, the Japan Society secretariat has also been supportive. Paul Norbury and the Curzon Press have been helpful, as they were to Professor Nish, at all stages of the production, including the initial trawl for authors.

Ben Thorne has already expressed thanks to those institutions that have enabled the Japan Society to continue this series, but I would like to add my own personal thanks as well. I should also express my appreciation to the Library of Congress and the Bodleian Library, for their willingness to make their catalogues freely available and to the inventors of the World Wide Web, who have provided the means of accessing them. The library of London's School of Oriental and African Studies, too, has proved useful. Finally, Susan has lived with this and three other manuscripts at the same time, as always with cheerful support and without complaint, for which I extend my thanks.

J.E. HOARE
London April 1999

1

Captain Broughton, HMS Providence (and her tender) and Japan 1794-98

J.E. HOARE

WILLIAM BROUGHTON'S voyage to the Pacific between 1794 and 1798 is not well known in Britain today. Yet his visits to Hokkaido in northern Japan in 1796 and 1797 are remembered locally with interest. In the Republic of Korea, the 200th anniversary of his visit to Pusan in October 1797 was celebrated as the first known visit by Britons to the Korean peninsula. This is an account of these visits, largely drawn from Broughton's own writings, together with some details of his life and the ships which went to Japan and Korea. Broughton may not be as important as Cook or Vancouver, but he deserves to be remembered for his sailing and surveying exploits.

BROUGHTON BEFORE 1794

Captain William Robert Broughton, Royal Navy, was one of a group of British naval officers who were sent on a series of survey expeditions to the Pacific and North East Asia during the latter part of the eighteenth century. They included such well-known figures as Captains James Cook and George Vancouver. Broughton, who had sailed with Vancouver, was in many ways equally distinguished, with a good record of survey work, as well as a moderately distinguished naval career. Broughton is little known today compared with some of his contemporaries, and his name, once prominent on maps, has now largely disappeared. Yet he made a major contribution to surveying knowledge in his day, and his work contributed to much nineteenth century cartography of East Asia.

* * *

He was born in 1762. By 1774, he was a midshipman in the Royal Navy. He served in the American War of Independence, when he was taken prisoner 'while trying to cut out an enemy ship in Boston harbour'. After his release, he served in the East Indies, where he was promoted to Lieutenant. In 1790, he was made commander of the brig HMS *Chatham* to accompany Vancouver in HMS *Discovery* on his voyage to the Northwest of America, which they reached in April 1792 via Capetown, Australia, Tasmania, New Zealand, Tahiti and Hawaii. The two ships engaged in a systematic survey of the area around Puget Sound, with Broughton responsible for work exploring the Columbia river. In 1793, Vancouver sent him back to Britain with despatches designed to encourage the government to authorize further survey work.

HMS *PROVIDENCE*

On arrival in Britain, Broughton was made commander of HMS *Providence* in October 1793, and instructed to rejoin Vancouver to continue the work of exploration and surveying. The *Providence* was a small ship, a sloop of some 420 tons with 16 guns. According to Broughton's own account, she had been intended for the West Indian trade, but had been purchased by the government 'for the express purpose of bringing the bread-fruit trees from the South Seas'. It was thought that the bread-fruit, discovered in Tahiti some years earlier by Cook, might prove a cheap way of feeding West Indian slaves. She had sailed for Tahiti in 1791, under the command of William Bligh. Bligh had four years previously been commander of HMS *Bounty* when a number of his crew had mutinied and set him and the remainder of the crew adrift in an open boat. Bligh commanded the *Providence* without trouble, however, despite almost succumbing to a nervous breakdown from delayed shock over the mutiny, and the ship had just returned safely with the bread-fruit when Broughton was given her to command. (The bread-fruit was successfully planted in the West Indies, but the slaves never took to it.)

Broughton was not over impressed with his new command. She was singly sheathed in copper, and he felt that ships engaged in distant voyages should be sheathed in wood, and the wood then covered with copper. In any case, she needed refitting after her Pacific voyage and so was moved from Deptford to the naval dockyard at Woolwich. It was not until early 1794 that she was ready. Her crew totalled 115, of which seventeen were marines, and one an astronomer. The crew, with one exception, were all volunteers. The exception was Patrick

Sherry, a seaman who had been pressed into service at Plymouth. He died on 5 June 1796, off San Francisco, when he fell from the mizen-top to the deck.

THE FIRST VOYAGE 1794-96

Broughton's instructions were to join Vancouver on the American Northwest coast and he finally set sail, with secret orders, on 21 October 1794. The expedition only got as far as Plymouth Sound, and there its members waited out most of the winter, not departing from British waters until 15 February 1795. By early May they were in the Canary Islands and the *Providence* reached Rio de Janeiro on 6 May 1795. From Rio, they sailed to the South Pacific, reaching Tahiti on 29 November and Hawaii on 1 January 1796. Broughton noted on leaving Hawaii two months later that the ships' crew were generally healthy, except for those 'who had become infected with venereal disease in the Sandwich islands (Hawaii), but the symptoms of the disorder were not very violent'.

More important to the success of his enterprise, however, was that Broughton at Hawaii learnt that Vancouver had left for Britain. Broughton nevertheless proceeded to the North American coast, and by June 1796 was at Monterey. There the Spanish authorities allowed him to re-provision the ship with plenty of meat, vegetables, milk and 'spruce beer' for the crew, but the Spanish commander remained aloof and unfriendly.

Broughton now had to make a decision. His instructions had been to explore the southern coast of the south west of America, in case Vancouver had not been able to do so. But, as he argued in his journal, Vancouver had good ships and had the time to take on this work. It was safe, therefore, to assume that the exploration was complete. If that were the case, Broughton believed that his instructions allowed him discretion to use the ship in the way he thought that would be most useful. He consulted his officers, and asked them to state in writing what they thought this would be.

Their views coincided with his own intention, which was:

> To survey the coast of Asia, commencing at the island of Sakhalin ... and ending at the Nanking river in 30 [degrees] N latitude. My intention was also to complete the survey of the adjacent islands viz. the Kuriles, and those of Jeso [Hokkaido] and Japan left unfinished at Captain Cook's last voyage.

This would be more use than going over ground already covered and would be welcomed by geographers, since knowledge of the Northern Pacific Ocean would be complete. He also felt that it would only be fair to give the astronomer a chance to practise his skills in unknown areas, as instructed, rather than in places already visited by Vancouver. Broughton estimated that the task he had now set himself would take until the middle of 1798 to finish. So he would continue working until Christmas 1796 and then return to Macau and Canton for new supplies before setting off again. Despatches recording what they had done so far, and setting out their new plans, were left with the unfriendly Spanish commander for forwarding to London as opportunity arose.

Broughton left Monterey for Hawaii on 20 June 1796, where he planned to check the expedition's time-pieces and take on water for the voyage to Japan. While in the Hawaii islands, they lost two marines who were killed for no apparent reason.

JAPAN

From Hawaii, *Providence* sailed towards the north-west coast of Honshu. After enduring the fiercest gale Broughton had ever experienced, and losing all the sails the ship was carrying at the time, land was spotted at daylight on 8 September 1796. On 9 September, they passed 'Port Nambu' (? modern Miyako) and then sailed on past 'Cape Nambu' (modern Cape Shiriya). They continued to the north, and on 10 September, they passed the straits between Honshu and Hokkaido, with the latter stretching away to the north. This was not new territory. Broughton had the benefit of charts dating back to the Dutch explorers of 150 years earlier. Nevertheless, his detailed observations remain of interest.

On 12 September, the *Providence* was visited by fishermen from this northern island. The people were clearly Ainu. They were 'of light copper colour, with dark hair, very thick and cut short behind. All of them had long beards, and expressive good natured countenances'. They had cloaks made from the barks of trees, with blue linen at the cuffs and collars. Each had a piece of cloth tied about the waist, from which hung a knife, and they had silver earrings. They were polite, not coming aboard until they had 'saluted us in a solemn respectful manner, agreeable to the Oriental custom of salaams'.

Asked if the island was called 'Matsmai' (Matsumae), the visitors indicated that was an area further west; they called the island 'Insu'. (At this point in his journal, Broughton gives a long account of how the island was called 'Jeso' or 'Jesso' in the west. He claimed that the Dutch gave it that name because of the hairiness of its inhabitants since 'Eso had the same significance in Dutch as Esau', a claim he would repeat when describing his return to the same area in 1797.) Broughton described the boats used by the fishermen as being like canoes, with additions fixed on them to increase their width.

For some days the expedition stayed in the area, exploring the bay which they called 'Volcano Bay' (modern Uchiura Bay). They were again visited by the fishermen, but this time a Japanese official arrived and told the Ainu to leave. Broughton gives detailed descriptions of the town and harbour which he called 'Endermo', which he said was the name used by the Ainu. From its situation (42 degrees 19 minutes N; 141 degrees 7 minutes E), this is modern Muroran. It was set in attractive countryside, with good soil, and Broughton thought that most things which would grow in England would grow there.

Broughton clearly liked the Ainu, who were gentle and inoffensive, and invariably polite. They spoke slowly and timidly, and he noted that their language contained many Japanese words. He described their food as mainly dried fish, boiled with a little oil, but noted that they also had wild berries and other plants. They kept bears and eagles in cages. He thought these were for food, since the Ainu would not part with them. He also felt that the local inhabitants were under tight control by the Japanese, who tried to drive them away when they approached the visitors, and he noted that the Japanese seemed to eat better than the Ainu.

Yet some of the Japanese also proved friendly and helpful, showing him maps and charts. One had a collection of coats-of-arms of the world, apparently obtained from the Russians, and was able to point out some relating to Britain. The next day, (25 September 1796), the Japanese returned and dined on board the *Providence*. In some secrecy, one presented Broughton with a Japanese chart, and he gave a copy of one of Captain Cook's in return. On 27 September 1796, the *Providence* left to sail north.

NORTH TO THE KURILES

Leaving Volcano Bay, *Providence* sailed east and then north along the coast of Hokkaido to the Kurile islands. This, too, was not new exploration, for the Dutch explorer De Vries had reached the area in the 1640s, while Cook and others had already been there even more recently. There were also maps and charts available, including relatively detailed ones produced some eight years previously by La Pérouse and Lesseps. Broughton described desolate land, with snow lying in the valleys – the year was now well advanced – and few signs of habitation. The weather added to the gloom, with thick fogs making it difficult to observe properly. There was an abundance of marine life, including whales and porpoises. On 17 October, they were off 'Maruchan' which also appears as 'Marikan', 'Marukan', which seems to correspond with the modern Shimoshir (Russian)/Shimushiru (Japanese) island, 'where the Russians are said to have a settlement'. A boat sent ashore found that the Russians were no longer there, but that crosses had been erected at various points and the Russian arms carved or painted at others. The native inhabitants seemed to be similar to those on Hokkaido, though they spoke a different language. They were gentle and seemed poor. They were dressed in bearskins, with Russian boots and cotton handkerchiefs on their heads.

Broughton fell and fractured his arm in a gale in the middle of October, and it was perhaps this, and the onset of winter, which now led him to turn back, rather than pressing on to the north. By the end of October, *Providence* was back at the straits between Hokkaido and Honshu, but the weather prevented her sailing through. Broughton, confined to his bed in pain, decided to retrace his route down the west side of Japan. On 14 November, they had 'a fine view of the famous Mount Fusi [Fuji]', and by 18 November they had left Japan behind. There was little or no attempt to record more than the weather and somewhat distant peaks.

WINTER IN MACAU 1796-97

By 10 December 1796, HMS *Providence* was once more in the islands near Macau. At this point Broughton summoned the officers and crew, and told them that

> ... it was necessary that they should deliver up to me their journals, remarks or whatever drawings that related to our proceedings since the first of September ult., and enjoining them also to secrecy since that period.

No doubt this was a sensible way of making sure that new information should not be broadcast abroad, but it may also have been that Broughton had an eye to his own eventual publication of an account of the voyage – others had done so.

Repairs were put in hand and there was much catching up on the news from home. Fortunately, the East India Company's packet, the *Crescent* was just in from England, with despatches and up to date news.

Once Broughton's arm had healed, towards the end of December, he was able to be more active. Hearing that there was a small ship for sale, he decided to buy her to accompany *Providence* on the 1797 voyage. As he explained in a letter to the Admiralty: 'The nature of maritime surveys frequently requiring a more close investigation than it might be proper to risk in one vessel only'. The ship was 87 tons, schooner rigged and copper-bottomed. She had been built at Shoreham in Sussex in 1788, and was named *Prince William Henry*. Broughton paid a total of £1500 for her; £1169 for the ship, with the balance going to pay off her crew. (Later, the story grew up that the schooner Broughton had purchased was none other than the schooner built by James Morrison and some of the *Bounty* mutineers in Tahiti in 1789-90. But Morrison's schooner was 18 tons, and the story seems to have been a case of mistaken ship's identity.) Events were to prove the wisdom of the purchase.

SHIPWRECK

For most of the period January-April 1797, Broughton remained ashore, writing up his account of the Kurile islands. Meanwhile, the two ships were prepared for the voyage. Fifteen months' supplies were taken on board, sails made and repaired, and new ropes prepared. This last work was done with the co-operation of the local Chinese, who allowed Broughton's crew to use their ropeworks and helped in the process 'at a reasonable consideration'. There were also social occasions, involving Royal Naval ships and East Indiamen, plus the senior staff of the East India Company's Macau factory. On one occasion, the Governor of Macau dined aboard *Providence*.

The ships were finally ready to sail in April 1797. Some of the crew were sick as were some of the herd of pigs. The latter had to be destroyed, leaving the crew without fresh pork for the first time since Tahiti. Broughton attributed the sickness to poor weather, and the lack of sunlight; others blamed the water taken on board at Macau. Sickness on board ship was clearly a major concern for Broughton, who, like Cook and Bligh, was a great believer in fresh fruit and vegetables, and the need to keep his crew healthy. Sickness apart, the other main problem was the discovery on 12 May that the mainmast of the *Providence* was completely rotten. It was bound up with iron hoops to keep it in service.

By now they were past Taiwan and in the southern Ryūkyūs. There, on 17 May l797, all other problems faded into insignificance. At about 07.30 that morning, the *Providence* struck a coral reef off Miyako island. Despite efforts throughout the day to save her, '... at half an hour after midnight, we quitted the *Providence*, leaving her a perfect wreck to the mercy of the sea'. Broughton felt that the officer of the watch, James Vashon, the third lieutenant, should have taken avoiding action. Vashon was court-martialled and dismissed the service, when he arrived with Broughton at Trincomalee in May 1798, but was later reinstated.

None of the crew was lost, though all their goods went down with the *Providence*, as did Broughton's books, papers and mathematical instruments. They returned to Macau, all crammed into the schooner, receiving help along the way from the generally friendly Ryūkyū islanders, who were, however, most reluctant to allow them to wander about at will. While carrying out necessary repairs to the schooner, and reprovisioning her, they had the somewhat disconcerting experience of watching part of the 'Providence' foremast and planking sail past. The mast was rescued, and the iron hoops so recently put on were taken off. The mast itself was 'perfectly rotten'. At Macau, Broughton got passage for some 30 of the crew on various East Indiamen, and 43 others on HMS Swift. Unfortunately, all those on the Swift were lost in June 1797 when she sunk in a typhoon.

JAPAN AGAIN – AND KOREA

The remainder of the crew joined the schooner – now referred to by Broughton as 'Providence, schooner' – to continue the planned expedition which set out on 27 June 1797. Although time had been lost, Broughton hoped to be able to explore the coast of 'Tartary' and Korea, and, he claimed, all the crew were in agreement. They sailed back to the Ryūkyūs – passing and describing, but not naming, the Diaoyutai/Senkaku islands on the way – and at the end of July, they were off Edo (Tokyo) bay, where several fishing boats came alongside to barter their fish for 'trifles'.

In August and September 1797, they again visited Volcano Bay and Endermo, to make new observations and soundings. They were visited by various Japanese from the town of Matsumae, including some of those they had met the year before. These were surprised to see how small a ship they now had. The Japanese, as before, tried to keep Broughton and his companions away from the Ainu, and also generally encouraged them to leave. But, as before, not all were hostile. Broughton noted that those they had met earlier were very civil, and one man supplied a complete map of the Japanese islands, with repeated requests for the gift to be kept secret. Others told them that the Japanese called their area 'Matsumae' after the town of that name, and that the proper name of the island of Hokkaido was 'Insu' or 'Insoo'. They were also told that the Russians traded at a port called 'Ago-dad-dy' [Hakodate], which had a much better harbour than that at Endormo.

When they sailed close to the town of Matsumae, they noted much activity by horsemen, and a body of troops were drawn up near to the landing place. They assumed that this was to prevent them landing. The town itself had a pleasing appearance, with banners flying from the temples, and coloured cloths laid out at other places. No doubt on the foreigners' departure, messengers were despatched to Edo, to report another successful repulse of barbarian intruders.

Because the season was advanced, Broughton abandoned a plan to sail again along the Kurile islands, and instead sailed towards the north of Sakhalin for a short period. He then turned south, and sailed down the coast of 'Tartary' [the Russian Far East and north east China], intending to survey the Korean coast to the Yellow Sea. He sailed fairly close to the Korean coast, but apart from noting the rocky nature of the land that was visible, recorded little of interest beyond the weather and various soundings. The expedition passed 'Tzima' [Tsushima], between Japan and Korea, on 12 October, with Broughton noting that there were fires alight in the early morning, 'a grateful sight, and what we had been long unaccustomed to on the coast of Tartary'.

The first contact with the inhabitants of Korea seems to have been on 14 October 1797. That day, fishing boats came out from the shore to investigate the ship, and the crew of one of these was persuaded to come aboard in the hope that they might be able to show a good place to land. This they did, indicating a way into a harbour past 'some stupendous black rocks some distance from the shore'. Broughton had reached Pusan. For the next two weeks, he and his companions would explore the area, attempt to trade, without success except for goods obviously needed for the ship's company, and generally observing the Koreans at every level from local officials to ordinary farmers.

Broughton wrote that this was the harbour of 'Tshosan' or 'Chosan', situated in the south east of Korea, at 35 degrees 2 minutes N, and 129 degrees 7 minutes east; clearly he confused the name of the country, Chosun, with that of the harbour. He thought that it was a good harbour, though admitted that he had been allowed few opportunities to study it properly and therefore the chart which he prepared was not very accurate. The land was cultivated 'in the Japanese manner' rising in ridges into the hills, for irrigation purposes, and there were trees planted in among the houses. Most of the hillsides, however, were bare except for a few scattered pine trees. Horses, pigs, poultry and black cattle could be seen. The houses were all one storey and thatched.

Eventually, however, noting the growing impatience of the Korean officials with whom they were dealing, and fearing that they might be subject to some form of attack, Broughton decided to slip away. They continued south east, noting the large number of islands through which they were sailing. 27 October saw them off 'Quelpart island' [Cheju-do], which Broughton wished to examine. He did not land, but noted the large number of dwelling houses visible from the sea, and the black rocks which seemed to run around the whole island. He also noted an absence of fishing boats compared to what he had seen among the islands. The Korean officials, meanwhile, had reported the visit to Seoul, though understandably claiming that they had compelled the unwelcome visitors to leave.

RETURN TO MACAU AND THE END OF THE VOYAGE

Around 30 November, Broughton left Korean waters and began the journey back to Macau. There were no difficulties, and they docked – 'in our old situation' – on 27 November 1797. From Macau, Broughton sailed for Madras and then to Trincomalee in Ceylon. He did not publish his account of this section of the voyage, pointing out that it would already be very well known to his readers. Broughton paid off the schooner at Trincomalee in May 1798, and returned to Britain in an East Indiaman, arriving in February 1799. He had been away for four years.

The schooner *Prince William Henry* was recommissioned at Trincomalee as HMS *Providence*, and four of the crew which had sailed with Broughton rejoined her. She served on the East Indies' station for a time, sometimes in surveying work, and eventually returned to British waters. In 1804, she was destroyed while in use as a fireship off Boulougne.

BROUGHTON'S LATER CAREER

Broughton, who had been promoted to Captain while away, served in a number of commands during the Napoleonic wars. According to his obituary, he commanded HMS *Batavia*, 54 guns, the frigate *Penelope*, 36 guns, the *Illustrious*, 74 guns, and the *Royal Sovereign*, a first-rate, that is, a major ship of the line. His duties included patrolling in the channel in 1805-6, and off the coast between Dunkirk and Ostend in 1808-9 in HMS *Penelope*.

In 1809, he was appointed Commodore, though probably only on an acting basis, to command HMS *Illustrious* on the East Indies station, where he arrived in 1810. He was present in the attack on Mauritius that year. In the spring of 1811, he was in command of the expedition against Java which assembled at Malacca and sailed on 11 June 1811. Broughton proceeded very cautiously – the 'most cautious navigator that ever wore a blue coat' – and the expedition was very slow. Almost as soon as the attack on Batavia had begun, Rear Admiral Stopford replaced Broughton as commander, to the latter's chagrin, but according to Lord Minto, governor general of India, travelling with the expedition, to the 'great relief of all in the fleet and the army'.

Broughton demanded a court martial against Stopford, for behaving in 'a cruel, oppressive and fraudulent manner' in depriving him of his command. The Admiralty did not agree, approving of Stopford's decision. Broughton returned to Britain. He never commanded another ship. He was made a Companion of the Bath (CB) in 1815, and appointed a Colonel of Marines; the latter was an honorary title for officers going no further.

He had married a cousin, and they had three daughters and one son. In his later years, he lived at Florence, where he died suddenly on 12 March 1821, some eight months after his father. He is buried at Florence. His tomb notes that his career was

> ... honourable to himself and beneficial to his country. In two voyages of discovery he traversed the Pacific Ocean with the perseverance and skill of a British Seaman. On the intricate coast of Java, as Commander in Chief of the English squadron, he steered his fleet to victory, and secured that valuable island to his sovereign ... .

The National Maritime Museum at Greenwich has a portrait of Broughton in Captain's uniform, presumably painted some time after 1798, but there are no details of when or by whom it was painted.

Broughton, like other navigators, such as Bligh, saw the advantages of publicising his work, and in 1804 he published his only book. The title page was more a summary of the contents than a title:

> **A voyage of discovery to the North Pacific Ocean in which the coast of Asia, from the lat. of 35° north to the lat. of 52° north, to the island of Insu (*commonly known under the name of the land of Jesso,*) the north, south, and east coasts of Japan, the Lieuchieux and the adjacent isles, as well as the coast of Corea, have been examined and surveyed. Performed in His Majesty's 's sloop *Providence* and her tender in the years 1795, 1796, 1797, 1798.**

Although there are some interesting passages of description in the book, it is largely a navigator's account, for fellow enthusiasts. As Broughton himself put it at the end

> ... [I] shall consider my exertions as amply rewarded, if this journal in the opinion of the scientific and geographical part of the world (however it may furnish little amusement to the general reader), is considered as adding to the stock of nautical information, and communicating a more extensive knowledge of the globe.

How well it sold is not known, and unlike some other works of navigation from the period, it has never been reprinted. His surveying work was incorporated into British Admiralty charts. It was known to Captain Hall and his colleagues who in 1816 sailed to the west coast of Korea and to the southern islands while waiting for the return of Lord Amherst's expedition to Peking. For whatever reason, the accounts published by Hall and John M'Leod of their visits to Korea and the Ryukyu islands had far more of an impact than did Broughton's. Both went through several editions in the nineteenth century, and served to bring knowledge of Korea to a wider audience than Broughton was able to reach.

Until recently, Broughton's voyage received very little attention. Occasional references occur in books about Japan and Korea, but they are usually slight and often inaccurate. Broughton's charts and descriptions of the Kurile islands have been used by some Japanese organizations seeking the return of the Habomai and Shikotan islands from Russia. Since the mid 1990s, both Muroran and Pusan have rediscovered this early Western contact, and have made much of the connection. Muroran celebrated his first arrival in 1996, and has erected a monument to mark the visit, while a major exhibition in Pusan in 1997 marked the maritime links between Britain and Korea. Two hundred years' on, Captain Broughton is at least achieving the recognition he sought.

2

Itō Hirobumi in Britain

ANDREW COBBING

'NEITHER choleric nor swashbucklerish', Japan's first cabinet prime minister was outgoing by nature, 'tranquil in manner and always with a friendly smile.' Prince Itō, as the German Doctor Baelz recalled him in later years, remained 'the unassuming and persistently cheerful little man that he had been thirty years earlier when I became acquainted with him as plain Mr Itō'.[1] Even from an early age, his elders had commented on this mild demeanour; in 1858, for example, Yoshida Shōin summed up his affection for the seventeen-year-old Itō by calling him 'sincere in temperament and without show'.[2]

During the course of a long career in public life including four terms as prime minister, Itō Hirobumi rose to become Japan's preeminent statesman and won international renown as the architect of the Meiji constitution. He travelled widely in Europe, America, China and Korea, and it was on his last fateful trip to Manchuria that he died on 26 October 1909, gunned down by a Korean at the railway station in Harbin. Of all his overseas adventures, however, it was his first trip abroad that did most to shape his political outlook when, in 1863, during the turbulent last years of the Tokugawa regime, he escaped with four companions from the Chōshū domain to embark on a student life in Britain.

Theirs was a dangerous mission; unauthorized overseas travel still carried the death penalty and utmost secrecy was required. It was also an unprecedented plan; they were the first Japanese students to arrive in Britain, and the first group of officers to be sent abroad by any single domain. Moreover, the timing of their venture was intriguing, as Chōshū was then orchestrating the xenophobic *jōi* movement bent on the expulsion of foreigners from Japan, and within days of their

13

departure from Yokohama, Chōshū guns began firing on Western shipping passing through the Straits of Shimonoseki.

Just 21 years old at the time, Itō was a fervent patriot himself, and ascribed the growing political unrest in Japan to the arrival of foreigners in the treaty ports. This reflected his contempt for the weakness of the *bakufu* authorities, or what he perceived as their treachery, in opening these ports at all without imperial consent, and so timidly surrendering the 'Great Peace' of the Tokugawa age. He was not just a passive observer; only six months before he left Yokohama on his voyage to the West, he was in the small band of Chōshū officers that attacked and destroyed the British legation in nearby Shinagawa. His motives for travelling abroad were thus somewhat ambivalent, but although he spent less than six months in Britain, this experience was enough to transform his perception of the West, as he then went on to show by demonstrating equal zeal in promoting foreign trade and closer relations with the treaty powers.

Following his return to Japan, Itō's new-found awareness of international affair's enabled him to carve a niche for himself as a mediator between Chōshū and British diplomats in the last years of *bakufu* rule, and later on behalf of the Meiji government in its relations with the outside world. In March 1868, for example, just weeks after the demise of the Tokugawa regime, the Emperor Meiji held audiences in Osaka for foreign representatives including the British minister Sir Harry Parkes. This was the first time any of them had seen the elusive figure they knew of as the Mikado and, even now, the young Emperor was seated at a distance, partially hidden from view beneath a canopy. Kneeling in front of the imperial dais in the role of interpreter and busy coordinating proceedings was Itō Hirobumi. He was still only 27 years old.

★ ★ ★

Itō came from a humble background in the Kumage district of Suō province. Born in October 1841 in the village of Tsukami as the only son of Hayashi Jūzō, his father's small plot of land yielded barely enough to survive. At the age of five, he and his mother were sent to stay with relatives nearby, while Jūzō set off alone across the mountains to the castle town of Hagi in a final bid to revive the family fortunes. After two years employed in a variety of menial tasks, he was able to summon his wife and child to join him there, and his young son, too, began the life of a servant engaged in a succession of samurai households.

In 1854, after years of faithful service to the Itō family, Jūzō inherited his master's name and house in Hagi. While this did not confer anything like full samurai status, the young Itō at least became eligible to serve in the lower ranks of the Chōshū domain. The arrival of Perry's 'Black Ships' the year before had alerted the *bakufu* to the weaknesses in Japan's sea defences, and instructions arrived from Edo for troops to be sent to guard the coast around Kamakura. In 1856, the fifteen-year-old Itō was among those ordered to join the Chōshū contingents there.[3]

Shortly after his arrival, he was placed under the command of Kuruhara Ryōzō, a former pupil of Yoshida Shōin. Kuruhara quickly recognized his potential, and it was through his influence that Itō's training in the samurai arts began in earnest. A strict daily regime encouraged him to develop a warrior's qualities of self-discipline and resilience, and when his term of service ended the following year, Kuruhara gave him a letter of introduction to present to Yoshida Shōin on his arrival back in Hagi.

Itō then spent a year at the famous Shōkason Juku school where the patriotic Yoshida, enraged by the *bakufu*'s capitulation to Perry's demands, exhorted his pupils to fight for the honour of Japan. It was there that that he came into contact with figures like Takasugi Shinsaku and Kusaka Genzui who were soon to become prominent Chōshū activists in the political struggles of the 1860s. They were among Yoshida's veteran pupils and his greatest hopes for the future, while Itō, then just sixteen, was still considered a rather junior figure in the juku's fine array of talent.

Meanwhile, Kuruhara's ongoing support gave Itō further opportunities to broaden his horizons. In late 1858 he took him to Nagasaki, where he received several months of military training at the mansion (*yashiki*) kept there by the Chōshū domain. On their return to Hagi in July 1859, Kuruhara introduced him to his brother-in-law, Katsura Kogorō (the later Kido Takayoshi), who was already a senior official based at one of Chōshū's *yashiki* in Edo. Katsura agreed to take him under his wing and they both left for the *bakufu* capital shortly afterwards. Itō spent the next three-and-a-half years with Katsura in Edo, and accompanied him on several visits to the imperial capital of Kyoto.

On personal grounds alone, the young Itō soon had good cause to harbour resentment against the *bakufu* authorities. His arrival in Edo coincided with the Ansei Purge, the brutal attempt by the Great Councillor, Ii Naosuke, to crush political opposition. Among the victims who were arrested and taken to Edo was Yoshida Shōin, and after just two weeks in the *bakufu* capital, Ito learned that his former master had been sentenced and executed. Together with Katsura, he was one of four Chōshū officers who, after much pleading, were allowed to collect his body and organize a funeral.[4]

15

In the service of Katsura in Edo, Itō was increasingly inveigled in a ruthless world of political intrigue, and met a number of extremists who had been stung into coordinating resistance to the *bakufu* by the painful memory of the Ansei Purge. Katsura, for example, was on familiar terms with several masterless *rōnin* from Mito, including those who waylaid and assassinated Ii Naosuke in 1860. When a similar attempt on the life of Ii's successor, Andō Nobumasa, ended in failure early in 1862, Katsura narrowly avoided charges of complicity in the plot himself after one conspirator fled to his Chōshū *yashiki* and promptly committed suicide there. Katsura remained silent throughout the following *bakufu* inquest, leaving Itō to concoct a tale insisting that his master had been out at the time. They both escaped with just a warning, but the faith that Katsura had placed in his young protegé on this occasion was perhaps an early indication of Itō's mediating skills.[5]

★ ★ ★

In a letter home to his father in 1861, Itō wrote: 'Ever since the arrival of the foreigners in such great numbers, all the people from the townsfolk to the peasants have been suffering great hardships'.[6] Like many of his peers in Chōshū, he was receptive to the growing calls for *jōi*, the slogan 'to expel the barbarian', and by extension, to attack the political authority of the Tokugawa *bakufu*. In January 1863, therefore, he listened with enthusiasm to Takasugi Shinsaku's plans for an attack on the newly completed British legation building on the hill of Gotenyama in Shinagawa. Itō became a member of the 'Mitategumi', a group of thirteen Chōshū volunteers formed by Takasugi for the task. Also involved were Shidō Monta (later known as Inoue Kaoru) and Yamao Yōzō, both of whom were to escape abroad with him less than six months later.

Takasugi was incensed by the duplicity of the *bakufu* authorities in pressing ahead with the construction of new diplomatic buildings, even though they had already received orders from the imperial court to expel foreigners from Japan. Such an attack, he hoped, could serve to unite opposition to the *bakufu* under the banner of *jōi*. Unlike Itō, however, he already knew that it was unrealistic to dream of closing the treaty ports by force; only months before, for instance, he himself had spent several weeks in Shanghai with a *bakufu* delegation, and had recorded conditions there in some detail. The scheme was calculated rather to embarrass the Tokugawa authorities without incurring excessive demands for reprisals from the British. After all, the legation building was still empty and protected only by native guards, so the costs of any damage would have to be met by the *bakufu*.

After dark on 31 January, the Mitategumi attacked and set fire to the

British legation; Itō later recalled how they broke through the perimeter fence using a handsaw which he had procured nearby. He was now committed to an active role in the unfolding struggle around him, whether it be in the name of expelling barbarians or for the sake of loyalty to the Emperor. Nine days later, he and Yamao waylaid and killed a scholar called Hanawa Jirō; according to rumour in Edo, the victim's crime was to have received orders from the *bakufu* to prepare a report on historical precedents for abolishing the imperial line.[7]

Soon afterwards, the Shogun bowed to mounting pressure from the court and finally undertook to implement the policy of *jōi*. The operation was due to commence on 25 June although, in the event, only Chōshū took any action. At the same time, Chōshū officials in Kyoto were already making plans to send some officers abroad, for some senior retainers were keenly aware of the need for knowledge of the West. Subu Masanosuke, for example, argued that, even if the treaty ports were successfully closed in the short term, a deeper understanding of the outside world would still be essential to meet the requirements of foreign relations in future years.[8]

The expedition was planned in May. It was perhaps Shidō Monta who first approached Chōshū officials on the subject, while two other officers, Yamao Yōzō and Nomura Yakichi (later known as Inoue Masaru), also arrived in Kyoto expressing a desire to take part in such a venture. Yamao had been overseas before in 1861 when he joined a *bakufu* expedition to inspect Russian-held territory north of Japan, while Nomura had already spent a year studying English in Hakodate. Subu Masanosuke soon informed them confidentially that the Chōshū authorities had approved their plan, and on 4 June, they received an order granting them five years leave to study abroad.[9]

Itō was also then in Kyoto, and Shidō urged him to join them in escaping to the West. Itō was not easily persuaded, however, and Kusaka Genzui for one told him that this was no time to be running off abroad. In the end, however, he could not resist such a chance to see the outside world for himself, as he had long since nurtured a desire to learn English and travel overseas. In a letter to Kuruhara in late 1860, for example, he had voiced his jealousy of Ishida Tarō, a Chōshū officer who had been sent to Nagasaki to study English. In a letter to Ishida the following year, he wrote of his wish to travel to Britain, and in 1862, shortly before the attack on the British legation at Gotenyama, he wrote with some emphasis that 'Shido is already thinking of going abroad'.[10]

Itō may have been dreaming of travel to Britain one minute and attacking foreign legations the next, but these were not incompatible ideas. Although bitterly opposed to opening the treaty ports, for example, Yoshida Shōin had encouraged his pupils to seek overseas knowledge, and in 1854, he himself had made an unsuccessful attempt to escape to America on one of Perry's ships moored off the coast of Shimoda. Languishing in prison shortly afterwards, he had written of his wish 'to go abroad and make a detailed study of every country so as to be able to devise a master strategy for the sake of Japan'.[11] Yoshida the patriot would have approved of Itō's bold words to his companions just hours before they left Japan in 1863 that their voyage to the West was not for Chōshū alone but for the sake of the Empire itself.[12]

The man chosen to help arrange the escape was Satō Teijirō, assistant manager at the Yokohama branch of Daikokuya, a merchant house operating under the patronage of the Chōshū domain. He was considered reliable enough to be trusted with such a delicate venture, for 'although a merchant, he was a man of letters'. Moreover, as Subu Masanosuke pointed out, he was ideally suited to the task because he had helped negotiate Chōshū's purchase of two ships from Jardine Matheson the year before, and already knew S.J.Gower, the company representative in Yokohama. On 18 May, Satō was summoned for an interview with Subu in Kyoto. 'I want you to buy some machines', Subu told him, 'but this time they are to be living machines.' Promising to guard these secrets with his life, Satō returned to Yokohama to broach the matter with Gower.[13]

Itō was not yet officially part of Chōshū's plans for the mission, and he was sent back to Edo shortly afterwards with orders to purchase foreign arms in Yokohama. The American merchants he saw there, however, showed concern over the growing threat of war against the treaty powers and he could find no one prepared to sell. Yamao was also back in Edo, and after visiting Gower in Yokohama on 18 June, he returned with more encouraging news. As arranged, Gower already knew of their plans through Satō Teijirō who had reached the treaty port five days before, and he was prepared to help them escape. Language proved to be no barrier, as Itō later recalled that Gower spoke excellent Japanese.[14]

Three days later, Shidō and Nomura arrived from Kyoto; an officer called Endō Kinsuke had also volunteered to join them, so there were now five Chōshū men planning to escape to Britain. On 22 June, Shidō went to Yokohama for further talks with Gower who introduced him to William Keswick, a Jardine Matheson colleague, and also to the captain of the *Chelswick*, a company ship that was due to sail for Shanghai on the morning of 27 June. He was shocked to learn, however, that they would each have to pay Gower a sum of at least 1,000 *ryō*; 400 *ryō* for their passage and 600 *ryō* to live and study in London for a year. In Japanese terms this was a fantastic sum, as a handful of *ryō* was usually considered enough to live on for several months, but unfavourable exchange rates made the cost of overseas travel forbiddingly high. As the Chōshū authorities had granted Shidō, Yamao and Nomura just 200 *ryō* each, they only had 600 *ryō* between them.

Nevertheless, Shidō left his samurai sword in Gower's keeping as a token of good faith and pledged to find the sum. Itō suggested they might use the funds originally intended for buying arms, but the procedure involved in obtaining this money from the Chōshū *yashiki* in Azabu was complicated and might unmask their carefully concealed plans. Instead, a draft of 5,000 *ryō* was covertly obtained from Daikokuya, supplied through Satō, while Ōmura Masujirō, a senior official, was persuaded to take personal responsibility for the debt on Chōshū's behalf.

On 26 June, the travellers gathered at a tea-house in Kanagawa where they all added their names to a detailed report prepared by Shidō. For Itō, this served as his official request for permission to go abroad. From there it was a short journey to Yokohama and Satō Teijirō's house where they changed into Western clothes. The choice was limited, and Itō recalled having to wear rough seaman's clothes and shoes several sizes too large for him. They also cut off their *chonmage* topknots, the distinctive status symbols of the samurai. After eleven o'clock at night, Satō escorted them to the Jardine Matheson office at House Number One on the Yokohama Bund and they lay in wait inside the garden which backed onto the quay. At last Gower appeared, only to report that the captain was having last-minute qualms, but he was swayed by their furious protests that it was already too dangerous for them to remain in Japan. Then he led them out across the waterfront and past the customs house to a small boat which carried them to the *Chelswick*. Once on board, they were hidden in the coal-hatch, and by the time they were allowed up on deck, it was already past daybreak and the ship was heading out to sea.[15]

★ ★ ★

Five days later, Itō and Shidō watched as Shanghai came into view. The harbour was filled with merchant vessels and giant warships, while imposing Western buildings stretched along the Bund. The scene made a deep impression on Shidō; faced with such powerful adversaries, he declared, there was no alternative but to abandon the campaign to expel foreigners from Japan. From Shanghai he sent a letter to this effect to Subu, who professed amazement at 'how quickly the leopard changed its spots'. Shidō, who was six years older than Itō, had also just taken the family name of Inoue. Standing beside him on the deck of the *Chelswick*, however, Itō remained unconvinced by his rhetoric and reproached him for uttering such heresies.[16]

19

After disembarking, the five men from Chōshū found their way to the office of a Jardine Matheson representative called Keswick. Only Nomura could understand a word he said and grasped that he wanted to know the purpose of their trip. 'Navigation' ventured Inoue in reply, recalling one of the few English words he knew, although he actually meant naval studies. Something else may have been said or at least implied, but on the strength of this exchange, they were divided into two groups with instructions to be given a practical training during the voyage. Itō and Inoue were put aboard the *Pegasus*, a three-hundred ton schooner with a cargo of tea, while the others left on the somewhat larger *White Adder*.[17]

The captain of the *Pegasus* determined that Itō and Inoue should do their share of the work on board, and was unmoved by their protests that they had paid for their passage to London. They were subjected to a punishing daily regime, spreading and lowering the sails, manning the pumps and washing the deck, while their diet consisted of salted meat, ship biscuits, tea and rainwater. At last Itō's health broke down, and in the high seas around the Cape of Good Hope, he was grateful for Inoue's support in helping him to survive. This was the start of a lifelong friendship, and in later years when they were both senior Meiji politicians, Itō remained loyal to Inoue in times of need and tended him when he was sick. Towards the end of their voyage, the two travellers at last grew accustomed to life at sea and spent more time communicating with the crew. This enabled Itō to discover the shortcomings of his dictionary, a work he called 'unsatisfactory and littered with mistakes'.[18]

At eight o'clock in the morning of 4 November 1863, after four months at sea, the *Pegasus* arrived in the London docks. The captain promptly disembarked with most of the crew, leaving Itō and Inoue to be collected by a Jardine Matheson agent. Several hours passed with no sign of anyone, and pangs of hunger eventually drove Inoue ashore in search of food. He returned with bacon sandwiches and soft-boiled eggs, although he needed some help to find his way back to the *Pegasus*. Then, after one o'clock, the agent finally appeared and led them to a hotel in American Square. To their amazement, Yamao, Nomura and Endō were already there, as the *White Adder*, which had left Shanghai a week after the *Pegasus* had reached London several days before.[19]

Itō and his companions were taken to meet Hugh Matheson who later recalled that 'only Nomura ventured at first to speak a little broken English'. They visited him frequently, sometimes at his home in Hampstead, and he was impressed by their 'most diligent use of time'. They also sought his help over the smallest details of survival in London, from asking 'How can we get our washing done?' to 'Where can we buy a pair of shoes?' Matheson entrusted their education to Professor Alexander Williamson of University College London who admitted them to his analytical chemistry class there. Inoue and Yamao boarded in the house of a painter called Cooper at 103 Gower Street near the college, while Itō and the others stayed at the Williamson family home in Belsize Park.[20]

The scales at last fell from young Itō's eyes when he saw for himself the industrial might of Victorian London. At weekends, a fellow student, perhaps called Carpenter, took them to visit places of interest. These included trips to Kew Gardens, the Houses of Parliament and Buckingham Palace, but inevitably, it was the huge shipyards and factories that arrested their attention most.[21] Life in England also fostered in Itō a sense of national awareness that transcended traditional loyalties to the daimyo, for although he could find no parallel for boroughs and counties in the Tokugawa world, they did remind him of the golden age of Heian Japan. 'When I went to study in Britain', he later recalled, 'I became all the more convinced of the need to overhaul the feudal order as I saw how the division of land into districts and prefectures had also brought prosperity to the nations of Europe'.[22]

Itō's own disavowal of *jōi* policy was now complete, so he and Inoue were dismayed one day to find a newspaper article reporting Chōshū's attacks on foreign shipping and learn of plans for a punitive expedition by the treaty powers. With their domain apparently bent on self-destruction, they resolved to hurry back to warn their daimyo of the futility of challenging the military superiority of the West. Matheson recalled how, in January 1864, 'they wrote me a formal letter, signed by them all, that, on careful consideration, they had decided that it was necessary two of them should go home'.[23] Williamson asked what such young men could hope to achieve by abandoning their training, and accused them of having tired of their studies, but they were unmoved by all efforts to dissuade them.[24]

Yamao, Nomura and Endō volunteered to join them, but Itō and Inoue argued against risking all their lives in such a reckless mission, and persuaded them to stay behind to campaign on behalf of their embattled domain from afar. In July 1864, for example, the remaining students were in contact with the Foreign Office, presenting a detailed defence of Chōshū policy and criticising the *bakufu* monopoly over foreign trade. In June 1865, they also visited a party of students from Satsuma that had just arrived in London, even as relations between their two domains were at last beginning to thaw in Japan. Endō returned home in 1866 while the others stayed until 1868, Nomura in London and Yamao in Glasgow. They were all to play key roles in developing Japan's infrastructure during the Meiji period, supervising teams of mostly British engineers.[25]

In April 1864, Itō and Inoue embarked on their return voyage on a Jardine Matheson sailing ship and finally reached Yokohama on 13 July. Still in Western clothes, they immediately called on Gower to explain their mission and, to avoid discovery by *bakufu* officials, arrangements were made for them to stay incognito in a Western hotel. Posing as Portuguese travellers, they were hard pressed to conceal their knowledge of Japanese when the local porters levelled insults at these unusual guests. Through Gower and a company colleague called C.S. Hope, they were then presented to the British minister, Sir Rutherford Alcock, who received them with courtesy. Announcing their determination to stop Chōshū from attacking foreign shipping, they asked for a safe passage home by sea as it was too dangerous for them to travel overland.[26]

The *bakufu* had already been given twenty days in which 'to give a satisfactory undertaking to re-open the straits'.[27] Impressed by the resolve of Itō and Inoue, however, Alcock consulted with the other ministers and agreed upon this final attempt to prevent hostilities. They were granted a passage on HMS *Barrosa*, accompanied by two interpreters, Ernest Satow and James Enslie, together with Satow's teacher, Nakazawa Kensaku. Between them they translated a memorandum which Alcock had written for Itō and Inoue to present to their daimyo, Mōri Takachika, on their arrival in Yamaguchi. This was effectively an ultimatum to cease bombardments or face the consequences. Sailing up the Bungo Channel, their ship moored off the island of Himeshima on 26 July, opposite the coast of Suō in Chōshū territory. As the two men made their way ashore, Nakazawa told Satow that 'the chances were six or seven in ten that their heads would be cut off, and that we should never see them again'.[28]

After a short but eventful journey during which they crossed the sea to the Suō coast in a fishing boat and borrowed samurai swords and clothes, Itō and Inoue arrived in Yamaguchi to the astonishment of Chōshū officials. Their sudden reappearance provoked bitter debate in a hurriedly assembled council, and on 29 July, they were admitted to an audience with Mōri himself. The daimyo confessed that he found their arguments compelling, but they were informed soon afterwards that the political climate in Chōshū was too volatile to accommodate any dramatic shifts in policy, as preparations for war were already well advanced.

Disheartened, Itō and Inoue returned to Himeshima and boarded HMS *Barrosa* on 6 August to announce their daimyo's reply, an evasive request for a three-month stay of hand to allow time for consultation with the court in Kyoto. Moreover, to the disappointment of the British, they had no formal letter to deliver. Satow recalled that he 'could not help feeling sorry for their failure to impress on their prince the warning which they had come all the way from Europe to impart'.[29] They returned ashore that same night, and an allied squadron of seventeen ships was soon on its way to Himeshima. An alarmed Mōri hurriedly despatched Itō and Inoue to sue for peace, but the fleet was just leaving Himeshima when Itō arrived, and by the time Inoue reached the Shimonoseki coast on 5 September, the bombardment and destruction of the Chōshū batteries had already begun.

Their mission may have failed, but this experience had allowed Itō to establish a working relationship with British diplomats, the role that was effectively to carry him into public office after the overthrow of the Tokugawa regime. He acted as Chōshū's interpreter during the following peace negotiations, and was on good terms with Ernest Satow, who he even entertained to a Western-style dinner in Shimonoseki later that year.[30] In 1865, he met the new British minister, Sir Harry Parkes, and also developed close ties with Thomas Blake Glover, the influential Scottish merchant in Nagasaki. As the arms race gathered momentum, he was sent to buy ships and guns from Glover & Co. on several occasions, once involving a brief trip to Shanghai.[31]

Increasingly, Itō was travelling on British vessels, and on 5 February 1868, just days after the outbreak of civil war and the flight of the last Shogun, it was on board a Royal Navy warship that he arrived in the newly opened port of Kōbe to begin a new life in the service of the Meiji state. In a letter to Kido, he wrote of his desire for a quiet stay and then perhaps a trip abroad. Circumstances in Kōbe prevented such plans, however, for only the day before, passing Japanese troops from nearby Bizen had created panic when they briefly opened fire on residents in the foreign settlement. Itō immediately called on an indignant Harry Parkes who, appalled by the chaos in Kōbe, was also sharply critical of the fledgling government for its impudence in failing to announce the transfer of power to the ministers in the treaty ports.[32]

When Itō hurried to Osaka to report these grievances to the new Meiji authorities, he was promptly enlisted in the foreign department. On 10 February, British diplomats were surprised to learn that he was to act as superintendent of customs and governor of the town of Kōbe. 'It seemed curious', thought Satow, 'that a man of certainly not very high rank should be thought fit for this double post'.[33] Barely a month later, Itō was receiving Parkes for his audience with the Emperor, and by mid-July, he held the powerful position of governor of Hyōgo prefecture.

Itō was perhaps not the most polished linguist of his generation, but as Satow recalled, his knowledge of English was 'a very uncommon accomplishment in Japan in those days, especially in the case of men concerned in the political movement'.[34] Moreover, he was indispensable to the new government because, through his experience abroad and as a mediator for Chōshū, he had managed to cultivate the trust of foreign diplomats sufficiently to help bridge the gap in understanding that Parkes had condemned.

In the early Meiji years, Itō was a prominent campaigner in the movement to replace the feudal order with a centralized state, and spent much of his time promoting the development of the Imperial Mint and the Ministry of Public Works. He was also one of the vice ambassadors during the Iwakura mission's travels in the West and, naturally, it was his role to deliver the official addresses in English on behalf of Iwakura Tomomi. The tour included four months in Britain in 1872, a time not without the pressures that inevitably accompanied the life of a Meiji politician, but nevertheless something of a triumphant return for Itō. During his stay, news arrived of the opening of the passenger railway service between Tokyo and Yokohama, the first in Japan, and a project he had worked hard to promote. Once again he called on Hugh Matheson for advice; no longer a student in search of shoes, this time he arrived as the Minister of Public Works, arranging the recruitment of engineers to teach at the Imperial College of Engineering in Tokyo.[35]

Kido Takayoshi observed in 1869: 'It is ironic that all those who went to the West are alive now, while more than half of their friends who stayed in Japan are guests in the land of *Yomi*, the land of the Dead.'[36] Only five members of Takasugi's Mitategumi lived to see the creation of the Meiji state; three of them, Itō, Inoue and Yamao, had gone to Britain in 1863. Not only did Itō and Inoue survive the perils of escape and life in London, but rather more surprisingly, they also emerged unscathed from their precipitous return. Itō's early career was blessed with some good fortune at critical moments and his close ties with Kido certainly helped, but it was a combination of adaptability and faith in the hard-won convictions he had acquired in Britain that paved the way for his emergence as an influential figure on the political stage of Meiji Japan.

3

James Summers (1828-91): Early Sinologist and Pioneer of Japanese Newspapers in London and English Literature in Japan

KOYAMA NOBURU

JAMES SUMMERS went to Japan to teach English literature at the Kaisei Gakkō (a forerunner of the Imperial University) with his wife and four children in 1873. This opportunity was offered by Iwakura Tomomi (1825-83), the leader of the Iwakura mission in 1872 while the mission was in London. He acquired the position of pioneer of English literature in Japan. Before his departure for Japan in 1873, Summers had been Professor of Chinese at King's College, London for 20 years since 1852. He was the third professor of Chinese in Britain after Samuel Kidd at University College, London (1837-43) and Samuel Fearon at King's College, London (1847-52). James Summers was the only professor of Chinese at this time since the Chinese professorship had ceased at University College in 1843. Also, he was the editor of the *Phoenix*, a monthly magazine for China, Japan and Eastern Asia.

In 1873 when he was 45 years old, Summers made a major decision to give up Chinese teaching in England and his editorship of the *Phoenix* in order to work in Japan. His new appointment was to contribute to the teaching of both English and English literature in higher education in the new Meiji Japan. As the result, Summers is known as a pioneer of teaching English literature in Japan, but especially as the person who introduced Shakespeare. He stayed in Japan with his wife and nine children for about 18 years. He died in Tokyo in 1891 at the age of 63. Thus 1873 marks the main turning-point in James Summers' life apart from his youth. Also, in 1873, before he left for Japan, he had published the *Taisei shimbun*, a Japanese language newspaper with Minami Teisuke (1847-1915) in London. This attempt was probably encouraged by the visit of the Iwakura mission to Britain. The *Taisei shimbun* was one of two earliest Japanese language newspapers published outside Japan. Summers' contribution towards the *Taisei shimbun* is often regarded as his most important achievement.[1]

EARLY LIFE AND CHINESE PROFESSORSHIP

According to his second daughter, Lily (Ellen) (1865?-1958), James Summers was born in 'Ritchifirudo' (in Katakana), England on 5 July 1828 as the only child of Edward and Catherine (or Katherine) Summers and was baptized on 30 July 1928. Adachi Shizue interviewed Lily Summers about James Summers' life in August 1939 and published as an article called 'Summers, Pioneer of Shakespeare Studies'.[2] However, Summers was registered in the records of the University of Oxford as 'o.s. (only son) Edward, of Titchfield, Hants, gent. Magdalen Hall, matric. 17 Dec., 1853 aged 25'.[3] The year of his birth is the same as 1828, according to both the sources, but the place of his birth differs. 'Ritchifirudo' in Adachi's article could be Titchfield, Hampshire, considering the similar names, but I could not find his name in the parish registers of Titchfield. Since James Summers himself mentioned 'Ritchifirudo' to his Japanese pupils,[4] 'Ritchifirudo' was possibly his birth place. However, I cannot identify where it is.

Lily Summers lived in Japan for 86 years, including the entire period of World War Two, working as a teacher of English. When she died at age of 92 in 1958, a newspaper reported her death as 'Mother of English has passed away'.[5] According to the 'Impressions of Japan in 1873: Told by Old Foreign Resident',[6] which was a series of three English newspaper articles about her life, James Summers' youth was described as follows:

> He had an interest in languages and after studying in Germany and France, became interested in the Far East, hoping to qualify for the diplomatic and consular service. In 1848 he went to teach in Hong Kong at St Paul's College, an Anglo-Chinese school and learnt both spoken and written Chinese, probably Cantonese and Shanghai dialects, but not Mandarin.

When he was in Hong Kong, the twenty-year-old Summers brought on the following incident.[7] In Macau where he made a short excursion from Hong Kong, Summers came across a Corpus Christi procession and, as a staunch Protestant, refused to uncover his head. Corpus Christi was an important festival of the Catholic Church which dominated this Portuguese colony, so this was considered a serious misdemeanour and accordingly he was jailed by the Governor of Macau on 7 June 1849. After negotiations failed, Captain Keppel of HMS *Mœander* and his men rescued him by force and, as a result, an unarmed Portuguese soldier was killed and three others injured on the following day. Because of this incident, he was described as '... the foolish lad Summers, whose childish obstinacy or idiotic bigotry led to these untoward events and the death of a fellow-creature'.[8]

Summers was appointed Professor of Chinese at King's College, London, in 1852 and advertized his course of instruction in the classical language and colloquial dialects of China in the 22 January 1853 issue of the *Athenaeum*. When this news reached Hong Kong, people were surprised because Summers '... was considered incompetent for the position, having only been a short time in Hong Kong and being even then quite a young man, and without experience of Chinese language', and more importantly, because he was 'the originator of the unfortunate affair at Macao in June 1849'.[9] Apart from whether he was competent for the position or not, Summers was indeed quite young for the post of Chinese professorship. He was just 24 years old. As I have already mentioned, he only matriculated in 1853 at Magdalen Hall, Oxford, as an undergraduate. Also whilst being Professor of Chinese at King's College, London, Summers worked for the India Office Library as assistant in 1858-59 and was appointed as a deacon at Rochester Cathedral and a curate at the church of Hitchin, Hertfordshire, after taking holy orders in 1863.[10] He worked for the Library of the British Museum as an assistant before 1863 as well.[11] So, considering his many activities whilst holding the Professorship of Chinese at King's College, one wonders indeed what was the nature of this post.

When Robert Morrison died in 1835, his friend and executor Sir George Staunton (1781-1859) offered the gift of Morrison's Chinese books to University College, London, on the condition that it appointed a Professor of Chinese for five years and Samuel Kidd was appointed as the first professor with a salary of £60 per annum.[12] Since the Professorship lasted for only five years, Staunton and others proposed to raise the endowment of a Chinese professorship at King's College, London in 1846 and the sum reached over £2,000 by 1856.[13] Samuel Fearon was appointed as the first Professor in 1846 and the salary of the post was £70.16s. 4d. per annum.[14] So, Summers' salary must have been approximately the same or similar. This salary was very small indeed. Fearon was not re-appointed in 1851 and was succeeded by the young James Summers in 1852.[15]

Since the salary of the Chinese professorship was so poor, Summers like other professors of Oriental languages at King's College was obliged to find work other than the teaching of Chinese. Probably most professorships of Oriental languages were low-paid at that time. For an example, the salary of a Chinese Professor at University College, London was merely £60 per year. So, *The centenary history of King's College London 1828-1928* describes the professor of Oriental languages at King's College as follows:[16]

> The professors were all of them busy men whose main centre of activities lay elsewhere – e.g., the India Office or the British Museum. The fees from King's College did not suffice to keep them from accepting anything else that offered. Hence changes were constant : there were ten within the years 1862-68.

So, like other professors of King's College, James Summers worked for the Libraries of the India Office and the British Museum besides taking holy orders and matriculating at Madgalen Hall, Oxford, while he was at King's College, London. Also, he took editorship of the *Chinese and Japanese Repository* (July 1863-December 1865) and the *Phoenix* (July 1870-June 1873) apart from the works of publications which were directly related with his Chinese teaching, such as *A handbook of the Chinese language Part I and II grammar and chrestomathy* (Oxford: OUP, 1863) and also his library work, such as the *Descriptive catalogue of the Chinese, Japanese and Manchu books in the Library of the India Office* (London: India Office, 1872). As the title indicates, the *Chinese and Japanese Repository* was to succeed the role of the well known *Chinese Repository* and also extended the areas of coverage to other East Asian countries, especially Japan which had already opened her ports to the West. The *Phoenix* was intended to supply information on the history, geography, languages and literature and religions of China, Japan, India and other related areas since the *Chinese Repository* and similar publications had ceased.

Summers also supplemented his meagre salary by student fees. So, if the number of students who studied Chinese under him was large, his income would be improved. In 1854 the number of students for Summers increased because the Foreign Office demanded training of Chinese language interpreters for eventual service in Hong Kong.[17] It seemed in 1859 that the numbers of students of Chinese would increase further due to the establishment of a legation in Peking but the result was the opposite. The first group of trainees could not cope in Peking with the Chinese they had learnt from Summers, because he spoke Cantonese and Shanghai dialect, not Mandarin.[18] He had been to Hong Kong and Shanghai, but never to Peking. So, when he was offered the new post in Japan in 1872, perhaps the decision was made easier by the fact that he could no longer hope to attract many students to his course at King's College. Ernest Satow was quite often referred to as a student of Summers at King's College, London but Satow himself was critical and dismissive of Summers' teaching. In the *Reay Report* (1909), Satow said, mentioning Summers' teaching, '. . . they only had an ex-missionary, the Rev. James Summers; he knew some Chinese, but I do not know whether he was able to give the correct pronunciation'.[19]

To return to the question why Summers made his decision to go to Japan in 1873, we should consider how the post was initially offered to him. Lily Summers remembered the following story.[20] Summers and his family lived at Sidcup, Kent, at that time. The Iwakura mission stayed in Britain from August to November 1872. Iwakura Tomomi sometimes called at Summers' house and one day he asked Summers whether he knew of a suitable teacher of English to work in Japan. Since Summers was interested in Japan, he offered to go himself. Officially, Summers signed a contract of employment with Terashima Munenori, the Japanese minister to Britain in London on 6 June 1873. This was the end of James Summers' career in England.

Why did Summers choose the new job in Japan? Of course, the conditions of the new post were a major factor. Another one was timing. The term of professorship of Chinese at King's College was five years; 1872 was the last year of his current term. One can assume that Summers made the major decision to go to Japan considering these matters. Summers and his family arrived at Yokohama on 10 October 1873 and travelled to Tokyo by the new railway which had opened in the previous year.[21] Summers arrived in time to attend the opening ceremony of the Kaisei Gakkō. His salary was 300 Japanese yen per month plus the expenses for travelling to and from Japan − 600 Japanese yen for each way.[22] The term of the contract was originally two years, but it was extended another year. Summers worked for the Kaisei Gakkō for three years from October 1873.

THE *TAISEI SHIMBUN*: A JAPANESE NEWSPAPER PUBLISHED IN LONDON

Before describing Summers' life in Japan, I would like to mention the *Taisei shimbun* which was published in London on 30 January 1873. The *Taisei shimbun* shares the position of early Japanese language newspapers published outside Japan along with the *Yo no uwasa* which was published by Leon de Rosny in Paris in 1868 and 1870. Only one issue of the *Taisei shimbun* was published, and around 1,000 copies of the first issue were reported to have been circulated, but only one copy is known to have survived. That copy was originally sent to 'Monsieur Ernest Seroux, Agent for Paris' who was probably in charge of the newspaper's Paris circulation.[23] This only surviving copy was eventually brought to Japan and was reproduced in 1927. Because of this only surviving copy, we can know the actual contents of the publication. Since the *Yo no uwasa* was also reproduced in 1934, we can compare the reproduced copies of both newspapers. The *Taisei shimbun* looks more like a proper newspaper and was more professionally produced compared to the *Yo no uwasa*.

In the 20 February 1873 issue of *The Times* there was an article on the *Taisei shimbun*. It says: 'A native Japanese paper is now being published in London under the imposing name of the *Tai Sei Shimbun* or *Great Western News*' and 'It is edited by a Japanese resident in London.' Then, the article mentions that Japan's advancement has brought about the opportunity to establish a newspaper in London as means of providing knowledge of the West to Japanese people. The new newspaper, *The Times* writer goes on to say, reflected the opinions of Japanese who have already seen the world and learnt European languages and the editors aimed to report political, moral and religious issues in the European countries and also to select articles of arts and inventions for Japanese readers. The illustrations were the important features of the *Taisei shimbun*, stating: 'The paper will be illustrated, so as to convey the most vivid ideas of the objects explained, and to simplify description', and 'Advertisements to a limited extent will be received in any European language.' Professor Summers of King's College who was the co-editor supervised those translations into Japanese. As regards the newspaper circulation of 1,000 copies, a large number would be distributed among the 700 Japanese residents in Europe and America, and the remainder sent to Japanese cities, such as Nagasaki, Osaka and Tokyo.

Who was the Japanese resident in London who edited the *Taisei shimbun* with James Summers? This person was Minami Teisuke. Minami was 25 or 26 years old, a student or former student. Also he was a director of bank. His bank was called the American Joint National Agency and its parent bank was called Bowles Brothers & Co. Both banks were closed down in November and went bankrupt in December 1872. A lot of members of the Iwakura mission, including Iwakura Tomomi and Japanese students, deposited their money in Minami's bank. Accordingly, they suffered a large financial loss from the bankruptcy of both banks. The Japanese Government borrowed £15,000 from the Oriental Bank in order to help the Japanese victims of the bankruptcy.[24] Minami went back to Japan in Spring of 1873. He probably left London in March 1873, a couple of weeks later after the article on the *Taisei shimbun* appeared in *The Times*. The new business of the *Taisei shimbun* was undertaken between the bankruptcy of Minami's bank and his departure for Japan. Although the Iwakura mission had already left England when the *Taisei shimbun* was launched in January 1873, its creation was probably encouraged by the visit of the Iwakura mission to England.

According to his short autobiography, Minami Teisuke described the launch of the *Taisei shimbun* as follows:[25] 'After consultation with Dr Summers, teacher of Chinese at King's College, London, I published a newspaper which was called the Taisei shimbun, making Japanese printing types and translating interesting news in the West into Japanese. This was the first Japanese language newspaper in the West.' *The Times* described the role of James Summers for the *Taisei shimbun* as the co-editor who superintended the translations of advertisements as well. Minami described Summers' role as the consultant of a new venture. However, if we study the actual *Taisei shimbun*, we can easily find out that Summers' role was larger than that of co-editor or consultant. On the first page there was a sort of prospectus which was partially cited in *The Times*' article. This prospectus was accompanied by Summers' name. His title was the *Shuji* (the person in charge) of the *Taisei shimbun* and Professor of the University of London. We do not know whether the actual Japanese prospectus was written by Summers himself or not, but we can assume at least the original prospectus was written by him in English. Also, we must not forget Summers' rich experience of publishing journals such as the *Chinese and Japanese Repository* and the *Phoenix*, particularly the latter which contains Chinese characters. Regarding the printing of Chinese characters, Summers gave F.V. Dickens assistance for the publication of the text in the original Japanese characters when Dickens published *Hyakunin isshu* in 1866.[26] Also, the *Descriptive catalogue of the Chinese, Japanese and Manchu books in the Library of the India Office* which contains Chinese characters was printed at the office of the *Phoenix* and the editor of the *Phoenix* was James Summers. Considering his experience, Summers was probably a leading expert in Britain of the printing of Chinese characters at the time.

ILLUSTRATIONS AND ADVERTISEMENTS OF THE TAISEI SHIMBUN

Next, I would move to the illustrations which are the feature of the *Taisei shimbun* and the advertisement which is mentioned in *The Times*' article. Through the illustrations and the advertisement, I would like to show how the *Taisei shimbun* was connected to two magazines, *Leisure Hours* and the *Phoenix*. *Leisure Hours* was a magazine published by the Religious Tract Society. In the *Taisei shimbun*, there are four illustrations (all are engravings) – Windsor Castle on the second page, Niagara Falls on the third, Louis Bonaparte Napoleon on the fourth and the Tuileries on the fifth, apart from the illustrations connected with advertisements. The engraving of Windsor Castle was borrowed from the Religious Tract Society. The illustration of Niagara Falls was reprinted by permission from *Leisure Hours*. The illustration of Louis Bonaparte Napoleon came again from *Leisure Hours*. So, did the illustration of the Tuileries. There seemed to be a close connection between the Religious Tract Society which published *Leisure Hours* and James Summers who took holy orders and was interested in both publishing and printing. When James Summers and his family went to Japan in 1873, he wrote a letter about his new life, the beginning of the Kaisei Gakkō and impressions of Yedo (Tokyo), etc. to the editor of *Leisure Hours*. His letter was published in *Leisure Hours*.[27]

The other journal that is connected to the *Taisei shimbun* namely, is the *Phoenix*. The address of both the *Taisei shimbun* and the *Phoenix* is the same, '3 George Yard, Lombard Street, London'. Also, I can demonstrate the relationship between these publications through their advertisements. Since the advertisements were mainly printed on covers and back pages in the case of the *Phoenix*, most of them were lost when the issues of the journal were bound. So, I use the advertisements which have survived so far. The January 1873 (No. 31) and April 1873 (No. 34) issues of the Phoenix included the following advertisement.

ENGLISH HOME FOR JAPANESE GIRLS

A clergyman's wife, assisted by a resident German lady of superior attainments, desire to receive a few Japanese girls to educate with her own daughter. The best Masters attend for accomplishments. Sound religious training, kind material care and a most comfortable home are offered. Terms, 100 guineas per annum. Distance two hours from London. – Address, W. R., 'Phoenix Office', George-Yard, Lombard-Street, London. E.C.

* References to a Japanese gentleman, and the Editor of the Phoenix.

The Japanese translation of the above advertisement appears on the fifth page of the *Taisei shimbun* although some religious aspects were erased. The terms were described as 100 pounds, about 500 *ryō*. Also it was added that the home which was advertised was well known among the Japanese students in England. It seems surprising that there was such an advertisement for Japanese girls in England so early in the Meiji period.

The January 1873 (No. 31) and April 1873 (No.34) issues of the *Phoenix* also included 'the protective and antifouling compositions for the preservation of ships' bottoms from Messrs. Peacock & Buchan, Southampton & London'. Exactly the same advertisement appeared on the seventh page of the *Taisei shimbun*. The eighth page (back page) of the *Taisei shimbun* is entirely dedicated to an advertisement of a hydraulic engineering firm, Messrs. John & Henry Gwynne, London. The advertisement of the same firm appeared in the August 1871(No. 14) issue of the *Phoenix*. Obviously, Summers was editor of the *Phoenix* and used the same advertisements for the *Taisei shimbun*. These advertisements clearly indicate the direct relationship between the *Taisei shimbun* and James Summers.

Either the idea to publish a Japanese language newspaper was initiated by Minami Teisuke or Summers might have been inspired by Leon de Rosny. Actually Minami was very good at finding new ventures, such as this one. Probably *The Times'* article was also initiated by Minami according to the contents which emphasizes the importance of Japanese residents in Europe. Although he had some knowledge of the commercial world, Minami did not have any experience of publishing, any connection with printing firms nor any clue about how to find advertisers. So, obviously, the printing business, particularly that involving illustrations and Chinese characters, and advertisements could only be done by James Summers. When the first issue of the *Taisei shimbun* was published, Summers was still publishing the *Phoenix*. So, he could use the printing facilities, printing technology, and even advertisers appearing in the *Phoenix* for the *Taisei shimbun*. However, the Japanese translation, particularly the checking of Japanese texts had to be done by a native Japanese, such as Minami Teisuke. Summers' command of Japanese did not seem to be sufficient to publish a Japanese language newspaper. In 1872, he published in the *Phoenix* a series of articles entitled 'Practical Lessons in Japanese'.[28] However, his Japanese ability did not reach the level of the *Taisei shimbun*. So, we have to conclude that the *Taisei shimbun* was the collaborative work of James Summers and Minami Teisuke. Lily Summers indicated that there was another Japanese who helped Summers to publish the *Taisei shimbun*.[29] That Japanese was called Masujirō and he was a kind of servant at Summers' home. However, I could not find any further information about him.

According to Lily, Summers wanted to continue the *Taisei shimbun* even after he went to Japan.[30] In fact, he actually brought the printing machine to Japan in order to publish a newspaper. But, Minami Teisuke refused to cooperate with him because he considered '*sekinin mondai*' (the issue of responsibility). Probably Minami was worried about the responsibility of publishers when newspapers were involved with political problems. Another matter was that Summers was not allowed to carry on other business affairs whilst he was a teacher of the Kaisei

Gakkō. Later, there was a fire in his house, so he sold the printing machine to Captain Francis Brinkley, the proprietor of *Japan Mail*. This marks the end of Summers' venture in Japanese language newspapers.

LATER LIFE IN JAPAN

Shiga Shigetaka (1863-1927) recorded in his diary (11 June 1882) Summers' emotional state when he was discharged from the Sapporo Nōgakkō (Sapporo School of Agriculture). Shiga had been one of Summers' pupils at the Sapporo Nōgakkō. He regarded Summers as a friend in his later life and wrote an obituary on Summers:[31]

> Afternoon; I went to Summers' house to say good-bye to him with Tmoto and Nakagawa, hearing that he would leave tomorrow because he was dismissed from the school. His daughter came to answer, but Summers seemed to be enraged and shouted 'I cannot meet anybody today. Shut the door, shut the door'. She closed the door accordingly. This was understandable, because his anger was great at this time. Summers did not expect the dismissal to come so early, and he had been suddenly told of it by Mr. Igawa. He appealed with a trembling voice as follows : 'Personally I do not want to stay at this school, but for "family conditions" – my wife is now getting used to the weather here, I would not be pleased to be dismissed after just one term. Please reconsider the decision and continue my employment.' But, it came to nothing after all.[32]

Shiga's diary continues to mention that Summers refused to meet the school officials at his house. However, Shiga remembered how upset Summers was when he visited Shiga's classroom next day before he left Sapporo for Tokyo.[33] Summers tried to say a word of farewell to his pupils, but he could not because he was tearful, even sobbing. Shiga later recalled happy memories of occasions when Summers and he would recite English poems in turn. Summers had been a memorable teacher for him.

For Summers, the Sapporo Nōgakkō where he worked from 1880 to 1882 was the last employment by the Japanese Government after the Kaisei Gakkō (1873-76), the Niigata Eigo Gakkō (1876-77) and the Ōsaka Eigo Gakkō (1877-80). Although Summers was one of early foreign employees (*Oyatoi gaikokujin*) , he suffered from the Japanese Government's policy of reducing the high cost of foreign employees. Summers was employed for a limited period in each institution and also his salary gradually declined. The monthly salary of the Kaisei Gakkō was 300 yen, those of the Niigata Eigo Gakkō 250 yen, the Ōsaka Eigo Gakkō 130 yen, the Sapporo Ngakkō 180 yen respectively.[34]

After returning to Tokyo, he purchased the house at Tsukiji, the foreign settlement in Tokyo.[35] Later he opened the school which was officially called the Ōbun Seikō Gakkan at his house. Usually it was called 'Summers School' or in Japanese Sammā Gakkō. The teachers of his school were mainly his family and himself although he continued teaching English privately to prominent Japanese. 'Summers School' was continued after Summers' death. It was run mainly by his wife, Ellen (1843-1907) and it was discontinued shortly after her death in 1907. Okakura Yoshisaburō, Osada Shūtō, Tanizaki Jun'ichirō and others learnt English at 'Summers School' which flourished as an English school. However, according to Uchida Roan, the reputation of Summers' family was not favourable among foreign residents at the Tsukiji foreign settlement, where most of residents were missionaries.

Sometime after settling down at Tsukiji, Summers seemed to devote a large part of his time to the compilation of dictionaries of Chinese characters besides the teaching of English. According to a directory (June 1884) of foreign residents at the Tsukiji settlement by occupation, his occupation was listed as 'Compiler of Japanese dictionary (under medical treatment)'.[36] Summers read a paper on Chinese lexicography, including the proposal for a new arrangement of the Chinese characters, at the meeting of the Asiatic Society of Japan on 23 January 1884 and generated 'a very animated discussion'.[37] In his paper, he described the compilation of his Chinese dictionary as his life-time work as follows:

> I began to wish for a rearrangement and adjustment of Callery's phonetics when I was a mere student in China in 1850. Fourteen years later I had the plan which I desire to lay before you sketched out : but I could not see my way to carrying out my method until within the last two years.

As Summers mentioned, he advertised 'Parts III and IV' of *A handbook of the Chinese language* on the volume of 'Parts I and II' in 1863 and 'Part IV' was a dictionary, but 'Parts III and IV' were never published.

Probably in the summer of 1884, he distributed the specimen pages of *A Chinese-Japanese-English dictionary*, *A Chinese-Japanese-English index-dictionary* and the advertisement for the subscription of *A Chinese-Japanese-English dictionary* to the people and institutions interested. These specimens indicate that the latter dictionary which costs five dollars is a kind of abridged version of the first one which costs 10 dollars. The advertisement for the first says: 'This dictionary is on an entirely new and scientific method of arrangement of the Chinese characters (about 12,000), following the order of strokes of a select number of primitives' and also: 'The advantage of the system is that each character is to be found at once under its Root-key.' Also, the advertisement emphasises 'The above work will be ready for publication in a few months, and will be sent to press as soon as a sufficient number of subscribers' are attracted.

In a letter of 14 August 1884, Summers wrote to Sir Harry Parkes who had been promoted from minister to Japan to that to China in the previous year, asking Parkes' support for his new venture in dictionaries.[38] He wrote: 'If you can bring the dictionary to the notice of any Chinese officials of influence who can support it, I shall feel greatly indebted to you. I am naturally anxious to secure a number of subscribers before going to press as the outlay will be considerable, and I have nothing to venture since the O.B.C. stoppage has locked up all my savings.' It seems that Summers could not attract a sufficient number of subscribers since these dictionaries were never published. Apart from the dictionaries of Chinese characters, also Summers continued to compile a dictionary of thirteen languages, including Japanese, Koreans, Tibetan, etc. in his later years, but he could not complete it, according to Lily Summers.[39]

Finally, in 1890, Summers brought about the so called 'Summers incident', reported in both *The Times* and in Japanese newspapers[40] or it would be more appropriate to say that he encountered it. Unlike the Macau incident, in this case he was a victim of the incident. By ironic coincidence, both incidents involved removing his hat to show courtesy. When driving in a pony carriage in Tokyo on 7 May 1890, Summers met a procession of the Empress Dowager. He drew to the side of the road and stood still, waiting to take off his hat at the appropriate moment, but a lancer, in the front of the procession, impatiently struck off his hat and injured his head. Though the lancer was punished and an apology was made, Saitō Shin'ichirō and other Japanese rebuked him for his disrespect. This incident was one of a string of anti-foreigner incidents which showed a changed situation in Japan, resulting from increased confidence and nationalism, a reaction against rapid Westernization. For a example, Dr Imbrie, an American missionary and a teacher at the Meiji Gakuin was attacked ten days later. So, Summers took refuge in Yokohama with his family in order to avoid troubles and decided to return to England.

Before departure for England, Summers was asked to visit the Imperial Palace with Count Kuroda because the Meiji Emperor wanted to confer a decoration on Summers for his contribution to English education in Japan.[41] However, Mrs Summers strongly opposed his visit because she was anxious about his safety. Even though Summers received a financial award from the Imperial Household Ministry, Mrs Summers returned it. Then, Summers and his family left for England in June. However, perhaps surprisingly, they returned to Japan only four months later in October 1890. By then, the troubles of the 'Summers incident' had already died down. About one year later, Summers died of a stroke on 26 October 1991. He was 63 years old.

James Summers is an interesting figure in the history of early modern Anglo-Japanese relations. Though his career was not completely successful, he has been remembered in Japan as a pioneer of the teaching of English literature and for the *Taisei shimbun*.

4

Fukuzawa Yukichi (1835-1901): The Finances of a Japanese Modernizer

NORIO TAMAKI

FUKUZAWA YUKICHI (1835-1901) a low-ranking samurai from Nakatsu, in Kyushu island, south west of Japan, was in 1890, at the age of 55 years, listed as the 231st richest man in Tokyo.[1] How could this be? Fukuzawa's wealth depended on the royalties from his books, his fees as a journalist and, above all, on his profits as an innovative businessman. Fukuzawa was the Japanese who, after three journeys to America and Europe, including six weeks stay in England, wrote on his return a series of books explaining to the Japanese people the life and times of *Conditions in the West*. Fukuzawa's published works sold in huge numbers in Japan. But Fukuzawa was also an entrepreneur of skill and daring. He was the man behind the formation of the Yokohama Specie Bank founded in 1880 (two years before the Bank of Japan) and the bookshop chain of Maruzen, which held in stock large numbers of books in English and other foreign languages. He was also closely associated with both the Mitsubishi Corporation (through Iwasaki Yatarō) and with the Mitsui Bank.

FUKUZAWA, THE TRAVELLING JAPANESE

Fukuzawa Yukichi first recognized the importance of the English language in the autumn of 1858 when he, then the head student of Tekijuku, a fine school for Dutch studies of Ogata Kōan (1810-63) in Osaka, was invited by his native Nakatsu domain to take charge of the clan's school in Edo (later Tokyo). Once in Edo, he visited Moriyama Takichirō (1820-71), the most competent interpreter of English for the *bakufu*, asking him to teach him the language.[2] Moriyama was in reality too busy with diplomatic negotiations to do much teaching but Fukuzawa's enthusiasm carried him steadily forward as his skills in reading English improved. He was in fact to become a member of three official overseas journeys, agreed by the *bakufu* government, which took place before 1868 and the Meiji Restoration.

In the autumn of 1859, Fukuzawa was told that a Japanese ship was to steam across the Pacific Ocean to San Francisco to accompany an American ship USS *Powhatan*, carrying the ratification of the Treaty of Amenity and Commerce between Japan and the United States of America. Thanks to one of his close friends, Katsuragawa Hoshu (1826-81), a doctor specializing in Dutch medicine, and brother-in-law of Commodore Kimura Yoshitake (1830-1901) who was the captain of the first Japanese ship to cross the Pacific Ocean, Fukuzawa succeeded in joining ninety or so others on board *Kanrinmaru*, in February 1860. He spent nearly two months, in San Francisco and its neighbourhood. In January 1862 Fukuzawa, in his capacity as a temporary member of the *bakufu* translators' staff, grasped an opportunity of joining the *bakufu* mission visiting France, Britain, the Netherlands, Prussia, Russia and Portugal to negotiate with them a postponement of the opening of the treaty ports at Edo, Osaka, Hyogo and Niigata. This second tour took a whole year and he spent six weeks in London. The third and last chance of going abroad for Fukuzawa came in February 1867 when he was able to join a mission to purchase warships in America. He stayed in New York and Washington for nearly two months. To succeed in making three journeys abroad in eight years, on official expenses, and on such nationally important missions, was extraordinary even by today's standards.

It seems clear that the young Fukuzawa was, at this time, the classic lower-ranking samurai who was, in his native Nakatsu, infuriated by the petty restrictions which dominated and restricted life. It was this spirit of rebellion which impelled him to importune his friends and allies so that he could escape from the stultifying atmosphere of old Japan and explore the wonders of the Western world.

Fukuzawa visited four big cities during his three overseas tours, in which English was the first language, that is San Francisco in 1860 and 1867, London in 1862 and New York and Washington in 1867. Of the four, London was crucial. The length of stay in London was the longest, and in every aspect of politics, economy and social science studies it was the best place for the enthusiastic scholar of social science.

FUKUZAWA IN LONDON, 30 APRIL-13 JUNE 1862

The Japanese mission, which consisted of three ambassadors and thirty-three followers, arrived in London via France on 30 April 1862. Fukuzawa was one of several translators. When the Japanese mission arrived in London, Queen Victoria was living in seclusion in Balmoral, Scotland, grief-stricken after the death of Prince Albert, the Prince Consort, in December 1861. Lord John Russell (1792-1878) greeted the party on behalf of Her Majesty. They were accommodated in grand style at Claridge's Hotel in Brook Street.[3]

Although the Japanese ambassadors were warmly received by Lord John Russell and others, the negotiations about the opening of the treaty ports did not start immediately. Rutherford Alcock, the British minister to Japan, was hurriedly making his way to London. Alcock was accompanied by Moriyama Takichirō, the best interpreter Japan had. During one month the ambassadors and their immediate attendants, guided by John McDonald (1831-66), attaché at the British legation in Japan, travelled north for a small expedition, visiting Newcastle-upon-Tyne, Birmingham, Liverpool and other cities. The rest of the Japanese group, mainly the lower-ranking samurai, including Fukuzawa, stayed on in London.[4]

The one month free of official duties gave a wonderful opportunity for Fukuzawa to explore London. A small group of Japanese, including Fukuzawa, was taken around London by Dr Chambers[5] and a Dr Johnson to look at various places on interest. They visited several hospitals, perhaps because many of the Japanese were former students of Dutch medicine. They visited King's College Hospital, St Mary's Hospital, the Blind School in St George's Field and two other hospitals. They also paid visits to the Great Exhibition of 1862, Greenwich, the Tower of London, London Bridge, the Thames tunnel, St Paul's Cathedral, the British Museum, London docks, a telegraph station and the arsenal in Woolwich.[6]

The visits to those places and institutions were invaluable. They gave Fukuzawa some appreciation of the importance of London as the capital and powerhouse of a great empire. A rare letter of Fukuzawa from overseas, writing to a senior officer, resident in the Nakatsu domain house at Edo, gives some idea of his reactions to his experience:

Bunkyu second year, fourth month, eleventh day (9 May 1862)

I was so fortunate to be able to join the Western tour which could not be done again. I have resolved not only to do research in this tour but also to look closely into conditions and customs of European countries. I have already made friends in both France and Britain and made enquiries about institutions of their countries, systems of army and navy, taxation and so on. Although everything is not necessarily clear to me, I could benefit tremendously from being able to look at things for myself which I had known only from reading books and it is the truth indeed that seeing is believing. ... In order to learn conditions in the West, it would be most useful to look at them on the spot, but it is almost impossible to do it by myself. There is no way but to buy books. I have already bought a considerable number of volumes of books in London. ... All the sum you kindly gave me in Edo will be spent on the purchase of books.[7]

Although he wrote that he had bought a number of books, Fukuzawa did not leave any records of what he purchased in London. The only book that we are able to identify, is the copy he no doubt bought in London of the two volumes of *English and Chinese Dictionary*, edited by W.H. Medhurst (1796-1857), printed at the Mission Press, Shanghei (sic), 1847 and 1848.[8] The inside cover of the copy of the dictionary contains the bookseller's label 'Trübner & Co., 60 Paternoster Row'. This label is indeed one of two rare records of the bookshops Fukuzawa visited and bought books. Another record is found in his leather pocket diary, on the first page of which Fukuzawa scribbled *W. and R. Chambers 47 Paternoster Row*. In a preface to one of the volumes of his *Conditions in the West*, he disclosed that the volume was a translation mainly from *Political Economy for Use in Schools and for Private Instructor*, published by William and Robert Chambers, London and Edinburgh.[9] He no doubt bought the volume at 47 Paternoster Row.

Fukuzawa did not leave any special comments on booksellers, Trübner or W. & R. Chambers. Both Trübner and Chambers were well known publishers and booksellers in Britain. Nicholas Trübner (1817-84), born in Heidelberg and trained under William Longman (1813-77), had arrived in London in 1843 and established himself in the book business. His catalogues on American and Oriental literature were invaluable for the scholarly world. William (1800-83) and, his younger brother, Robert (1802-71) Chambers were born in Peebles. The book business was started first by Robert at the suggestion of William, but later in the early 1860s, shortly before Fukuzawa and his colleagues turned up there.

Robert Chambers may have shown Fukuzawa the Paternoster Row bookshop on his St Paul's Cathedral tour. No doubt Fukuzawa returned again and again to the bookseller. From Claridge's Hotel, Fukuzawa could easily walk to Paternoster Row within ninety minutes.

What books did he purchase at Paternoster Row booksellers? We may well reconstruct the list of books with the prices by looking into two sources, namely his own later writings and the 1862 issue of the *English Catalogue of Books*.[10]

W. Blackstone	*Commentaries on the Laws of England* Hargreaves éd. 1844. £3 15s.
H.T. Buckle	*History of Civilization in England* 2 vols. 1861. £1 17s.
J.H. Burton	*Political Economy for Use in Schools and for Private Instruction* 2s 6d.
W. & R. Chambers	*Chambers' Encyclopaedia* 5 vols. [A to L] 1860/62. £2 5s.
	Information for the People 2 vols. 1857/58. 16s.
W. Ellis	*Outlines of Social Economy* 1860. 1s 6d.
Encyclopaedia Britannica	8th ed, 21 vols & Index. 1853/61. £25 12s.
F.P.Z. Guizot	*History of the Origin of Representative Government in Europe* 1852. 3s 6d.
	History of Civilization in Europe 3 vols. 1856. 10s 6d.
J.R. McCulloch	*The Principles of Political Economy* 1849. 15s.
	A Dictionary, Geographical, Statistical and Historical, of Various Countries, Places and Principal Natural Objects in the World. 1854. £3 3s.
	A Dictionary, Practical, Theoretical and Historical, of Commerce and Commercial Navigation. New Edition. 1860. £2 10s.
W.H. Medhurst	*An English and Japanese and Japanese and English Vocabulary.* 1830. 10s.
	English and Chinese Dictionary 2 vols. £5.
F. Wayland	*Elements of Political Economy* New ed. 1859. 2s.
	Elements of Moral Science 1860. 3s 6d.

All in all, Fukuzawa paid £46 10s 6d, that is some 200 ryo or 200 yen.[11] This was quite a large sum, two-thirds of the money he was given in Edo. This library, expensive for Fukuzawa to acquire at the time, was perhaps the first of its kind in Japan and proved to be invaluable for Fukuzawa when he was writing *Conditions in the West*.

FUKUZAWA'S ACCUMULATION OF CAPITAL

Returning from the long journey in Europe in January 1863, Fukuzawa produced four books on the West *before* the Meiji Restoration; *Seiyōjijyō* (Conditions in the West) in 1866 and 1867, *Seiyō tabiannai* (Guide to tour in the West), 1867, *Jōyaku juichikokki* (Eleven nations with which treaties are concluded), 1867, and *Seiyō ishokuju* (Everyday life in the West), 1867. The latter three books were small having seventy-four sheets (that is 148 pages), twenty-five (50 pages) and nineteen (38 pages) respectively. Not only the length of the three books but also the contents suggestive in the titles are self-explanatory to the effect that they were the by-products of the master work, *Conditions in the West*.

Fukuzawa wrote in retrospect in his preface to his first *Collected Works*, five volumes, published in 1898:

> Once those who had no knowledges (on arts and literature) accomplished a formidable task of the Restoration, they had to face the aftermath. Although they had resolved to discontinue the foolhardy seclusion policies, they did not know how to proceed to the civilized world. It was at this very moment that these talented people in dismay encountered *Conditions in the West*. The book instantly interested them and convinced them that it provided with them materials on which they would be able to prepare their plans of civilization. Once one realized it, the realization spontaneously spread among the rest. A copy of *Conditions in the West* could not be dispensed with by any one, either in or out of power, who at all argued for the Western civilization and the opening of the country. *Conditions in the West* was indeed a teacher in the uneducated society. Not a negligible number of new policies of the Restoration government come out of this tiny book. It may sound odd, but there was only my humble book at that time in Japan that could introduce new Western ideas.[12]

Conditions in the West, full of new ideas and fascinating for the Japanese, sold very well indeed. According to Fukuzawa, all in all 150,000 copies of the first book (each copy holding together three volumes) were sold.[13] The price of a copy was 3 bu, that is three-quarters of 1 ryo, and the whole proceeds of book sale amounted to 112,500 ryo, or 112,500 yen. Fukuzawa's royalty was 20%[14] and he could earn 22,500 ryo or 22,500 yen from the first book alone.[15] It is believed that copies of extra (four volumes and 4 bu) and second books (three volumes and 3 bu), also sold well.

For the rest of the early publications there remains no information as to the numbers sold or the profits made. They certainly sold quickly. As is suggested by Fukuzawa's letter, dated 31 May 1868:

> Book bindings of *Guide to tour in the West* are not able to catch up with the sales.[16]

In a letter dated 5 July 1868, he wrote:

> Nowadays, shutting up doors, I stay at home the whole day and am engaged in translation. ... All copies of *Eleven nations with which treaties are concluded* have sold out. A lot of pirate editions of *Guide to tour in the West* made their appearances.[17]

There were no regulations to protect copyright, and Fukuzawa suffered considerable financial loss. He was, understandably, one of the earliest supporters of an author's copyright in Japan. Before 1875 there seemed to have been no censorship in force involving any of his publications. But he was afraid of possible assassination by the hands of 'Expel the Barbarian' extremists.[18]

The success of his publications encouraged Fukuzawa to undertake translation work on demand. Requests came from domain offices and ex-lords. He wrote in a letter dated 26 July 1868:

> Regardless the volumes, I propose to accept translation works on your behalf. At the moment the arrangements are as follows;
> 1. Books on arms, physics, geography and chemistry and newspapers
>   Fee   1 ryo per sheet (10 lines with 20 characters on each line)
> 2. Books on politics, economics, international laws and military
>   Fee   1 ryo 3 bu per sheet (do)[19]

Fukuzawa, was one of the first samurai to throw away his two swords, and so embrace the spirit of the new age. During the turbulent years of the Restoration, Fukuzawa devoted his whole time to the translation of Western writings on various subjects. It is a curious reflection that by withdrawing from public life, until the new regime became more settled, Fukuzawa was, in fact, making himself a wealthy man.

In September 1867, shortly before the collapse of the *bakufu* administration, a new revised salary payment for the high officials was introduced. They were to be paid in cash instead of rice. According to the salary list, the senior counsellor was to be paid 10,000 ryo per annum; junior counsellor 4,000; Nagasaki commissioner 4,000; Kanagawa commissioner 3,000; Hayashi Digaku no Kami (head of *bakufu* Confucians) 700.[20] Salaries of lower-ranking samurai like Fukuzawa were still given by the *bakufu* in kind, that is to say in rice. Lower-ranking samurai were given cash only occasionally, say, at the end of the year as a bonus, for example the sum of which in the case of Fukuzawa was 15 ryo in 1864.[21] 22,500 ryo, the size of Fukuzawa's income from publication say, of the *Conditions in the West* is therefore astonishing. It was thirty times larger than the head of Hayashi family.

Imaizumi Mine (1855-1937), the second daughter of Katsuragawa Hoshu, well remembered Fukuzawa, who was among the frequent visitors to her father. She commented on Fukuzawa's wealth, writing:

From that time (1869) on, various books by Mr Fukuzawa were published. As they sold pleasantly, Mr Fukuzawa suddenly became so rich and busy that he could rarely come to see my father.[22]

What outlets did Fukuzawa have for his accumulating wealth? A top priority was no doubt the demands of his growing family. Fukuzawa and his wife, Okin (1844-1924), had two sons before the Restoration and were expecting a third child in the summer of 1868. As it happened, while Okin was eight months pregnant, the Fukuzawas and the school had to move out of the Nakatsu domain house in Tsukiji, Edo, because the land had been appropriated for foreign settlement. Fukuzawa bought an estate in Shinsenza, near the shogunal seaside villa at Edo Bay, and built premises and moved there in April 1868 when his school was renamed as Keiō College.[23] Fukuzawa took all responsibility for the college. Fukuzawa's action in taking over the former Nakatsu domain school and making it his own university demonstrates his business initiative. He was soon looking beyond his college to the wider business world.

FUKUZAWA AS BUSINESS PROMOTER

In the aftermath of the Satsuma Rebellion of 1877, Japan suffered from disastrous hyper-inflation. Soaring prices mitigated further international competitiveness of Japanese products and naturally badly affected Fukuzawa and his college. The number of students fell away and, early in 1879, Fukuzawa asked for assistance from the Ministry of Finance. No help came from the ministry. But Fukuzawa was consulted by Ōkuma Shigenobu (1838-1922), then Finance Minister, who asked, 'how can we overcome this runaway inflation?' It is evidence of Japan's lack of understanding of international finance that Ōkuma, a good man but one who had never travelled abroad, should be in charge of Japan's monetary affairs. It was therefore natural that Ōkuma should consult Fukuzawa with his wide experience of travelling in the West.

Looking at the market in Yokohama, Fukuzawa wrote Ōkuma a letter, dated 2 August 1879:

It is good to see that the price of the Mexican dollar at Yokohama continues to be stabilized since the uproar in the last spring. But it would eventually go up again unless the cause of the rise is not removed... Discussions I have had with several of my friends on the matter have produced an idea which is laid down in a paper enclosed.[24]

Fukuzawa's idea was brought to the consideration of Finance Ministry officials. As his letter of 12 September 1879 explained:

> I told Koizumi about the matter of a bank. He will let you know about it. The matter stands as I spoke to you the other day. I have not disclosed it to any other people. If you think it needs to be done immediately, both Koizumi and Nakamigawa will do it to your satisfaction.[25]

Koizumi Nobukichi (1849-94), then a junior officer at the Ministry of Finance, and Nakamigawa Hikojirō (1854-1901) at the Ministry of Foreign Affairs were both Keiō graduates and eager to follow Fukuzawa's suggestions.

Within a month from mid-September the plan of setting up a Specie Bank, based in Yokohama, was quickly developed. On 5 October Fukuzawa recommended that Nakamura Michita (1836-1921) should be head of promoters.[26] This was accepted by Ōkuma. On 13 October Fukuzawa proposed that the government should also contribute funds to the Specie Bank so that it could be safely launched.[27] Ōkuma agreed. In the same letter, Fukuzawa wrote:

> While, receiving your official announcement, Nakamura and his fellow promoters are prepared to submit the application, we do ask you to give us privately further directions. The plan is a great enterprise, and if there occurs any mistake, I will lose the trust of my friends in myself.[28]

The procedures were finalized, and the plan of founding a Yokohama Specie Bank was submitted by the Finance Minister, Ōkuma, on the table of *Dajōkan*, the Meiji cabinet, in November 1879. This was in fact the last financial question Ōkuma tackled because he had to resign as Finance Minister on 28 February 1880 and was ousted finally in October 1881.

What did Ōkuma and Fukuzawa achieve in founding of the Yokohama Specie Bank? With this bank, they thought they would be able to provide the Japanese economy with a market for specie, particularly silver, the effective standard for Japanese currency, and thus to draw into circulation precious metals previously hoarded by Japanese citizens inside Japan. Whatever the validity of their idea of mobilising the hoarded specie within Japan, the bank plan was the first serious attempt to tackle Japan's urgent specie question.[29] Heavy imports, which had exceeded exports since the opening of the ports in 1859, constantly put Japan's balance of payments in the red, and Japan suffered a shortage of means of payment, that is, specie.

The bank opened its doors in February 1880 with a paid-in capital of ¥1,906,580, composed of 30,000 shares and 282 shareholders. As Fukuzawa had urged, the Ministry of Finance supported the bank by subscribing a huge amount of 10,000 shares. Fukuzawa himself took 100 shares. Among the rest of the shareholders, there were notable rising businessmen; Yasuda Zenjirō (1838-1921). 450 shares), founder of the Yasuda Bank; Iwasaki Yatarō (1834-85). 300 shares), head of the new Mitsubishi business; Godai Tomoatsu (1835-85. 100 shares), founder of the Osaka Chamber of Commerce; Hirose Sahei (1828-1914. 100 shares), manager of the Sumitomo business; Ōkura Kihachirō (1837-1928. 90 shares), founder of the Ōkura construction and trading companies; Hara Rokurō (1842-1933. 70 shares), founder of the 100th National Bank of Tottori; Masuda Takashi (1847-1938. 50 shares) and Minomura Risuke (1843-1901. 50 shares), managers of the Mitsui business. Eight directors were elected, and Nakamura Michita assumed the presidency and Koizumi Nobukichi, leaving the Finance Ministry, took the office of vice president.[30]

What was significant, but not clear from the list of shareholders, was the involvement of a solid group of Keiō graduates, that is, Fukuzawa's disciples. Except for the governmental shares, their holding amounted to 8% of the total and 11% of the Tokyo-Yokohama area's. Fukuzawa's business initiative had thus promoted a nationwide project.

Encouraged by the successful launching of the Specie Bank, Fukuzawa proceeded to make another proposal of setting up a trading company to export silk with financial support from the bank. Fukuzawa again consulted Ōkuma who gave consent to the scheme. This time Fukuzawa also involved Iwasaki Yatarō, the founder of the successful Mitsubishi business. In July 1880, Yugensekinin Bōekishō-kai, or Trading Company Ltd. was founded at a site at Nihonbashi, at the very centre of Tokyo. Hayashi Yutekei (1837-1901), Keiō graduate and Mitsubishi man, became the manager. Of the total capital of ¥200,000, Iwasaki contributed ¥80,000 and the rest was put up by Fukuzawa and his associates.[31] The company immediately appointed agents in London, New York and Vladivostok. Fukuzawa's enterprise produced a set of financial and trading institutions, vital for the development of Japan's modern economy.

Fukuzawa had become known to Iwasaki Yatarō, probably from May 1875 when Iwasaki Hisaya (1868-1955), the first son of Yatarō, entered Keiō College. Thereafter, friendship between the two developed. In a letter dated 20 November 1876, Fukuzawa wrote that 'The other day Iwasaki Yatarō visited me and we talked about various matters.'[32]

What made their cooperation stronger was the Takashima Coal Mine problem. The mine had been started in 1868, as a joint venture between the Saga domain and Glover & Co., and after the abolition of the domain system in 1871 it fell into the hands of the Meiji government. Later, in 1874, it was bought by Gotō Shōjirō (1838-97) as the owner. Unfortunately, the failure of Glover & Co. did great damage and left a huge debt on the books of the Takashima Coal Mine. Even worse, Gotō, though talented in politics, was incompetent in business and had borrowed heavily from Mitsubishi. Gotō's son-in-law, Iwasaki Yanosuke (1851-1908), younger brother of Yatarō, was vice president of Mitsubishi.[33] This involvement of the Mitsubishi business in such a business disaster angered the formidable Iwasaki Yatarō, and could have implications for the family. At this stage Fukuzawa took the opportunity of intervening.

Fukuzawa wrote to Shōda Heigorō (1847-1922), Keiō graduate and a Mitsubishi manager, a letter dated 7 October 1879:

> What I would like to say is a matter of Mr Gotō's mine as you implicitly know. I have kept talking to Mr Ishikawa of Mitsubishi confidentially since last October, but I could only recently realize the complications of the problem. From the outset of the problem emerging, it has been my thought that if the Takashima Coal Mine could be obtained by Mitsubishi it would be satisfactory to both Mr Gotō and Mitsubishi... what is going on in Mitsubishi? if you think my idea is worth trying, I would like to discuss the matter. If this could be done, the government would not lose face though Mitsubishi would suffer for a short while. As Jardine, Matheson & Co. had already cleared everything, it would be a matter of money.[34]

Fukuzawa's idea was eventually accepted by Mitsubishi. Through arbitration, involving Ōkuma, the matter was finalized in March 1881. Shortly before the final decision to be made by Iwasaki Yatarō, Fukuzawa wrote to one of his close friends

> Yesterday *Small Rock* (Iwasaki Yanosuke) came to see me. I note everything is going very well. Now let us see how *Large Rock* (Iwasaki Yatarō) makes up his mind.[35]

The mine was sold to Mitsubishi at the price of ¥600,000.

Fukuzawa's relationship with another *zaibatsu*, the House of Mitsui, was less direct. Because Fukuzawa and the Keiō men were seen as part of Ōkuma's group, Nakamigawa Hikojirō, Fukuzawa's favourite nephew, left the Ministry of Foreign Affairs in the wake of the political upheaval of October 1881. Since then Nakamigawa had changed jobs several times, perhaps Nakamigawa's dissatisfaction related to the fact that he, together with Koizumi, had spent more than three years in London.[36] While he was president of the Sanyō Railway Co. connecting Kobe with cities in the far west towards

Kyūshū, Nakamigawa was offered in 1891 a managing directorship at the Mitsui Bank via Inoue Kaoru (1838-1915), chief adviser to Mitsui.

Before accepting the offer, Nakamigawa asked advice from Fukuzawa who immediately sent a telegraph of congratulations and wrote a detailed letter dated 24 June 1891 to him:

> A letter you wrote in the evening of 22nd has just reached me. I immediately sent a telegraph to you. The Mitsui question is very delicate. The other day when I met Takahashi, I asked him in a casual manner about the progress of their reform. Although he did not give any details of it as they are keeping it confidential, it would not be difficult if you could do it. The cleansing of a *Cathedral* that size could never be done by Takahashi. He is no more than a clerk. Even Koizumi would not be able to do it. Only you could do it. Only worry is how Masuda and Shibusawa would think of you, but I think you could leave them for Inoue. The other worry is the attitude of insiders, both seniors and juniors... What matters most is honesty and kindness. As far as businesses are concerned, the status of Mitsui would put any amount of money under their control. There has been a lack of serious management on the one hand, and their awkwardness towards the government on the other hand, which has resulted in their incurring various public commitments. All this has damaged their business. If you could sort it out, you might enjoy the job. Anyhow, if you can, you should accept the offer. You need not worry about Sanyo.[37]

Takahashi Yoshio (1861-1937), another Keiō graduate, was a journalist-turned banker with Mitsui, with only a few years experience. Shibusawa Eiichi (1841-1931), one of the most energetic entrepreneurs in the Meiji era, was invited to assist the Mitsui Bank as an adviser. Masuda Takashi, a competent officer at the Mitsui Bussan, or Mitsui Trading Co., was also dispatched to the bank as an adviser. Therefore Fukuzawa had every reason to worry about Nakamigawa because he was much younger than Masuda and Shibusawa and had no experience in banking.

Nakamigawa was a success for Mitsui but unfortunately he died young in October 1901. During the decade he served Mitsui, Nakamigawa laid a solid foundation on which Mitsui would build. That Mitsui was reborn as a modern *zaibatsu*, a huge corporation of firms in various industries, was, at least partly, through the direction of Nakamigawa on the advice of his uncle Fukuzawa.

Then last but not least Fukuzawa was important in the foundation of Maruya Shōsha, or Maruzen. When Hayashi Yuteki (1838-1901), another Keiō graduate, moved to Yokohama he intended to open a shop in which to sell Western books, clothes and stationery. It is believed that Fukuzawa drew up the prospectus of Maruzen when it opened its doors in January 1869. Fukuzawa stressed that Japan and her people must abandon entirely the seclusion policies and must promote foreign trade on their own account in order to enhance their wealth, and also that the institution would serve as a college of commerce for training people. Taught by Fukuzawa the principle of 'united we stand, divided we fall', Maruzen was founded as a joint stock company with limited liability.

Maruzen not only learned from Fukuzawa the Western method of organizing a modern company but also borrowed a large sum of money from him. Fukuzawa's 'general account' tells us that he was probably one of a few lenders to Maruzen in its early years. Fukuzawa's lending stood at ¥961 in October 1872; ¥17,691 in January 1873; ¥1,134 in July 1873; and ¥41,146 in October 1873.[38] Fukuzawa's general account book continued to record Maruzen borrowings, but increasingly Fukuzawa's investments were made in other commercial concerns.

The success of Maruzen's business resulted in the establishment of the Maruya Bank at Nihonbashi, Tokyo in September 1879. The bank was to have a capital of ¥50,000 composed of 500 shares, but was over-subscribed and eventually had ¥70,000 capital with forty-eight shareholders. The two largest shareholders were Hayashi Yuteki and Fukuzawa himself, who invested ¥18,000 and ¥10,000 respectively.[39]

As a shop supplying books, Maruzen was crucial for Fukuzawa himself and for his school. Keiō College required books; Maruzen supplied them. Without this import of English language books, Fukuzawa could not have maintained the high standard of learning at Keiō College. Maruzen also became a proving ground for young would-be businessmen. Nakamura Michita and Hayashi Yuteki, both trained at Maruzen, subsequently assumed the presidency of the Yokohama Specie Bank and of that Trading Company respectively. Maruzen and Maruya Bank were important early business ventures which later encouraged Fukuzawa to embark on grander projects like the Yokohama Specie Bank.

FUKUZAWA'S BALANCE SHEET

The more involved in business activities Fukuzawa was, the less his earnings from writings became. It was inevitable that sales of his books would decline as new writers on new subjects entered the market. Even so the profits from his own newspaper *Jiji Shimpō*, launched in March 1882, soon became important. Ironically, the newspaper had its origin in a proposal made in 1879 by Itō Hirobumi (1841-1909), then Home Minister, to Fukuzawa. Itō was intent on encouraging his countrymen to understand the government policies through a nationwide newspaper and chose Fukuzawa as the editor. But the political upheaval in 1881 destroyed Itō's plan, which was brought to fruition in Fukuzawa's hands. *Jiji Shimpō* under Fukuzawa's guidance was critical of the government which was still controlled by the *Sat-Cho* oligarchs. Censorship was introduced and in June 1882 the newspaper was banned for five days. However, thereafter, *Jiji Shimpō* kept the censor at bay and proved to be successful, emerging as one of the most influential newspapers in Japan. It was also profitable.

By the 1880s Fukuzawa, in his mid-forties, became a shareholder of many important companies including the Bank of Japan, Yokohama Specie Bank, Kanegafuchi Spinning Co., Oji Paper Manufacturing Co., Sanyō Railway and Kyūshū Railway Companies. He owned several plots of land in Tokyo including those in Ginza, Shiba, Shirokane and Hiroo where land values were constantly rising, which he rented out. He kept deposits of considerable amounts in prestigious banks including Mitsubishi, Mitsui and Specie Banks, some of which gave him a particularly favourable rate of interest.[40] When he was preparing *Conditions in the West* in the early 1860s, he was almost penniless as he was when he first arrived in Edo from Osaka. Once *Conditions in the West* was published, he was in receipt of a modest income. Over time, through a series of judicious business initiatives, he became a rich man.

In a ranking list of millionaires in Tokyo (1.6 million population), prepared in 1890, Fukuzawa was listed 321st out of 4,289 rich people in the capital of Japan. His ranking was well within the upper 8%. Fukuzawa accomplished this without taking any office in the government. It was indeed a remarkable achievement. Although Fukuzawa learnt much from talking to businessmen in the West during his travels, credit must be given to him for his intelligent interpretation of Western business ideas to suit Japanese circumstances. His contribution to the development of Meiji Japan must be thought of not only in terms of his intellectual achievements but also in relation to his business initiatives.

That a low-ranking samurai from Nakatsu domain should have made such a contribution to the new Meiji Japan, and made a personal fortune into the bargain, is indeed a matter of note.

5

Thomas Wright Blakiston (1832–91)

SIR HUGH CORTAZZI

THOMAS WRIGHT Blakiston spent over 20 years in Japan (between the end of 1861 and 1884) mostly in Hakodate in Hokkaido. He was an entrepreneurial businessman, an active engineer, an adventurous and hardy explorer/traveller and an outstanding ornithologist/zoologist. His discovery of the differences between the fauna of Hokkaido and Honshu led to what came to be called the Blakiston line, an imaginary line drawn through the Tsugaru straits between Hokkaido and Honshu. The fauna of Hokkaido were, he concluded, palearctic deriving from Siberia while those in Honshu were 'partially special or peculiar' and partially assimilating otherwise to Asia and the tropical islands to the southward'.[1]

BLAKISTON'S CAREER BEFORE COMING TO JAPAN

Thomas Wright Blakiston[2] was the second son of Major John Blakiston (1785-1867).[3] Major Blakiston married in 1814 Jane, daughter of Thomas Wright, Rector of Market Harborough after whom his second son, born in 1832 at Lymington in Hampshire, was named.

Thomas was educated at St Paul's school in Southsea, Hampshire, and at the Royal Military Academy at Woolwich. He was commissioned in the Royal Artillery in December 1851. After serving with his regiment in England, Ireland, and Nova Scotia, he was sent to the Crimea.

In 1857 Blakiston was asked to join an expedition for the exploration of western Canada. The expedition was under the command of John Palliser (1817-87).[4] Blakiston was mainly engaged in taking observations on the magnetic conditions, temperature and other climatic details. In 1858 he crossed independently two of the passes in the area the expedition was exploring. In 1859 he published at Woolwich an account of his travels under the title 'A Report of the Exploration of two passes through the Rocky Mountains'.

After his Canadian expedition, Blakiston was sent to China where he had command of a detachment of artillery at Canton during the war [of 1859] with China. At Canton he organized an expedition to explore the middle and upper reaches of the Yangtse River. His aim was to ascend the river as far as the Min, and then cross the province of Szechuan (Sichuan) and reach north-western India through Lhasa and Tibet. The party of eleven set out from Shanghai on 12 February 1861 escorted by a Royal Navy squadron which left the expedition at Yo-chau on 16 March. They reached Pingshan on 25 May having travelled eighteen hundred miles from Shanghai. They then had to turn back as the surrounding area was disturbed by rebels. They left Pingshan on 30 May and reached Shanghai on 9 July. Blakiston produced a chart of the river from Hankow to Pingshan which was 'surprisingly accurate'.[5] This was published in 1861 and for this he received in 1862 the Royal (Patron's) Medal of the Royal Geographical Society. In October 1862 Blakiston published an account with illustrations and scientific appendices, under the title *Five Months on the Yangtse.*

As Blakiston described over twenty years later[6] 'rendered sleepless from the partiality of China mosquitoes for white blood, and the intense heat of Shanghai' caused him 'to decide on migrating to cooler regions'. 'As luck would have it, there was a vessel on the point of leaving for Hakodate.' Despite the smell of dried fish and seaweed his first impression of Hakodate was favourable. It was cool and remote. Hokkaido (Yezo as it was then called) had not been explored by Westerners and he was attracted by the thought of travelling in wild country among different peoples.

When he arrived there were only some twenty foreigners in Hakodate of which 'four were women', two of whom were Russians.

> 'There was generally a Russian vessel-of-war lying in the harbour, which added its officers to the society of the place, and its drunken sailors to the streets of the town. Naturally, in so small a community, all nationality was dropped, and the residents were more like members of one family, such etiquette as formal invitations and calls being discarded, for the more open and cordial hospitality being induced by a common feeling of being strangers amongst a treacherous and deceitful race; and all seemed to look to one another for mutual protection.'

He was most hospitably entertained and enjoyed his stay 'excessively'. He took the opportunity to join a few expeditions to the surrounding country and 'devoted much of his time to collecting birds'.

Blakiston decided to resign his commission and settle at Hakodate.

BLAKISTON IN JAPAN

Blakiston established with J. Marr, another British businessman in Hakodate, Blakiston, Marr and Company.[7] The company was set up to trade with Russia and China, manufacture ice and process timber.[8] In 1864 Blakiston imported a steam sawmill and European engineers to put it up. He invited the Japanese government to place its mechanics at the plant to learn about steam machinery under these engineers and urged Japanese people to visit and inspect the mill. In 1871 he negotiated a contract for a sawmill and steam engine for the government in Hokkaido and arranged for its delivery. Contemporary advertisements show that his firm was dealing in paint, selling and renting real estate, and offering for sale the salvage from ships wrecked off the coast.

Blakiston made 'plans for the harbours of Hokkaido; the founding of a regular shipping service between Hakodate and Aomori: and planning a water system for Hakodate'. He 'inaugurated the annual sailboat race in Hakodate harbour for the purpose of developing sailing techniques'. He also 'interested the Japanese in meteorological observations and led to the establishing of Japan's first meteorological station at the home of his friend Fukushi Unokichi'.

Blakiston kept an open house for travellers, especially those with scientific interests. One of his scientific friends was John Milne, described as the father of modern seismology, (1850-1913).[9] Blakiston's knowledge of Hokkaido 'was of tremendous value to Milne during the latter's first tentative sorties into the interior'. He also got to know John Batchelor, missionary and Ainu scholar, whose knowledge of the Ainu he respected although it is doubtful whether they had much in common other than an interest in the Ainu. Blakiston seems to have got on reasonably well with the many Ainu he met He was struck by their 'subdued nature'.[10] 'Careless and good-natured as they are, they appear to have lost all idea of independence, and to have assigned themselves almost as slaves to the more civilized Japanese.' His comments on the Ainu in his writings were not scholarly but should not be overlooked by students of the Ainu.[11]

Blakiston, although at first favourably impressed by the small foreign community in Hakodate, became disillusioned. At the end of his stay[12] he had this to say:

A most healthy climate permits of no disease in the body,
but the mind broods over its own cares, and it must be

added – the cares of others. The latter begets scandal, the first insobriety. People who should live as one family – two dozen foreigners in the midst of thirty-seven thousand natives – exist as cats and dogs. Some wear brass collars, such as consuls, some wear black coats, such as missionaries, some would be industrious dogs if they had enough to do, some would be sleepy, quiet cats if their tails were not trodden upon.

It is easy to surmise that Blakiston, a tough individualist who spoke his mind and went his own way, did not fit easily into such a small community.

Blakiston had his ups and downs with officialdom and before his departure made some scathing comments on consular officials. He noted[13] that 'with the exception of of one or two notable examples' Hakodate 'had been usually blessed with some of the worst specimens of foreign officials it would be easy to select'. In an earlier passage[14] he had commented:

> ...our consuls, feeling that they might not be backed in straightfoward and firm conduct by the minister at the capital, were forced to have recourse to diplomacy, at which the Japanese invariably beat them; or when there was any doubt...they sided with the Japanese. Such is, of course, very disagreeable to mercantile men, and great and frequent were the complaints against the mode in which British interests were looked after in Japan.

As the two episodes, summarized below, show Blakiston was inclined to take the law into his own hands and disliked any attempts to curb what the consuls no doubt saw as his high-handed behaviour.

In February 1873 Blakiston was accused of the manslaughter of a Japanese boy. Inquiries revealed that Blakiston had caught a boy whom he suspected of theft. The boy had confessed but had refused to give any details or his name. Blakiston had then whipped him and tied him up in his godown. After the boy had been whipped again he gave his name. Blakiston went out and when he returned the boy was dead, apparently having strangled himself. Blakiston who complained that the Japanese authorities did nothing to deal with cases of theft also seems to have locked up and whipped a boatman whom he suspected of being involved in the robbery. Blakiston was eventually tried in the consular court on charges of assault rather than manslaughter and fined 400 dollars on one charge and 100 dollars on a second charge. The Japanese authorities protested vainly against the leniency of the sentence.[15]

In 1875 Blakiston came into conflict with the local authorities over the issue by his firm of coupons (*shoken*) promising to pay the bearer

Japanese money on demand. Such coupons had been issued in the past by foreign trading companies and local daimyo, but the banking regulations isued in 1872 had prohibited such action by the daimyo and the local commissioner considered that the regulation should apply to Blakiston, Marr and Company and prohibited the use of their coupons. This led to various diplomatic arguments but eventually Sir Harry Parkes, the British minister, and the Japanese foreign minister agreed that the issue of such certificates should be stopped and Eusden, the British consul in Hakodate, was ordered to issue a prohibition order to Blakston, Marr.[16] This no doubt riled Blakiston greatly.

Blakiston's business interests 'eventually suffered seriously from his inability to collect the generous loans he had made to Japanese civilians' thus causing him to leave Japan in 1884.[17]

After a visit to Australia, New Zealand and England Blakiston decided to retire to the Unted States eventually settling in New Mexico. In April 1885 he married Anne Mary, daughter of James Dunn of Dundaff, London Ontario, by whom he had a son and a daughter. He died at San Diego, California, on 13 October 1891.

BLAKISTON, TRAVELLER AND EXPLORER

Blakiston's *Japan in Yezo*, published at Yokohama in 1883 records his journeys in and around Hokkaido with detailed accounts of Hokkaido as he found it in those days. It also includes a record of a journey which he made round Hokkaido in 1869 which he had read as a paper entitled 'A Journey in Yezo' to the Asiatic Society of Japan on 12 February 1872. He read to the Society a second paper entitled 'A Journey in North East Japan' on 17 June 1874.

The first journey which took Blakiston round Hokkaido, began on 15 September 1869 when he left Hakodate on board the *Akindo*. They ran into a head wind and heavy swell but at sunrise on the 17th they rounded Cape Erimo, the southern tip of the Hidaka mountains. Blakiston noted that the existing charts including that produced by the British Admiralty were 'not only imperfect but so untrue' that they could hardly be said to be a guide at all for navigation in those waters. Even so foreign charts had to be used as the Japanese produced a map of Hokkaido in four sheets which had 'no pretensions to a coast chart' although 'as a map of the interior it is most elaborate'. But Blakiston thought the map 'considerably in error in latitude, and probably much more so in longitude'.

The *Akindo* stopped at Akkeshi bay (referred to by Blakiston as Akis). Here he and the ship's captain called at the *Kaisho*, the office of the *Kaitakushi*, the Japanese government agency in Hokkaido. They encountered many Ainu and observed the Ainu habitations. Blakiston commented that 'A well-fed Aino [sic] is not a bad specimen of humanity, but the women are not to be compared with them', although he had seen 'some young girls very good-looking, save and except always their lips which are invariably tattooed'. He noted that the Ainu were all 'subsisted' by the lessee of the fishing coast. This meant that they received a daily allowance of rice in return for performing various menial services. The Ainu 'generally hunt with bows and arrows'. 'Most of those I met spoke Japanese, more or less.'

At Akkeshi Blakiston observed the seaweed fishery and the *Akindo* was able to load a cargo of seaweed (*konbu*). From Akkeshi they sailed on to Hamanaka bay, 'a great fishing district' by Cape Kiritappu. Blakiston was 'left alone at the eastern end of Yezo with a fowling piece, powder, shot, and bullets, a couple of pairs of blankets, a change of clothes, a good pair of boots, a pocket compass and note books, and a Japanese map of the island, to pursue a journey hitherto unattempted by any foreigner'. The country had hardly begun to feel the effects of the Japanese colonization efforts.

Blakiston started out early on 7 October 1869. He rode one pony and on another on top of his pack saddles rode a Japanese who was to act as his guide and escort. There were hardly any roads. Generally 'the sea beach, or the rough mountain-side, with the trees cut away sufficiently to allw of the passage of pack-horses in single file, are the "roads" of Yezo'. They passed two or three small 'rest-houses, usually mere sheds, kept up for the accommodation of travellers'. At one they stopped for half an hour to rest their ponies and eat some cold rice and fish. He was then in the Nemuro district and picked up an Ainu guide who 'took great delight in doing showman' at Ainu settlements. The Ainu 'seemed gratified to find my appearance somewhat resembled their own people, and this fact has doubtless a good deal to do with the friendliness on all occasions displayed by the Ainos towards foreigners'. Throughout his journey on land of 54 days (of which he travelled for 43 days) and covered 367 *ri*, or about 895 miles, he 'was invariably treated with civility and kindness by Japanese as well as Ainos'.

Blakiston went on to Shibetsu opposite to the island of Kunashiri and on 9 October, a wet morning, he set off up the Shibetsu valley with a party of six Ainu and a Japanese, mounted on ponies. Their provisions consisted principally of fine salmon.

> The Ainos were a merry lot of fellows, and their spirits being more than usually elevated by an extra dram served out before starting, they kept up a round of jokes among them, and occasionally enlivened the still woods with a song.

Blakiston was in some discomfort as he was perched on top of his baggage with his legs hanging down on either side of the horse's neck with the pommel of the saddle right under him and the cautle against his spine. He urged all future travellers to take their own saddle and boots. Fortunately, he was wearing

> ... thick, good, strong, corduroy trousers, which, tucked into a pair of English-made knee-boots, with a flannel shirt, an Aino cloth coat, a red worsted sash round my waist, an old felt hat, and a loose wrapper to put on in wet weather, completed a costume which, if not pictureque, was both comfortable and serviceable.

The party came across the Shiretoko peninsula reaching the sea again at Share. On their way they startled a deer and later came on a whole herd. At Share he rested for a day, taking the opportunity to wash some of his clothes in the river. At Abashiri he was 'invited to take a warm bath – a luxury which native travellers never refuse, and which officials demand as a right – which I enjoyed in a nice wash-room, fitted up in the style of a first class native hotel. I may observe, however, that this was a luxury I seldom resorted to, preferring the clear running-stream of some cold mountain torrent to the enervating "furo"'.

Blakiston's route took him via Mombetsu along the coast towards Cape Soya. He recorded that, the rivers being swollen by the rains, the fords were deep. 'My horse fell once this day, sending me flying over its head with my gun in my hand, but owing to my carrying it detached – my usual practice – it fortunately sustained no injury, while I had become so accustomed to such mishaps that I thought little of it.' It was by now getting cold and Blakiston found the dwellings put up by the Japanese ill-suited to the climate.

Near Cape Soya Blakiston met an official from Hakodate who had been in charge of the Soya station when HMS *Rattler* was wrecked in the autumn of 1868.[18] He was of the opinion that the vessel ought never to have been run so close on shore, even supposing entire ignorance of the existence of reefs – a judgement which, after inspection of the locality, I believe can hardly be gainsayed.

Blakiston remained at Soya during 25 October to inspect, on the orders of the Japanese government, the guns, stores, and material saved from HMS *Rattler*. He found

> ... a house which had been occupied by Captain Stevenson and the officers of that ill-fated ship, with a flagstaff erected in front of it, and the royal arms and other devices from the vessel stuck on the gate posts. The stores and material, consisting of rope, blocks, wire rigging, boarding pikes, cutlasses, revolvers, chairs, tables, a fire-engine, smith's

forge and tools, cooking utensils, crockery, lanterns, compasses, salt provisions, biscuit, shot and shell, flags, sails, a turning lathe, sponges and rammers, and some books, in two houses and a shed covered with sails, were all as they had been left when the officers and crew were taken away by the French corvette *Dupleix*.

The doors had been nailed up and nothing had been removed, but as a result of the weather '. . .most of the sails and many other perishable articles were more or less damaged'.

Some spars, five anchors, a quantity of chain cable, with five of the ship's boats were outside, partly covered with thatched roofs. What guns had been saved were ranged up in two lines on their carriages. A portion of the *Rattler* was fast on the reef to the south of the entrance into the small harbour, and the whole shore was still strewn with fragments from the wreck. Many of the things were moved and distributed under my superintendence, and I left word with the two officials then at Soya how to dispose of the remainder: the whole of these stores having been presented to the Japanese government by orders from England.

Blakiston mislaid his compass while he was at Soya, but he was able to give a Japanese who accompanied him on the next section of his journey guidance about where he might have left it. It was delivered back to him by an Ainu three days later. Blakiston's route took him down the west coast via Rumoi to Ishikari. He was impressed by the beauty of the autumn colours:

. . .the lateness of the season had turned the oak leaves a deep rich brown, the birch yellow, and the mountain ash the brightest lake colour, which, with the berries of the last a rich scarlet, and some of the grasses a violet hue, made up such a mixture of colours, and so beautifully distributed, that an artist would have been at a loss to exaggerate them. As I gazed on this scene, recollections of similar views in the more northern regions of America came fresh to my memory, but I believe I can say with truth I had never seen anything to excel the fall colours of Northern Yezo.

On this stretch Blakiston met more people travelling than he had on the north coast. He discerned a couple of officers travelling on horseback at a long distance by the rays of the sun on their bright lacquered travelling hats '. . .They civilly stopped and spoke to me, asking me to "give their greetings to their friends at Hakodate"'. At one point as there was already deep snow on the mountain passes, he had to take a small boat part of the way along the coast, sitting on the bottom between two oarsmen.

From Ishikari Blakiston went on to Otaru. He noted that there were 'but one or two houses, and but few fishing-huts, along this shore'. He was, however, much impressed by the bay and its potential as a harbour.

He then went on to the little village of Yoichi (where Nikka whisky now has its main distillery) and in the river valley he saw Ainu expertly spearing salmon. On his way to Iwanai he decided to walk despite the cold and snow as the horse provided was 'shaking with cold'. He left his fowling piece to be fastened to his baggage This turned out to be an unfortunate decision as while trudging along he came across three bears in his path. When he shouted and waved the 'old one mounted on her hind legs' to 'take a better look' at him. Hardly had they moved than he encountered another big bear who only waddled off after he had thrown a handful of dried mud in its direction.

At Iwanai he visited the coal mines which had been reopened following a visit there in 1866 by E. H. M. Gower and his brother who was then British consul at Hakodate. The work on the mines had been interrupted by the civil war in 1868, but in the autumn of 1869 work had resumed under the direction of a Mr James Scott. Blakiston 'had the gratification of seeing the first coal run down the tramway; in fact I may say, the opening of the first rail-road in Japan'. He believed that 'Iwanai coal will come into general use in the north of Japan for steam purposes' as it was superior in quality to most other kinds of Japanese coal.

On his way back to Ishikari Blakiston 'fell in' with the newly-appointed governor of the region who 'was travelling in grand state'. In crossing the mountains between Iwanai and Yoichi he 'had no less than 17 horses and 160 coolies'. The governor wanted Blakiston to go with him to Sapporo 'where they had decided to make the seat of government', but pleading the lateness of the season Blakiston declined.

On his way across to the east coast Blakiston met many friendly Ainu. It was now late November and the snow was hard and crisp. At one point he let an Ainu girl ride on top of his baggage while he walked. They came across some deer. 'As one troop crossed the road in front of us, a fine stag stopped and looked at me, some 70 yards distance.' Blakiston shot him 'full in the forehead, and he dropped like a stone. The Aino, the girl and I, set to work at once, skinned and cut up the deer.'

At Muroran, Blakiston saw some small batteries constructed by the Tokugawa who had held Hakodate in the previous winter. 'What they could have seen in this locality, either as a defensible position, or having any other recommendation, I cannot see.'

Blakiston, who was anxious to get back to Hakodate, pushed on via the coast road. This was one of the worst he had passed over in his journey. Fortunately, on this stretch he had a good horse 'that climbed like a cat'. He travelled on one stretch for some time after dark:

> In the shade of the woods it was so dark that it was impossible to see a few yards distance. I left it all to the horse, contenting myself with shielding my face from blows of branches of trees, which I could not see, and holding on with the other hand to the cantle of the saddle to keep myself in position when descending the steepest places.

Blakiston eventually got back to Hakodate late on 29 November 1869 after a journey of nine hundred miles 'almost entirely over ground hitherto untrodden by any foreigner'.

*   *   *

The above summary account gives mere highlights of Blakiston's journey. They show him as tough, resourceful and arrogant.

Blakiston's 'A Journey in North East Japan' took place between 28 October and 9 November 1873. The journey followed the ship-wreck of the PMSS *Ariel* off Toyoma point in what is now Fukushima prefecture. Blakiston records the event:

> When Captain Newell and myself slid down a rope from the fore chains, the vessel had sunk so far aft that the water was on the upper deck forward of the paddle boxes, and the whole after hurricane deck was submerged. Fortunately there was little swell, so that all the boats in the darkness of the night reached the shore, and chanced to strike parts of the beach between the reefs. The head-man of the little village of Toyoma whom I found with the assistance of a fisherman and his paper lantern, made arrangements for the accommodation of the eighty-four shipwrecked people, and the villagers were all extremely civil.

On the next morning only one of the mastheads of the vessel was visible. Blakiston 'after a breakfast of beef and ship-biscuit' hired a man to carry 'a small leather-bag, which my next cabin neighbour had saved for me' and started on foot for Taira, the chief town of Iwasaki-ken some 7½ miles away.

Blakiston went to the government office in Taira where he was civilly received. The chief official promised to have quarters prepared for all the shipwrecked people and to arrange for them to be forwarded to Edo (Tokyo) about 138 miles distant. Blakiston, however, was on his way to Hakodate and saw no reason why he should return via Yokohama. To travel overland at this period he needed a special passport but the official demurred. Bakiston '...therefore left him and put up at a native hotel where I ordered a horse, purchased a blanket, a Japanese pipe and tobacco, and was nearly ready to start when Captain Newell and the rest of the people arived. As the ship's interpreter had not yet come on, I assisted in getting them billeted.'

About half-past two an officer came to see Blakiston and told him that his plan to travel north was '*muzukashii*' (too difficult). Blakiston had, however, made up his mind and told the official that he would proceed without a passport. This put the officer 'in great tribulation'. Blakiston arranged for his scanty baggage to be carried on a horse with a man and followed on foot. Outside the town he mounted on the pack saddle and with the horse led by the man he began his journey.

Blakiston took the Hamakaidō which like the Tōkaidō was lined with pine trees. He hoped that 'the unsparing and barbarous hand of an impoverished government' would not be laid on these pine trees and that '...this great feature of the scenery of Japan will not be civilized off the face of the earth...After the almost bloodless revolution which changed Japan from a feudal to a monarchical government, it should be the study of those in power to retain at least some of the time-honoured features of a state which has passed away.'

Blakiston stopped for the night in an inn. He was 'hardly surprised' to find the next room to his occupied by two *yakunin* who had come post haste to overtake him. One of these asked him if he had a travel permit which he answered in the negative. The official then produced '...a Japanese document which was unintelligible to me, and said if I *was* going on, he had been deputed by the chief official at Taira to accompany me.' They soon became 'the best of friends' and after breakfast they set off.

Blakiston followed the 'road' via Ichinoseki towards Morioka. They stopped one night at a place called Kurosawa where 'they were comfortably lodged in a good large house'.

They passed not far from the '...Yachingashira farm, where Messrs Lucy and McKinnon, in company with two Japanese officials, are raising stock and grain...Their isolated situation may be imagined when I say that I was the third white man Mr Lucy has seen for the last two years.'

Blakiston spent the greater part of his final day on foot as it was very cold with snow and sleet. He had hitherto tried to avoid walking as much as possible as he had only one pair of thin boots and had been unable to buy en route any boots suitable to rough travelling. 'My two Japanese companions, unaccustomed to a northern climate, were nearly frozen, and looked most miserable.'

Blakiston travelled some 352 miles overland to Aomori at an average of 27 miles a day.

BLAKISTON AS AN ORNITHOLOGIST AND ZOOLOGIST

On his first visit to Hakodate in August, September and October 1861 Blakiston began his study of the local bird life and contributed articles[19] about Japanese birds to various ornithological journals including *Ibis* and *The Chrysanthemum*. He also sent boxes of birds for study and comparison to Mr R. Swinhoe, an authority in London on the birds of East Asia. His main work which was done jointly with Mr Harry Pryer of Yokohama was a 'A Catalogue of Birds of Japan' which was first published in *Ibis* in 1878.

In the introduction to their paper for the Asiatic Society in 1880 Blakiston and Pryer referred to the *Fauna Japonica* by Temminck and Schlegel between 1845 and 1850 which had hitherto been the standard work on the birds of Japan and covered all the species obtained by Dr Franz von Siebold between 1823 and 1830. The authors did not claim that their catalague was complete and said that they would be 'happy to receive specimens, either skinned or fresh, of any birds whatever and will undertake to furnish the senders with the names, when known, or any other information in their power.'

The compilers noted that foreigners often remarked on the paucity of birds in Japan and complained that those which were found were 'not remarkable for either beauty or song.' They agreed that this was to some extent true of the neighbourhood of the settlements, but it was 'a great mistake to suppose that Japanese birds are at all deficient, either in numbers or other respects, in the wilder parts of the country.' On a visit to the Fuji area, 44 species were obtained during a few days and a number of others observed. Among those obtained were several specimens of *Tchitrea Princeps*. 'When alive, this bird rivals in beauty any denizen of the tropics.' 'Three species of Thrushes, all good songsters, abound on Fuji-san.'

They noted that 180 of the species they had observed found also occur in China, and 'about 100 are identical with those of Great Britain'.

Seebohm in his '*Birds of the Japanese Empire*' (London: Porter, 1890) listed 381 species of birds, not including sub-species. '*A Field Guide to the Birds of Japan*', (Tokyo: Wild Bird Society of Japan, 1982), noted that 524 species of birds had been recorded in Japan by the time the book was published.

One or two Japanese species still have official names given by Blakiston such as the *ketupa blakistoni* or Blakiston's fish owl known in Japanese as the *shima-fukuro*. Blakiston's eagle owl or *bubo blackistoni*

(Seebohm No 184) is listed in the field guide as a *bubo bubo* or *washi-mimizuku*.

Blakiston gave specimens of the birds he collected to the Hakodate museum, to the Natural History Museum in London (see note 19) and to the United States National Museum. He also sent living animals to the Zoological Society of London.

In the nineteenth century ornithologists tended to collect specimens for museums. Nowadays, ornithologists generally try to preserve living species and study birds in the wild taking photographs with telescopic lenses. Blakiston, of course, had no such equipment and his catalogue lacks illustrations. Seebohm includes a few drawings. *Birds of Japan* includes colour reproductions of the various species.

THE BLAKISTON LINE

In the course of his studies of the birds and fauna of Hokkaido Blakiston reached the conclusion that there were substantial differences between the fauna of Hokkaido and Honshu This led to what came to be called the Blakiston line. He published the results of his studies in his paper for the Asiatic Society of Japan entitled 'Zoological Indications of Ancient Connection of the Japan islands with the Continent' which he read to the Society on 14 February 1883. He stressed that his paper was not intended to be definitive. He hoped that it would 'be looked upon as an inquiry into the possibility of evidence leading to certain inferences'.

Blakiston began by looking at the geography of Japan and the proximity of parts of Japan with continental Asia. He had had the benefit of the observations of Professor Milne, the seismologist. The main island of Japan seemed distinct and 'we should naturally expect to find it with special or peculiar fauna. However, it is not so entirely, but only partially; assimilating otherwise to Asia and the tropical islands to the southward'. It appeared to him that the deep seas around Japan might 'be bridged, or floated over' in ways which would 'account for the non-peculiar zoological forms. The first by the freezing of the Strait of Tsugaru, and the second by the Kuro-siwo [Kuroshio] ocean current'.

Blakiston did not think that the Asian elements in Japanese fauna arose because of a connection between Hokkaido and Honshu, but he did think that there had been a land connection between Hokkaido and Sakhalin, thus making Hokkaido part of Siberia during 'the warm period'. During the subsequent cold period 'animals would be gradually driven south' and when the Tsugaru straits were bridged with ice have migrated into the Japanese islands. It seemed to him that the descendants of the animals which had travelled south would have found themselves cut off from returning north by the melting of the ice in the Tsugaru strait. These animals 'would necessarily become localized'. He went on to give examples to prove this hypothesis.

Blakiston deduced from his researches that the animal life of Hokkaido was Siberian and had 'arrived there doubtless subsequent to the glacial period'. He concluded that there was 'an absolute dissimilarity of the two islands [Hokkaido and Honshu] zoologically'. He recognized, however, that there were exceptions to 'the otherwise very marked distinction between the fauna of the two islands, and, as it were, leaves a small gap in the otherwise decided zoological line of division as marked by the Strait of Tsugaru'.

Blakiston summed up by saying that his paper was

> . . .an endeavour without assuming physical changes of great magnitude in very recent geological time, to account for zoological indications in Japan which point principally towards the neighbouring continent and thereby necessitate a connection at some period; in considering which, the conclusion has been forced on us that Yezo and more northern islands are not Japan, but, zoologically speaking, portions of north-eastern Asia, from which Japan proper is cut off by a decided line of demarcation in the Strait of Tsugaru.

At the Asiatic Society meeting on 14 February 1883 when Blakiston's paper was read, Professor Milne commented that

> Captain Blakiston's paper would be regarded by all naturalists as a valuable contribution to zoology. . .Captain Blakiston had shown the clear distinction between the fauna of Yezo and that of Niphon. The straits of Tsugaru were shown to form a new zoological line which might appropriately be called 'Blakiston's line', just as the line between Bali and Limbok was called Wallace's line.

According to Dr Yuma Masahide of the Centre for Ecological Studies in the University of Kyoto[20] 'the discovery of the ecological line by Blakiston has been regarded as "a classical work" among naturalists in the world'. 'It is as valid now as it was when Blakiston was active, since there are still notable and important differences in fauna and flora across the line.' 'Blakiston stands as the major pioneer in Japan on this stage.'

6

Frederick Victor Dickins (1838-1915)[1]

PETER FRANCIS KORNICKI

I T HAS TO BE admitted that Dickins is today a forgotten figure. In 1956, at an address delivered at the School of Oriental and African Studies in London, Sir George Sansom identified the pioneers of Japanese studies in the West as Ernest Mason Satow (1843-1929), William George Aston (1841-1911), Basil Hall Chamberlain (1850-1935) and Karl Adolf Florenz (1865-1939). Satow and Aston were fellow members of the consular service who arrived in Japan in 1862 and 1864 respectively; Chamberlain arrived in Japan in 1873 and taught English at the Naval Academy and was later the first professor of Japanese at Tokyo Imperial University; and Florenz reached Japan in 1889 and taught German language and literature at the Imperial University for more than 25 years.[2] Yet Dickins was in Japan before any of them apart from Satow, he published the first scholarly translations from Japanese into English, and he was the first in any language to take Hokusai as a subject of study. Furthermore, when practising as a lawyer in 1872 he was indirectly responsible for what contemporary newspapers termed the 'abolition of the Yoshiwara [pleasure quarter]'. He did not, it is true, produce a synthesis like Aston's' *A history of Japanese literature* (1899) or Florenz's *Geschichte der japanischen Literatur* (1904-6), but he did publish a number of scholarly translations which reveal him to have been a serious literary scholar. It is certainly appropriate to reassess his career, which included the practice of medicine in Japan as well as law and active membership of the foreign community in Yokohama in the 1870s, and to reconsider his contributions to Japanese studies.

★ ★ ★

Frederick Victor Dickins was born on 24 May 1838 in Manchester; in 1855 he became an apprentice at Manchester Royal Infirmary, and he took his medical degrees at London University. He served as medical officer on a steamer sailing to Australia and then, in 1859, qualified as a Member of the Royal College of Surgeons. On 13 May 1862 he joined the Navy as an acting assistant surgeon and was attached to HMS *Euryalus*, which was the flagship of rear-admiral Küper on station in the East Indies and China. From 5 January 1863 he was employed on HMS *Coromandel*, the tender for the *Euryalus*, and it was in this year that he first set foot in Japan. From 10 October 1864 he was detached from his ship and was appointed the sole surgeon at, and effectively in charge of, the naval sick-quarters in Yokohama. He remained in this position until 1 February 1866, when he resigned his post and brought his naval career to an end.[3]

Whilst serving on the *Coromandel* Dickins was responsible for keeping the medical and surgical journal of the ship, in which he noted that syphilis was the disease which caused him most trouble among the crew. He came across no cases of smallpox on board, but he added to the journal an essay on smallpox in Japan, which he found to be 'endemic and extremely prevalent': 'I have obtained,' he declared, 'a knowledge of the Japanese language and have thereby been enabled to gain some information upon Small Pox as it exists among the natives.' He had evidently by this time formed some acquaintance with Japanese doctors for he also wrote an assessment of their qualities:

> Japanese doctors are of two classes, one of which learns the Western system of diagnostication and therapeutics from Dutch books. The other adheres to the old system introduced by the Chinese. I prefer the latter class, for the knowledge of the former is purely book-knowledge unfounded on any acquaintance with anatomy chemistry or physiology, and they are eminently unpractical, and apt to make strange havoc in their misapplication of the maxims they get from Dutch books, most of which by the bye are of ancient date. While the former (*sic; sc.* latter) are for the most part given to the exhibition of harmless herbs, powdered snakes, etc which have little bad effect beyond sickening the stomach.[4]

By the time he had written this, showing his lack of sympathy for Chinese medicine, Dickins was in charge of the sick quarters at Yokohama.[5]

Little is known about Dickins' activities in Japan at this time. After his death in 1815 his wife followed his instructions that all his letters be destroyed saving those received from Satow, which are now in the Public Record Office, but it is unclear what became of the diary he is known to have kept. A passage he cited later from an entry written in 1863, 'if ever these people [i.e., the Japanese] get out of their present tyranny [the Shogunal government] they will astonish the world', reveals that early on he had been much impressed by what he found, and he wrote later that he had 'fallen in love with things Japanese in the early'60s'. In another letter to Satow written in 1909 he recalled a small monastery at the end of Bluff in Yokohama and some of the acquaintances he had had in those days:

> The old priest there in the sixties was a great chum of mine and many delightful hours I spent with him. . . . I also knew a man named Utanosuke, a subordinate civil servant of the Mito clan, very intimately and through him a small circle of men, all enthusiastic 'seers'.[6]

Quite how and when Dickins began his studies of Japanese is unknown. According to an article published in England in December 1864 Dickins at the time of writing already had 'thirteen months' experience of the language', so he must have begun his studies in mid 1863. In this article Dickins referred in passing to the writings of Léon de Rosny and Rutherford Alcock on the Japanese language, and, more impressively, to several Japanese works, including an encyclopaedia, *Wakan sansai zue*, and a guide to letter-writing, *Shōsoku ōrai*. This article appeared in the *Chinese and Japanese Repository*, a journal founded by James Summers (1828-91), who, in 1851, was appointed to teach Chinese at King's College, London. He already knew some Japanese well before his first visit to Japan in 1873 and he provided Dickins with an outlet for his first writings on Japan, including his translations from *Hyakunin isshu*, mentioned below, and a survey of the temples of Kamakura.[7]

Dickins' studies of Japanese were evidently motivated by his interest in the 'rich and extensive literature of so intelligent a people as the Japanese', and he made rapid progress in applying his knowledge of the language to literary work. In 1865 he published his first translations of Japanese literature, which are amongst the first ever made from Japanese into English. These translations were of the 100 poems in *Hyakunin isshu*, an anthology of one hundred *waka* poems each written by a different poet which was supposedly compiled by Fujiwara no Teika (1162-1241). Dickins' translations consisted of renderings of the poems into English verse, together with literal translations and notes. They appeared in successive issues of the *Chinese and Japanese Repository* and then in 1866 they were published in London in a handsome volume which also included the texts of the poems in Japanese script, lithographically printed, and a picture of Mt Fuji on the cover. Dickins acknowledged that he had used the text and commentary contained in a recent edition of the poems, *Hyakunin isshu mine no kakehashi* (1806), but in order to do so he would have had to familiarize himself with the cursive forms of Japanese writing as used in blockprinted books, which in the 1860s were all that was available in Japan. Although his contemporaries, including Satow, had to do the same, it was a considerable achievement to have reached this level so quickly.[8]

On the title-page of the book Dickins described the poems as 'Japanese lyrical odes'. Further, he also quoted from Horace, *'carmina no prius audita canto'*, 'I sing songs not heard before', presumably referring to his role as a pioneer in the translations of Japanese literature. His use here of the word 'odes' and his reference to Horace suggest that he was trying to famliarize Japanese poetry for British readers by presenting it as akin to the odes of Horace.

While he was in Japan, Dickins seems to have decided to abandon his medical career, although his reasons for this are unknown. He returned to England in 1866, where he joined a warehousing company in Manchester to learn the ways of business. He had not been there long when he switched course again and began reading for the bar; according to his obituary in the *Lancet*, this was because he had heard that there would be openings in Japan for English barristers, presumably in connection with the consular courts. At this time he was living in lodgings in Wimbledon, and he recalled later that in 1866 and 1867 various students from the Satsuma and Chōshū domains then in London had frequently come to his lodgings to read books in English with him; he does not identify them, but states that some of them later rose to high office. On 21 November 1867 Dickins was admitted to the Middle Temple, one of the ancient Inns of Court in London, and on 10 June 1870 he was called to the bar and became a barrister. By this time he had a wife, for in May 1869 he had married Mary Jane Wilkinson, who was the second daughter of William M. Wilkinson of Manchester and with whom he was to return to Japan.[9]

While back in England, Dickins disposed of some Japanese books he had acquired in Japan. In 1867 he sent his copy of Iinuma Yokusai's *Sōmoku zusetsu* (1856-62) and 'such specimens of Japanese plants as are remaining in my possession' to Canon Richard Durnford (1802-95), who was later the bishop of Chichester and had 'a rare knowledge of botany and horticulture'. In his letter to Durnford he stated that he considered the book 'so strong a proof of the advances made by the Japanese in science' and expressed the wish that Japanese achievements might be better known so that 'the position to which Japan by her intelligence and industry has a right might be freely accorded to her by my countrymen'.[10] In 1871 Dickins evidently sold some or all of his remaining Japanese books to Bernard Quaritch, the leading antiquarian bookseller of London. Quaritch immediately offered them for £25 to

Lord Lindsay, the 25th earl of Crawford and Balcarres, whose collection of oriental books was already extensive and who had since 1862 been asking Quaritch to find him Japanese books. At any event, while in England studying law Dickins was by no means neglecting his Japanese studies, for his translation of *Kanadehon Chūshingura*, which was published in Yokohama in 1875, was in fact completed in England, and part of it appeared in the *Westminster Review* in 1870.[11]

Dickins returned to Japan late in 1871. Shortly after his arrival at Yokohama a notice appeared in the *Japan Mail* in November 1871, one of the three English-language newspapers published in Yokohama, to the effect that he had been admitted to practise in the British consular courts. By 1878 he clearly had a solicitor working for him, but in July of that year he suffered a breakdown of some sort and on 1 January 1879 the Dickinses left Japan with their three children, as it happened, for good. The 1880 directory lists him as absent, most likely because he had the intention of returning to Japan, as will be clear below.[12]

Dickins first appeared in court in Japan in December 1871 and for the next seven years practised extensively in Yokohama, not only in the British consular court but in other courts as well. Most of his work seems to have been in the consular courts of Yokohama, and therefore inevitably concerned the foreign community, but he also worked in Japanese courts in Yokohama and Tokyo in cases where foreign residents were suing Japanese companies or individuals. However, his impressions of Japanese courts and judicial practice were unfavourable.[13]

During his years in Japan as a lawyer the most famous case with which he was involved was undoubtedly that concerning the Peruvian ship, *Maria Luz*. This ship was on its way from Macau to Peru, carrying several hundred Chinese labourers, or coolies as they were then called, when its mast was damaged in a storm and it put into Yokohama for repairs. Some days later one of the Chinese jumped ship. According to the court report this man, 'wishing to escape the cruelty he alleges he suffered jumped overboard, to swim ashore', and was rescued by the British naval vessel, HMS *Iron Duke*, where he 'prayed for security' and claimed that the Chinese labourers were being held against their will and in inhuman conditions. This claim was backed up by a second escapee, and both the British and American diplomatic representatives in Japan at the time urged the Japanese government to investigate. The foreign minister, Soejima Taneomi, instructed Ōe Taku, an official at the local Kanagawa prefectural offices, to launch a judicial enquiry: Ōe impounded the *Maria Luz* and had the Chinese 'passengers' disembark for their own safety. The consequences of this action were, however, to rebound on Japan in connection with the indentured prostitutes of the pleasure quarters.[14]

There was heated controversy about the *Maria Luz* in Yokohama, and the issue drew excited attention outside Japan, too, as the first legal case in which Japan was claiming jurisdiction over foreign property by virtue of its presence in Japan, or, in this case, in Japanese waters. As an editorial in the *Japan Weekly Mail* put it, 'there is no moral doubt about the nature of this trade as carried on from Macao. . . . It is characterized by a wholesale system of kidnapping, and half the contracts signed by the coolies are extorted from them by intimidation. . . . this vessel is a slaver'. On the other hand, there was doubt about the jurisdiction of Japanese courts over foreign vessels, and there were other arguments that could be brought to bear as well. Dickins was retained by Ricardo Hereira, the captain of the *Maria Luz*, and protested that, 'even were the *Maria Luz* an actual slaver with slaves on board the Japanese Government would have no right to detain her or to hold any inquiry relative to her except as to acts done while in a Japan port'.[15]

On 18 September Dickins presented his most telling argument, and although it did not win him the case it had important repercussions. Stating his view that 'contracts made for work and service for a term' were 'enforceable according to Japanese law or custom', he gave three examples of this drawn from Japan. The first was the case of labourers who, he said, were frequently hired by the Japanese Government itself 'at less than market prices to be employed on public works, and any labourers so hired refusing such employment can be, and frequently are, punished and forced to labour on such works'. The second was the case of Japanese citizens who he claimed were forced to emigrate to Hokkaido as part of the land-settlement programme. But these two cases were overshadowed by the third:

> [T]here is one species of contract exceedingly common in Japan – a contract between private persons for the rendering of services the most disgusting that any human can be called upon to perform, that is enforceable by Japanese law, and is constantly and most strictly enforced. . . . I refer, it will be understood, to prostitution contracts made with brothel-keepers of the Yoshiwara. . . . The Japanese government not only derives a revenue under this system and acknowledges the validity of such contracts, but lends its aid towards their daily enforcement.

This argument was rejected by the court on the ground that the import and export of slaves was an entirely different matter from the domestic matter raised by Dickins, and the court found in favour of the Chinese labourers. This was not the end of the matter, for the Peruvian government protested and the case was submitted for arbitration to

Tsar Alexander II, but the Japanese handling of the case was in the end upheld.[16]

Although Dickins lost the case, his arguments seem to have been directly responsible for the abolition of the indenture system operated in houses of prostitution in Japan. After the conclusion of the case in Japan in 1872 the presiding judge, Ōe Taku, who was also the governor of Kanagawa Prefecture, sent a memorial to the government urging that courtesans be freed. Before the end of the year *Dajōkan*, which was the highest organ of the Meiji state, issued an ordinance banning the sale of people to others, which effectively outlawed the indenture system under which courtesans suffered, and the Ministry of Justice explicitly banned the practice. These changes, however, which Dickins' speech had undoubtedly occasioned, were shelved within a year, and although the anti-prostitution movement grew in strength in Japan over the following years, under the influence of Western missionaries and Japanese Christian activists such as Niijima Jō, it failed to force any fundamental changes in the conditions of courtesans. Further, Dickins' argument relating the *Maria Luz* case to the courtesans was omitted both from the official account of the case published in the form of a book in 1874 and from the selection of *Gaimushō* (Japanese Foreign Ministry) papers on the case published in the *Dainihon gaikō monjo* series in 1939.[17]

Dickins' years in Japan in the 1870s were filled with other activities as well as his legal work, but they were mostly confined to the international settlement at Yokohama, a world that was detached from its Japanese setting and which adhered to different values. Towards the end of his residence in Japan Dickins also became involved in the lively world of English-language journalism in Yokohama, which at that time boasted several papers. In 1878 he succeeded W.G. Howell as editor of the *Japan Mail*: he had earlier represented Howell in the British consular court when Howell sued the *Japan Gazette* for libelously suggesting that the *Japan Mail* was in the pocket of the Japanese government. It is likely that Dickins was responsible for at least some of the translations and unsigned articles that appeared in the *Japan Mail* in the 1870s, but it is not possible now to identify his contributions. In any event, under his editorship the paper gradually lost ground to its rivals, the *Japan Herald* and *Japan Gazette*. Finally, after lengthy negotiations, Charles Rickerby, who had recently relaunched the *Japan Times*, persuaded Dickins in July 1878 that the two should be merged, and the result was the *Japan Mail and Times*. This change, however, coincided with the onset of Dickins' 'severe and painful nervous disposition' and Dickins had probably been unable to give the paper much of his energy.[18]

During the 1870s Dickins continued his studies of Japan, although it was after his return to England that his most important work was done. When the Asiatic Society of Japan was founded in 1872, Dickins was one of the founder members, along with Ernest Satow, who was later to achieve fame both as a japanologist and diplomat and who remained in correspondence with Dickins for most of his life. Dickins served on the Society's Council in 1872-3 and 1877-9, but his contributions to the *Transactions* were few. They included, however, an important contribution to the debate on transliteration of Japanese, a question that seems to have exercised the membership in 1879-90. In 1879 Satow had proposed that Japanese be represented in roman letters with close adherence to the historical spellings represented by the *kana*, but Dickins argued for a phonetic representation of Japanese words. Satow was not convinced: he allowed that Dickins' system was more economical and more practical 'for books intended merely to teach colloquial', but maintained that 'for persons who study the written language the *kana* spelling is the most convenient', and himself spelled Osaka 'Ohosaka' to reflect the current *kana* usage. Nevertheless, it was the phonetic system that eventually became the standard, and it had the effect, as Dickins had argued, of making Japanese more accessible phonetically.[19]

Dickins returned to England in 1879. Once his health was restored to him he began establishing himself in legal practice, but it seems that he missed Japan and, partly because he was finding it difficult to make enough money, was thinking of returning to legal practice in Japan. At some point he went to Egypt and practised in the law courts there. However, the outbreak of Arabi Pasha's rebellion in 1882 prompted him to return once more to England, and he was thereupon appointed Assistant Registrar of the University of London in 1882. He became the Registrar in 1896 and on his retirement in 1901 he went to live in Seend in Wiltshire, where he died in 1915.[20]

Dickins' involvement with Japan and scholarly work as a japanologist continued well after his return to England, indeed until the end of his life. In 1879 he completely revised his earlier translation of *Chūshingura*, having recourse to a different text from that used for the previous edition but noting that his revisions had been made 'without the advantage of the usual native assistance in its preparation': it seems clear from this that Dickins, like other European scholars grappling with Japanese texts in the nineteenth century, made use of scholarly assistance furnished by Japanese whose contributions were only acknowledged in passing. As mentioned above, Dickins had long been an advocate of the adoption of an accessible romanization system for Japanese, and he appended to another of his translations a romanized transcription of the text complete with a sketch of Japanese grammar, grammatical notes on the text and a vocabulary: his intention was clearly to present the text as one would a Greek or Latin text, with the apparatus to enable the students to construe the text, but just how many students might there have been then ready and able to tackle such a text? A similar intention, much more ambitiously articulated, lay behind his *Primitive and mediaeval Japanese texts*, which was published in 1906 in two volumes and which consists of transliterated texts of the *Man'yōshū*, *Taketori monogatari* and other works, together with translations and notes. Although his efforts may have been premature, it is clear that Dickins had faith in the future of Japanese, or at any rate classical Japanese literature, as a subject of academic study well before serious instruction in the subject was ever offered at a university in Britain.[21]

From this time onwards, Dickins' publications on Japan were extensive and continued to break new ground. In 1880, for example, he published a study of Katsushika Hokusai's *Fugaku Hyakkei*, a collection of a hundred views of Mt Fuji by Hokusai with accompanying texts. Until at least 1909 he was the regular reviewer of books on Japan for the *Athenaeum*, and in the academic year 1909-1910, when the University of Bristol created the office of reader for distinguished people whom it wished to associate with the University and who were expected to give occasional lectures, he was one of the first two scholars appointed to this office. In 1911 he consequently gave a series of three lectures at the University on 'Old Japan'.[22]

In the 1890s Dickins had come into contact with the famous folklorist Minakata Kumagusu (1867-1941), who was living in London in somewhat straitened circumstances and whom Dickins was able to help financially. They cooperated on a translation of *Hōjōki*, and it is clear that he also gave Dickins considerable help with his work on the *Man'yōshū* which was included in his *Primitive amd mediaeval Japanese texts*: Dickins wrote to Satow about its progress in 1904 adding that he was 'waiting for some studies from Japan now being made for me by a very remarkable man . . . a bonze named Minakata Kumagusu – certainly a man of extraordinary erudition'. Yet Dickins noted in the same letter that 'I got him back to Japan with great difficulty and am not anxious for him to reappear'.[23]

Dickins' continued engagement with Japan in terms of scholarship did not, however, make him sympathetic to the attempt made by the Japanese government in the 1880s to renegotiate the 'Unequal Treaties', the treaties concluded with the Western powers in 1858. These provided for fixed tariffs outside the control of the Japanese government and such other conditions as extraterritoriality, making foreigners accused of crimes in Japan answerable only to consular courts, which were perceived in Japan to compromise Japan's sovereignty. Sir Harry Parkes, the then minister at the British legation in Tokyo, was opposed to revision and Dickins agreed with him. In 1881 he wrote at length to a leading Japanese newspaper expressing his sympathy for the government's aspirations but arguing that Japan was still 'not in a position to claim the full exercise of sovereign rights as against foreigners', because 'the criminal code is such that no civilized state would dream for a moment of subjecting its citizens to it: the procedure of criminal Courts is repugnant to the commonest principles of justice, there is no civil law, no independent judiciary, no safety or guarantee for persons or properties, no power to travel in the interior even for pleasure without express permission' and the new proposals 'offer no amendment of any one of the above matters'. Dickins went on to argue that he knew of not 'a single instance of Consular partiality in favour of the foreigner' and to reject the argument that extraterritoriality had caused any harm to Japan. He also considered the Japanese language to be a major obstacle to the abolition of extraterritoriality, for the Japanese had chosen to shroud [their] language, not in itself a difficult one, in an almost undecipherable character, instead of simply romanizing it, at all events for public purposes, as might very easily be done.' Dickins was by no means alone in holding these views about the treaty question, and there were even Japanese resident in England, such as Suematsu Kenchō, who were of the same opinion. However, he was out of touch with opinion in Japan and betrays his identification with the interests and attitudes of the foreign community in Yokohama.[24]

The ambivalence towards Japan that can be detected in Dickens' writings on the extraterritoriality question seems to have become more pronounced in his later years. In 1904 and 1905 he wrote to Satow of his disillusionment and his return to the world of the Greek tragedians and comedians:

> I now know that my falling in love with things Japanese in the early '60s was a terrible misfortune for me – there is nothing in Japanese literature to compensate one for the energy and time lost in its mere decipherment.
>
> I shall do nothing more in *re japonica* . . . properly speaking, Japan has no history, it has merely annals. Nor is there any literature *qua* such worth the trouble of working it out. . . . I have plunged into the Greek drama with enthusiasm. It is hard to go back to anything Far Eastern after the *Frogs*, *Agamemnon*, the *Bacchae* or *Antigone*.[25]

Had Dickens lost faith in Japan by 1905, twenty-five years after he had last been there, or were these merely the symptoms of passing doubts? On the one hand, it is of course true that he continued to write on Japan until a few years before his death: his study of the Hokusai *Manga* came out the following year, and in 1912 he published his translation of *Hida no takumi monogatari* as *The story of a Hida craftsman*, noting of the author in the preface that 'like others of his craft he was a skilled plagiarist'. He clearly continued to be busily involved in *re japonica* after all. On the other hand, like most of his contemporaries, he could never rid himself of the view that European literature, and especially the Greek and Latin classics formed the standard against which non-European literature had to be measured, and that Japan failed to meet the standards of European civilization. His engagement with Japan, then, which may have been a misfortune for him personally, nevertheless signalled the engagement of an intellect that may at first have 'fallen in love' with Japan but that subsequently sought to apply the highest standards of scholarship to the study of Japan. Although he managed in his writings to avoid exoticizing Japan, his approach was imbued with the outlook and methods of classical scholarship. Further, his advocacy of the use of roman letters for writing Japanese, although it did not originate with any failure on his part to come to grips with the difficult written language and although the *Rōmaji-kai* in Japan was of the same view, nevertheless reflects a paternalistic view of what is best for Japan. In 1892 he said,

> That sooner or later the roman character will be adopted in Japan I cannot doubt. Japan cannot go on for ever contented with a mode of recording its highest thought that, translated into speech, would be unintelligible.[26]

He is careful here to leave the initiative to Japan and not to preach, but his conviction that the Japanese language should conform to the norms of European languages is obvious.

By the time of his death the milieu in which japanologists worked had changed immeasurably, even though most of them were still amateurs with other professions rather than holders of university teaching positions. The Japan Society had been founded in 1891, providing a forum for those with a serious interest in Japan; in 1892 the ninth international congress of orientalists had been held in London, with a section on Japan and with Dickins as a member of the organizing committee; and in 1902 relations between Britain and Japan had been put on an equal footing with the conclusion of the Anglo-Japanese Alliance. In 1903 J.H. Longford had been given the title of professor of Japanese by King's College, London, and in 1909 J.H. Gubbins had been appointed to a lectureship in Japanese at Oxford: although they did little or no teaching, their appointments bespeak acceptance of the study of Japan as an academic subject. By the time Japanese was being taught at the City of London College and four Army officers were being selected annually to spend two years in Japan learning Japanese. In 1909 also the Reay Committee, which had been appointed to look into the teaching of 'Oriental' studies in Britain, had recommended the establishment of a school of oriental languages in London, in which Japanese would be taught by one professor and one 'native assistant'. In 1907, in evidence to the Committee, Satow had referred to four Englishmen competent to hold such a professorship, of whom one is unmistakably Dickins.[27] He was without doubt a pioneer, not only as a translator of Japanese literature but also, for all his later doubts, as a scholar with the convictions that Japan was worth studying and should be brought within the horizons of Western scholarship.

Kawanabe Kyōsai (1831–89), the Painter, and the British

OLIVE CHECKLAND

KAWANABE KYŌSAI (1831-1889) was brought up and trained as an artist and a painter under the old regime, in a Japan effectively cut off from the outside world. He was 37 years of age when, in 1868, the Restoration of the Emperor ushered in an era of great change which promised a new Japan. It is of interest to explore Kyōsai's response to the new challenge; was his involvement with the British his answer to the changes in Japan going on around him?

Despite the uncertainties of the newly emerging Japan, Kyōsai remained essentially a traditional Japanese artist, revelling in his virtuosity. This was sometimes displayed at the day-long painting parties, at which he was the star. During these exhibitions Kyōsai would dash off, for a fee, a series of paintings, bought then and there, by patrons who made an admiring audience. Kyōsai was initially anti-foreigner, as were most Japanese, but in course of time his views seem to have moderated. It is believed that Yamaguchi Tōru (18?-1893) an official of the Imperial Household Agency, introduced Josiah Conder to Kyōsai. Conder (1852-1920) was an *oyatoi*, a man hired by the Japanese government as professor of architecture at the Imperial College of Engineering in 1877, who remained in Japan for the rest of his life. After some initial resistance Kyōsai accepted a request from Josiah Conder that he, Conder, should become Kyōsai's pupil. Through Conder and Frank Brinkley, also a permanent resident of Japan, Kyōsai received other foreign artists and art historians, from France as well as Britain. Remarkably, articles on Kyōsai and his work appeared in British art journals over 100 years ago. Indeed, it could be said that for British artists at the end of the nineteenth century, Kyōsai, then, was the best known contemporary Japanese artist.

Kyōsai's name and work was kept in the public eye as long as Conder was alive. But after 1920, when Conder died, knowledge of Kyōsai's oeuvre dropped from public view. The recent rehabilitation of Kawanabe Kyōsai as a great artist, has depended on the dedication and determination of his great grand-daughter Kawanabe Kusumi.[1] Between December 1993 and early 1994, her dream of an exhibition in the West of Kyōsai's works came true when the British Museum held an exhibition *Demon of Painting, the art of Kawanabe Kyōsai.*[2] The catalogue reveals not only the breadth of Kyōsai's work but also his many artistic skills. In Japan his great grand-daughter has opened a Kyōsai art centre in Warabi (Saitama Prefecture) north-west of Tokyo, where she not only shows his work, but also arranges for lectures to be given interpreting his work. Kyōsai's 'eccentric genius' has also attracted the attention of Brenda Jordan, an American art historian, who has explored Kyōsai's character and his art and has added another dimension to an understanding of this artist.[3]

KYŌSAI'S TRAINING

Kyōsai was born at Koga in the province of Shimosa in 1831. His parents called him Shiuzaburō. His father apparently changed his name to Kawanabe 'on being made a small retainer of the Fujiwara clan'.[4] From all accounts he was an infant prodigy, from earliest days 'observing and mentally retaining natural form'. So marked were his talents that, at the age of seven, his father, who had initially been unwilling to accept that his second son should become an artist, brought him to Edo and to the studio of Kuniyoshi Ichiyusai. Kuniyoshi accepted Kyōsai as a boy of seven, and for two years he studied with the great master.

Kyōsai's interest in the macabre, which remained with him all his life, is reflected in the awful story of the boy finding, and fishing out a hairy human head floating down the Kanda river. His father discovered the head and, horrified at his son's shocking prize, insisted that it be returned to the river. This was done but not before the boy had made his drawings of it.

When he was eleven years old, his parents succeeded in getting him accepted into the studio of Kanō Tōhaku. The members of the Kanō school were, by tradition, painters to the Tokugawa regime. There were several branches of this school, all led by members of the Kanō family. All members had to be *shizoku*, that is of samurai descent; no-one of the merchant class was admitted. Kyōsai remained under the guidance of the Kanō masters until the age of 27. He then left perhaps following a disagreement, but always retained great respect and reverence for the work and the artists of this school.

It should be noted that the training of young Japanese artists at this time essentially consisted of copying, and re-copying, the work of former masters, in this case of the Kanō school. Kyōsai's observations from nature whether of the severed head, or of the carp, which he had caught but which he refused to eat, were a breakaway from Japanese tradition at that time.

It is not surprising that by the age of 27, a year before the treaty ports in Japan were officially opened to foreigners, Kyōsai wanted to be independent. Kyōsai, by removing himself from the deferential atmosphere of a tradition-dominated school of painting, demonstrated his unwillingness to conform which was characteristic of the man. In setting up his own school Kyōsai expected his students not only to copy from work of the old masters, but also to work directly from nature. It is said that the garden ground around his studio were full of animals which students could use as models for their drawings.

In 1867 Kyōsai made the first of his many journeys into lesser known parts of Japan. In the course of these travels he received hospitality from religious leaders and was often requested to undertake great painting projects at temples, or monasteries. In this sense, he was a flamboyant artist willing, after due thought and consideration, to undertake huge commissions for theatres or religious buildings. For all these great exhibitions, when he painted as the 'demon of painting', Kyōsai drank large quantities of saké. He became notorious as a painter of great talent who worked all the better when liberally supplied with rice wine. In 1870, when showing off at one of the many painting parties, he got very drunk and made pictures which the authorities thought were disrespectful. He was arrested and imprisoned. This proved to be a frightening experience given the brutality of the prison regime. Kyōsai was eventually released, but his harsh treatment had damaged his health.

After his detention Kyōsai remained unorthodox. This he demonstrated by continuing to paint satirical pictures, and by his willingness to talk to, and to teach the British.

CONDER, PUPIL TO KYŌSAI, THE PAINTING MASTER

The relationship of Kyōsai to Conder was that of master and pupil. This is remarkable in an age when the Japanese were engaged in a major exercise to learn from Western experts. Conder's willingness to transform himself from professor of architecture into Kyōsai's pupil was an unusual reversal of roles.

Kyōsai's diary entry (Kyōsai Gadan) explains the painter's response to Conder's initial request:

In his own country, the Englishman J.Conder studied the
practise of oil painting and diligently learned the rules of
draftsman-ship until he had truly absorbed expert techniques. But he loved Japanese paintings which demonstrated
deft brush control. He loved the serenity of a Soami (?-
1525) painting of an egret, a Tan'yu (Kano, 1602-1674) of
an egret and other types of old paintings which he
collected. Whenever he had free time, he looked at them,
feeling there was no greater pastime.[5]

Some time ago he came to Japan where he became
employed by the government. Happily this gave him the
chance to study the laws of Japanese painting from ancient
times and to collect works by master artists from those times
for further study.[6]

But beyond reflecting on these things he tried to begin studying
under Kyōsai. Kyōsai replied, 'I have long since heard about Conder's
great abilities in oil painting as well as draftsmanship. I don't have either
the energy or the place to teach such a man'. Kyōsai declined several
times without yielding. In the end, however, it was agreed that they
become teacher and student. During the 1880s Conder and Kyōsai
became close. Kyōsai apparently went to Conder's house on Saturday
mornings to teach and advise.

The two men made several journeys together to study art and to
paint and draw. One of the expeditions was to Nikkō, a mountain
town north of Tokyo, where the first Tokugawa Shogun, Ieyasu, is
enshrined. Kyōsai and Conder paid their respects to the third Shogun
Iemitsu, and admired the beautiful stonework. They walked up many
stairways all decorated with intricate stonework, before moving on to
Lake Chujenzi where they did many drawings. They also spent many
hours trying to capture the magic of the many spectacular waterfalls
there. There is no doubt about the spectacular sight of these falls. There
are various descriptions of these, one of which explains:

'About 3 *ri* (12 kilometres) northwest of Mt Futaara is
Kirifuri Falls. The water falls in three tiers. Pine and cedar
grow in dense profusion by the upper falls; the next falls is
in a deep valley, the lower part of which is shaped like a
yagen (mortar). Three tiers of water burst over stones
sending up spray just like a misting rain.

In this way Kyōsai and Conder spent some days visiting
and sketching many waterfalls. Kyōsai, through these
sketches, has shown young students the force of the
current. If students examine the brush strokes, it will surely
be instructive in many ways.[7]

This journey to Nikkō was one of several which Kyōsai and Conder did together. They also travelled to Enoshima, and Kamakura, neither far from Tokyo. The relationship was also a family affair, Conder's daughter, Helen, who was given the name Kyōzui, also worked under Kyōsai. The Conders lived in a fine house so that it is not surprising that the Kyōsai family should be entertained there. Kyōsai's daughter Kyōsui was also friendly with the Conders, and the family connection flourished.

Kyōsai died in 1889 and Conder continued his professional life as an architect. But he was much enthralled by Japanese culture. He presented papers to the Asiatic Society of Japan on 'The History of Japanese Costume' (1881); 'The Art of Landscape Gardening in Japan' (1886); and 'The Theory of Japanese Flower Arrangement' (1890). During these years Conder was himself collecting Kyōsai paintings. As he remarked, most of these were works which Kyōsai had painted in the years when Conder was a pupil and Kyōsai, master. That is in the 1880s. Conder was anxious to commemorate Kyōsai the painter with whom he had worked. In 1911 Josiah Conder's book *Paintings and Studies by Kawanabe Kyōsai* was published. This contains 34 black-and-white plates and 87 half-tone illustrations. These, together with chapters on Kyōsai's life and methods, make up the book.

There are three chapters on 'Painting Materials', 'Painting Methods' and 'Examples of Technique'. In the chapter on painting materials, Conder not only discusses the paints which Kyōsai used but also the paper and silk on to which he worked. As Conder explained:

> The paper usually employed for paintings is a smooth brownish-white fabric called *Toshi-gami* ... it was originally of Chinese manufacture, but now an imitation is made in Japan. It requires lining to give it thickness and stiffness, and this is done with a Japanese paper called *mino-gami*. This lining, and the coating of the surface with a wash of alum and size, is done by the paper dealers who sell it prepared for the use of painters. There is a superior paper, called *tori-no-ko*, which is thicker, smoother, and of a whiter colour than *Toshi-gami*. This is much used for scroll paintings and album painting, being specially suited for fine and delicate work, and for the application of gold. ...[8]

Conder also explained, when painting on silk, the importance of having 'a thin material, woven in close and even thread.[9] The use of silk was very popular, particularly for *kakemonos*, and wall-hangings, but the stretching, framing and pasting of the silk to make it a suitable surface for painting was and is, a long and highly demanding process.

The Japanese painter then used charcoal to 'rough out his proposed work. The variety of brushes available and the ink used were also important. As Conder commented: 'The best black ink comes from

China and is distinguishable by its extreme blackness and fineness.'[10]
Conder also gives 'the colour pigments which Kyōsai used'.

Ai	Indigo, a dark blue pigment, rubbed from the cake or stick.
Rokusho	A powder of emerald green colour, produced from copper ...
Kongo	Blue carbonate of copper ... ... the best *Kongo*, seen in old paintings, ... is of a deep *lapis-lazuli* blue ...
Shiwo	Gamboge, imported from China, in lumps.
Odo	Yellow ochre, used always in powder.
Shido	Red oxide of iron, a powder of 'Indian red' colour.
Taisha	Burnt sienna used in a cake or the stick.
Hi	Vermilion (sic) powder, the best being imported from China.
Tan	Red oxide of lead, an orange-red powder, the best comes from China.
Shoyenji	A Chinese vegetable dye of colour resembling rose-madder.
Kiyenji	A powder of a purple brown colour.[12]

The final explanation of Kyōsai's use of colours relates to the importance of the use of gold powder, or gold leaf.

The relationship of Kawanabe Kyōsai and Josiah Conder is one of the most intriguing links between East and West in Meiji Japan. It was a rare instance of a close friendship between a Japanese and an Englishman where the former was teacher to the latter. In this case, Conder, with his status as a permanent resident in Japan, and his fluency in the Japanese language, was able to persuade Kyōsai to accept him as a pupil. As the classes took place on Saturdays at Conder's home, a real rapprochement between the Kyōsai and Conder families grew up across the cultures in the last years of Kyōsai's life.

And the family connection, however tenuous, still lives on. Josiah Conder and his wife are buried in the grounds at Gokokuji temple Tokyo. This grave has been maintained and cared for by Dr Kawanabe Kusumi.[12]

Other British art lovers and artists also beat a path to Kyōsai's door.

KYŌSAI AND WILLIAM ANDERSON

In the 1870s William Anderson, medical officer to the British legation in Tokyo and professor of anatomy and surgery in the Naval College, was perhaps the first of the British to recognize Kyōsai as a gifted artist.

Anderson visited Kyōsai and commissioned a series of paintings which were completed in 1878 and 1879.

Anderson tells the story of Kyōsai's crow, a painting submitted to the first Art Exhibition at Ueno in 1877. Kyōsai put the price of ¥100, a very large sum in those days, on the painting. As Anderson explains:

> ... the self-constituted official judges turned their heads aside and remonstrated at so exorbitant a price being attached to a painting of a common crow. Kyōsai replied that the sum was not the price of a common crow, but a small fraction of the price of the 50 years of study that had enabled him to dash off his picture in this manner.[13]

Anderson emphasises Kyōsai's eagerness to paint the 'humorous or the horrible'. One picture Anderson explains, 'the Snake and the Frogs', illustrates the principle of 'retributive justice'. In this picture 'a band of frogs have captured their natural enemy the snake, and, having lashed him firmly to a couple of stakes, are avenging past terrors by dancing, drumming and swinging on his body, pulling his tail, tickling the savage jaws with a straw, and otherwise jubilating over his impotence'.[14] There are indeed many examples of this kind of subject in Kyōsai's work.

Anderson regarded with severe disapproval Kyōsai's devotion to the saké bottle, believing that Kyōsai's ability to paint while getting wildly drunk affected the quality of his work. Most other people regarded the saké as a stimulus to Kyōsai's work. Nevertheless Anderson sums up Kyōsai and his work favourably concluding:

> In spite of his eccentricity he was a man of liberal ideas, for although he wisely adhered to the art principles which from childhood had been part of his being, he saw clearly their limitations. He realised in his drawings of birds how much beauty lay in truthful observation and he understood how much was lost by the failure to carry that observation into the representation of higher motives ... and he admitted that the science of the West might be studied with advantage in place of the conventions which had retarded the evolution of the art of the Far East. As a painter, he was second to none in his school in the skill and swiftness with which he yielded his brush; and his work has qualities of sincerity, strength and originality that will give it a high value in the eyes of every lover of art of every nationality'.[15]

William Anderson had artistic interests and so became curious about Japanese art. Was Anderson a genuine admirer and collector of Japanese art, or was he collecting Japanese art in Japan as a business venture? On his return to London, he carried in his baggage a collection of Japanese art work. Part of this he sold in 1881 to the British Museum for £3,000. The Trustees of the British Museum requested Anderson to make up *A Descriptive and Historical Catalogue of Japanese and Chinese Paintings in the British Museum* which the British Museum published in 1886. This massive work of 544 pages demonstrates the variety of objects collected by Anderson.

It is worth noting that on his death in 1900, William Anderson left an estate valued at £11,282-3s. After his return from Japan he had worked at St Thomas Hospital and he lived at 1 Harley Street, where he may have been a private medical consultant. Did the substantial fortune which he left come from his successful medical career or from the sale of his Japanese art? Apart from his 'large bronze dragon' Anderson makes no reference to any Japanese or other Eastern art in his possession at his death.[16]

KYŌSAI AND MORTIMER MENPES

It was Mortimer Menpes (1856-1938) who brought Kawanabe Kyōsai's work directly to the attention of James Abbott MacNeill Whistler (1834-1903). Menpes was a 'follower' that is student, adviser, or assistant to Whistler when, without informing Whistler, in March 1887 he left for Japan. Menpes made much of decision to travel to Japan, ignoring any obligation to Whistler, on the grounds that he had 'a career to make and was determined to succeed'.[17] Menpes arrived in Japan in the late spring of 1887. It is most likely that he had an introduction to Conder who presented him to Kyōsai. Menpes thus learnt of Kyōsai's work not long before his death in the spring of 1889.

In 1887 Menpes first met Kyōsai 'at Captain Brinkley's' and then spent 'an entire day observing Kyōsai at work'.[18] As Kyōsai explained to Menpes:

> I watch my bird, and the particular pose I wish to copy before I attempt to represent it. I observe that very closely until he moves and the attitude is altered. Then I go away and record as much of that particular pose that I can remember. Perhaps I may be able to put down only three or four lines, but directly I have lost the impression I stop. Then I go back again and study the bird until it takes up the same position as before. And then I again try and retain as much of it as I can. In this way I began by spending a whole day in the garden watching a bird and its particular attitude, and in the end I have remembered the pose so well, by continually trying to represent it, that I am able to repeat it entirely from my impression – but not from the bird. It is a hindrance to have the model before me when I have a

mental picture of the pose. What I do is a painting from memory and it is a true impression.[19]

Menpes greatly enjoyed his visit to Japan. He did much work on his 'Japanese' painting.

On Menpes return from Japan, Whistler greeted him sourly. 'Well Sir, excuse yourself', he cried. Menpes advised Whistler that, in Japan, he had found another master. Whistler replied: 'How dare you you call this Japanese a master on your own responsibility? Give me your reasons. What do you mean by it?'. Menpes, then and there, began to explain Kyōsai's methods as he had seen them. 'That is my method' interupted Whistler. 'No, that is Kyōsai's method' said Menpes. 'I told him that Kyōsai displayed enormous facility and great knowledge. A black dress would be one beautiful broad tone of black, the flesh one clear tone of flesh, the shadows growing out of the mass forming part of the whole'.

'That is my method' Whistler broke in volubly; 'that is exactly my method. I don't paint my shadows in little blues, and greens, and yellows until they cease to be a part of the picture. I paint them exactly as they are in nature, as a part of the whole. This Kyōsai must be a wonderful man, for his methods are my methods. Go on Menpes, tell me more'.[20]

In this way Mortimer Menpes brought knowledge of Kyōsai's technique to those in Britain who were active artists and interested to know how Japanese painters worked.

Kyōsai's methods were those of Japan where the artist in training spent his time copying the work of the old masters of, in Kyōsai's case, of the Kanō school. It should however be stressed that although Kyōsai did work in the Japanese way 'from memory' he also worked directly from nature.

Western artists visiting Japan usually secured a recommendation and introduction either to Frank Brinkley or to Josiah Conder. Brinkley was not a regular pupil of Kyōsai but he was an authority on Japanese and Chinese porcelain. Anyone introduced at this level was, before his death in 1889, usually taken on to meet Kyōsai and thus saw him at work.

The first such introduction would appear to be that of Emile Guimet and François Régamey. Once Guimet's book *Promenades Japonaises* (Paris: 1878) was available to the artistic community Kyōsai's name and work were known about in the West. As Elisa Evett has noted 'Kiosai (sic) was important to Europeans because he was a rare specimen, a contemporary Japanese painter who had come to be known by Guimet and Régamey.'[21] This personal contact was enriched by Kyōsai's own eccentricity and by his vistuosity as displayed in his exuberant exhibitions of paintings. His willingness to play 'to the gallery' of foreigners watching him may have been encouraged by his rather cool reception by nervous officials in Japan.

Kyōsai's status as an artist in the changing world of Meiji Japan has been closely examined by Brenda Jordan. Her recent work demonstrates the importance of this artist. As she writes:

> Kyōsai's art in and of itself is often a source of fascination and interest for scholars and laymen alike. The variety of themes and styles, the lively brush-work, active figures, and the unexpected twists and turns on tradition make him an artist worth looking at for the art alone. However, Kyōsai's creative and individualistic approach to his art came at a time when Japan was going through one of the most important and dramatic periods in her long history.[22]

Kawanabe Kyōsai, perhaps because of his uneasy relationship with Japanese officials in Tokyo, showed himself willing to make contact with British and other Western artists. His generosity to those Western artists who, through Josiah Conder or Frank Brinkley, sought him out, earned him a fine reputation in the West over 100 years ago. Not until 1993-94 was it possible for this generation of Westerners to see a major exhibition open at the British Museum, on the art of Kawanabe Kyōsai. That he was 'One of that small but most distinguished band of great personalities in Japanese art'[23] was amply demonstrated at the exhibition under the title *The Demon of Painting*.

8

James Alfred Ewing and his Circle of Pioneering Physicists in Meiji Tokyo

NEIL PEDLAR

'I WANT TO MASTER PHYSICS, which is the basis of all science' the 22-year-old Tanakadate Aikitsu wrote to his father in 1878.[1] The times were rapidly changing in Japan with the coming of Western science and technology, and the young and serious students were wrestling with the dichotomy between modern Western learning newly available in Tokyo and traditional Oriental learning based on Confucian concepts. The first son of a samurai who taught military tactics, Tanakadate (1856-1952) received an early education in Nambu fief (modern Iwate Prefecture) in swordsmanship, calligraphy and the Chinese classics. But the old fief schools all closed after the Meiji Restoration, government and education became centralized, and 'Western Science, Eastern Ethics' was the slogan of the time.

The Tanakadate family had moved to Tokyo in 1872, the father now becoming a merchant and concerned about the right education for his six children. 'I hope by your choice you can make some contribution to mankind throughout the world' was his reply to Aikitsu, recognizing new horizons beyond the confines of Japan.[2]

Young Tanakadate realized that a new order was coming to Japan, and new skills and knowledge would be needed to survive in it, so he applied to take a degree course in physics at the new University of Tokyo, founded the previous year. He had resolved his inner conflict involving the two accepted Oriental methods of studying: '*seisoku*' (the exact way) and '*hensoku*' (the altered way). In the first, basics are learned and built upon in a logical progression, whereas in the second the student neglects basics and plunges into topics relevant to immediate needs. Tanakadate accepted only '*seisoku*'.[3]

Financial constraints as well as ideological considerations also influenced young Tanakadate's decision to study physics under Western teachers. The private traditional school he was attending, Keiō Gijuku, required fees much higher than the new government-run University staffed by Western foreigners! However, he was told that in order to enter the latter he would need to know English as well as the elements of algebra and geometry. Accordingly, he obtained books and studied mathematics on his own, and employed the wife of Montague Fenton, a teacher of Western music, to instruct him in English.

INFLUENCE OF PROF. EWING

Meanwhile, in Scotland, James Alfred Ewing (1855-1935), just one year older than Tanakadate, had completed his course at Edinburgh University as the first holder of an Engineering Scholarship from Dundee High School. He spent the following three summer holidays on a ship laying submarine telegraph cables to and around Brazil and on the River Plate in the employment of his main teachers at Edinburgh, Sir William Thomson (Lord Kelvin) and Fleeming Jenkin. During the winter months the three of them '... investigated a novel type of internal combustion engine which had every merit except that it would not go'.[4]

J.A. Ewing was the youngest son of James Ewing, minister of St Andrew's Free Church, Dundee, and a former pupil at Dundee High School. Family conversations were 'chiefly clerical and literary' but young Alfred later wrote:

> 'I took my pleasure in machines and experiments. My scanty pocket-money was spent on tools and chemicals. The domestic attic was put at my disposal. It became the scene of hair-raising explosions. There, too, the domestic cat found herself the unwilling instrument of electrification and a partner in various shocking experiences.'[5]

He became interested in '... the stages by which science had risen on stepping-stones of its dead self to positions that command a wider view'.[6] Like Tanakadate, Ewing chose to study an exact science rather than theology or Greek and Latin Classics which were then popular choices for future British Empire administrators. His two elder brothers, Robert and John, became ministers of the church.

When the agent of the Japanese government, Masaki Taiso, enquired at Edinburgh if a Professor of Engineering and Physics for the faculty of science in Tokyo University could be recommended to replace Robert Henry Smith (1851-1914) who was the very first professor and who had organized the whole of the engineering department, Jenkin nominated the 23-year-old Ewing and invited him to a dinner party so as to meet Masaki and discuss the proposed appointment.[7] Almost immediately the adventurous Ewing signed a three-year contract. This was to bring Tanakadate and Ewing into intimate contact as scientists and life-long friends, and influence subsequent developments in both Japan and Britain.

From 1877 Ewing had been a close friend of Robert Louis Stevenson, a failed engineering student who later, as author of *Treasure Island* and *Kidnapped*, was to become famous for his writing about life in remoter parts of the earth. Masaki, the Japanese agent in Edinburgh, met Stevenson at the home of Jenkin who was also present at the dinner party. The author and Masaki communicated well, due to their concern with natural living in a technological world. A Japanese folk tale told to Stevenson by Masaki led to the former writing the inspirational and popular story, about Yoshida Torajirō (Yoshida Shōin) who was an heroic patriot and adventurer, later published in his volume of essays entitled *Familiar Studies of Men and Books*, (1882). Stevenson was moved by two lines from a classic Japanese poem that heartened Yoshida while in prison awaiting execution:

'It is better to be a crystal and be broken,
Than to remain perfect as a tile upon a housetop.'[8]

On arrival in Japan, Ewing discovered a nation '. . . venerable in its traditions, its arts, its manners, its high standard of patriotism and personal duty, but almost painfully young in the veneer of Western culture'.[9] He was given the use of a wooden bungalow, No.7, in a group occupied by Western staff protected by gateways located about 2 km. north-west of the university. He bought furniture at the local auction, a great social feature in Tokyo at the time, for the foreign population fluctuated greatly and everyone wondered how much they would make when their time came to leave. Professor Chaplin, who taught civil engineering, lived at No.6 while on the other side of Ewing lived Professor Morse from America, a naturalist. At No.3 lived Reverend Dr Edward W. Syle, his wife Rebecca, and her daughter by a previous marriage called Annie Washington, aged 24. Syle was the main force behind the founding of the Asiatic Society of Japan (ASOJ) in 1872. He had spent time as a missionary in China and then Yokohama, before accepting the post of Professor of Moral Philosophy at Tokyo University. Ewing made two special friends soon after arriving. One was Basil Hall Chamberlain, the Professor of Philology, the first person to analyse the structure of the Japanese language and set out its rules of grammar, and the other was Lieutenant Thomas Henry James, R.N., an engineer, who taught Japanese naval cadets the elements of navigation on British-built training ships. These friends spent their leisure hours riding horses around the surrounding countryside, playing tennis or visiting each other at their homes. On Thursdays, Sir Harry Parkes, the British minister, received all members of the British colony at the legation.

The two-storied university buildings were at Hitotsubashi, standing apart from the rest of the city and enclosed by high wooden palings. Between the gates and the main porch in the front were ornate gardens with flower-beds, shrubs and mounds of grass all separated by a maze of twisting paths. Ewing's classroom was at the open extremity of the central wing, for the plan of the building resembled an 'E', and this overlooked the playing field, the open-air gymnasium and the dormitories. Ewing later wrote:

> To an inexperienced teacher, there was a stimulus and help in pupils (undergraduates) whose polite acceptance of everything he put before them was no less remarkable than their quick intelligence and receptiveness... For quite half a century, two or three of these Japanese youths of 1880 have kept in touch with me as a friend.[10]

Tanakadate was one of these. Of the total of 200 students attending the university, Ewing had a class of just 16 at first and was timetabled to lecture for 20 hours per week, but he did not finish at any stated time for he knew the signs of flagging attention or a high point that came when he emphasized an important concept. He was constantly aware that English involved a constant strain for his students.

To Ewing, brought up to search for truth through the scientific tradition, the love of research and the desire for new knowledge seemed natural. The hope of revealing and unveiling, and perhaps explaining, some of the unknown mysteries of nature was passionately desirable and vital to him, but the same attitude did not exist in Japan at the time. Yet he managed to communicate to Tanakadate and many others of his Tokyo University students his thrill and excitement in this activity, and by his inspirational teaching and insistence that they actually take an active role in his research projects (of which there were many), they were eventually accepted and respected as physicists and engineers on the international scene.

Although Ewing was employed in Japan by the Ministry of Education (Mombushō), he was in close personal and professional contact with other British scientists and engineers employed in Tokyo by the Ministry of Public Works (Kōbushō), sometimes called the Ministry of Industry and Technology, at the College of Engineering (Kōbu Dai Gakkō) with Henry Dyer as academic principal. Here, the Professor of Natural Philosophy (the old name for Physics)) was William Edward Ayrton who had arrived with Dyer in 1873, and who had a special interest in electrical engineering, having worked in the

Telegraph Service in India and attended courses on electricity in Glasgow University. The great Michael Faraday, pioneer of inventions concerning electricity, current and magnetism, who had first formulated several laws relating to them, had died only in 1867, and so research in this area was still new and fairly basic in the 1870s. It had been just 50 years since Faraday had built the first primitive electric motor and 40 years since he had demonstrated electromagnetic induction and constructed the first dynamo. But '. . . these ideas were not taken up on the practical side for almost 40 years, after their mathematization in the early 1860s'.[11] The mathematization was done by James Clerk Maxwell (1831-79), and his four second-order linear differential equations discovered in 1865 relate all electrical and magnetic phenomena to light and other waves (electromagnetic radiation).

It was in 1876 in the USA that an electric arc lighting system was first demonstrated at Philadelphia Centennial Exhibition. In Japan, at a banquet given at the Hall of the College of Engineering on the evening of 25 March 1878 to celebrate the opening of the Central Telegraphic Communication Office, three of Ayrton's students lit a large arc-light to illuminate proceedings.[12] Unfortunately, after the dark banqueting hall was lit up like broad daylight for a few seconds, the arc broke with a hissing sound and darkness ensued again. The students made unsuccessful attempts to relight the arc. Despite this, the Electrical Association later decided to call 25 March 'Electricity Day' in Japan.

Ayrton had designed and had built a laboratory for teaching physics in Tokyo, and his colleague John Perry, a teacher of civil engineering, explained:

> When I arrived in Japan in 1875, I found a marvellous laboratory, such as the world has not seen elsewhere. At Glasgow, at Cambridge, and at Berlin, there were three great personalities; the laboratories of Kelvin, and of Maxwell, and of Helmholtz, however, were not to be mentioned in comparison with Ayrton. Fine buildings, splendid apparatus, well-chosen a never-resting keen-eyed chief of great originality: these are what I found in Japan.[13]

Another commentator claimed that '. . . the centre of electrical science moved from England to Japan'[14] and:

> 'Ayrton played a leading role in developing the electrical power industry in Japan as well as in training scholars and engineers in this field. . . He was indeed the prominent personality in the field of electrical science in Europe (on his return to England in 1879).'

92

Sir Norman Lockyer (1836-1920), the founder in 1869 and first editor of the British scholarly science magazine, *Nature*, a famous astronomer and foremost organizer of science in Britain, quickly realized '... the significance of the establishment by the Japanese in 1872 of an Engineering College at Tokyo, where W.E. Ayrton established the first laboratory in the world for the teaching of applied electricity... He saw that the Japanese technological university (sic) was becoming the largest institution of its kind in the world.'[15] He remarked in *Nature* (7 May 1877) that: 'It is somewhat singular that this country (Britain), foremost as it has always been in matters of engineering enterprise, should be so behindhand in the systematic education of its engineers.'

Ayrton was also a prominent member of the Asiatic Society in Tokyo and read several papers to members as well as being secretary and treasurer from 1875-77. However, he did cause controversy when several of his papers and those of his scientific colleagues were deemed too technical and specialized to be of general interest to members. Subsequently, a special Physical Section of the Society was formed, but soon disbanded. Ayrton's first wife, Matilda Chaplin Ayrton (1846-83), was the first woman to read and present a paper to the previously all-male Society. She was a fine medical scientist in her own right, and while in Japan she opened a school for midwives, in which she lectured with the aid of an interpreter.[16] She also wrote many articles about the politics and customs of Japan for the *Scotsman* newspaper.

Back in England in 1879, Ayrton became a professor at the City and Guilds Institute and continued to work with John Perry on numerous electrical devices.

MAGNETISM AND EARTHQUAKES

In Tokyo Ewing taught courses in mechanics and on heat engines to engineering students, and lectured on electricity and magnetism to students of physics. Unlike his Scottish friend at the Engineering College, Henry Dyer, James Ewing carried out many research projects and had numerous articles published by the scientific academic press back in Britain. In the laboratory he investigated magnetism and discovered the phenomenon of 'hysteresis' – a word he introduced into scientific language. (Actually it was later shown that the phenomenon had been researched before, unknown to Ewing.) It involves the way a material, like iron, becomes magnetized when placed in an magnetic field produced by electricity flowing in a coil, which is increased from zero to a high value and then reduced so that it is in the opposite direction. Measurements taken can be represented on a hysteresis curve or loop.

In this research Ewing invited and encouraged his Japanese students to participate and express their own ideas. This gave them invaluable experience and training but also, more importantly, inspired in them the confidence that Japanese could make original discoveries and contribute to the mainstream of international science. Much later, an understanding of hysteresis would be essential in the construction of audio tape-recorders of the 1950s and video recorders of the 1970s, both of which use magnetic tape developed in Japan.[17] He did, however, study one of Thomas Edison's 'tin-foil phonographs' which he took to Japan with him and where '. . . its capacity to speak Japanese with a slightly nasal twang was a double passport to popularity'.[18] However, in one lecture he gave on the telephonic transmission of sound which he illustrated by using the phonograph, he remarked that '. . . no desirable results of a practical nature, had yet proceeded from Edison's contrivance'.[19]

Ewing also investigated earthquakes. This work led him to help the telegraphy expert at the Engineering College, T. Lomar Gray, and the rest of the team there which included John Milne, to develop a seismometer that could plot a continuous record of the earth's movement as it shook. Again, his young and eager students were invited to participate in and contribute to this. There appears to have been very close cooperation between foreign academic staff at the Engineering College and Tokyo University at this time.

Ewing may have been frightened by the 300 earthquakes he experienced in Tokyo, but he was not fatalistic and simply devised ways of observing and measuring their activity. Certainly, his fear of injury or death by earthquakes could not have been too strong for he soon proposed marriage to his next-door neighbour Anne Maria Thomasina Blackburn Washington and, after a trip to Yokohama to buy a diamond ring, they married on 14 May 1879 at the British legation in the presence of Basil Hall Chamberlain as best man and E.C.W. Stevens, the American chargé d'affaires, with the ceremony officiated by the Rev. John Piper and Sir Harry Parkes.[20] The bride was a great-great grand niece of George Washington. She owned once-prosperous farms in America's South, but the Civil War had devastated most of them, drastically reducing her income from them. It was not until August 1879 that the Ewings had their honeymoon. Leaving sweltering Tokyo by rickshaw they made for Hakone, using pack horses and a *kago* (palanquin) on the final steep slopes. On 19 August they decided to climb Mt Fuji, and at 5.00am they set out, accompanied by Kano, their cook, three coolies, guides and baggage carriers. After 12 hours climbing they reached the summit and spent the night there, cold and bitten by fleas, but were impressed at dawn by the sunrise and the chanting of hundreds of religious pilgrims. Then came the rapid descent through ankle-deep lava dust, and a hot bath in Subashiri.

Later a son, Alfred Washington, and a daughter, Maud Janet, were born to them in Tokyo. It was at this time that Ewing became fearful of the quality of the water supply and the sewerage system in Tokyo and proposed new improvements to the government authorities. But despite cholera panics, indifference and economic restraints were the order of the day.

★   ★   ★

Ewing's circle of acquaintances was broadened when he became a member of the Asiatic Society of Japan. Here he met other scientists from Europe and America who were working at many different locations throughout Japan, as well as missionaries, school-teachers, diplomats and business people. During 1879-82 Ewing was the Recording Secretary in Tokyo. He served first with the Rev. E.W. Syle as president, then under Dr Edward Divers, the professor of chemistry at the Engineering College, followed by J.G. Kennedy, the chargé d'affaires at the British legation, and finally with Sir Harry Parkes. Ewing read one paper to members at a meeting of the Society on: 'Notes on some Recent Earthquakes' which was published in the 1880-81 Transactions. Many papers presented by Asiatic Society members of this era dealt with problems of the day in Japan – including various prevalent diseases and their cures, and construction materials as well as landscape gardening by Professor Josiah Conder – rather than with purely academic subjects.[21] The meetings at this time were lively and all were outspoken, opinions clashed, and the Japanese academics present gained an insight into the nature of Western-style debate.

A final project in Japan was the establishment, with the involvement of students and other staff, of an observatory in the lowest part of the Vale of Edo. Seismological results from there were published in the Memoirs of the Science Department of the University of Tokyo in 1883.[22]

RETURN TO ENGLAND

Ewing's three-year engagement in Japan was extended to five, and this ended in 1883. He was presented with personal gifts by the Emperor and later was awarded the Order of Precious Treasure. His post in Tokyo was taken over by another brilliant young scientist from Edinburgh, Cargill Gilston Knott (1856-1922) who also did some research with Tanakadate. Back in his native Dundee, Ewing was appointed Professor of Engineering at the newly-opened University

College where he continued teaching and researching for the next seven years. Today, the Ewing building, which formerly housed the Department of Electrical and Electronic Engineering, is now one of the main teaching and research areas in the university.[23]

Then, in 1890, the professorship of Mechanism and Applied Mechanics fell vacant at Cambridge University, and Ewing successfully applied for the chair. He became embroiled in delicate university politics at Cambridge. Here there was an argument and conflict concerning the suitability of engineering, and its associated workshop practice, as part of the studies at so ancient a university. In the stormy rhetoric many thought that the Chair of Mechanism and Applied Mechanics should be terminated, for it was considered unacademic (as well as too expensive) for students to operate noisy machines in the workshop as part of their studies.

But as Ewing had been elected to his professorship he had strong backing and support, and persuaded the authorities to develop the Engineering School at the university despite the expense. By 1892 the Mechanical Sciences Tripos was established and the workshop designated an Engineering Laboratory under the guidance of Ewing in 1894. In the following decades these initiatives proved invaluable to such pioneering scientists as J.J.Thomson and others who needed to construct apparatus to make discoveries about the nature of electrons, basic research on which the electronics and computer industries are founded. For following an understanding of electric current with its associated magnetism, pure scientists then focused on the deeper nature of electricity and its relationship to atoms and the light spectra produced by excited ones, i.e., to finding out the very structure of the building blocks of material objects, atoms, and atomic physics was born.

In 1899 Ewing was offered the post of director of the National Physical Laboratory. He refused it. In 1903 the British Admiralty had decided to provide all naval officers with a new scheme of training so that they could understand the scientific and technical principles behind the construction of their ships and weaponry. Ewing accepted the post of Director of Naval Education, and based on his experiences in Japan and at Cambridge, he devised new systems for teaching science and engineering which was 'of immense benefit in promoting the efficiency of the service'.[24] Afterwards, at the beginning of The Great War, he was the key figure in 'Room 40' in the Admiralty for deciphering enemy coded messages, and he ended his career as principal of Edinburgh University. A few days after his death in 1935, his past students at Tokyo University hung his portrait next to that of engineer James Watt as they celebrated the 'Watt-sai' (anniversary festival) in a ceremony of ancestor worship.

SEED SOWN IN JAPAN

Meanwhile in Japan, Tanakadate pursued answers to the questions revealed by Ewing's research into magnetism. In 1888 he was sent abroad to study by Tokyo University, now prefixed with the name 'Imperial'. With Ewing's help he became a fellow of the University of Glasgow to study under the direction of the great Lord Kelvin (William Thomson) and continued the experiments in electricity and magnetism which he had begun in Japan. The result was a number of papers published in English in *Philosophical Magazine* concerning new knowledge about the magnetization of soft iron. During these two years in Glasgow he admired Thompson who made a deep impression on his thinking. Then he moved to Berlin for one year, where he went to lectures given by Hermann von Helmholz (1821-94), famous for devising a pair of coils of copper wire that produced a uniform magnetic field between them and for expressing new concepts in thermodynamics. He also attended talks by Professor Fuchs, and a colloquium held by Max Planck (1858-1947), founder of quantum theory, and August Eduard Eberhard Aolph Kundt (1839-94) famous for his experimental glass tube capable of measuring accurately the speed of sound in various gases.[25]

Tanakadate arrived back in Japan in July 1891 where he was promoted to full professor at the Imperial University, and the following month was awarded the D.Sc. degree. He remained at the university as Professor of Physics until 1916, when he retired aged 60.

When Tanakadate left Tokyo to continue his studies at Glasgow University in 1888, Nagaoka Hantarō (1865-1950) had continued his research, devising many ingenious experiments to investigate the phenomenon of magnetostriction. As a result Nagaoka was invited to report on his discoveries to the First Physics International Conference held in Paris in 1900.

Ewing and Tanakadate through their studies and careers had become brothers in science even though they were from different races from opposite ends of the world. Each created events in their scientific apparatus unseen before, and explained them through the common means of communication with mathematical equations and carefully chosen words that described new laws of science. A new vision of the world and the universe had emerged by this means. Yet they were forced to live through a turbulent era of nationalistic conflict in which their discoveries were sadly abused and misused to the detriment of the human species. It was the Japanese minister in Paris, Motono, who remarked with sadness: 'As long ago as we Japanese consecrated ourselves to the work of an intensive civilization, producing only men of letters, men of science, and of art, you treated us as barbarians. Now we have learned to kill, you call us civilized.'

Although Professors Ewing and Tanakadate are not remembered by many today, their basic work in physics research a century ago is apparent everywhere. Magnetic recording tape used both in the entertainment industry and in computers where the magnetic hysteresis cycle is undergone millions of times per second could not exist if the early experiments had not been done and the nature of magnetism understood. But Ewing's lasting achievement was to be one of a dedicated team to teach and inspire the first generation of modern physicists in Japan through his desire for adventure.

9

Captain Francis Brinkley (1841-1912): Yatoi, Scholar and Apologist

J. E. HOARE

W H E N   C A P T A I N Francis (Frank) Brinkley died aged 73 in Tokyo in October 1912, the anonymous commentator in the *Annual Registrar* wrote that he had been the 'chief interpreter of Japanese ideas and views to the Western world', through his journalism and scholarship.[1] Brinkley's long residence in Japan, spanning over forty years, his varied interests, reflected in his published works, his links with some of the great leaders of the Meiji period, and his journalism, all seemed to qualify him as one who would rank with Satow, Aston and Chamberlain as one of the giants of Britain's involvement in Japan.

Today, however, Brinkley's name, while occasionally remembered in Japan, especially as a journalist – he features in the Kodansha *Encyclopaedia of Japan*, for example – is hardly known outside a very small circle in the West. His books on art and history have never been reprinted. Only his *Dictionary*, which in 1896 replaced the earlier dictionary by J. C. Hepburn as a prime tool for foreigners learning Japanese, remains in somewhat limited use as a guide to Meiji usage.

THE SOLDIER AND YATOI

Brinkley was born in Ireland, and went to school in Dublin. There are no available details of his family background, although at his death there were references to his coming from a 'good Irish family'. Although the editor of the *Japan Punch*, in 1883 lumped him in with Parnell as a 'self boiled lost potato', suggesting that he return to join other potatoes,[2] evidence from editorial writing in the *Japan Mail*, the newspaper which he owned from 1881 until his death, indicates that

Brinkley came from a Unionist rather than a Nationalist background; the *Mail* regularly attacked Irish revolutionaries and Irish ingratitude at British rule, and was particularly scathing about the activities of Irish-American groups. It was also generally unsympathetic to Roman Catholic missionaries, which perhaps points to Brinkley coming from a Protestant background.[3]

Brinkley joined the army, passed out from the artillery school at Woolwich in south London, and joined the Royal Artillery as a second lieutenant. In 1867, he went to Hong Kong as private secretary and ADC to the Governor, Sir Richard MacDonnel, who was almost certainly a relative.[4] He appears to have held this post for only one year, for all records agree that he was in Japan by late 1867. He was not 'part of the legation guard', as is sometimes claimed, but was a member of the British garrison stationed at Yokohama since 1863 to protect the foreign community from attack. Although an artillery officer, he was attached to the 10th Regiment of Foot.[5]

From his earliest days in Japan, Brinkley applied himself to the study of Japanese, and by the early 1870s, when he was asked by the Fukui *han* to become a gunnery instructor, the British legation noted that he was completely fluent in the language.[6] Brinkley was keen to take up the offered post, and asked to be placed on the seconded list. The Foreign Office had no objection; indeed it was the policy of the British minister in Japan, Sir Harry Parkes, to get as many Japanese posts as possible into British hands. The War Office, however, would not agree to such a move at Brinkley's request; the impetus had to come from the Japanese authorities. Although the files examined show no evidence of such a formal request, presumably one was made, for by the end of 1871, the way was clear for Brinkley's appointment.[7] His name remained on the *Army List* as a lieutenant on secondment as a drill instructor (*sic*) employed by the Japanese government.

By the time Brinkley was free to take up his appointment, the *han* had been abolished, but he was instead offered a post with the newly-established naval college as an artillery instructor. Later, from 1874, he taught English at the same institute, and from 1878–80, he joined the Public Works Department as a teacher (sometimes described as 'Professor') of mathematics in the Engineering College.[8] Perhaps he remained most attached to the navy; in later years, his newspaper was certainly a strong supporter of the build-up of the Japanese Navy.

Brinkley's *yatoi* career followed the standard path for Japan's foreign employees. He moved from one post to another, was reasonably well-paid although his salary dropped somewhat each time he moved, was accorded a moderate amount of respect, and dismissed when there were suitable Japanese replacements.[9] Perhaps understandably, the definition of *yatoi* in his 1896 *Japanese-English Dictionary*, was less than fulsome: 'Yatoi: ... a government employé (not a regular official); lowest grade of officials ...'.[10]

Whatever the drawbacks, Brinkley had time for study and writing, and during these years he established a reputation as a scholar of things Japanese. As a side product of his teaching at the engineering college, he produced a textbook, *Go-gaku hitori annai*, ('Lessons in English for Japanese'). Evidence of his ability in Japanese was shown in the various translations he published in the treaty port press, including the 'Tales of Taikoo', while Ernest Satow, the Japanese secretary at the British legation, acknowledged his help in compiling a Japanese dictionary.[11] The loss of his library, of 'over a thousand volumes' and many manuscripts in a fire in 1877, must have reduced his output.[12]

He was active in other ways. He was a founder member of the Asiatic Society of Japan in 1873, and remained a member until his death. For many years, until illness took its toll, he was clearly an active participant in the Society's affairs. After 1881, he also provided support through his newspaper; the *Japan Weekly Mail* carried the minutes of the Society's meetings and often the full text of papers delivered. Brinkley's only known contribution to the Society's formal activities was an unpublished paper presented during the 1880-81 season on 'The history of Japanese keramics'. He also contributed papers to other journals.[13]

During his period as a *yatoi*, Brinkley, like many of his contemporaries, acquired a Japanese mistress. She was Sei, the daughter of Wakabayashi Tahei. They had a son, Harry, born in 1878, but Sei died soon after. Later that year, Brinkley concluded a marriage contract with Tanaka Yasu. Although she was a Christian, there was no Christian wedding and no attempt to register the marriage for some years after they had set up house. That he was married to a Japanese and had a Japanese family, was one of the reasons Brinkley would cite later for his positive and supportive view of Japan, but it brought with it its own difficulties.

These were two-fold. One related to the status of the marriage. Theoretically, since the arrangements between Brinkley and Tanaka Yasu had not been registered with either the Japanese or the British authorities, there was no marriage in the eyes of either country. This was resolved, as far as the Japanese were concerned, when Yasu applied for the marriage to be registered with the Tokyo authorities in 1884. It was more difficult to persuade the British, but in 1890 the British government accepted that the marriage was valid, since Brinkley had gone through a form of marriage recognized as such by the Japanese authorities. The resolution of the Brinkley case had an importance beyond the Brinkley family for hitherto the British authorities had refused to recognize such 'local law' marriages.

The second problem related to the children. Tanaka Yasu settled the issue of Harry's status by adopting him as her son, and he was thus entered on her family register, as was the Brinkleys' daughter, Dorothy, born in 1881. When the marriage was registered by the Japanese, however, Yasu ceased to be the head of a household, and six-year old Harry took on the role. The Brinkleys wanted the children registered as British but this was refused until the marriage was recognized. Then the Japanese authorities refused to recognize the children as Japanese, and for the rest of their days, they remained British citizens.[14]

JOURNALIST AND APOLOGIST

When Brinkley left Japanese government employment at the end of 1880, he underwent another career change, for he purchased a Yokohama newspaper, the *Japan Mail*. At the same time, he remained an army officer, not resigning until forced to do so in late 1881 – though he would later claim that his resignation dated from 31 December 1880. In 1883, a correspondent to the Royal Artillery magazine, *Broad Arrow*, writing from Japan, noted that Brinkley's name still appeared in the *Army List*, and enquired whether it was possible to be both a newspaper owner and an army officer. The *Broad Arrow* editor replied that Brinkley was no longer on the *Army List*, and the *Mail* was in 'capital hands'. Brinkley reprinted this in the *Mail*, with a note claiming that he had resigned from the Royal Artillery on 31 December 1880, having been eligible for a retirement pension from 23 June 1880.[15] In fact, Brinkley's promotion to Captain and resignation from the Royal Artillery was not carried in the *London Gazette* until November 1882 (and then only because he had been given the choice of resigning or returning to his regiment). For over two years, therefore, he had owned and edited the *Japan Mail* while still, in theory at least, in the British army.[16] It was perhaps not surprising that some felt Brinkley was not to be trusted.

In taking over the *Japan Mail*,[17] Brinkley did not entirely sever his links with the Japanese government. The *Mail*, founded in 1865, and originally called the *Japan Times*, had acquired a somewhat doubtful reputation. It was a good newspaper in terms of literacy and general content, at least when set against the relatively low standards of Japanese treaty port journalism. Since 1870, however, when the original proprietor had sold it to a consortium made up of Horatio Nelson Lay, the first foreign commissioner of the Chinese Imperial Maritime Customs, and W. G Howell, late of Shanghai and Hakodate, there were suspicions that the *Japan Mail*, as the new owners renamed the *Japan Times*, had links to the Japanese government. The exact relationship was never clear, and Brinkley denied on several occasions that he received a direct subsidy. But it had been admitted in court in the mid-1870s that the Japanese government subscribed to five hundred copies of the *Japan Weekly Mail*, no small boost to a newspaper operating in the world of the treaty ports. The fact that the newspaper could boast in 1883 of the largest circulation in Japan, and the long runs of the *Mail* from the 1880s to c.1906 existing in a number of overseas libraries outside Japan, indicate that this was one way the Japanese government helped Brinkley. Another may have been through payments to allow the *Mail* to subscribe to Reuters' telegrams; from 1883 until the late 1890s, only the *Mail* was able, or willing, to do this. (The benefits of having this exclusive service were undermined by the flagrant copying of the telegrams by both foreign and Japanese newspapers.)[18]

Contemporaries had few doubts on the score, and however many denials were issued, Brinkley was regarded as in Japanese pay. Whatever his motives, the *Mail* under Brinkley followed a consistent pro-Japanese line on all major issues. Whether it was policies towards Korea or China, or questions of more immediate interest to his theoretical readership in the treaty ports, such as treaty revision, or the merits of the British minister in Japan, Sir Harry Parkes, Brinkley favoured the Japanese position. It was this constant support that seemed remarkable to observers. Few were surprised at occasional shifts to a pro-Japanese position; that could be bought by judicious purchase of advertising space. But Brinkley's steady support for so long a period required another explanation, and again, it was seen as lying in Japanese government funds. As the British vice-consul in Tokyo wrote in 1893 when Brinkley was considering renouncing probate over the will of his friend and fellow supporter of Japan, Major-General Palmer: 'Some of the assets will be in the nature of claims on the Japanese Government which it would be difficult for [Brinkley] to press adequately with due regard to the interests of the estate.'[19]

As well as supporting the Japanese position through the *Japan Mail*, Brinkley did so as an occasional correspondent for the London *Times* from 1885 to 1897, and thereafter from 1897 to 1912, as its permanent Tokyo correspondent. Before Brinkley, the *Times* permanent correspondent had been his friend Major-General Palmer, and for several years, therefore, the *Times* advocated similar policies to those supported by the *Japan Mail*. The link did not go unnoticed. As one newspaper put it, the two might seem to be independent of each other, but 'the *Times*' letters are the reverberation and distant echoes of the *Mail*'s thunders ... [T]here is one voice only, and that is the voice of the scholarly editor of the *Japan Mail* ...'.[20]

Brinkley's importance as a correspondent for the *Times* is hard to judge. Palmer's work was certainly valued; the British minister reported in 1890 that the main reason behind his employment on the Yokohama waterworks project in 1887 was his support in the *Times*. Brinkley was perhaps less useful, since his appointment as correspondent was well-known, as was his ownership of the *Mail*. He was never the only *Times* correspondent in Japan; there were others at Yokohama and Kobe, who were often less favourable in their estimate of Japan and Japanese policies. His pro-Japanese views certainly fitted in with the paper's editorial line during the years 1895-1905, and his support for an Anglo-Japanese Alliance was well-known and vindicated by the conclusion of just such an agreement in 1902. The official history of the *Times*, however, barely mentions him. More influential on Japanese matters were its China correspondent, G. E. Morrison, and Valentine Chirol, the foreign editor.[21]

A lesser charge against Brinkley was that of aloofness and distance from his readers. Some argued that although the *Mail* continued to be published in Yokohama and claimed to speak for the 'thinking' foreign community in Japan, or to represent 'the best views' of the treaty ports, Brinkley was out of touch with those views. Though there was some truth in the charge, for Brinkley never lived in Yokohama after 1871, and rarely visited the port in later years, he defended himself vigorously. In an editorial in 1891, after the *Japan Gazette* had raised the issue, the *Mail* dismissed the implied claim that Yokohama was the centre of the universe. Since the *Mail* could not afford to employ many reporters, the editor had to collect news himself, and the place for news was Tokyo, not Yokohama. It was also 'a trifle childish' to argue that he was unaware of the views of foreigners: 'Tokyo has a foreign community not altogether undeserving of consideration at the hands of an editor.'[22]

In his later years, however, the charge became more accurate as Brinkley left the day-to-day running of the paper to his managing editor, J. E. Beale. In 1912, the *Japan Times*, in paying tribute to his long years of support for Japan, also pointed out that by the time of his death, many of the senior Japanese he had known, such as Itō Hirobumi, had passed from the scene, and that Brinkley had become out of touch with modern Japanese thinking. By then, Brinkley was not just out of touch with the foreign community in Yokohama; the London *Times*' obituary in 1912 noted that it was thirty years since he had visited Europe. It could have added that it was many years since he had even visited the Chinese ports.[23]

THE SCHOLAR

Brinkley's involvement with Japan was not confined to journalism. He had many contacts amongst the senior statesmen who made up the

Meiji oligarchy. During one of the Korean crises of the Meiji period, he accompanied the then foreign minister, Inoue Kaoru, to China in 1885. As so often with Brinkley, his role is not clear, but whatever it was, the Japanese government were ready to decorate him, until stopped by British objections. The *Japan Punch* suggested that he should adopt Japanese costume on such occasions, just as the Korean government's German adviser, Paul von Moellendorf, had taken to wearing Korean clothes.[24] As well as being on good terms with Inoue, Brinkley was believed to have close links with Itō Hirobumi.[25]

He was also an adviser to Nippon Yūsen Kaisha (NYK), the Japan Mail Steamship Company established in 1885, (as were a number of other prominent Western journalists in Japan), though it is not clear in what capacity or for how long; he was still listed as a foreign adviser in 1906 but by then he was already ill. Neither he nor other foreigners employed as advisers are mentioned in the most recent history of the company, which makes clear that by 1900 even foreign professionals such as ships' captains were being dismissed from the company.[26]

Whatever his links with NYK, a company strongly associated with Mitsubishi, for many years he lived in a house in Azabu owned by Baron Mitsui, which he filled with Chinese and Japanese antiques – a visitor shown part of the collection in 1889 felt that 'Brinkley's godown [warehouse] had no bottom'.[27] At his death, Brinkley's contribution to scholarship was widely regarded as every bit as important as his journalism in educating the world about Japan. He devoted much effort to assembling collections of Japanese and Chinese art and artefacts. Despite the fires that periodically sent him back to the beginning, by the mid-1880s he had a well-established reputation as a connoisseur, always willing to show his collection to those interested. Ceramics were his first love, but he also assembled an important collection of woodblock prints. He had always held sales of parts of his collections, but in the last decade of his life, he seems to have made a systematic effort to sell or give away much of the remainder. His Chinese ceramics were sold to the Iwasaki family, for example, and much of his woodblock collection went to the New York Public Library.[28]

To some extent Brinkley's scholarly writings derived from his collections, and he published at least one catalogue based on his holdings. He continued translating, publishing versions of various *Noh* and *Kyogen* plays, and the official *History of the Empire of Japan*, produced by the Education Ministry for the 1893 World's Columban Exhibition in Chicago. In 1896, he published *An unabridged Japanese-English dictionary*, a 1687-page work, produced with help from a number of Japanese scholars. Many dictionaries have appeared since 1896, but Brinkley's remains important as a record of the Japanese language at the end of the Meiji period. As such, it still retains value for scholars, and was reprinted in 1963.[29] In 1897, he edited a twelve-volume account of history, art and social customs written by Japanese.[30]

He produced two other main works. One was a twelve volume account of *Japan and China: their history, arts and literature*, which appeared between 1901 and 1904. Volumes 1-8 dealt with Japan, 9-12 with China. The work was lavishly illustrated with photographs of places and objects, and there was an original watercolour frontispiece for each volume. The second, published after his death, was *A history of the Japanese people from the earliest times to the end of the Meiji period*, produced in collaboration with Baron Kikuchi Dairoku (1855-1917), a distinguished scholar and Education Minister from 1901 to 1903. It, too, was big and lavishly illustrated.[31]

Neither has lasted. Even though Brinkley was an acknowledged art expert, his methods and approach have long been superseded. As for his work as an historian, it was not even held in high regard at the time. Basil Hall Chamberlain wrote of the history of China and Japan that parts of it were interesting, but that the volumes on China could be ignored as slight. As for those on Japan, while Brinkley 'let in light' on the neglected art history and the social customs of the Japanese, the work as a whole was flawed:

> ... in the domain of history proper his loose method, his failure to quote original authorities, and above all his lack of the critical faculty render him an unsafe guide, except for the events of the last forty years whose gradual unfolding he has personally watched.

Chamberlain in practice made more use of Brinkley's works than this might imply, but it was a damning indictment, published while Brinkley was still alive.[32]

CONCLUSION

Brinkley died on 22 October 1912. Just before his death, he received the Sacred Order of Merit and the Double Rays of the Order of the Rising Sun in recognition of his services to Japan. (He had previously held the Order of the Scared Treasure, Third Class, a standard award for foreign employees.) The obituaries were fulsome, noting his support for Japan over many years and his scholarly interests, but there were frequent references to a man who had been left behind as the world changed rapidly around him. In his last years, he suffered from Parkinson's disease, and had steadily withdrawn from journalism. He dispersed his art collections and saw fewer people.

Japan, too, was different, and no longer needed foreign apologists.

In 1899, new treaties replaced the 'unequal treaties' of Bakumatsu days. The 1902 Anglo-Japanese Alliance accorded Japan international status undreamed of when Brinkley bought the *Mail* in 1881. The Russo-Japanese War (1904-5) completed acceptance of Japan as one of the 'powers'. Since 1897, in any case, it had its own English-language newspaper, the *Japan Times*, to put forward its views.[33] Even as a journalist, Brinkley no longer counted.

Nor did he count in other ways. Few of his British contemporaries in Japan held him in much esteem. His fellow editors attacked his pro-Japanese views and mocked his scholarship. Scholars who shared his interests were less vitriolic in public, but equally contemptuous. Basil Hall Chamberlain, writing in 1906, felt that Brinkley was an awful warning of what happened if one got stuck in a rut. Satow generally tried to avoid him, and wrote privately after his death that he had not trusted him.[34]

Few now read his scholarly works, which, lacking the depth of his contemporaries such as Chamberlain and Aston, have long since been replaced. His main monument remains the *Japan Mail*, still valued as a source for the history of the Meiji period and, thanks to the Japanese government, relatively widely available. As Britain and Japan grew apart in the 1920s and '30s, Brinkley's support for Japan, if remembered at all, was seen in a hostile light, and his reputation has never recovered.

10

The Archdeacon and the Bishop: Alexander Croft Shaw, Edward Bickersteth, and Meiji Japan

HAMISH ION

'Japan is a most interesting country; the almost wild rush of the whole nation towards Western civilization and towards Xtianity makes it of supreme importance to the Church there that her affairs be managed with all possible wisdom.
ROBERT READE TO BISHOP OF TRURO, 6 OCTOBER 1885.[1]

THIS PAPER deals with two British missionaries who played a crucial role in managing the affairs of the British Anglican missionary endeavour in Japan (and particularly in Tokyo) as that country was seemingly rushing towards Western civilization but not, as it turned out, towards Christianity.[2] The first of these is the Canadian-born and educated Archdeacon Alexander Croft Shaw (1848-1902), one of the two pioneer missionaries belonging to the Society for the Propagation of the Gospel in Foreign Parts (SPG, High Church) who came out in Japan in 1873.[3] A man much admired by the British congregation of St Andrew's Church, Shiba for his gentle courtesy and self-forgetfulness, Shaw has been described as exemplifying '... the very spirit of the [SPG] Society in his calm wisdom, his patience, his dauntless courage and his unflinching fidelity to the Catholic Church'.[5] The second missionary is Edward Bickersteth (1850-97),[6] who was consecrated in February 1886 as Bishop in Japan. In 1887 Bickersteth was responsible, together with his Virginian counterpart, Bishop Channing Moore Williams (1829-1910)[7] of the American Church Mission, for the formation of the Nippon Seikokai, the Anglican Church in Japan.

While the experiences of Shaw and Bickersteth were different, both left an indelible mark on the emerging Japanese Anglican Church.

Around Shaw coalesced the so-called Shiba Sect in Tokyo which included among others Arthur Lloyd (1852-1911),[8] Imai Judō (1863-1919),[9] Yamada Sukejirō, Herbert Moore, Armine King, Lionel Cholmondeley and even perhaps, R. D. M. Shaw (Shaw's own missionary son). Professor Cyril Powles has suggested that the British Christianity of the Shiba Sect was 'church-centred, theological, aristocratic, liberal humanist and permissive (i.e., it accepted Japanese culture as valid, if imperfect)' ... and stood in sharp contrast to American Protestantism which was 'Messianic, ethical or non-theological, republican and dialectical (i. e. challenging)'.[10] The Shiba Sect view of Japanese culture was clearly expressed by Imai in 1905 who stressed when investigating bushido that there were many good elements in Japanese culture but Christianity was needed to make it perfect.[11] They recognized as valid such elements in Japanese culture as Shintō, Ainu religion and Buddhism and studied them with interest. This does not mean, however, that the attitudes of Shiba Sect missionaries were not free from cultural conditioning. The books on Buddhism by Arthur Lloyd,[12] for instance, investigate Buddhism from the standpoint of Western thought. Yet Shiba Sect writings are free of the stilted images of quaint Japan popularized by Victorian observers of Bakumatsu and early Meiji Japan and continued on by authors such as Lafcadio Hearn into the early twentieth century.[13]

The Shiba Sect missionaries, in the main the products of public schools and Oxford or Cambridge Universities, identified with the Japanese who formed the political and educational elites in Meiji Japan. All viewed, for instance, the Emperor-family-centred Japanese society in terms of their own paternalistic rural British society with its strong identification with the monarchy and awareness of class distinctions. There were times when they were unable to see that cultural differences between Japanese and themselves could lead to future difficulties. An obvious example of this was the prayers to the Emperor in the Nippon Seikokai Prayer Book which were virtually the same as those offered by Britons to the British Royal Family despite the obvious differences in the relationship of the two heads of state to the Anglican Church.[14] In general, the Shiba Sect missionaries were happy to cooperate with Meiji leaders in such areas as education rather than establish independent institutions like American missionaries. Although there was an element of self-interest involved, both Shaw and Bickersteth were deeply concerned with the improvement of Anglo-Japanese relations and became early and staunch advocates of treaty revision.[15] Overseas, however, they were prepared to accept uncritically Japanese imperialism and military adventurism which manifested itself in the Sino-Japanese War of 1894-95.

The Shiba Sect missionaries were very much a visible part of the British community in Tokyo. Many of the leading diplomatic, business and educational figures within that community were members of the English congregation of St Andrew's Church, Shiba which Shaw built in 1879. The original St Andrew's Church building was brick with stained glass windows. It housed both a Japanese and an English-speaking congregation and afforded '. . . to the surrounding population a public proof of the power of the Christian religion to unite wholly alien races on the ground of the same faith'.[16] Indeed, it was reported after Shaw's death that he had taken special delight over the fact that excellent relations had always existed between the Japanese and British congregations '. . . and only the insuperable difficulty of the language prevented all from at least occasionally meeting together for worship at the same time'.[17] However, when it came to the design of St Andrew's Church or its furnishings, Shaw made no concessions to Japanese sensibilities for British Anglican traditions were maintained intact even to the surpliced choir which was the first of its kind in Tokyo. Close by, St Andrew's Mission House with its Senior Common Room atmosphere (impressive as it must have been to young Japanese enquirers) also served as a meeting place for the British community, especially those who were young and new to Japan. The missionary compound in crowded Shiba was a little British oasis, and this was definitely part of its attraction to both Japanese and Britons.

Shaw's career in Japan reflected the dual nature of SPG missionary work for he became honorary Chaplain to the British legation in 1879 as well as working as a missionary to the Japanese. Moreover, whatever else he might have done, Shaw is famous for being one of the first Westerners to visit Karuizawa[18] which became a popular hill station for foreigners and later for Japanese wanting to escape the summer heat of the coastal cities. However, taking summer holidays in the hills and catering to the spiritual needs of the British diplomats and other Britons in Tokyo was only part of what he did.[18]

FIRST YEARS IN TOKYO

Shaw and his colleague, William Ball Wright, were among the first missionaries to reside outside the treaty port confines in Tokyo. Soon after their arrival in Japan in 1873, they found, with the help of the British legation, living quarters in the Daishōji temple in the Mita district of central Tokyo.[19] Indeed, it was there on Good Friday, 11 April 1874 that Shaw began regular services for the English-speaking community in Tokyo.[20] In early 1874, an opportunity for Shaw appeared that had a profound impact on the future of his work. Shaw wrote to the SPG authorities in London that:

> I have accepted the offer of a Japanese to live with him and
> teach his three children English... the father of my pupil
> truly if not the most prominent man in the country as far as
> educational matters are concerned, has established large
> schools at several of the principal cities and is altogether
> very liberal minded and progressive.[21]

As well as tutoring his children, Fukuzawa Yukichi (1835-1901)
allowed Shaw to teach ethics and Christianity at his private school,
Keiō Gijiku. Keiō students were also drawn into the Sunday school
classes that Shaw and Wright held in the Daishōji temple including
Ozaki Yukio (later one of Japan's most famous parliamentarians) and
Tajima Jutarō (later elected to the first Diet) both of whom Shaw
baptized at Christmas 1875.[22] Shaw stayed with Fukuzawa and his
family for two years. The link to Keiō did not end, however, when
Shaw moved into a home of his own. In 1876 Fukuzawa gave Alice
Hoar, the first female SPG missionary in Japan, 'the use of the upper
part of his house, where he opened a small school for her to use in
teaching Christianity'.[23]

During the 1880s and afterwards, when most missionary societies
had rejected working in Japanese-run schools and begun to establish
their own institutions, a succession of SPG missionaries continued to
teach part-time at Keiō. Among them was Arthur Lloyd whose long
association with the school began in 1885 as a teacher of English with
the right also to teach Christianity.[24] Given the anti-Christian
pronouncements of Fukuzawa, it might appear surprising that Shaw
and his Shiba Sect colleagues maintained their ties with Keiō.
However, the personal relations between Shaw and Fukuzawa always
remained cordial, and Fukuzawa's public and political stance against
Christianity did not appear to translate into any restrictions on the
activities of Lloyd and others who taught at Keiō. Indeed, on certain
political issues Shaw and Fukuzawa shared common views, particularly,
at the beginning of the 1890s, on the need for treaty revision.[25] Further,
Cyril Powles has suggested that the Shiba Sect missionaries generally
interpreted the rise of *kokusui shugi* after 1889 as a preoccupation with
politics to the neglect of faith rather than direct opposition to
Christianity.[26]

Shaw had realized from the first that the connection with Keiō
provided contact with students who would possibly become part of a
future elite within Japanese society. Yet, he was equally aware that
even though he might attract a good many students to take an interest
in Christianity, few would remain Christians. During the first years in
Tokyo, there had been no apparent difficulty in attracting converts,

both students and others, for between 1873 and 1877 Shaw and Wright, baptised 150 people.[27] However, Shaw's primary concern was not numbers of converts but rather the creation of a strong central church that could serve as a foundation for future growth. He objected to the more diffusive methods of Wright who was eager to expand Christian work beyond Tokyo.[28] Shaw preferred to concentrate on developing a strong faith within a few of the brightest of the young people with whom he came into contact. In 1878, in order to prepare properly candidates for the priesthood, the SPG, CMS and American Church Mission came together to form a single theological college in Tokyo. It was to the training of Japanese clergy that Shaw and the SPG missionaries in Tokyo would devote much of their energy.

A growing Japanese Anglican community was already in existence in Tokyo when Edward Bickersteth arrived in Japan in late April 1886 as Bishop of Japan in succession to the late Arthur W. Poole (1852-1885).[29] Unlike Poole, who had lived in Osaka, Bickersteth chose to reside in Tokyo. For the first eighteen months, Bickersteth lived in Shaw's home and Shaw's *deshi*, Imai, often acted as his interpreter and translator.[30]

THE MAKING OF A BISHOP

Edward Bickersteth owed his Bishop's mitre to the pleading of his father, Bishop Edward Henry Bickersteth of Exeter[31] with Edward Benson, the Archbishop of Canterbury, to appoint him to Japan. Lacking a determined prelate for a father, Arthur Lloyd, whose name was also put forward, never stood a chance. In 1883 Bickersteth, sometime Fellow of Pembroke College, Cambridge, and founder of the Cambridge University Mission to Delhi, had been invalided home after six years of missionary work in India. Despite being warned by his doctors not to go back, Edward decided in the summer of 1885 to resume his work in the sub-continent even though it meant almost certain premature death. A worried Exeter informed Archbishop Benson that '... my son argues that civil and military men dare greater risks for their duty's sake, and he ought not to hang back.'[32] Exeter was resigned to the fact that his son wanted to be a missionary but did not want him to return to fever-ridden India.

By chance or by providence, on the same day in July 1885 that Exeter received a letter from Edward announcing his intention to return to India, he learnt from Mrs Poole[33] that Bishop Arthur Poole was dying and had already resigned from Japan. For Exeter this news was almost too good to be true, and he wrote immediately to the Archbishop that:

Now I confess the thought flashed upon me, can it be

possible that God will call Edward to labour in that temperate climate. . . . I think he possesses very many of the qualifications you might seek in a successor to Bishop Poole, theological learning (for he was first in the Theological Tripos and has been an eminent student ever since), missionary experience, sympathy both with the S. P. G. and with the C. M. S., and I know I may add an ardent love for souls.[34]

Edward's theological views were seen to be more in sympathy with those of the High Anglican SPG than the Low Church Church Missionary Society (CMS) for his work in India had been associated with former society. However, Edward made it clear that he had always '. . . maintained in India that the CMS method of giving the native congregations an early opportunity of acquiring partial independence and of progressively withdrawing foreign aid was the right one, and have worked to move in that direction at Delhi', . . . and he saw no difficulty with working with CMS missionaries in Japan if they were the same type as the CMS men that he had known in India.[35] India and the CMS approach there had also made him a believer in the idea that '. . . that churches like children would never learn to walk alone, unless they were allowed to try!'[36] Indeed, this was a policy that he would quickly adopt in Japan.

His future policies were not a concern for the SPG. Henry W. Tucker, the Secretary of the SPG, who was mainly worried about the impact of language study on Bickersteth's health, had '. . . implored him to take warning from the many men, who have broken down through too close a study of the language in a climate that is very exciting to brain and nerves'.[37] Bickersteth, of course, had no Japanese and, perhaps taking Tucker's warning to heart, never did acquire much facility in it. However, he came to Japan with a recognized talent for picking up Asian languages rapidly. In 1883 Exeter had boasted Edward '. . . has considerable power in acquiring languages having been able to preach in Urdu the Easter of his arrival [in India] i. e. in less than six months, and since then he has gained some insight into Arabic and Persian'.[38] Among those in Japan, Lloyd was also noted for his linguistic ability and that his '. . . great knowledge of languages has enabled him to known the leading thinkers and teachers in Japan. Buddhist priests, university professors, doctors, officers and lawyers are among his pupils.'[39] Lack of Japanese language, however, did not prove a barrier either to Bickersteth's appointment or to his ability to be a successful Bishop. The attraction of Bickersteth, Shaw and Lloyd to young Japanese was not their fluency in Japanese language but rather they were *gakusha* with an impressive breadth of knowledge that was not limited to things Christian. Their very Britishness was also part of their appeal.

At the end of October 1885, on the eve of departing for India (for he was tired of waiting to hear about Japan), Bickersteth received a letter from the Archbishop asking him to be Bishop for Japan, an offer which he accepted with alacrity.[40]

BICKERSTETH AND THE NIPPON SEIKOKAI

In June 1886, soon after his arrival in Tokyo, Bickersteth wrote to Archbishop Benson that '... I have come to Japan at a very critical period in the history of its Christianity. A widespread desire for union has recently sprung up among the various Christian bodies in this country.'[41] He pointed to the recent union of all the American and the one Scottish Presbyterian missions into a single Japanese Presbyterian Church. In the light of this development, Bickersteth, after talking to and winning the support of Bishop Williams of the American Church Mission, felt that it was expedient to unite the Anglican work of the two British and one American missionary societies into a single Japanese Anglican Church. Bickersteth had detected among Japanese Anglicans a feeling of depression and a want of energy in evangelistic work, as well as a serious waste of resources owing to the lack of cooperation between the three Anglican missions. Further, he thought that '... the great majority of the more educated Japanese, who became Christians, knowing little or nothing of the special claims and privileges of the Anglican Communion, naturally attach themselves to bodies which are regularly organized and offer then a share in counsel and administration'.[42] In order to counter this, Bickersteth and Bishop Williams agreed to call a conference of delegates in July 1886 to discuss the matter of a new Church organization. At this conference, it was decided to hold a Church Synod in Osaka in February 1887 to formalize a Constitution and Canons for an independent Japanese Anglican Church.

In September 1886 Bickersteth stressed to Archbishop Benson that the strong Japanese desire for independence and self-government '... comes out very remarkably in the rapid advance, which the nation as a whole is making toward a constitutional form of civil government, and the widely expressed resentment at any interference of foreigners in the civil domain,' and he added that '... there is a corresponding demand for ecclesiastical independence and self-government among the Japanese Christians'.[43] Yet, it was not simply that the Anglicans should follow the Presbyterians in the formation of a Japanese Church independent of foreign control. Bickersteth saw another reason to hurry to form an independent Church for he believed that '... efforts will be needed before very long in Japan to establish a Body which will unite the various Christian denominations', and when that happened unless a Japanese Anglican Church already existed, '... the acknowledged and essential principles of our Communion would have no chance of obtaining any general acceptance'.[44] As it turned out Bickersteth proved to be a little too prescient. It was not until 1941, and only then under government pressure, that a union of all Protestant denominations was effected with the creation of the Nippon Kirisutokyodan. When, at his instigation, the Synod meeting in Osaka placed on record 'the desire for the establishment in Japan of a Christian Church which by imposing no non-essential conditions of communion, shall include as many as possible of the Christians in this country', it met with little support from other missions in Japan.[45]

While other denominations in Japan rejected union with the Anglicans, Bickersteth's efforts to form a Japanese Anglican Church also did not initially meet with universal support in England. In December 1886 Canon B. F. Westcott (who had greatly influenced Edward Bickersteth's own Christian beliefs) wrote to Archbishop Benson that '... I find it most difficult to realise the circumstances which have made this hasty action wise or necessary. It is not obvious that the union of the congregations requires such a scheme, and there is no evidence that the desire for independence, so far as it is wise, has been satisfied in the first mention of it', and he added that '... I don't think that the impatient desire for independence is wholly healthy'.[46] The CMS headquarters in London was also concerned that the proposal for a Japanese Church was being pushed ahead too quickly. The CMS correctly pointed out that because there were so few Japanese clergymen connected with the three Anglican missions any Church proposed for the Japanese '... would be distinctly foreign in its origin and character'.[47] However, Bickersteth was not deterred.

Any concerns that the CMS might have had over the formation of a Japanese Church disintegrated with the Synod in Osaka in February 1887. A. B. Hutchinson, a CMS missionary delegate from Kyūshū, wrote that the meeting '... seems to me to mark an epoch in the history of the reformation. For it is the endeavour to set up an independent Church in a heathen land not merely a branch of the Anglican Communion in a Christian Country. It seems a successful attempt to combine episcopal Churchmen of all shades of Thought, in an organization securing to all their freedom'.[48] For his part, Bickersteth was careful to point out in the framing of the constitution and canons of the new Church that he had in no way compromised any British Anglican beliefs. Although the American Church authorities wanted the 39 Articles omitted from the Constitution, he had won a compromise that '... a resolution, to be recorded between the Constitution and Canons, declaring that the Japanese Church adopts for the present the Prayer Book and Articles of the Anglican Communion'.[49] Importantly, he pointed that he believed that such were the difficulties of changing the resolution that it would not be done until after the Japanese Church was able to exist without foreign aid. Further, he added that the Japanese delegates had agreed '. . . to remain in the position which they at present occupy in relation to the Anglican Communion, and at the same time have found for themselves in conjunction with the Foreign Bishops and clergy a Synod for counsel and action in matters of common and practical interest'.[50] He feel that this would '. . . keep them as nothing else could have done from irregular action and a premature desire for complete independence in the coming period of their Church's history'.[51]

Yet the fear that the Japanese Anglicans might take independent action was obviously there. Later in 1887 Bickersteth suggested that an ecclesiastical Province of China and Japan be formed by joining the dioceses of Victoria, Mid China, North China and Japan together. He thought when Japanese bishops were consecrated (and Bickersteth saw this happening soon) that it was '. . . undesirable such native Bishops should be able to act wholly independently of the Anglican episcopate,' and '. . . a provincial organization should be in existence in which they would naturally find a place, and the members of which would have agreed not to take individual action without common counsel'.[52] However, Archbishop Benson was not about to create an ecclesiastical Province of China and Japan, but he did agree to the formation of the Nippon Seikokai (as the new Church was named after lengthy debate). Despite his early reservations about the speed at which Bickersteth was bringing about change, Benson was won over as was Canon Westcott.[53]

Bickersteth modestly took no credit for the creation of the new Church stating that '. . . I neither originated the idea nor has it been worked out entirely on lines which I should independently have chosen, but as in itself good and suitable to the very exceptional circumstances of Japanese Christianity, and approved by Bishop Williams and the whole body of missionaries'.[54] Yet it would seem highly unlikely that the Nippon Seikokai would have been created at that time and in the form it was without his determination and energy. Bickersteth had realized from the start '. . . the impossibility of acting in an independent country like Japan, which has never known a Master and all whose people are zealous asserters of independence, exactly as would be suitable in India, where there is British rule and an Establishment, and whose people have not for nearly a thousand years been without an "overlord"'.[55] Bickersteth was impressed by Japanese Christians. Writing to the Archbishop of Canterbury, he noted rather patronizingly that they '. . . are as a rule independent of foreign help in getting a livelihood, educated, and many of them, as our Conference proved, thoroughly able to debate a question, with a keen appreciation of the points at issue. On the other hand they are ready to accept sympathetic guidance and teaching'.[56] To Bickersteth perhaps the last point was the really important one. Nevertheless, he made it clear that the different circumstances in Japan required a different response from missionaries from that suitable in India or elsewhere under British colonial rule.

STRENGTHENING THE CENTRE

If Japanese Christians were different, Bickersteth still felt that a University Mission on the same lines as the Cambridge Mission to Delhi would be effective in Tokyo. In particular, his desire to combat the anti-Christian feeling at Tokyo Imperial University was one of the reason for establishing such a Mission. In 1887 Bickersteth founded the Missions of St Andrew and St Hilda, and the Guild of St Paul was established in England, in order to help support them.[57] St Andrew's was '. . . designed for graduates of universities and St Hilda's for ladies of culture as well as of devotional life and zeal'.[58] The object of these two Missions was to reach the educated classes of Tokyo and to form a convenient centre for general mission work. St Andrew's Mission Brotherhood served to train deacons and priests. It also sought to reach students and office workers through English language classes and lectures held in its night school. Further, the Mission tried to strengthen the Anglican congregations in Tokyo through pastoral work.

From the start, however, there was difficulty recruiting clerical members for St Andrew's. It might well be a reflection of the decline of Bickersteth's own influence in clerical circles at Cambridge that all those who did joined St Andrew's beginning with Lionel Cholmondeley, Bickersteth's chaplain, in 1887 were graduates of Oxford or Toronto Universities until the arrival of Basil Woodd of Trinity College, Cambridge in 1896.[59] Although the members of St Andrew's Mission Brotherhood did not take a vow of celibacy, initially the members lived communally at the Mission House in Shiba, and it was a surprise and disappointment to them when Bickersteth in 1893 during a visit to England married Marion Forsyth, the daughter of a London barrister.[60] Despite Bickersteth's departure into married quarters, St Andrew's Mission continued to form the centre for SPG work in Tokyo.

Its sister institution, St Hilda's, also came to play an equally important role in the development of SPG educational work for women, social work and parish visiting. In regards to work among

Japanese women, Bickersteth in 1888 expressed concern that '... as yet our Church has scarcely touched the ladies of the Japanese higher classes', and was very pleased with '... the number of highly trained and talented English ladies' who had offered to work in Japan.[61] Unfortunately, because of financial considerations, it was only possible to accept a few of those who put their names forward. This was perhaps doubly unfortunate for the female missionaries of St Hilda's such as Susan Ballard, the sister of the well-known Admiral, leave the impression that they worked much harder and were more evangelistically inclined than their male counterparts at St Andrew's. St Hilda's had none of the difficulties that St Andrew's had in finding suitable candidates.

Bickersteth's Cambridge connections obviously helped in engendering support for a Canadian Anglican mission in Japan. The first steps towards Canadian Church participation in missionary work in Japan occurred in 1888 when J. Cooper Robinson, sponsored by students at Wycliffe College, Toronto, came out. Bickersteth's personal ties were with Trinity University within the University of Toronto where his friend from Cambridge days, C. W. E. Body, was Provost.[62] It was a great help also that Shaw was a graduate of Trinity and that Lloyd taught there between 1890 and 1893. In 1890 J. G. Waller, a Trinity graduate, arrived in Japan to begin work with official Canadian Church support. Bickersteth himself visited Canada in the autumn of 1888 on his way back to Japan from attending the Third Lambeth Conference in England. In September 1891 he visited again, and in 1893 he honeymooned at Niagara. So eager was Bickersteth for Canadian help that in 1894 he held out the possibility of a Canadian Bishopric if the Canadian Church expanded its mission work in Japan.[63] Bickersteth's last visit to Canada was on what turned out to be his final journey from Japan in late 1896 on his way back to England.

Much of Bickersteth's time was spent travelling back and forth to England which he did five and a half times between 1888 and 1897 via Canada, the United States or India (in 1892). He also had to travel great deal within Japan. In late November 1892, after visiting the Ryūkyū Islands, Bickersteth complained that '... my most northern station is over 2000 miles from the most southern. As things are, my time in Tokyo and the greatest cities is much too short and my visits hurried and too infrequent. I have been travelling with slight intervals since last March. With the numerous questions that ought to be thought out and sometimes studied at leisure in Japan, I feel that a bishop should not always be moving from place to place.'[64] Already, in 1889, he had created archdeaconates making Shaw Archdeacon of Tokyo and C. F. Warren Archdeacon of Osaka, but, by 1892, Bickersteth was convinced that there was a need for more British bishops in Japan. This was supported by Shaw and the most senior CMS and SPG missionaries who suggested that two new bishoprics be formed, one for Hokkaido and the Kurile Islands and the other for Kyūshū and the Ryūkyū.[65]

In 1894 Henry Evington, a long time CMS missionary, was named Bishop of Kyūshū, and a second veteran CMS missionary, William Fyson, was appointed Bishop of Hokkaido in 1896. Shaw did not think highly of Fyson as a choice for bishop, and wrote to Archbishop Benson in October 1895 that '. . . Mr Fyson, though an amicable man, and a good Japanese scholar, can in no sense be called a Churchman'.[66] Yet, if the CMS obtained two bishops, the SPG also got one. In 1896 William Awdry, the Bishop of Southampton, was named the Bishop of Osaka. When asked for his opinion of Awdry, the Archbishop of York cattily noted '. . . I have always thought well of Awdry – but is he not a little old? and I should have thought rather *dull* and lacking in energy and enthusiasm for a position such as Bishop of Osaka. . . . Mrs. Awdry is charming'.[67] Beyond the the concerns about Awdry, the Archbishop was also of the opinion that the Church might be overdoing the creation of bishops in Japan. Indeed, by1896 there were four British and two American Bishops associated with the Nippon Seikokai, and the number of Bishops would keep on growing in the future.

Much more important than simply consecrating too many Bishops was a deeper concern. York damningly but still presciently wrote that '. . . I have a considerable distrust of Japanese Christianity. I believe the day may come, and before long when they will be tired of Europeanism and will throw us over and our Christianity at the same time.'[68] That day would come in 1941. However, in 1896, after ten years as Bishop and as the major missionary driving force for change in the Japanese Anglican Church, Bickersteth (now Bishop of South Tokyo as the result of the diocesan division because of the creation of new Bishops) must bear some responsibility for failing to remove that 'considerable distrust of Japanese Christianity'.

Sadly, there was no more time left for him to try to remedy this failure. Bickersteth died in England in the summer of 1897. He had been in a hurry to create a Church in Japan independent of foreign control. In reality, however, the Nippon Seikokai only gave Japanese Anglicans limited independence for it remained very much under the control of foreign missionary Bishops. Further, his concern to ensure the preservation of Anglican traditions and values in Japan led to the creation of a static type of Church organization. Consequently, it was only in 1923 that the first two Japanese Bishops were consecrated, and not until just before the opening of the Pacific War that a Japanese became Presiding Bishop of the Nippon Seikokai.

Bickersteth's desire for an independent Japanese Church was

predicated on a very positive attitude towards the transformation of Japan into a modern state. The affirmative approach towards Japanese society and culture that the Shiba Sect held also helped to sustain this attitude. The open gratitude of Fukuzawa Yukichi and other prominent Japanese to Shaw for early advocacy of Anglo-Japanese treaty revision as well as the overall improvement of Anglo-Japanese relations after 1894 could only further reinforce Bickersteth's optimism about Japan. Yet Bickersteth was naïve to believe that what he considered to be the Westernization of Japan meant also the Japanese would accept Christianity.

The fact remains, however, that Bickersteth and Shaw strove to bring Japanese and Britons together on terms of equality in the religious sphere. In doing so, they helped to lay the foundations of the Nippon Seikokai, a Church which still continues to flourish. This independent Japanese Church stands as a living legacy to the commitment of Bickersteth and Shaw to the development of Anglicanism in Japan and to the generosity of those tens of thousands of Britons, both in Japan and at home, who gave their hard-earned money to support the British Anglican missionary endeavour in Meiji Japan.

11

Henry Dyer at the Imperial College of Engineering Tokyo, and afterwards in Glasgow

OLIVE CHECKLAND

HENRY DYER (1848-1918) was appointed in 1872, at the age of 25, to establish, and to become Principal of, the Imperial College of Engineering[1] in Tokyo. After ten years he returned to Glasgow, where, for the rest of his life, informally, he acted as guide, counsellor and friend to the many Japanese engineers and scientists who came at that time to the West of Scotland for post-graduate experience. For half a century, whether in Tokyo or in Glasgow, Dyer made an important contribution to the success of the nascent engineering profession in Japan.

Henry Dyer was born at Muirmadkin, Bellshill, in Bothwell, Lanarkshire on 16 August 1848.[2] The family moved to Shotts Ironworks in Lanarkshire where Henry was educated at Wilson's Endowed School at Shotts, before being apprenticed to James Aitken and Co., foundrymen, of Cranstonhill, Glasgow. It is not known who made the suggestion that Henry Dyer should apply for university entrance to study engineering. The University of Glasgow (founded 1451), had had, in the name of the Queen, and, in the teeth of opposition from the *Senatus Academicus*, in 1840, a Chair of Engineering imposed upon it, by the London government. By the 1860s, under the guidance of Professor W.J.M. Rankine,[3] engineering was becoming an important subject at Glasgow. It was fortunate that, at that time, Joseph Whitworth, engineer of Manchester, had left money for Engineering Scholarships. Henry Dyer was awarded a Whitworth Scholarship[4] and so had the financial support necessary to attend university. It should be noted that Dyer's scholarship was awarded to him as 'workman' not as 'student'. He was a good student, gaining class prizes and other honours.

In 1872 when Dyer was recruited for service in Japan, his qualifications were CE (Certificate of Engineering, the then qualification for Engineers), MA and BSc.[5] Henry Dyer was an ideal candidate to become principal of the Imperial College of Engineering in Tokyo. As an apprentice engineer he had worked, as a mechanic, with his hands, over several years and he had attended night classes at Anderson's College for workmen. Subsequently, he had studied for years at the University before graduating. In addition, and of significance to his career with the Japanese, he was helpful, conciliatory and cooperative in his dealings with his Japanese employers.

It is believed that Dyer, on his sea voyage to Japan, in 1873, with other colleagues already appointed, discussed the organization of the College in Tokyo. On his arrival he was greeted by Yamao Yōzō,[6] (then Vice Minister of Public Works in the Japanese government) one of the original Chōshū five, who had, (between 1866 and 1868) studied in Glasgow and worked in Napier's Shipyard on the Clyde. On meeting Yamao, Dyer recognised the man who had also attended workmen's evening classes with him, at Anderson's College, in Glasgow.

Between them Dyer and Yamao created the highly successful Imperial College of Engineering[7] in Tokyo, which, before becoming the Faculty of Engineering (in 1886) at the Imperial University of Tokyo, had an independent life of some thirteen years.

The staff at the Imperial College of Engineering 1873–86

1.	Dyer, Henry	Dean, Engineering
2.	Divers, Edward	Dean, Chemistry
3.	Ayrton, W.E.	Physics, Telegraphy
4.	Milne, John	Geology
5.	Marshall, David H.	Physics
6.	Brinkley, Frank	Mathematics
7.	Conder, Josiah	Architecture
8.	Alexander, T.	Civil Engineering
9.	Thomson, A.W.	Civil Engineering
10.	Perry, John	Civil Engineering
11.	West Charles D.	Engineering
12.	Angus, W.M.	Engineering
13.	Cawley, George	Engineering
14.	Dixon, J.M.	English
15.	Dixon, W.G.	English

16.	Craigie, William	English
17.	Brindley, G.S.	Superintendent of Engineering Workshop, Akabane
18.	Gray, Thomas	Telegraphy
19.	Mondy, Edmond F.	Drawing
20.	Barr, W.	Drawing
21.	Clark, Robert	Drawing
22.	King, Archibald	Model-making
23.	Jones, R.D. Rymer	Surveying, Preliminary Course
24.	Hamilton, G.	Preliminary Course
25.	Sandeman, F.	Preliminary Course
26.	George,	Preliminary Course
27.	Luckden, ?	Preliminary Course
28.	Macrae,	Preliminary Course

Source: Tokyo University (ed.) Historical Materials On the Imperial College of Engineering, 1871-1886 (Tokyo: Tokyo University Press 1931), pp.353 and 354; H.J. Jones, 'The Meiji Government and Foreign Employees, 1868-1900' (PhD, Michigan, 1967) and Live Machines, Hired Foreigners and Meiji Japan (Tenterden: Paul Norbury Publications, 1980).

Most of the staff listed here remained in Japan for a few years, others preferred to stay on. None of the staff named were in service from 1873-1886.

Henry Dyer himself was married in Yokohama in the spring of 1874. His fiancée, Marie Ferguson, arrived in Yokohama on 19 May 1874 and the marriage took place, at the British legation on 23 May 1874, according to the rites of the Church of England. Harry Smith Parkes, the British minister, was present and signed the certificate. The witnesses were David Marshall (from the College), William Walter Cargill, Edwin Wheeler and one other.[8]

On their departure from Japan, Mr and Mrs Henry Dyer 'and four children and servant in cabin' left Japan on the British steamer Arabic on 14 July 1882 for San Francisco.[9]

THE IMPERIAL COLLEGE OF ENGINEERING

Students at the Imperial College of Engineering were to undertake a six year course.

Years 1 and 2 The first- and second-year courses which all students attended included, English (language and composition), geography, elementary mathematics, elementary mechanics (theoretical and applied), elementary physics, chemistry, and drawing (geometrical and mechanical).

Years 3 and 4   At the beginning of the third year each student chose to specialise in one of six options – civil engineering; mechanical engineering; telegraph engineering; architecture; chemistry and metallurgy, and mining engineering.

Years 5 and 6   The final two years were to be devoted entirely to practical work, although special lectures as well as examinations were also organised in the College.

YEARS 1 AND 2

It would be surprising if there were no difficulties in teaching these pioneering engineering students. At this time all the teaching was done in English and inevitably some students must have been ill-equipped to speak and understand English. No doubt the quality of the teaching was good, the English professors were all capable men. But in the last quarter of the nineteenth century it was, by modern standards, unimaginative and uninspired. Natsume Sōseki made a sharp comment on J.M. Dixon's teaching 'I was often reproved by Professor Dixon for my wrong pronunciation in reading English composition. He asked such examination questions as "How many kinds of Shakespeare folios are there?" and "Mention the works of Scott in chronological order". Such questions are of no use in the study of English literature.'[10]

It seems likely that the first two years tuition gave the staff ample opportunity to learn the strengths and weaknesses of their students. Japanese students had previously been trained to learn everything by rote, which was not a good precedent for those planning to be engineers. The future of modern learning, at ICE, required students who could use their knowledge of a subject, or a project, to work out how best to proceed.

The staff had nothing but praise for the 'respectful demeanour' and 'earnest attention' of the students. Indeed the students were believed to be consistently overworking. Professor Ayrton, who taught natural philosophy at the College from its opening until 1878, was also enthusiastic, commenting that his Japanese students were 'much quieter in their manner, more earnest in their studies and have greater application 'than those of the West'. But he also sounded a note of caution, observing that 'the Japanese boy labours under the disadvantage that he is not observant ... all his knowledge is formal knowledge as learnt in class, and he is comparatively ignorant of any information that he has not acquired from set lessons'.[11] Ayrton's sensitivity to the responses of his Japanese students is a reminder of the enormous leap which his students were required to make, living as they did in a pre-industrial Japan without any acquaintance with those machines which were part of everyday life in the West. The compromises between the old and the new which these men were required to make imposed their own strains.

It is clear that there were other difficulties, even among so eager a group of pioneering students. Practical engineering work in the West required that engineering managers, which these students were to be, should themselves learn how to do the manual tasks normally done by craftsmen. The engineers had to be ready to get their hands dirty. Those reared in the samurai tradition found it difficult to accept the need to learn through doing what were to them menial tasks. This introduction of heuristic education, that is being able oneself to undertake menial tasks, cut across some traditions of old Japan.

It is difficult to judge the standards of work which were achieved by the Japanese students. The best were able to respond to the demands made on them by teachers like William Ayrton and John Perry. A proportion of the graduates from ICE subsequently received government grants to study further in the West. The best of these won prizes in Western universities where they were in direct competition with Western students.

Certainly the young professors teaching the Japanese were highly competent and enthusiastic. In almost all cases they later had distinguished careers at home.

YEARS 3 AND 4

It could be said that the critical decision for each student came at the beginning of the third year. These years, 3 and 4 of the course, were the core of the teaching at ICE. It was hoped that the two years spent mastering the chosen subject would bring the Japanese students to a satisfactory level of competence. Inevitably the students were taught in Western idioms.

It is not known whether the students were allowed to choose their specialism independently. Those choosing Civil Engineering could expect to work on roads or perhaps railways, factories needed mechanical engineers, and the new telegraph systems operating in Japan and elsewhere, required telegraph engineers. Modern mining engineers were essential in a country where mines were still simple pits dug out of the ground. Modern industry, chemical and textiles in particular, required trained chemists and metallurgists were essential if the mining industry was to be modernized.

YEARS 5 AND 6

Given the non-industrialized state of Japan in the 1870s and 1880s the College had no option but to train its engineers on its own premises. Usually, in the West, such students would have sought practical experience in factory or workshop. This option was not available in Japan at this time.

The laboratory provision originally could, apparently, accommodate between forty and fifty students. Professor Divers so organized the work that the chemistry laboratories were shared between third-year students of mining and telegraphy and fourth-year students of applied chemistry and metallurgy. As Professor Divers reported '... all necessary apparatus and chemicals being supplied by the College to the students, free of cost, with each student having the exclusive use of a complete set of them'.[12] In addition the General Drawing Office and the Architectural Drawing Office were available for trainee engineers and architects.

But it was William Ayrton's laboratories for the teaching of Natural Philosophy which aroused the most surprise and admiration. As John Perry explained:

> When I arrived in Japan in 1875, I found a marvellous laboratory, such as the world had not seen elsewhere. At Glasgow, at Cambridge, and at Berlin, there were three great personalities; the laboratories of Kelvin, and of Maxwell, and of Helmholtz, however were not to be mentioned in comparison with Ayrton. Fine buildings, splendid apparatus, well-chosen, a never-resting-keen-eyed chief of great originality: these are what I found in Japan.[13]

Laboratories were of great value but engineers needed more. Because there were in Japan no modern factories, workshops or shipyards yet further provision was made.

The Akabane Engineering Works were set up as the workshop provision for the Imperial College of Engineering. It can be said with confidence that Henry Dyer was fortunate in running the Imperial College of Engineering under the Ministry of Public Works in Tokyo in the 1870s. The engineering workshops were to play an increasing role in the establishment of engineering industries in Japan. But in the early years as an adjunct of the College they had several important functions. They enabled the College students to have practical workshop training, and they also employed a large number of workmen and apprentices, who were to become the nucleus of a new generation of technician engineers in Japan. Once the workshops were fully operational it would appear that between 320 (in 1876) and 370 (1884) 'workmen and apprentices' were being trained.[14]

For Dyer at Akabane these were the golden years. In 1881 an illustrated catalogue was produced under the title of *Akabane Engineering Works*.[15] It featured a large number of engines, including steam engines, marine engines, locomotive boilers, pumps of various kinds, fire engines, cranes, sugar-cane-crushing mills and many mechanical engineering tools, as well as ironwork and ornamental railings and gates.

The catalogue contains descriptions of each machine in Japanese and English together with a scale drawing of the machine. The book is similar to many such produced by manufacturing engineers and their agents in the Western world to illustrate what was available. The catalogue, perhaps prepared by Brindley, the workshop superintendent, on Dyer's instructions, was a demonstration of the range of machinery which could be used. It is not suggested that all these machines could be made at the Akabane Works although in the case of a number of items the claim was made.

Clara Whitney, an American girl in Meiji Japan gave an insight into the arrangements in the College when she wrote:

> Then we went to look at the College, going through classrooms arranged like a theater, – the seats being graded from those at the lowest to those almost touching the ceiling, while the teacher's desk was below. We visited the Chemist's department and the drafting room, where a lot of boys were at work on architectural plans.[16]

The Imperial College of Engineering did a remarkable job in training this first cohort of modern engineers in Japan. The enthusiasm of the students and the dedication of the young professors did produce men who excelled as pioneers. The Japanese government enabled the best of these Japanese engineers to study abroad. 'Study' usually meant practical training in factory, office or shipyard as well as classroom learning.

Who were these students for whom such lavish provision was made? This first generation of Japanese engineers were young men whose fathers had decided to educate their sons for the future rather than the past. Most of them came from South and West Japan, that is from areas and clans associated with the rebellion against the old regime.

Two examples of students at ICE will be given.

Watanabe Kaichi (1858-1932) graduated from ICE in 1883 before proceeding to Scotland in 1884 for further study at the University of Glasgow. He later worked for the civil engineering firm, Benjamin Baker,[17] then designers for the proposed Forth Railway Bridge (completed 1890). Watanabe features as the central figure in the well-known picture demonstrating the cantilever principle used in making the Forth Bridge. On his return to Japan he was appointed chief engineer of Japan Public Works Company (*Nippon Doboku Kaisha*). Watanabe was later director of Sangu and Narita railway companies and Tokyo and Kyoto Electric railway companies.

Another promising physicist was **Shida Rinzaburō** (1855-92), a first-class graduate from the Imperial College of Engineering in 1879, who had worked with J.W.Ayrton at the laboratories in Tokyo, specializing in telegraph engineering. Shida was based in Glasgow in the early 1880s working under Kelvin[18] on electromagnetism and telegraphy. He travelled widely, carrying introductions from Kelvin to German scholars. On his return to Japan in 1883 he became Professor of Natural Philosophy at ICE, a post which had remained vacant since 1879 when Ayrton had returned to London. Shida was also much involved with the technical development of telegraphy in Japan. He died in 1892 at the age of 37. The loss of young men like Shida, after heavy investment in his education to an advanced level, from diseases such as tuberculosis, was not uncommon in Japan at this time.

THE HEARTACHE OF RE-SETTLEMENT

At the age of 35, Henry Dyer left Japan in the summer of 1882, never to return. The Japanese government was generous in its praise of Dyer's achievement. He was awarded the Order of the Rising Sun, third class, and the title Honorary Principal of the Imperial College of Engineering, Tokyo. He re-settled himself in Glasgow, where he remained for the rest of his life.

Unlike most of the other young British professors at the Imperial College of Engineering in Tokyo, Dyer did not succeed in returning to full-time paid employment in academic life. Twice, in 1883 and 1886, he applied for the newly established Chair of Naval Architecture in the University of Glasgow. His applications were not successful.[19] It seemed unfortunate that he should attempt to become professor of naval architecture when, for ten years, he had been in charge of a general college of engineering in Tokyo. The design of ships and their engines was changing rapidly. Dyer's ambition of being professor of naval architecture seems to have been ill-judged. Dyer also applied for the post of principal of the newly re-organized Heriot Watt College in Edinburgh. This would have suited his talents. He lost this opportunity by the casting vote of the Lord Provost of Edinburgh.[20] There seems no doubt that Dyer urgently needed the support of a patron, some senior figure like McQuorn Rankine who had died in 1872, who would have advised him and recommended him.

The price which Dyer paid for being the Principal of the Imperial College of Engineering for ten years in Tokyo, was high. Nevertheless he was never idle. He gave great service to the old Anderson's College[21] and helped transform it into the Royal College of Science and Technology (now the University of Strathclyde) in Glasgow. From

1887 to his death in 1918, dyer was a life governor of the College. Henry Dyer has recently been honoured by the unveiling at the University of Tokyo and the University of Strathclyde, of two newly sculpted heads by Kate Thomson. The celebration of Henry Dyer at the University of Strathclyde took place on 16 November 1998. Dyer became a much-respected educationalist who responded to many calls on his time and who was a member (latterly Chairman) of the Glasgow Education Board. Throughout the 35 years of his 'retirement' in Glasgow, Dyer supported the Japanese students who were studying in the city.

★   ★   ★

Henry Dyer also had an important late career as an author. His first writing[22] was a necessary part of his position as Principal of the Imperial College of Engineering, when he prepared *The General Report by the Principal* (Tokyo: Imperial College of Engineering, 1877). This was followed by *The Education of Engineers* (Tokei: Imperial College of Engineering, 1879) and, after he returned to Glasgow, a number of other pamphlets relating to the education of engineers. He also wrote papers on marine engines (reflecting his interest in naval architecture), the teaching of science, and on the need for a Faculty of Engineering in a University.

In 1895 with the publication of *The Evolution of Industry* (London and New York: Macmillan), Dyer moved into a different league. This was followed by *Dai Nippon, the Britain of the East* (London, Glasgow, Dublin and Bombay: Blackie & Son Ltd., 1905) and in 1909 *Japan in World Politics* (London, Glasgow, Dublin and Bombay: Blackie & Son Ltd.).

In *The Evolution of Industry*, Dyer takes a rather radical approach extolling a kind of socialism. As he concluded: 'The Society of the not very distant future will have an admixture of individualism, trade unionism, cooperation, and municipal and State socialism.' He seemed to be advocating a 'socialized individualism' which will, in course of time, 'bring about the ideals of thoughtful Socialists'.[23] But he was harsh in his judgement of 'idlers and parasites who fatten on the degradation of their fellow creatures'.

Dyer, among other themes, considered the position of women (Chapter 6, pp.110-123). He wrote sensibly about women working, in factories and so on, but like others, he reflected the values of the age in which he lived. As he concluded (p.123) '... the womanly woman is a good mother, a devoted wife, a gentle sister and a quiet guardian of the family hearth and thus has a most profound influence in moulding human destiny'.[24]

In his next book *Dai Nippon*, (Great Japan) *the Britain of the East* (1905), Dyer wrote admiringly of the extraordinary progress which Japan had made since 1868. As *Dai Nippon* was published after the Russo-Japanese War ended it is not perhaps surprising that Dyer should be so pro-Japanese. In fact Dyer and his colleagues could claim some credit for Japan's achievements through their pioneering work in Japan in the early Meiji years.

Henry Dyer's final book *Japan in World Politics*, published in 1909, is a study of Japan in relation to the rest of the world. There is no doubt that Dyer had read widely and that he understood a good deal of the arms race then afflicting the Western world, in the years approaching the First World War. But his view of Japan in East Asia, was for example, rather one-sided. In discussing Formosa, (Taiwan) which became part of the Japanese empire in 1895 after the defeat of China in the Sino-Japanese War of 1894-95, Dyer acknowledges that Japanese rule is firm, but that the 'Savage aborigines' and some of the Chinese, were unwilling to accept Japanese rule. In the case of Korea, Dyer puts his trust in Prince Itō, although he does recognize that many condemned Japan's repressive government in Korea.

THE JAPANESE IN GLASGOW

Glasgow remained a Mecca for Japanese engineers, scientists and shipbuilders at least until 1914 and the outbreak of the First World War. At Dyer's spacious home, at 8 Highburgh Terrace, in the west end of Glasgow, within a few minutes of the University on Gilmorehill, there was always a welcome for the Japanese. In addition, from 1890 (to 1941) there was an honorary Japanese consul in Glasgow. The first consul, A.R.Brown, was, until his death in 1913, equally hospitable to the Japanese.

Glasgow was favoured by the Japanese for a number of reasons. William John McQuorn Rankine, who held the Chair of Engineering from 1855 to his death at the end of 1872 was a distinguished engineer who worked closely with the Clyde shipbuilders, notably John Elder. McQuorn Rankine's successor in the Regius Chair of Engineering, from 1873-89, was James Thomson, Lord Kelvin's brother.

And, most important of all, in 1883, following a petition by the shipbuilders on the Clyde, Isabella Elder endowed the John Elder Chair of Naval Architecture, the first such in the world. The availability of this speciality in the University of Glasgow confirmed for the Japanese Glasgow's supremacy at that time. In addition internationally known William Thomson, Baron Kelvin of Largs, occupied the Chair of Natural Philosophy from 1844-99. The availability of Kelvin, and his kindness to Japanese students, was well-known in Japan.

There can be no doubt of Dyer's usefulness to the Japanese. In 1901 he approached the University Court on behalf of Japanese students requesting that the University make Japanese a language acceptable for those wishing to matriculate into the University. The University agreed and thereafter papers in Japanese were taken by those Japanese who wished to make use of this provision. During his stay in London, in the early 1900s, Natsume Soseki was the examiner. He was paid four guineas for his services.[25]

It seems certain that Hugh Matheson, of the great eastern trading house, Jardine Matheson, in London, first alerted Itō Hirubumi,[26] in the 1860s, to the rich opportunities for engineering education available in Glasgow. As a young man, Matheson, a Scot, had been a private student at Glasgow College. He was also a relation of Lewis Gordon, the first professor of Engineering at Glasgow.

The agreement in late 1872, or early 1873 that Henry Dyer should leave Glasgow for Tokyo to head the new engineering college there was the defining moment in making Dyer the link between the nascent engineering profession in Tokyo with that of Glasgow. For more than forty years there were always Japanese engineers in Glasgow. Dyer himself, until his death in 1918 was an essential part of the support network for Japanese engineers in Glasgow and the West of Scotland.

Dyer's rise from humble beginnings was also remarkable, for he was the son of an Irish labourer, who left his native County Cork in Ireland to better himself in West Scotland. John Dyer met and married Margaret Morton. Henry Dyer's scholarly progress was encouraged at Wilson's Endowed School, Shotts and later his university career was made possible by a Whitworth scholarship. In later life Dyer became a highly respected figure in Glasgow society. And in Tokyo, in engineering circles, the name and achievements of Henry Dyer are nor forgotten.

12

Aoki Shūzō (1844–1914)

IAN NISH

WHEN COMMODORE PERRY visited Japan, Aoki Shūzō (1844–1914) was nine years of age. He was born in Hagi in the western part of Honshu island and went in his teens to the Chōshū clan academy, Meirinkan, and then to medical school, Kōseidō. As was the common practice at the time, he was adopted by a prominent family, in this case that of the famous president of the school, Aoki Kenzō. Taking the name of Shūzō, he moved to Nagasaki in 1867 to complete his studies in medicine and was instructed to go to Prussia for three years for further study at the expense of the Chōshū clan. He reached Marseilles in December 1868 and proceeded to Berlin. Aoki soon found himself in a country at war and became 'intoxicated' (as he said) with the Franco-Prussian War and the contrast between the performances of the Prussian and French armies.[1]

Because of Aoki's first-hand observation of the conflict, his career pattern changed. He began to study politics and his status changed to that of a *ryugakusei* (student abroad) for the central government of the New Japan in the New Germany. In 1873 he became a first secretary in the Gaimusho (Foreign Ministry), and entered the central government bureaucracy for the first time. In August of the following year he was appointed minister to Germany at the absurdly early age of 30 and was to spend much of the first half of his working career there.

While still a student acquiring the German language and the know-how about the most progressive nation on the continent of Europe at that time, he was much in demand from the Iwakura Mission which visited Europe in 1872–3. One of the influential members of that star-studded mission was Aoki's clansman, Kido Takayoshi (Kōin). In August 1872 Aoki visited the commissioners soon after they reached

London and briefed Kido about what the mission might expect on the continent. He obviously had an insatiable curiosity and his enthusiasm clearly impressed Kido. When they reached Berlin in March, Aoki's help was indispensable both because of his fluency in German and his sheer knowledge of the country.[2] Moreover the group of those studying in Germany had already acquired a circle of foreign friends who admired 'the fast progress that the 70 or so Japanese studying in Berlin had made'. They praised their high motivation and their good examination results. As a reward for Aoki's enthusiasm he was allowed to accompany the mission on its travels to Russia in April. Presumably his ability as an interpreter in German was deemed to be useful on the long rail journey to St Petersburg.[3]

After a spell of leave he returned to Germany as minister in the autumn of 1874. He had from time to time additional responsibilities as minister to Austria, Holland, Denmark and Norway. In 1877 he married Baroness Elizabeth von Rade and this was useful for his diplomatic activities in Germany where court diplomacy was important. Two years later his daughter Hanako (Hanna, sometimes Hanni) was born. From this point Aoki's life-style became increasingly Europeanized; and it was said that the language which was most frequently heard in his household was German. This makes it strange for him to be included in this book. But, if Aoki was a Germanophile, there is a strong current running through his diplomatic career of concern with Britain. This was only to be expected in the light of Britain's dominance in world affairs and the large number of British nationals who lived and traded in the treaty ports of Japan.[4]

It was a sign of Aoki's standing that during a period of leave he had a memorable talk in Inoue's residence with Sir Harry Parkes, shortly before he left Tokyo. In 1880 he returned for another five-year stint in Berlin. At the end of his life he wrote an incomplete memoir of part of his career which was not published during his lifetime. In it he tells of a memorandum he wrote, arising out of discussions with the redoubtable Lord Ampthill, who as Odo Russell served as the British ambassador in Berlin from 1871 till his death in 1884. Aoki ruminated that Japan, if she were to grow as a nation, needed an alliance with either Britain or Germany. France, he wrote, was not in the running after she had been defeated in the Franco-Prussian War and while she was engaged in war with China, though she had made approaches to Japan with that in mind. He gives an account of conversations he had with Bismarck, the German chancellor, on this point. He was conscious that Japan could become a most useful ally to a European power in the east. Above all, he wanted Japan to attain equality with the powers. His long-term objective was to align his country with Britain and Germany and prevent Russia's southern expansion.[5]

Since this was a time of alliances centring on Bismarck and the New Germany, it was not unnatural that Aoki should address the problem of how Japan should fit into the European alliance system. It was to remain a great political concern for him right down to the turn of the century. It is of course very relevant to the later Anglo-Japanese Alliance that experienced Japanese diplomats like him were already in the 1880s acknowledging the need for Japan to have an ally or allies. It may seem odd that a person who was so Germanophile should consider the merits of a British alignment so seriously at this time. But that, I believe, was a mark of the Realpolitik with which Aoki had become imbued during his stay in Germany.

On his return to Japan in 1885, Aoki assisted in the ministry. It was at this time that he penned the above memorandum and spoke along these lines to Inoue Kaoru as foreign minister. He was appointed vice-minister in March 1887. His main task was to assist in pushing ahead with plans for treaty revision. But Inoue resigned in July. Aoki, however, continued to serve under his successor and concerned himself with the treaties.

FOREIGN MINISTER

On 24 December 1889 Aoki was promoted to foreign minister in the first cabinet presided over by Yamagata Aritomo. This appointment was due to his clan connections. There were various factions associated with the Chōshū clan and Aoki belonged to the Yamagata branch whose moment had now arrived. This was in itself a notable development because Aoki was the first foreign minister who came from the corps of diplomats rather than what could loosely be called 'politicians'. It was to set a trend that was to be followed in cabinets down to 1945 with remarkably few exceptions, namely that the foreign minister would come from a background of diplomatic service.

It was the renegotiation of the treaties of early Meiji that had the highest priority in Japan's diplomacy at the time. The subject had been discussed from time to time over the previous two decades without any results; but it took on a new urgency with the coming of the new Imperial Diet which was due to open in 1890. In the elections which were held that summer, the new opposition parties latched on to the populist issues and attacked particularly the failure of the previous government to make any headway over treaty revision. The first Diet was convened on 29 November and attacked the government on many issues. The Diet had powers which forced the administration to act cautiously in adopting new approaches in diplomatic negotiations. Constitutionally it became necessary to obtain the approval of a majority of Diet members in order to bring new treaties into force. So it was essential for any government negotiating agreements to remember that they would in due course have to obtain ratification by the Diet.[6]

Aoki hated and feared the Diet. He did not enjoy appearing before it. Yet as a good diplomat he emphasized its xenophobic attitudes over treaty revision to his own advantage. He left the powers with the impression that, if they did not give concessions, the treaties would be denounced as a result of the new strong parliamentary opposition which was spreading to public opinion and that the foreign communities would stand to lose everything.

Aoki decided to concentrate initially on Britain which had a bad reputation for holding up treaty revision in previous decades and abandoned the multi-national approaches which had hitherto been followed. His aim was to recover for Japan judicial and tariff autonomy simultaneously. He approached Britain first because it was she who held the most pronounced views on the need for reforming the judicial system before she would give up extraterritorial rights for her nationals and on the need for assurances over tariffs because she was Japan's largest trading partner.

A few days after taking up office, Aoki passed on his personal plans to Hugh Fraser, the British minister in Tokyo. After he had secured cabinet approval he presented the proposals formally on 28 February 1890. On 15 July after the complex matter had been scrutinized in London, Fraser responded by passing over the draft of a treaty of commerce and navigation and a protocol drawn up in Whitehall.[7]

In the tense political atmosphere of the early Diet period, the Yamagata cabinet adopted on 3 March 1891 a comprehensive government policy on a possible revised Anglo-Japanese treaty. It was passed on to Fraser who rather optimistically expected negotiations with London to proceed smoothly since the British draft of the previous July seemed to have met the Japanese demands halfway; but domestic political turmoil in Japan prevented the matter being settled so quickly. Yamagata resigned on 9 April and, though Aoki continued under his successor, he too resigned on 29 May assuming responsibility as foreign minister for the violent knife attack on the Russian Crown Prince at Otsu during a visit to the Japanese countryside. Whether Aoki need have assumed the responsibility for the notorious Otsu incident is a moot point; but he was a man of conscience and the Foreign Ministry was one part of the administration involved with the tsarevich's reception. Although the incident was small, it was the symbol for a lot of anti-foreignism and violence against foreign nationals which followed the opening of the Diet.[8]

These incidents led the British and Japanese governments to identify a common interest. Both wanted to hold the negotiations away from the penetrating and predominantly hostile gaze of the new Diet members and the urban crowds which supported the political opposition. On 26 May 1892 Minister Fraser took the initiative to suggest 'a resumption of negotiations in London through Viscount Kawase, rather than in Tokyo'.[9] While the Japanese certainly wanted to avoid negotiating in Tokyo, they regarded Kawase who had been minister in London since 1889 as unsuitable to steer through talks of this complexity. They replied that Viscount Aoki who had just been posted to Berlin on 27 January as envoy had more knowledge of the matter than his colleague in London and would be transferred for this purpose. Kawase who had served as the first president of the Japan Society of London following its foundation in 1891, was now recalled and became adviser to the Privy Council (*sumitsu komonkan*).[10]

BRITISH TREATY REVISED

Mutsu Munemitsu, who became foreign minister in August 1892 was ready to build on Aoki's earlier talks with Fraser on this subject. On 15 September 1893, Aoki was instructed to go over to London for talks on treaty revision. Fraser and the other stalwart of the treaty negotiations at the Tokyo end, John Harrington Gubbins, had by prior arrangement returned to Britain on leave.[11] From his initial talks with Aoki, Fraser concluded that Japan was not yet ready to make enough concessions and felt that Britain should not accept the radical terms which she was proposing. Mutsu had therefore to go back to the drawing board and present fresh proposals in November. Aoki visited Britain again in December in order to have further discussions with Fraser before the latter departed again for Japan at the end of the year and convinced him that the revised proposals were a sufficient basis for negotiations. When it looked as though these preliminary parleys would succeed, Aoki was appointed as temporary minister to Britain with plenipotentiary powers to discuss treaty revision on 5 December. He finally presented his credentials on 22 February 1894.[12]

Aoki was active at the London legation from February onwards. The legation was at that time so small that Aoki had to do most of the negotiation himself, ably assisted by the young Uchida Yasuya behind the scenes.[13] By the very nature of the subject Aoki had a considerable discretion; and on a few occasions acted against the wishes of Minister Mutsu and Vice-minister Hayashi Tadasu in Tokyo. On the British side, the main negotiator was Francis Bertie, assisted by Gubbins. The official negotiating sessions began on 2 April and were held in secret at roughly fortnightly intervals through to July. After six months the negotiations were complete. The new Anglo-Japanese Treaty of Commerce and Navigation was signed on 16 July. Extraterritorial jurisdiction by consuls was abolished; Japan beyond the treaty ports was to be opened to British and foreign traders; and new legal codes were to be introduced before the treaty came into force, perhaps in five years' time. Ratifications were exchanged with great expedition on 25 August.[14]

Although Aoki had made a decisive contribution to the revision of the British treaty, the ultimate accolade for achieving the treaty with Britain went to Mutsu Munemitsu.[15] There is some justice in this. Aoki rightly deserves the credit for conducting the tricky negotiations on a highly technical subject in London where things were made difficult by the known opposition of the British merchants in Japanese ports who wanted to preserve the status quo. In recognition of his endeavours, Aoki and his colleagues, Baron von Siebold and Uchida, were awarded Japanese decorations.[16] On the other hand, Mutsu had to face Japanese politicians and the public who were unhappy about many of the aspects of the new treaty which they chose to interpret as 'a Japanese concession'. At both ends it was a most difficult political operation.

Perhaps its acceptance in the Japanese Diet was eased when war broke out between Japan and China at the beginning of August. Since all the European powers had advised Japan against going to war, it suddenly became important for Japanese diplomats to try to win friends for their cause and influence public and press opinion abroad. Aoki with his vast experience of European courts was, like his amanuensis Baron von Siebold, adept at this as the following telegram to Tokyo will indicate:

> Daily Telegraph friendly; Times and other leading papers changing tone on last information being judiciously employed; secured the cooperation of several press and telegraph agencies beside Reuter. English authority Westlake expressed publicly Naniwa was right by international law. ... You should supply me with about £1000 sterling for secret service.

When one considers that £1000 in 1894 is equivalent to £70,000 today (1998), it is apparent that Aoki had mastered some of the gentle arts of persuasion in the London press world.[17]

Aoki was ordered to return to Germany at the end of the month after one year's responsibility in Britain. His appointment as minister plenipotentiary to Britain terminated on 23 November. This was partly because of the war crisis and partly because Germany was next on the list of powers with which treaty negotiations were to be taken up. Mutsu found that the reactions of the European powers to the war were very difficult to interpret and depended greatly on the advice and good judgement of his representatives overseas. The powers which called on Japan for restraint against China during the war tended to be Britain and Russia. Russia was allied with France which was likely to support her ally. Was it likely that Britain or Germany would ever consider intervening on Russia's side?

These speculations came to practical reality after 17 April when China and Japan signed the Treaty of Shimonoseki. Some of the powers because of sympathy for China and their national interest felt that Japan was demanding too much. Mutsu, who had been expecting outside intervention all along, felt confident from his success over the British commercial treaty (1894) and other evidence that Britain would not join Russia and guessed that Russia would not act on her own. What he had not bargained for was the strong support which Germany decided to give to France and Russia in making up the *Dreibund* or Triplice of intervening powers. When asked his views on the likelihood of Germany's intervention, Aoki gave Mutsu a very conceited answer to the following effect: 'So long as I stay here I will never allow Germany to stand against Japan. Please do not worry yourself so much about it.' As it turned out, Germany took a leading part in the intervention. Soon after the German protest was made in Tokyo in very forceful terms by her minister, Freiherr von Gutschmid, Mutsu sent Aoki a telegram saying teasingly : 'What did you mean by your previous message reading. . . . ?'[18]

To be sure, Aoki changed his tune at the very last minute on 13 April and conceded that Germany was inclined to be more interventionist. But his optimistic reports over the previous months appear to have seriously misjudged the situation; Germany's overtures to join Russia and France in intervening had already been underway since mid-March. This illustrates the self-confidence and rashness of Aoki and the hostility underlying his relationship with Mutsu.[19]

Meanwhile, Aoki was busy negotiating the German-Japanese treaty which was based on the British model. It was signed on 4 April 1896. To his consternation Aoki was on 1 September 1897 ordered to return to Japan because he had exceeded his authority on the occasion of the signing the German treaty. On 8 February 1898 he left his posts as minister to Germany and Belgium (where he had also been responsible for concluding a new commercial treaty).

The British and German treaties formed the core of treaties with all the trading powers whose revision was celebrated in Tokyo in the summer of 1899. These were the culmination of a quarter-century of hard work and determination. Aoki's contribution to resolving this, the most important issue of the first half of the Meiji period, was substantial and has to be recognized at three levels: his period at the Foreign Ministry where the ground plan was sketched; his personal negotiations with Britain which were tenacious (from the British perspective); his negotiations elsewhere in Europe.[20]

Nonetheless, Aoki's diplomatic career in Europe ended unhappily. At this exalted stage of his career, Aoki found it very hard to accept directions from Tokyo where he felt that those in charge were his juniors. The telegrams he sent from Berlin to the Foreign Ministry were often couched in a rather superior tone. But Mutsu had as a result of the Japanese victory in the war with China been made a Count. When he received an over-confident telegram from Aoki who had the misfortune to be still only a Viscount, he responded by sending him a telegram saying that Counts did not expect counter-instructions from mere Viscounts.

FOREIGN MINISTER AGAIN

On Aoki's return to Japan, he again benefited from a strange reversal of fortune. On 8 November 1898 he was appointed foreign minister in the second Yamagata cabinet, the same position that he had occupied in the first. It must be assumed that he was again favoured because of his Chōshū connections and the goodwill of Yamagata. He brought to the task a fervent hatred of Russia and a predisposition towards Russia's rivals. Also he became in 1900 head of the *Dai Nippon Butokukai* (Great Japan Martial Arts Association), which may suggest that he was recognized as belonging to the right-wing.[21]

His frequent conversations with Sir Ernest Satow, the British minister in Tokyo, show that he – and Japanese opinion – was watching every move by Russia in Korea, the Liaotung Peninsula in China and the East generally. He appeared anxious to act along with Britain. His notion was that the powers were anxious to take advantage of Britain's entanglement in the South African War and were likely to try to capitalize on the uproar in China connected with the Boxer Rebellion from 1899 onwards.[22]

Britain, embarrassed at the simultaneous outbreak on two fronts, took the lead in asking for Japan's assistance by sending troops to north China to join the international expedition for the relief of the foreign legations in Beijing. Aoki was inclined to be positive. He supported the sending of a Japanese expeditionary force to China on 15 June 1900. But, when Britain asked for the Japanese force to be increased, he faced substantial disagreement in the Japanese cabinet which decided that Japan should first take soundings among the world powers. They responded half-heartedly, on the whole urging Japan evasively not to take independent action.

On 8 July Britain, thinking that Japan's reluctance was caused by financial constraints, took the unprecedented step of offering to defray

Japan's necessary expenses in sending a division of troops to take part in the international force. Aoki was swayed by Britain's appeal but also by his acute suspicion of Russia's actions if Japan alone were to send such a large force. He often judged things in European terms and appears to have thought that Britain's enemies were forming a continental coalition and that these enemies were the same enemies that Japan had faced in the 1895 Dreibund. He again proposed that Japan should respond favourably to the approach, urging that she would become 'a partner in world history and in the progress of the world'. In spite of serious disagreements within the cabinet and words of caution from Yamagata and General Katsura Tarō as minister of war, reinforced by the *Genro* (Elder statesman) Itō Hirobumi, Aoki's approach surprisingly prevailed. The Japanese decided to mobilize the 5th Division for sending to China. The British money was, however, not accepted. While Japan was serving her own national interest in joining Britain and the powers in their endeavours in saving the legations, she was also responding to a rather special vote of confidence from Britain for powers only distribute largesse to trustworthy partners. And Aoki acknowledged that fact.[23]

The Boxer Rebellion ended with much recrimination between those powers who had troops on Chinese soil, puffed up with the success of relieving the Peking legations. Britain and Japan were at one in distrusting the actions of the Russian armies in the north. In this Britain found an unexpected ally in Germany and concluded an Anglo-German agreement on China (known to the Germans as the *Yangtse Abkommen*) on 16 October 1900 which proclaimed the territorial integrity of China and the importance of the Open Door there. We can imagine that Aoki liked this treaty between the two countries closest to his heart and would as foreign minister have wanted his country to join in it. But the Yamagata cabinet which had only stayed in office to see through the Boxer emergency offered its resignation on the 19th. It was left to Aoki's successor to adhere formally to this agreement on 29 October, which was to prove a most significant stepping-stone on the way to the Anglo-Japanese alliance. But possibly Aoki made his views known before he left office.[24]

Aoki became a privy councillor in November 1901 but was offered no other posting straightaway. He lived in aristocratic style which reflected the nature of diplomacy at the time. He had houses at Kami Nibancho in Tokyo and in Chuzenji. His daughter Hanako, at the age of 25, married Count Hatzfeldt, a diplomat at the German embassy in Tokyo, in one of the great social events of December 1904, though it was at the height of the Russo-Japanese War.[25]

CODA OF DISENCHANTMENT

The status of Japan's major legations around the world was raised after the Russo-Japanese War on a reciprocal basis. The allocation of the new embassies was worked out during the final weeks of the Katsura ministry and on its recommendation. On 7 January 1906 Aoki was appointed as ambassador to Washington. He might have expected to be promoted to the senior post of ambassador to London but that was being reserved for the retiring foreign minister, Komura Jutarō. Sir Claude MacDonald who was also promoted to British ambassador at this time wrote: 'Viscount Aoki will be much missed by Diplomatic Society in Tokyo where he has dispensed hospitality on a most generous scale.'[26]

It cannot be said that Aoki's new assignment was an easy one. When he reached Washington in April, he found that relations with the United States were soured because of disputes over the Open Door in China but, more significantly, over the various problems associated with Japanese immigration into California. Tokyo, proud of its achievement in defeating Russia, bombarded him with demands to call on the US administration for a speedy end to discrimination against Japanese. Public opinion in both countries was running high, though both governments were conscientiously trying to work out some settlement. Aoki often found it necessary to tone down his superior's instructions.[27] Immigration legislation was passed with the Root amendment. The anti-Japanese Californian riot of May 1907 was answered throughout Japan by anti-American outbursts. After Aoki had been in the US for 18 months, he reported that he had in his personal capacity suggested to President Theodore Roosevelt a solution to the problem by way of an American-Japanese treaty along certain lines and that this had been favourably received. In Tokyo, Foreign Minister Hayashi noted that the proposal did not take account of the immigration issue which was, in his view, the sole issue requiring attention. The matter was presented to the Japanese cabinet who rejected Aoki's personal initiative. Hayashi, therefore, replied to Aoki, dishonouring his approaches and ultimately recalling him to Tokyo for taking the law into his own hands without receiving instructions.[28]

Aoki's remorse was great and he sent three strongly worded defences of his position though not denying that he had taken an initiative not mandated by his government. But in vain : Hayashi had not forgiven him for some of his actions in London in 1894.

Aoki's humiliation was widely-known. Commenting on his return from Washington, the British embassy reported that '... he is being recalled owing to his having exceeded his instructions in the Immigration question having accepted the principle of reciprocity in the matter of immigration without consulting his Government' and that he '... sometimes wrote in the most overbearing tones to his Chief'.[29] In high dudgeon Aoki left his post at the end of 1907 and resigned from the diplomatic service at the age of 63. He was again appointed a privy councillor (*sumitsu komonkan*). This seems to have given him some retirement income. At one level, it was the case of a senior man being dismissed for exceeding his powers and failing to accept the discipline of his appointment. At another, it seems to have been part of the bitter personal feuds in which Aoki, probably the seniormost member of Japan's diplomatic service, frequently got involved.

But Aoki was able to mobilize the support of influential friends who sympathized with their clansman. Soon he was able to turn the tables on his political enemies as he had earlier done in 1898. A Chōshū-based cabinet came into power under Katsura on 14 July 1908. Katsura himself became the main force in policy-making and, in effect, adopted Aoki's line. He immediately agreed to conclude a treaty with Washington, the so-called Root-Takahira pact, which generally follows the ideas put forward by Aoki. The latter could take some comfort in his disheartening retirement that he was not without support in the clan-ridden politics of the day.

Aoki was not happy in retirement and leaves little account of his doings in his fragments of autobiography. But these fragments, which were not published in his lifetime, reflect a little of his thinking. They contain a chapter on religion written late in life in which he praises Protestantism to which he turned from Catholicism towards the end of his life. Not unexpectedly, therefore, he was a believer in '*kojinshugiron*' (individualism) to which he devotes a chapter appended to that on religion. Unusually for a Japanese, he extols the merits of personal freedom.[30]

Aoki died on 16 February 1914 aged 71 just before Japan declared war on Germany, which he described as his 'second country'.[31] Ambassador MacDonald summed up Aoki by writing that he was '... unpopular with the authorities at the Foreign Office [Ministry] owing to the independent position he takes up vis-a-vis that department, and also to his somewhat dictatorial manner and his distinct but sometimes indiscreet pro-foreign proclivities'.[32] Yet he had great achievements. He had served overseas as minister countless times and as ambassador once and had twice been foreign minister. He was a good negotiator as his performance in 1894 showed. But he was a bad parliamentarian: he lacked the politician's capacity for public debate. In the early days of the Diet he attended reluctantly and left when the going got rough. Perhaps he was not a perfect diplomat because he was too independent-minded. He was more attuned to formulating high policy for himself than to consulting his superiors. As we have seen in this essay, he had, on two occasions at least, 1894-6 and 1907, taken risks and been punished for his transgressions. On the first occasion he managed to vault back, becoming foreign minister. The second time, he was pushed into oblivion prematurely. He felt it deeply and bore a grudge till his death.

Like many of the distinguished sons of Chōshū and men of Meiji, Aoki was a highly individualistic Japanese. He did not come within the front-rank of Meiji leaders. He was basically an official and politician who never rose to the commanding heights of Meiji political leadership.[33] But he seems to represent some of the characteristics that Japan has lost. The interest of his personality lies in the fact that he was so independent-minded and so direct. Of course, these qualities led to accusations of arrogance, self-importance and, as some thought, indiscipline. Perhaps his marriage and his long service abroad made him unusually international in his approach and sympathies. To some Japanese he seemed to have been out of the country too long; he did not seem to be fully at ease with his own people. Yet his positive qualities are refreshingly similar to contemporaries elsewhere in the world.

Aoki's place in Anglo-Japanese relations was historically significant. At many crucial junctures, he seems to be pointing the way to the Anglo-Japanese alliance. Although his residence in London was comparatively short, he did affect relations beneficially in 1894. For twenty-five years in the Meiji period, Britain had not appeared to be a friend of Japan over revising their treaties; indeed she was the major obstacle among the powers. Yet Britain was the big fish who had to be caught if Japan was to win back her international self-respect. And Aoki was the lucky fisherman.

13

The Douglas Mission (1873-79) and Meiji Naval Education

IAN GOW

JAPAN'S NATIONAL ISOLATION policy from the early seventeenth to the mid-nineteenth century, together with its destruction of and ban on further construction of ocean-going ships, resulted in Japan approaching the modern era with no real naval expertise beyond coastal shipping. Thus from a position of almost parity with the maritime West in the early seventeenth century Japan now found itself with neither the technology, tradition nor trained manpower in matters naval. Whilst the Bakumatsu armies and even the early Meiji army could utilize elements of the samurai heritage in terms of military leadership, these were hardly appropriate to a professional, technologically sophisticated navy. Yet, from a base formed from those early experiments in ship purchase, ship construction and training in the Bakumatsu period Japan was able, within half a century, to create a modern, technologically sophisticated naval force, professionally officered and capable of defeating first the Chinese and then the Russian navy. In no small part this was due to the tremendous mentoring by British naval training missions as well as contributions from a myriad of serving British naval personnel, former naval and army personnel, as well as civilians who tutored and supported the nascent Japanese navy. In terms, however, of manpower development perhaps the most important contribution was the second British Naval Mission, the Douglas Mission (1873-79) which laid the foundations of basic naval officer training and education.

BAKUMATSU NAVAL EXPERIMENTATION AND THE FIRST NAVAL MISSION

The heightened awareness of the Western naval threat following the traumatic intrusion by Perry's 'black ships' triggered a frantic search for knowledge, expertise and equipment within Japan in terms of the creation of naval forces. However this naval boom, actively encouraged in the various *han* by a Shogunate desperately short of funds created a domestic naval arms-race in ship construction between outer domains and the Shogunate. It was this domestic competition rather than any real belief, at least in the short term, that they would be able to effectively combat Western naval power with their own indigenous forces that fuelled the explosion of training of naval forces and the study of foreign navies now given a major priority both within the domains and within the Shogunate itself. Initially, and naturally the Japanese turned first to their long time guests and former great naval power, the Dutch, for their first naval training missions.[1] In 1854 a Captain Fabius and other Dutch staff began instructing retainers from both the *bakufu* and some of the domains. In 1855, a *Kaigun Denshujō* (Naval Training Establishment) was established at Nagasaki and a Dutch team began teaching there. The students were from the *bakufu*, and *fudai* and even *tozama* domains and received training in maths, navigation, ship construction gunnery and seamanship. A second Netherlands detachment arrived in 1857 and stayed until March 1859 when Dutch tuition of Japanese naval personnel in Japan came to an end. Japanese students who had studied under the Dutch established a new naval school at Tsukiji near Edo (Tokyo) in 1857. It was first called the *Gunkan Kyōjujō* (Warship Teaching Institute) and shortly afterwards renamed the *Kaigun Sōrenjō* (Navy Training Institute). In 1859 the Nagasaki training establishment closed, the students were transferred to Tsukiji and the Dutch instructors left Japan. Shortage of funds was officially given as the reason for releasing the foreign instructors but it is more probable that the Japanese were dissatisfied with the level of instruction and moreover were becoming more confident of their own abilities. In 1860 the Japanese-crewed *Kanrin Maru* sailed across the Pacific to the USA. In 1863 the *bakufu* sent students abroad for naval training and, no doubt reflecting in part the assistance from American crew furnished during the *Kanrinmaru*'s voyage, the United States was selected as the most suitable country. At this time the American Civil War prevented this and instead the students were sent to Holland. The *bakufu* at first had decided to try and persevere themselves after the 'failure' of the Dutch missions but many of these initiatives were short-lived and ineffective.

Indigenous Japanese efforts in this area were, however, by no means limited to the Dutch model. Lord Shimazu Nariakira of Satsuma, later to be the most influential *han* in the Meiji navy, researched the British navy and recommended it as the most likely to be of most beneficial to Japan.[2] The first involvement directly by the British was when the British Minister Alcock was asked to provide training for the army. The British, suspicious of the Japanese, procrastinated and in 1865 the French were successfully approached to provide this service. Alcock's successor, Harry Parkes, ever mindful of the dangers of allowing the French any advantage within the region, pressed the Japanese to change their mind. He was aware no doubt of the French instructors employed on naval training and when the Japanese refused to reconsider British training for the army, he switched his efforts to persuading them to accept naval tuition. Japanese naval officials such as Katsu Kaishū, who initially favoured Dutch tuition, tried unsuccessfully to argue that they did not wish to rely on just one country but rather to seek the best teachers from any Western power. This seems to have been a smoke-screen to cover their possible embarrassment since the Shogunal authorities were in fact concealing the fact that they had actually already engaged a third Dutch naval mission. This arrived in Japan, was paid the full contract, and sent home. In their anxiety to extricate themselves from a difficult diplomatic situation, the Japanese eventually succumbed to pressure from Parkes. A British naval mission of 17 officers and men arrived, under a director, Cdr. (later Admiral) Richard Tracey, and his deputy Lt. Arthur Wilson (later Admiral of the Fleet Sir Arthur Wilson) 'one of the greatest naval commanders of the 19th century'.[3]

There were three major groupings, seamanship/navigation, gunnery and engineering. Interestingly, Anglo-French sensitivities were immediately tested on Tracey's arrival. Apparently, the French had previously sought parity and status since Tracey outranked his French army counterpart. The British were unsuccessful in their attempt to block a request that the French army mission director be given equivalent rank.[4] Unfortunately, although there were positive signs of Tracey's mission achieving progress in laying the foundations of modern naval education for the *bakufu*, the Japanese civil war erupted. The naval mission not only had to withdraw and observe neutrality but also to watch their former pupils fight, and often die, on opposite sides. The mission withdrew to Yokohama and Katsu Kaishū then announced:

> Regarding your naval instructors there is a contract but it is with the Tokugawa house not the country. I do not know if the government which will follow will honour that contract. For this reason, although we may dismiss the

instructors we cannot (afford to) send them home. We have already paid the salaries and various expenses so please understand our predicament.[5]

This first major attempt to provide British naval training in Japan, therefore, ended prematurely although it is perhaps unfair to state that it achieved little.[6] It made a beginning and probably helped to make later decisions to favour the British more likely. However, two former Royal Navy personnel, Lt. Albert Hawes R.M. and Lt. John M. James continued in the employ of various han and made a significant contribution to shipboard training, influencing the first Japanese instructors at the Shogunal, han and Meiji naval academies. These men were later to enter the employ of the Meiji navy.[7]

EARLY MEIJI NAVAL TRAINING

The first years of the Meiji era were ones where the navy found its growth greatly constrained by the government's financial difficulties. Furthermore the greater part of available funds were devoted to an army first (rikukaigun) policy for internal security reasons. The shortage of funds for the navy was one reason for initially placing greater emphasis on training rather than purchasing ships at this time.

In 1870 the *Kaigun Heigakkō* (Naval Academy) was established at Tsukiji but there were serious problems. The courses were too theoretical, too bookish, and the Japanese instructors lacked sufficient experience. Students were sent abroad to the USA and Germany, but the majority went to Britain. In 1871 twelve students were sent to England but the Admiralty were unable to offer them places at Royal Navy establishments and they were assigned to merchant navy instructors. Some did eventually serve as midshipmen in the Royal Navy. The most famous of these first students was Tōgō Heihachirō who served aboard the training ship *Worcester* of the Thames Nautical School and was to become the 'Nelson of Japan'. Japan had also placed midshipmen on Western naval vessels and two were serving on HMS *Audacious* in 1870.

For the new Meiji government the most important naval task was to decide which countries would provide a model for the new army and navy. The French model was immediately selected for the army (later replaced by the Prussian/German model) but there was some doubts as to the most effective for the navy. Both the Dutch and the British models were suggested but in the end the British model was selected. Real documentary evidence as to the reasons why the British model was selected is lacking. However, Britain was obviously a far more potent naval power than Holland at this time and some of the successful *han* had utilized the British model, especially Satsuma *han* which had even translated the admiralty regulations into Japanese in the Bakumatsu period. In August 1870, the Military Authority had requested that the British system be studied further and then sought the views of its serving captains as to the most appropriate model for the new navy. From the replies of ship captains, it would seem initially that both Holland and Britain were candidates. However, it is probable that, at least in terms of naval training and education, the real deciding factor was the return of overseas students who had studied with the Dutch navy and who indicated dissatisfaction with the Dutch model.[8] Eventually, in October 1871 the Japanese naval authorities announced '...the present standing forces are to be organized on the British model for naval forces and the French model for land forces'.[9] This decision to adopt the British system, whilst it did not make it inevitable that Japan request direct assistance from the British Admiralty, made it much more likely.

Having decided on the British model there were a number of options open to the Meiji government. The first, as stated above, was to send students abroad. The second was to teach them in Japan possibly using British instructors. In fact the first British personnel employed by the Japanese navy on navy-related duties predated the Douglas mission. They were Thomas Snowden, who was employed on marine transportation issues, and Joseph Taylor, who advised on refloating sunken vessels.[10] In addition, the Naval School employed two British English teachers in 1872 prior to the Douglas mission arriving, David and John Hare. They were not the first teachers of English since a Dutchmen was originally employed for those duties. One month after their appointment an American, Pilkington, was also hired. A British naval doctor was hired for naval medical matters. Artlllery Lieutenant Frank Brinkley taught gunnery at the academy from 1871, and former Army Bandmaster Fenton started a naval band movement. The first navy trained personnel was actually Lt. Albert Joseph Hawes, hired by the Meiji naval department in 1870. He taught aboard a training ship, and is apparently credited by the Japanese with outlawing the *hibachi* (charcoal heater) and tatami matting on Japanese men-of-war. He entered Meiji Navy employ and he performed outstandingly. Later, Basil Hall Chamberlain who was the first English teacher hired by Douglas for the Naval Academy (1874) and Hawes' co-author of a guide to Japan, stated:

> This officer, had tremendous organisational powers and on the ship... and after that concerning other positions, apart from training of marines was active in a great number of other respects. We can probably think of him as the true father of the Japanese navy.[11]

This high praise is echoed by a number of authorities on Japanese naval history.

The second was a former naval lieutenant, John Mathew James, who had been employed by a number of *han* and also worked for the lighthouse bureau surveying Japanese coastal waters prior to entering navy employ as a foreign employee in May 1872. Edwin Wheeler, the first British naval doctor, arrived in Japan in 1870. He acted as a physician to the British legation and he was employed from 1871 at the Navy Hospital. He was certainly the first to introduce the latest naval medical science from Britain and went on to become Chief of the Tokyo General Hospital. He remained in Japan until he was killed in the 1923 Kantō earthquake. William Anderson was the first British doctor employed at the Navy Medical School. He arrived in Japan in 1872 and within the year was employed as an instructor attached to the Hospital.[12] He returned home in 1880 after some 15 students had graduated, but returned to Japan and continued his studies of beriberi, a disease in which Japanese medical doctors maintained a worldwide reputation in later years. He also published a major study of Japanese painting.

THE DOUGLAS MISSION 1873-79

The Japanese naval authorities, having decided on the British model, began to investigate how they might achieve this particular objective and their thought naturally turned to naval training. As mentioned previously, the last students returning from Holland had expressed dissatisfaction with training in Holland and, we can assume, training abroad generally. The first communication dated 6 April 1871 was forwarded to the Japanese consulate in London and asked for 11 instructors, a mission chief, and specialists[1] for gunnery, engineering, boatswain, 3 artificers, 2 gunnery assistants. The British government delayed matters. This was, in part, a lack of trust in the Japanese exacerbated perhaps by the financial losses incurred in getting the Tracey mission home. Almost one year later, shortly after the departure of the Iwakura mission, a new Minister Plenipotentiary, Terashima, sailed for London with specific orders to use his best efforts, and those of members of the Iwakura mission, to get a decision from the British government. By then the number of instructors requested had risen to 21. Terashima apparently enlisted the assistance of Itō Hirobumi, then with the Iwakura mission, but their efforts did not progress matters. In October Terashima, acting on the instruction of the navy authorities, then wrote to the Foreign Office stating:

At this time we lack Japanese officers with the requisite

experience for teaching. This applies to all areas of naval science, seamanship etc. For these reasons the Japanese navy strongly wishes to employ from the British government 10 officers and 11 NCOs.[13]

Sir Harry Parkes, home on leave in England, also supported the Japanese. He explained his fears of other countries seizing the opportunity to take up this offer if Britain did not move quickly. He felt that a first-class team immersed in naval tradition should be sent. Lord Granville, the foreign secretary, then agreed, stating his earnest desire to improve Anglo-Japanese relations and no doubt motivated by ensuring that other foreign powers would not seek advantage. Final discussions were concluded by 7 April 73 but apparently the mission leader, a Lt. Cdr. Archibald Douglas, had already been selected in late March.

Douglas (1842-1913) was a very interesting choice.[14] He was not perhaps a typical naval officer of his generation. He had neither public school background nor establishment connections. Although often referred to as an English naval officer he was in fact a Canadian/Scot. Born in Quebec, Canada, the son of an émigré Aberdeen doctor. He was personally recommended by the Governor General of Canada and became the first Canadian-born cadet to serve in the Royal Navy. He entered the navy at the age of 14 and was immediately sent to sea. He early on excelled in navigation and seamanship although his gunnery skills were somewhat weaker. This defect was later remedied and he became a senior staff officer instructor at the Cambridge gunnery school. He had not apparently spent any time in Asia in his years at sea, and appears to have been a highly competent, very practical officer destined for higher rank, but not necessarily Flag rank. He had seen no major naval action although had been involved in anti-slave trade activities off Africa, but this was gunboat diplomacy, not major naval warfare.

Douglas received his instructions from the Japanese minister in London, Terashima, and was responsible to Japan's navy minister, not to the British Commander-In-Chief China Station although he clearly did report to the latter and sought his cooperation. Prior to his departure Douglas withdrew temporarily from active service on half pay and also requested that the warrant officers be placed on the books of HMS *Iron Duke* (China Squadron) for the duration. He also requested 34 revolvers; no doubt concerned regarding the personal danger of a place such as Japan. There is no record of these being received, although Douglas is recorded as always sleeping with a loaded shotgun at his bedside. He also requested that, when necessary, he could exchange subordinate officers and men with crew from the China Squadron but this never actually occurred.

The Douglas mission arrived in Japan in 1873 after, for many of the ratings, a most uncomfortable voyage for which Douglas obtained compensation for them. Douglas and his men were confronted by a very difficult situation in human terms as well as educationally. The school comprised some 115 students and 34 instructors, including some who had fought on opposite sides in the recent civil war. Some students apparently found it difficult to deal with instructors who had no combat experience when they themselves had recently been fighting. However, it has been suggested that the internal dissension evaporated for the most part, largely due to the Japanese wish to show a united front and give a good impression to the foreign experts. But discipline and dress codes were poor, the learning experience was far too bookish and the students lacked fitness. Douglas and Chief Engineer Sutton commented on the abstract knowledge, Sutton immediately arranged for training for engineers in the dockyard where the French were most helpful.[15]

The Head of the School, Nakamuta Kuranosuke, gave Douglas almost complete freedom to change the system. The Douglas team immediately set about replacing the Dutch regulations with British Admiralty regulations and with routines and dress and eating codes more appropriate to officers. Douglas dropped the training of senior non-commissioned officers, choosing to focus almost exclusively on the creation of a disciplined, well-trained officer corps.[16] The Japanese did not find it easy to adjust to the new regime. Language was a problem, and Douglas immediately augmented the English teaching. One of his very first appointments was Basil Hall Chamberlain. Japanese trainees also objected to saluting and especially responding to bells and whistles, apparently feeling that this was more appropriate to training animals than people.[17] He also introduced stricter dress codes and regulations such as the five-minute rule (be there five minutes in advance of all classes). Although shore-based, the teaching was not classroom-based but practical as far as possible, with mock-up ships equipment and guns ashore as well as extensive training aboard cutters and Japanese warships. Douglas has been accused of being rather old-fashioned and less advanced technologically, but in fact he quite rightly regarded rigorous sail training as mentally and physically good for these officers, inculcating a sense of discipline and routine.[18] Douglas also introduced compulsory competitive sports. This was commented on most negatively in the local Japanese press, which was particularly scathing about such things as three-legged races and blindfold races. However, this was no mere effort to introduce English school games, but rather a belief, held by Douglas and his instructors, that Japanese naval officers who were far from fit when his team arrived had to be physically as well as mentally superior to their men. Douglas also introduced the training mission idea whereby midshipmen served as crewmembers on trips abroad, adding to their seagoing and international experience. No doubt the latter was also used for intelligence gathering in terms of mapping out foreign harbours an so forth. In addition, Douglas introduced such very English things as billiards, British national holidays, including Easter and the Queen's Birthday, and also Sunday prayers. This latter innovation was not liked at all by the Japanese trainees.[19] It has been suggested that Douglas actually introduced public school education characteristics. This may well be true, although he himself was not from that background and Britain at the time had still not introduced college teaching ashore at Dartmouth incorporating such ideas. There is no doubt that even in the two years that Douglas was in charge, tremendous progress was made, under very difficult circumstances, in terms of discipline, seamanship, navigation, gunnery and engineering as well as naval medicine. Douglas, whilst clearly greatly respected by all although he did clash at times with the head of the college. In his memoirs Count Nakamuta stated:

> Douglas liked to interfere in everything. If someone did not listen to him he became very upset. It was very difficult to calm him down.[20]

However, he went on to write that the teaching received by the Japanese was undoubtedly the very best available. This is a tribute not only to the thoroughness of Douglas's approach, but also the very high calibre of the team selected. There were no doubt considerable tensions and whilst some have put this down to personality clashes and even arrogance on the part of Douglas, this seems less likely than the obvious problems of teaching in a foreign land, in a foreign tongue and building a new system from the bottom up in as short a period as possible. Douglas himself does not seem to have sought to understand things Japanese in the way that many *oyatoi gaijin* (hired foreigners) did. He was single-mindedly focused on creating a system as close a possible to best British practice. Based on a view that first one disciplines students into shape, he could hardly afford to be too sensitive to Japanese feelings. Since the Royal Navy had been engaged in the past in training other navies, Douglas probably knew how far he had to push foreign trainees to ensure a successful outcome. He was also accused of arrogance since he stated apparently '... we are not here simply to instruct in techniques. The creation of the new Japanese navy rests on our shoulders.'[21] This may have reflected the rhetoric of a man in command of a team far from home rather than arrogance.

Douglas and his men still had to put up with a distrust of foreigners. They had experienced this outside the school when at times they were hissed at in the streets, but there was also a student movement to have the British naval instructors dismissed. This was led by Yamamoto Gonnohyōe, later Navy Minister and Prime Minister.[22] This group of students were fearful that Douglas and his men were spies but probably were resentful of the discipline imposed on them and the hard life. Of course it was nowhere near as hard as the life for a Japanese aboard Western naval warships where suicides were recorded as students buckled under the far greater difficulties of adjusting to Western lifestyles aboard men-of-war. The student movement came to nought but there was clearly at times an undercurrent of resentment and in a certain sense shame.[23] Douglas himself, it has often been assumed, returned home because he had fallen out with the authorities and retained a sense of resentment although there is no clear evidence for this.[24] Whilst there were undoubtedly clashes with the Japanese authorities from time to time it is reasonable to assume that Douglas' decision to resign one year early was motivated not by Japanese circumstances but by his need to return to active service for promotion considerations. He had been promoted to commander during the mission, but it was not active service and he urgently needed this to ensure promotion to captain and to flag rank. He wrote:

> The great unforeseen changes that have taken place in the active list of the Royal Navy since I accepted this appointment make it imperative that I should return to my service or relinquish any prospect of future advancement.[25]

His family had settled well in Japan and his second daughter had been born there. His son later recorded that 'mother would have liked to have stayed on' and it is therefore reasonable to assume that his wife would have preferred this life to one where her husband would spend many more years at sea. Nevertheless, the reasons given by Douglas are far more logical and sensible than any hint that he did not get on with the Japanese. On his departure he was granted an audience by the Emperor and according to his granddaughter, awarded the Order of the Rising Sun First Class. The official statement of thanks stated:

> ... Since then you have discharged diligently the duties devolving upon you and it is due to you that the studies of the cadets have reached their present state of progress. We have great pleasure in heartily commending the result, being as it is the basis for the development of our navy.[26]

However, these warm words were rather more welcome than the last encounter with British officials authority in Japan. When he arrived immediately prior to departure 'in white civvies' to pay his respects to the British minister and the Japanese foreign minister, Parkes apparently was furious:

> While I am waiting the little man comes in and flies into a passion and says he won't present me (to the Foreign Minister) in that dress and I ought to be in uniform. He was in such a rage that I could not get him to listen to me. When the Foreign Minister then appeared and I see him but when he sees me Parkes jumps out of the room. I make my interview as short as possible and am met at the door by Parkes, white with rage calling me 'begone sir, begone'.[27]

Whilst one might immediately make judgements here about Parkes, the other distinct possibility is that once again Douglas, talented as he was, was supremely unaware of the need for proper sensitivities when dealing with senior Japanese officials and Parkes was very aware of these.[28] Parkes was possibly also not too happy with Douglas breaking his contract but Douglas certainly seems supremely unaware of (or unconcerned about) Japanese ways and manners at this stage. Indeed, on his way home he demurred from giving a lecture on Japan. This again hints at his insularity, possible lack of knowledge of things Japanese, and total focus instead on the creation of a Royal Naval environment within the college. Douglas was clearly upset by this encounter with Parkes, coming at the end of a difficult but successful tour of duty in Japan. Later, Douglas apparently was somewhat placated by a supportive letter from Parkes. Ironically, having sought active service Douglas was then posted (exiled his son called it) to the China squadron for a number of years, many of which were spent off or close to Japan. He did land in Japan again and was feted by his former pupils and colleagues who had remained behind.

Douglas rose eventually to the rank of admiral and actually chaired a major committee on British naval education, the Douglas committee, and his experience with the development of engineering and other officers is clearly indicated in the documentation of this committee. He clearly however, had been most impressed with the progress of the Japanese, writing:

> The Japanese appear to possess the requisite elements of making good seamen. They are hardy, fearless and active and easily controlled. Up to the present time, for lack of sufficient officers they are badly trained and disciplined, ...
> In conclusion I may remark that the Japanese navy had made a very fair start, and it will only remain for time to prove whether the impression made by the training during the last two years will be a lasting one.[29]

The Douglas mission continued until 1879 building on the great work Douglas had started. Chief Engineer Sutton is well remembered as the founding father of the naval engineering school in official naval histories. Chief Gunner's Mate Frederick Hammond also contributed to the development of torpedo training. Members of the mission also stayed on to continue to contribute to Meiji Japan's development in a myriad of ways and some contributed to scholarship on Japan. The ending of the mission also coincided with the beginning of dramatic reductions of foreign employees in Japan as the government now began, not least for financial reasons, to move away from expensive missions and to replace foreigners with trained Japanese personnel. The total numbers of foreigners employed by the Meiji Navy was 182 of whom 130 were British.[30] The British contingent peaked in 1874 at 96, and by 1900 those in direct employ had been reduced to three.

The Douglas mission clearly had laid excellent foundations in terms of basic training and the Japanese now believed they were capable of taking on these tasks themselves. The next level was more advanced training in terms of strategy etc. This was initiated, in 1876, by a Lt. Cdr. Willan who introduced teaching on fleet movements.[31] He was actually employed as a gunnery instructor ashore and afloat. A small amount of higher level teaching had therefore been carried out whilst the Douglas mission was at the Naval Academy but it was only in the 1880s that the navy began serious planning of more advanced postgraduate study. The result was the transfer of the *Kaigun Heigakkō* (Naval Academy) to Etajima and the establishment of the *Kaigun Daigakkō* (Naval War College) at Tsukiji. In 1886 the Japanese Navy Minister Saigo Tsugimichi formally requested a British adviser and Captain John Ingles was selected to assist in the development of higher and technical naval education.[32] The Ingles mission lasted from 1887-93. It seems that that Ingles was generally pleased with what one might call the Douglas legacy in the navy in terms of good order, discipline and cleanliness at the training establishments. However, he did not rate their fleet movement activity highly and was a little critical of their gunnery expertise. At the same time, he felt that they had the great advantage of an officer corps not carrying all the mental baggage of the British naval officers trained in an age of sail. According to Perry he was '... used as a walking encyclopaedia and as a means of obtaining encyclopaedic information from the Royal Navy', facilitating a steady flow of useful documents on all aspects of naval life.[32] Ingles contributed greatly to Japanese technological expertise, urged them to create specialist engineering officers rather than line engineering, but his greatest contribution was possibly in tactics and strategy. His lectures were published in Japanese in 1894 as *Kaigun Senjutsu Kōgiroku* (Transcripts of naval tactics).[34] Despite their very considerable contribution to Japanese naval officer development, Royal Naval officers were not placed in command of Japanese vessels as they had been with the Russians, and indeed later were to be used with the Chinese. Whilst not perhaps a deliberate policy, it does perhaps indicate a more sensible approach to officer development. It is also true that the calibre of those sent on the missions to Japan was unquestionably of a very high order indeed.

The contribution to Japanese naval development of the three naval missions was very great but needs to be set in the context of the overall British contribution, in Japan as well as in Britain. Many of them went on to contribute beyond naval matters on academic writings and medicine, (Chamberlain, Anderson), in journalism (Brinkley), and Western band music (Fenton). Training in accountancy and other skills was provided aboard British ships, especially on the China squadron. Training was also provided in Britain, in the naval schools and for steaming crews in the dockyards. In addition those who had served on the naval missions in Japan were excellent contacts for Japanese naval attachés in Britain when the latter sought to expedite ship deliveries, gain access to the latest technological developments etc. This was especially true of the likes of Tracey, Wilson, Douglas and Ingles who rose to very high rank. Many Japanese naval officers were naturally proud of the fact that their former *sensei* (teachers) reached such high ranks in the world's leading navy.

Japan's naval successes against a major European power in the Russo-Japanese War (1904-5), following on from earlier successes against the Chinese navy, finally indicated to the world that the Meiji navy had come of age. British naval officers took considerable pride in the fact that their former pupils and alliance partners had achieved so much in so short a time. The Meiji navy now provided the new Japan not only with international status but also a mechanism for first obtaining and then developing naval technology. This, in turn, acted as a major modernizing tool through technology transfer and diffusion within and beyond the navy. It also nurtured the development of a vast number of technically competent personnel capable of managing the most advanced equipment of the day. Furthermore, having achieved membership of the super-power club of élite nations of the world through the Anglo-Japanese Alliance, Japan now, through her naval achievements, looked set to become a major maritime power in her own right. In all this Japan owed a very considerable debt to Western nations such as Holland, France, the United States and, most importantly, Britain.

In 1906, in the aftermath of the naval victories against Russia, along with the Frenchman Emile Bertin, three British naval officers were decorated by a grateful Japanese government, Lt. James, Admiral Ingles and Admiral Douglas.[35] The Japanese Prime Minister had written to the Palace recommending that Admiral Sir Archibald Lucius Douglas be honoured for his role in the making of the Meiji navy:

> This person, at the time of the establishment of the Meiji navy, responding to the request of our government, took up matters of education with his officers and non-commissioned officers and provided the base for training and development of our officers and engineers for which we are most grateful.[36]

He was awarded the Order of the Rising Sun (First Class). His award was of course also recognition for the tremendous work done by members of the second Royal Navy mission to Japan (1873-78). In later years his photograph hung in the Naval Academy at Etajima. It was lost in the Great Kantō Earthquake of 1923 and, following a request to the Douglas family, was replaced in 1929.[37] Again, it was lost during the occupation of Japan and in 1961, photographs were again requested from the Douglas family and are now at the Maritime Self-Defence College at Etajima and on board the preserved national treasure, the battleship *Mikasa*. In an era when overseas training missions, by taking officers out of the mainstream of naval service and often on half pay, often narrowed or ended their chances of promotion to high rank, no less than four officers, Richard Tracey, Arthur K. Wilson, Archibald Lucius Douglas and John Ingles, all with senior responsibilities for naval education in Japan, attained Flag rank as Admirals and Wilson and Douglas were knighted. Of course the training of other navies was no new thing for the Royal Navy leading one naval historian Laird Clowes to suggest that Britain was not only the mother of parliaments but also the mother of navies.[38] Writing just before the outbreak of the Russo-Japanese War, Laird Clowes had also stated rather prophetically that of all the nations which turned to Britain for aid in naval matters none was more successful than Japan.[39] For the Japanese navy of the time and even for their successors in the Maritime Self-Defence Forces, the work of Douglas (and the team he selected) continues to occupy an honoured position in Japanese naval education.

14

British Naval and Military Observers of the Russo–Japanese War

PHILIP TOWLE

THE BRITISH ARMED FORCES made a greater effort to observe the Russo-Japanese War than they made for any foreign war before or since. In the half century before the Japanese attack on Russia in 1904 Britain had not been involved in a war with a major power. Its army had vast experience but only of fighting colonial wars, its navy had not been tested against another modern navy for almost 100 years. No wonder that the Admiralty and War Office were hungry to learn what they could from the conflict between the Tsar's forces and the Emperor's.

But there were other reasons which explain the magnitude of the British effort. Between 1899 and 1902 British forces had been humiliated by the Boers in South Africa and the defeats there caused a general conviction that fundamental reforms were needed in British tactics and equipment. At sea the British were facing ever increasing threats as new navies were developed by Russia, France, Italy, the United States, Germany and Japan. The period of effortless maritime dominance was over. Finally, Britain had been Japan's ally since 1902 and might be drawn into the war with Russia if the French sent forces to help their Russian allies. Thus London had a very immediate need to know how the conflict was developing in Asia.

When war broke out in February 1904 Britain already had Naval and Military Attachés in Tokyo, Captain E.C. Troubridge, Captain Ricardo and Lieutenant Colonel C. Hume. Troubridge was a difficult man who tended to boast about his influence with the Japanese and completely misunderstood Admiralty instructions in 1904.[1] Nevertheless, after the Russo-Japanese War, he became Chief of the Naval

War Staff in 1912 and commander of the Cruiser Squadron of the Mediterranean Fleet the following year. As such he was blamed for the escape of the German cruisers, *Geoben* and *Breslau* to Turkey in 1914. He was exonerated by the court martial but never regained a sea command, serving with the Serbian forces for the rest of the war. His chief successor in Tokyo, William Pakenham, had a happier career, serving as Fourth Sea Lord from 1911 to 1913, commanding the Australian Fleet until 1916, serving at the Battle of Jutland and then as commander of the First Battle Cruiser Squadron.[2] Charles Hume was an Asian specialist. He had served as A.D.C. to the Commander-in-Chief in India from 1885 to 1892. Subsequently, he had acted as adviser to the Crown Prince of Siam and after the Russo-Japanese War he returned to that country. Hume was supported by a number of more junior army officers seconded to Tokyo to learn Japanese.[3]

But neither the Admiralty nor the War Office regarded the presence in Tokyo of Troubridge, Ricardo, Hume and the language officers as enough. The Admiralty sent Captain Pakenham to join Troubridge and Ricardo. But their plans went awry. Prickly as always, Troubridge decided that Pakenham had been sent to replace them. Troubridge and Ricardo started for home and were extremely reluctant to return to Tokyo. The First Lord of the Admiralty, Lord Selborne, was furious. He told the commander of the British Fleet on the China station that appointment of attachés was his personal responsibility, that the three naval officers had been particularly chosen by him and that Troubridge and Ricardo had not been given permission to leave Japan. 'We should be failing in a most obvious duty if we did not exhaust every opportunity of acquiring information about the war.'[4] Eventually, Captains Hutchinson and Jackson were sent to join Pakenham. The Admiralty also sent Captain Eyres to observe the war from the Russian side. However, the Russian fleet was bottled up in Port Arthur and Vladivostok and, even when Eyres reached Vladivostok, there was little to see. Not surprisingly, given that Britain was allied to Japan and that Russian forces were suffering so heavily at Japanese hands, Eyres was looked upon by the Russians with grave suspicion and, to the embarrassment of the British, he was eventually captured in Manchuria by the Japanese army.[5]

The War Office decided that it would make an even greater effort than the Admiralty to observe the conflict and a whole stream of officers went out to join Hume in Tokyo. The most senior of these were General Sir Ian Hamilton and Sir William Nicholson. The War Office's intention was that they would accompany the Japanese armies in the field while some of the language officers remained in Tokyo. Two problems supervened, friction between Hamilton and Nicholson, both of whom acquired followers amongst the other British officers in

Tokyo, and, much more importantly, the reluctance of the Japanese to allow the foreign officers to go to the front.

It was hardly surprising that Hamilton and Nicholson would disagree. Hamilton was a fighting general with a fascination for infantry tactics. As a young officer, he had so impressed Lord Roberts, then the most famous and successful British general in India, with improvements in the musketry of his regiment, that he had been made Assistant Adjutant General for Musketry in India. Ever afterwards he remained very close to Roberts who helped further Hamilton's career at the expense of antagonizing those, like Nicholson, who were not in Roberts' circle.[6] Hamilton was wounded in the first Boer War in 1881 and served with distinction in the second. In between he had served in the expedition to rescue General Gordon, in fighting in Burma, and on the frontiers with Afghanistan. In 1903 he was appointed Quarter Master General in the War Office but lost his post during the organizational reforms following the Boer War. He was then encouraged by Nicholson to go out to Japan in the hope of being accredited to observe the war. While he was on his way eastwards, Hamilton learnt that Nicholson had been appointed senior observer. It was an inauspicious beginning.

Nicholson was a desk-bound general and an engineer. He served as Director of Transport during the second Boer War and subsequently became Director of Military Operations at the War Office. But, like Hamilton, he lost his post in the great reforms of 1903-4 and thus was free to observe the Asian war. From the start Hamilton believed that Nicholson, now nearly 60 years old, would be unable to stand up to active campaigning with the Japanese in Manchuria. However, he could not say so as others felt he was jealous of Nicholson's seniority.[7]

Nicholson's closest associate in Japan was Colonel Aylmer Haldane, a cousin of the future War Minister, R.B. Haldane. Haldane was one of the most articulate of the British observers of the war. Unfortunately, he was on bad terms with Ian Hamilton and his distrust inflamed relations between Hamilton and Nicholson. Haldane thought that Hamilton had blocked his promotion during the Boer War and was now trying to prevent him going to the front by suggesting that one of the senior officers should stay in Tokyo to collate reports. Haldane wrote to his mother that he was watching Hamilton carefully as he was a 'very tricky character'.[8] Hamilton and Haldane were to disagree profoundly and vociferously about the tactical lessons to be derived from the Japanese successes in Manchuria.

In any case it took a long time before they were allowed to leave Tokyo and to observe the war. On 11 February 1904, three days after the war had begun, the British minister in Japan, Sir Claude MacDonald suggested that Japan might allow the four British language officers in Tokyo and the military attaché to accompany their forces. On the following day the War Office told MacDonald that they had selected 12 officers to join the Japanese.[9] Subsequently, he was told to ask the Japanese to permit two officers from India and a Canadian officer to come as well. On the 15 February the Japanese begged MacDonald to keep the number down to 10 plus Nicholson. At the beginning of March the Japanese agreed that Hamilton could join them as a representative of the Indian army 'at the special request of Lord Roberts' and they also eventually accepted an Australian officer. All this time they were under pressure from every other developed nation to be allowed to send observers. No doubt they would have preferred to have no foreign observers at all as they would just be an encumbrance and might release secrets. But they had to keep the sympathy of the other Great Powers and of the British in particular. They needed to raise loans in Britain, Germany and the USA in May and November 1904 and in March and July 1905.[10] They also depended on the neutrality of the Great Powers. Thus they allowed the various officers to arrive in Tokyo but kept them there as long as possible.

It was not until April 1904 that Hamilton left Tokyo for the front with Captains B. Vincent and J.B. Jardine. Hamilton had wanted to take officers from the Indian army and suspected the minister of being prejudiced against them, but MacDonald believed officers who could speak some Japanese would be more useful and Hamilton eventually came round to agreeing with him. Berkeley Vincent was an efficient officer. He had served as a staff officer with three mobile columns in South Africa. He eventually rose to command the Sixth Inniskilling Dragoons and retired from the army as a brigadier general after the First World War. Hamilton found Jardine better with a horse than a pen but he believed he was 'a sensible chap and his opinions are worth attention'. Jardine also retired as a brigadier general after the First World War.[11]

After Hamilton left for the front, Nicholson and the rest of the British and foreign officers were kept waiting in Tokyo. Haldane became more and more furious with Nicholson whom he suspected of not wanting to suffer the rigours of the campaign: '... foreign officers and correspondents look to Sir William to get a move on, but he remains apathetic, sits in his room all day reading novels and smoking cigarettes. He is comfortable here and does not want to undergo the discomforts of the field'.[12] At the end of June Haldane persuaded Nicholson to complain to Sir Claude MacDonald. At the beginning of the following month the British boycotted the departure of the Japanese General Staff for the front as a sign of their irritation.[13] It was only at the end of July that the rest of the attachés and journalists were allowed to depart for Manchuria, by which time the Japanese had lost most of their sympathy, and the rivalries and disputes between the various officers had intensified.

Colonel W. Apsley Smith, Major Crawford from India, Captain C.A.L. Yate and Captain Sir Alexander Bannerman were sent to observe the Japanese siege of Port Arthur. The other officers joined the field armies. Captain Bannerman was to be promoted for his work on the fortifications and to go on to command the Air Battalion of Royal Engineers from 1910 to 1912. Nicholson was accompanied by Haldane, Captain Tulloch from India and the medical officer, Colonel Macpherson. Nicholson liked Macpherson which was fortunate because he quickly had need of his services. As Hamilton wrote: '... poor Nicholson has been sent back very sick indeed... it was a wicked shame sending a man of his habits and constitution at a time of year when the climate is tropical and with a rice-eating army'.[14]

While Nicholson managed only two months campaigning, Haldane and Hamilton enjoyed their time with the Japanese, despite their frustration when information was hidden from them. Hamilton told one of his correspondents: '... professionally this is the best time of my life. For more years than I like to think of I have been engrossed in routine, detail and hard work for others'.[15] As the autumn turned into winter he became increasingly angry with the pessimistic mood of the other attachés. As he told his wife, he was '... buried in the icy depths of a Manchurian winter with foreign officers who have never been away from home before and who daily, hourly almost become more silent and triste'. Even so great an officer, as the German Max Hoffmann grumbled, '... the only bliss in life does really not consist in establishing the most practical method of delivering an infantry attack and we grow old here waiting'.[16]

At the beginning of 1905 Hamilton and Nicholson were recalled to take up new duties in Britain while Haldane asked to stay at the front. Nicholson went on to become Chief of the Imperial General Staff from 1908 to 1912 and to be made a Field Marshal and a Baron. Hamilton took over the Southern Command of the army in 1905, served as Inspector General of Overseas Forces from 1910 to 1914 and commanded the ill-fated attack on the Dardanelles the following year. This, unfortunately, blighted his reputation but he was an unusual officer combining considerable military and intellectual talents.

While the Russo-Japanese War continued, a steady stream of officers flowed out to Manchuria both from India and Britain. Some replaced the colonial attachés, Hoad and Thacker, whom the British criticised heavily. The Canadian, Thacker, copied one of Hamilton's reports which leaked to the press. Later, he had to be invalided home. Hoad quickly asked to return to Australia after making a few superficial reports on the campaign. He then used his exiguous experience in

Manchuria to become Inspector General of the Australian Forces.[17] The remaining officers in Manchuria came under the command of General C.J. Burnett who was sent to Japan in 1905. Like Nicholson and Hamilton, Burnett had served for much of his career in India where he had concentrated on improving the living conditions of his men.[18] He was not a distinguished tactician like Hamilton or an administrator like Nicholson but he carried out his role in Manchuria to the satisfaction of the War Office and his colleagues.

The War Office considered it natural that the Japanese should allow their allies to observe the conflict; it was less sure how far the Russians would cooperate. The India Office was permitted to choose two senior officers, General Sir Montagu Gerard and Colonel W.H.H.Waters, to observe the war from the Russian side. Both were selected because of their previous connections with the Russian court. Gerard had served as Military Attaché in St Petersburg in 1892. He was a keen sportsman and published a lively account of this side of his life in 1903.[19] After disagreements with the British ambassador in Russia, Gerard was succeeded in St Petersburg by Waters who remained there until 1898. Waters was less sporting and more literary than Gerard and also succeeded in building up good links with the court. The two British officers were about as friendly as Hamilton and Nicholson. Waters made fun of Gerard's Russian and suspected him of wanting to become ambassador in St Petersburg. Gerard suggested that Waters might like to travel to the front via the USA. Waters disagreed and they travelled uneasily together via Russia, having an interview with the Tsar on the way.[20]

Both Waters and Gerard expected Russia to be victorious and Waters admitted to actually hoping that this would be the case.[21] Despite their bias, both attachés had to work very hard to overcome the suspicions of their hosts. Rumours were prevalent that British officers were advising the Japanese and even that British regiments were cooperating with Japanese forces. In one sense the Russians were right to be suspicious because Gerard was specifically asked to assess the extent of the Russian threat to India. He was also to report on particular items of Russian equipment which the British regarded as notably effective and thus threatening.[22]

The third and more junior officer sent to observe the war from the Russian side was Major J.M. Home of the Gurkhas. Home was asked to report on the efficiency of the Russian railway system and the support it could give to a Russian army menacing India. Unfortunately, Home had to be invalided home with a nervous breakdown which followed a serious stomach complaint. Gerard was reluctant to allow Home to depart as he knew how long it would take to replace him and indeed Major Mockler did not arrive in the theatre until March 1905 and Captain Holman even later.[23] This meant that Waters and Gerard were for most of the time the only British military observers on the Russian side.

The War Office ordered Waters home to write a report on the progress of the war in the middle of the winter. Waters interpreted this as a sign that he was regarded with greater favour than Gerard, although it is just as likely that the army wanted to keep the most senior officer at the front. Having finished his report Waters tried to return to Manchuria early in 1905. Again he had an interview with the Tsar but this time, despite his imperial backing, when he reached Irkutsk, he was prevented by a minor bureaucrat from going to the front.[24] In any case he would have been too late to see the great Japanese victory at Mukden. Waters was, however, more fortunate than Gerard. In May 1905 Gerard reported that ten foreign attachés had left the front through ill health. He himself died on the way home at Irkutsk. His memorial service in St Petersburg was attended by the Tsar but, when his coffin arrived in Scotland, his personal possessions had been taken and any observations on the campaign, which he had not already sent to the War Office, had been lost.[25]

Gerard's death and the illnesses suffered by Nicholson, Thacker and Home showed that the campaign was certainly not without its dangers and difficulties for the attachés. But the War Office was keen to have their reports and to publicize them. Many of the reports were printed and circulated within the army. The War Office wrote an official history which was later incorporated into a larger history sponsored by the Committee of Imperial Defence. The Admiralty had the most distinguished British naval historian of the day, Julian Corbett, write an unpublished naval history of the campaign.[26] The problem was not that the British armed forces were instinctively unwilling to learn from Manchuria but that each observer tended to draw lessons which reinforced his own beliefs and the interests of his regiment or corps.

The Russo-Japanese War broke out at a time when military technology was advancing rapidly and beginning to threaten many vested interests. The Boer War had been fought at very long ranges. Bayonets had been little used and the infantry had been forced to entrench and to resort to dispersed formations in order survive. Quick-firing artillery was coming into service, machine guns were becoming more plentiful, and the Japanese used very heavy artillery to pound the defences of Port Arthur. During the Russo-Japanese War cavalry usually fought dismounted with their rifles rather than with the *arme blanche*. But was this because warfare had changed fundamentally and cavalry were as out of date as the longbow or was it because the Russian and Japanese cavalry was so incompetent ? Here the line was drawn between the progressive and the conservative schools with the cavalry officers arguing determinedly that the war had not undermined the value of their arm.[27]

The progressives were undoubtedly led by Hamilton and Gerard, the conservatives by Haldane and the cavalry officers. Most of the attachés noted that the Russians and Japanese adopted wider formations in the face of the fire of their enemies, though the conservatives believed that this change could be exaggerated. One wrote from the Japanese side, '. . . after the Shaho battle, the Japanese began to consider whether, after all, the close formations as taught by the Germans. . . were the best for fighting in such flat open country. They had our experience in South Africa to help them and they decided to try what more open formations would do'. Similarly Holman concluded from the Russian side, '. . . after the battle of Mukden loose formations were practised, but up to the last it may be said that the Russians had not learnt how to use ground and they still moved slowly presenting a good target'.[28]

The observers' views were also deeply coloured by the vantage point from which they viewed the war. The British observers on the Russian side believed the war showed that artillery would dominate future battlefields. As Major Home put it: '. . . the greatest impression made on my mind by all I saw is that artillery is now the decisive arm and that all others are auxiliary to it..other things being equal that side will always win which has the best artillery'. Waters agreed that it was Japanese artillery which had defeated the Russians, while Gerard reported 'artillery now has the preponderating influence on the battlefield'.[29] The officers with the Japanese were more sceptical. Indeed Haldane and Hume believed that the effect of artillery had been exaggerated, and Haldane fought against the use of high explosive by the British artillery. The First World War was to show that infantry could only advance from their trenches in dispersed formations and with the backing of massive high explosive artillery barrages. The army was to pay dearly for the influence of the conservatives and for its failure to pay sufficient attention to the reports from the Russian front in the Russo-Japanese War.

For the Royal Navy the situation was very different. While the Russo-Japanese War was being fought, the First Sea Lord, Sir John Fisher, was beginning to revolutionize the British fleets to prepare them for twentieth-century warfare.[30] In the nineteenth century, because the Navy lacked conventional challenges, it could spread its gunboats around the world on imperial duties. It could also afford to lag behind technical innovations because having the largest fleet meant that it had time to catch up, it also meant that innovation could potentially outdate its fleet and give its enemies the advantage. Now Fisher believed that it could afford neither to deploy gunboats broadcast across the world, nor to lag behind its enemies. Fisher brought the gunboats home and scrapped them. He also planned the introduction of new fast capital ships. These would be equipped with very large guns, all of the same calibre which would make every battleship afloat obsolete. This was the origin of *Dreadnought* and all its successors.

The war largely confirmed the wisdom of Fisher's policies. At the outset, two small Russian warships were easily attacked and destroyed by the Japanese off the coast of Korea, confirming the vulnerability of such dispersed vessels.[31] Troubridge emphasized the very great range at which Port Arthur was bombarded by the Japanese from the start of the war: 'The most remarkable feature of the operations ... is the great range at which ships and forts now engage. It may be doubted whether any ships of any navy have ever practised firing at 8,000 metres and yet at that distance three Russian cruisers were driven into harbour.'[32] Pakenham reported that the key battle of 10 August 1904 was fought at even longer range. On this occasion the Russian fleet based in Port Arthur tried to escape to Vladivostok before the Japanese armies destroyed it in harbour. It nearly succeeded until the Russian flagship, *Tsarevitch*, was disabled at very long range. 'Firing begins to look possible at 20,000 metres, reasonable at 14,000, close range may begin at 10,000 metres and at 5,000 ships might as well be alongside each other as far as appearance and sensation of proximity go.'[33]

Thus Pakenham confirmed that ships needed very large guns, as Fisher had predicted. But Pakenham and Fisher were not always in agreement and the 'lessons' of the naval war were not always so clear. The final and most famous naval battle of the war, Tsushima, was fought at much shorter range. The Japanese so dominated Rojestvensky's squadron, which had struggled round the world from the Baltic, that it was able to close to 3,000 yards and destroy the Russian fleet in the straits between Japan and Korea.[34] Not only was this particular battle confusing to many analysts but Pakenham was not in favour of firing the guns in a broadside as Fisher and other reformers intended at the Admiralty. Their view was that, if all the guns fired together, the fall of the shot would be easier to spot and corrections to the aim could be made more easily. Pakenham and Jackson reported that 'spotting' had failed completely during the war and doubted the wisdom of the central control of the guns.[35] Fisher argued, quite rightly, that this was because the guns were of different calibres and the firing system used by the Japanese was now out of date. Fisher also had to struggle against the distinguished American naval writer, Admiral A.T.Mahan who argued that the battle of Tsushima had shown that speed was not a major factor in modern engagements. Here Pakenham and Fisher were in agreement that superior speed enabled the Japanese admiral to overcome the mistakes of his cruisers who initially misinformed him about the direction of the Russian ships.[36] It also made it possible for him to concentrate his fire on the Russian vessels. *Dreadnought* was to be very fast as well as heavily armed.

If the influence of the observers on British naval and military policy is thus a complex one, so is their influence on political relations between Britain and Japan. The British press generally greeted Japan's victories with euphoria. The courage of the Japanese troops, the efficiency of their fleets and the determination of the small island state to defeat the Russian 'bully' were all deeply admired. But there were reservations. In 1904 Angus Hamilton's classic study of Korea criticized the behaviour of Japanese merchants and others in the 'Land of Morning Calm' in the strongest possible terms: 'They are debauched in business, and the prevalence of dishonourable practices in public life makes them indifferent to private virtue... The modesty, cleanliness, and politeness, so characteristic of the Japanese, are conspicuously absent in their settlements in this country.'[37]

Not only were there doubts about the character of Japanese imperialism, doubts which grew stronger with the passing years, but the Japanese lost the sympathy of many of the correspondents and military officers who came to observe the war. Nicholson warned against the bias of the returning journalists: '... many of them are out of temper – God knows why – and have gone back openly boasting that they will do their best to injure Japan in the estimation of the British public'.[38] The journalists' complaints were, quite surprisingly, often dismissed by the British press which saw that belligerents had to impose censorship and that the Japanese had done their best to accommodate the 100 or so foreign correspondents who descended on Tokyo.[38]

If the press was divided about the nature of Japanese politics and its emerging world role, so were the military observers. Sir Ian Hamilton's published account of his time with the Japanese, *A Staff Officer's Scrapbook*, suggested that he was distinctly pro-Japanese. As he wrote in the introduction: '... our allies are war-like by taste and tradition; and upon the patriotism, which they have absorbed with their mother's milk, their government has been careful to graft initiative, quickness and intelligence'.[39] Hamilton admired Japanese education, which he said was in advance of British, but in private he warned the editors of *The Times* about the Japanese mistreatment of the Koreans and about Japan's long-term intentions which he construed were anti-British.[40] Haldane appears to have been almost as cautious. On the other hand, many of the language officers were deeply sympathetic towards the Japanese and plainly loved and admired their society. Writing in 1924 M.D. Kennedy, who had served as a language officer in Japan from 1917 to 1920, dismissed claims that the Japanese were militaristic and their policy in Korea and Manchuria was repressive and brutal.[41] Another officer, who served for extensive periods in Japan, F.S.G. Piggott continued to defend his Japanese officer friends even after the Second World War.[42]

Was the British effort to learn from the Russo-Japanese War cost-effective from their point of view? The British service ministries were obviously disappointed with the sales of the official histories and they never again made such an effort to learn from a foreign war.[43] Yet the effort was fully justified. After such a long period of peace and with major threats emerging, the British armed forces needed to learn everything possible from the fighting between Russia and Japan. If Admiralty and War Office expectations were disappointed, it was because they were unrealistic, even naïve. Vested interests within the British armed forces themselves blocked the acceptance of some of the tactical, strategic and political 'lessons', but more than enough was learned to justify the effort involved.

From the Japanese point of view, the hospitality offered to the military attachés and correspondents was the price they had to pay for their exposed international position. They continued to raise money on international exchanges and they kept the other powers neutral. They were regarded in Britain as the 'Davids' who had slain the Russian 'Goliaths'. Some of the officers involved became firm and lasting friends of Japan who did their utmost in the 1920s and 1930s to prevent Anglo-Japanese alienation. The disadvantages included the anger of many of the correspondents because of Japanese secrecy and dilatoriness, and distrust of Japan engendered by the reports of the Japanese behaviour in Korea. Tokyo undoubtedly gained from the observers' presence in the short run; in the long run the advantages and disadvantages were more finely balanced.

15

Natsume Sōseki and the Pre-Raphaelites
The depiction of Ophelia in Sōseki's The Three-Cornered World

SAMMY I. TSUNEMATSU

FIFTEEN YEARS after Commodore Perry arrived in Japan with his five Black Ships in 1853, the Meiji government was established. During the closing years of the nineteenth century and the beginning of the present century, the Meiji government sent groups of Japanese overseas to learn from the countries of the West. The main destinations of these students were first of all, the United States, Britain and France, but from 1861, increasing numbers went to Germany. Their main object of study was research into military science, pure science and shipbuilding with the aim of catching up with Western civilization, but there were also numbers of students of the humanities including law, economics, literature and education. Those who came to Britain to study the humanities included Kanda Naibu, Baba Tatsui, Shimamura Hōgetsu, Tsuchii Bansui, Okakura Yoshisaburō and Natsume Sōseki.

The two great figures of modern Japanese literature are indisputably Mori Ōgai and Natsume Sōseki. Both studied in Europe in the latter part of the nineteenth century. As a military doctor, Mori Ōgai went to Germany in 1884 to study hygiene for four years at government expense. Sōseki was the Japanese Ministry of Education's first overseas scholar in Britain, and spent two years and two months there, from 28 October 1900 to 5 December 1902. Reading Ōgai's *German Diary*, one is struck by how positive his account is in comparison to Sōseki's and how he enjoyed his studies overseas to the full. I have previously discussed[1] why it should be that two people should have such different experiences of their study abroad, but undoubtedly their respective ages at the time, family situations, and differences in personality resulting from their birthplaces were all factors. Ōgai's study was medicine and his field hygiene, a very practical area with universal application. Despite some linguistic difficulties he could clearly see his studies progress. On the other hand, Sōseki studied English literature with linguistics, concentrating on the vague area 'what is literature?' So it is perhaps unremarkable that Ōgai and Sōseki's attitudes to their research and their lives as students overseas should be as contrasting as light and darkness.

* * *

A portrait of Sōseki was used for the Japanese 1,000 yen note put out in 1984, and most of his works have been translated into Chinese, Korean, English of course, French, German and Italian, yet sadly in the UK his name is probably less well known than those of Mishima Yukio or Endō Shūsaku. Sōseki wrote:

> The two years I spent in London were the most unpleasant years of my life. Among English gentlemen I lived in misery, like a poor dog that had strayed among a pack of wolves. I understand the population of London is about five million. Frankly speaking, I felt as if I were a drop of water amid five million drops of oil. If a clean white shirt fresh from the laundry gets stained by a drop of ink, the owner is sure to be angry ... My departure from England on the completion of my period of two years there may be compared to the return of a wild goose in spring'.[2]

From this most scholars have taken the view that Sōseki did not take full advantage of his stay in London. But were the two years of Sōseki's study in London really a failure? The truth may lie somewhere else, because after Sōseki went back to Tokyo, he often took his wife Kyōko and daughter Fudeko to musical concerts in order to learn Western manners.[3] In this paper, I would like to explore how Sōseki's time in London influenced his works and the world view that informed his life.

Sōseki's student life in London is described in his *Diary* and *Letters*, while a number of works are the direct fruits of his studies, including *London Tō* (Tower of London), *Carlyle Hakubutsukan* (The Carlyle Museum), *Jitensha Nikki* (The Diary of a Bicycle Rider) and a number of essays from *Eijitsu Shohin* (Sketches of a long spring day) such as *Geshuku* (Lodgings), *Kako no nioi* (Smells of the past), *Atatakai Yume* (Warm Dreams), *Kiri* (Fog), *Inshō* (Impressions), and *Henka* (Change). Aside from these, in Sōseki's autobiographical novel *Botchan* (1906), which is well-known to almost every Japanese, there is a scene where Botchan and Red-shirt go fishing together. There is a conversation where Red-shirt says to Noda: 'Look at that pine tree. Its trunk is so straight and it spreads upwards like an open umbrella. Turner would have drawn such a tree.' and Noda replies: 'Yes, it is a genuine Turner. What a perfect curve! A Turner itself!'[4] The work they are referring to is Turner's 1832 'Child Harold's Pilgrimage – Italy' where it really does open up like an umbrella. Turner is the water colourist, J.M.W.Turner (1775-1851) and it is likely that during his stay in London, Sōseki would have turned his steps to the Tate Gallery to see the Turner paintings.

Another passage, from the unfinished novel *Meian* (Light and Darkness), suggests the influence of Sōseki's stay in England in his literary imagination. Mr Okamoto went to the outside of Mansion House to see the coronation of Edward VII and Alexandra. But he was too short to see the coronation so he sat on the shoulders of his landlord to watch it British style:

> You probably were too heavy and crushed the poor foreigner. If that had happened he'd have been proud of it, but instead he merely hung on to this large man's shoulders, in the middle of a London crowd, while everyone was staring at him amazed. He did it to see the procession.
> Okamoto still did not laugh.
> What story are you cooking up? When in the world is this supposed to have happened?
> At the time of coronation of Edward VII. You were standing in front of the Mansion House trying to see the procession. But, unlike us, people over there are all much taller than you, so out of desperation you asked the owner of the boarding-house who'd gone with you if you could get on his shoulders.
> Don't tell such silly stories. It was somebody else. I know perfectly well the fellow who did that. It was that Monkey-face.[5]

In Japan at that time it would doubtless have been considered disrespectful to look down on the coronation of an emperor. In fact this incident which appears in Sōseki's work was an actual happening, for Sōseki had sat on the shoulders of Mr Brett, his third landlord, to watch the funeral procession of Queen Victoria in Park Lane. In his diary he writes: 'It's the coronation today but I was so horrified by the crowds at the funeral procession of Queen Victoria that I have decided not to go.'[6] From this we can see that Sōseki used his own experiences in London in a number of his works. In the last of his works like *Meian* these were literary embellishments and details, which would not have existed if Sōseki had not spent time in London.

Sokuten kyōshi (to forsake the self and follow Heaven) could be described as Sōseki's motto but it is not widely known that the experiences that resulted in that world view were those he encountered in London:

> My next step was to strengthen – perhaps I should say to build anew – the foundations on which I stood in my study of literature. For this, I began to read books that had nothing whatever to do with literature. If, before, I had been other-centered, it occurred to me now that I must become self-centered. I became absorbed in scientific studies, philosophical speculation, anything that would support this position. . . .
>
> Having been born into the world, I had to find something to do. But what that something was, I had no idea. I stood paralyzed, alone and shut in by a fog, hoping that even more that I could turn a searchlight outward and find a lighted path ahead, however narrow. But wherever I looked, there was only obscurity, a formless blur. I felt as if I had been sealed in a sack.
>
> Once I had grasped this idea of self-centerednes, it became for me an enormous fund of strength, even defiance. Who did these Westerners think they were anyway? I had been feeling lost, in a daze, when the idea of ego-centeredness told me where to stand, showed me the road I must take. Self-centeredness became for me a new beginning, I confess, and it helped me to find what I thought would be my life's work.[7]

Another work which bears the imprint of Sōseki's time in London is *The Three-Cornered World*. I shall now explore here the depiction of Ophelia in this story. Sōseki once told an American who was conducting research for an English translation of his work: 'Sorry. There is none of my works I wish to be read by Americans',[8] though one must read in that comment an element of Japanese self-deprecation.

The Three-Cornered World was first published in the September 1906 edition of the literary magazine *Shinshōsetsu* (New Novels). Sōseki wrote it in a mere 15 days, beginning on 26 July and completing the work on 9 August. At the time Sōseki was teaching at Tokyo Imperial University and Meiji University, so it was just the time of the summer vacation: 'I didn't set out with the idea that writing novels was my real work, but it was as though there was something that I had wanted to write for a long time but which had been stifled and once I began to write, it all came pouring out at once.'[9] Of the content of *The Three-Cornered World*, Sōseki himself said: 'There is no plot and nothing really happens'.[10]

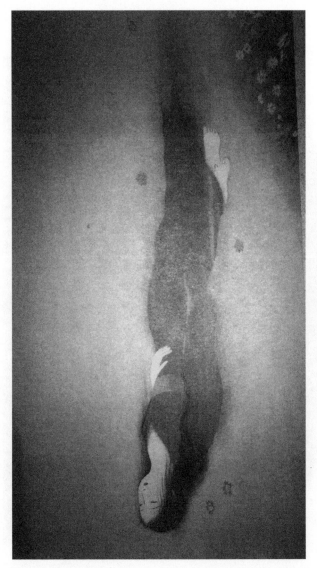

Figure 1.3 : Ophelia in the stream by Yamamoto Kyujin (p.7)

Figure 2.3: Ophelia by John Everett Millais (p.12)

Figure 3.3: Hogsmill where Millais painted the background of his Ophelia (p.12)

If there is anything we can call a story, it begins when the painter, who has begun climbing a mountain path in his search for the state of detachment from humanity, reaches a tea house in a mountain pass. As he rests there, the artist overhears the old lady talking to the pack-horse driver Gen about his new bride and is overwhelmed with curiosity. He tries to paint a picture of the bride:

> Strange enough, although I had a clear impression of the clothes, the hair-style, the horse and the cherry tree, the one thing I just could not picture was the bride's face. I was searching my mind of a face that would fit, trying now one type, now another, when suddenly the face of Millais' Ophelia came to me, and slipped neatly into place beneath the high 'Shimada' hair-style. 'No, that's no good,' I thought, and immediately allowed my carefully built up picture to disintegrate. The clothes, the hair-style, the horse and the cherry tree, all completely disappeared in an instant from the scene I had created. Somewhere deep within me, however, the misty figure of Ophelia being carried along by the stream, her hands folded in prayer, remained. It was as indestructable as a cloud of smoke which, when you beat at it with a fan, merely thins and becomes less palpable.[11]

The Millais referred to here was John Everett Millais (1829-96) one of the founders of the Victorian art movement, the Pre-Raphaelites. (His painting of Ophelia was loaned for exhibition in Japan for the UK98 Festival, where it was very popular.) Ophelia was completed in 1852, with Elizabeth Siddle, later to be the wife of Dante Gabriel Rosetti, as the model. The painting is an attempt to visualize the watery death of Ophelia as told by Queen Gertrude in Act 4 Scene 7 of Shakespeare's *Hamlet*. The sudden reference to Ophelia (Chapter 2, *Three-Cornered World*) may seem somewhat incongruous to today's readers, but at the time Sōseki was writing the novel, Tsubouchi Shōyō's translation of *Hamlet* was very popular in Japan.

But why Ophelia? We must first not overlook the fact that Millais' Ophelia comprises three elements, the tragic love of a young girl, her death and '*the sight of her floating in the water*.' Sōseki wrote a short story called *Kairokō* (A dirge) in 1905, in which the character, Elaine, portrayed in the last section *Fune* (The boat) behaves in much the same way. 'The pitiful Elaine' who spends her years in 'the old castle Astolat, like a violet unseen by humans' grows weary of this world because of her unrequited love for Lancelot and, refusing to eat, chooses death. On her deathbed she asks her father and brother to put her remains on a bark and float it towards Camelot:[12]

On and on, the boat drifted along with no destination, only

a cargo: a beautiful corpse surrounded by silks and flowers and accompanied by a silent old man, as lifeless as a wooden doll. Apart from his arms, which moved rhythmatically, dipping the long oar into the calm waters, he showed no sign of life.[12]

This scene appears in Tennyson's epic poem *Idylls of the King* subtitled 'Lancelot and Elaine'. John Atkinson Grimshaw (1836-93), an artist with close links to the Pre-Raphaelites, painted the same scene. The second section of *Kairokō*, entitled *Kagami* (*The mirror*) is a working of the story of the Lady of Shallot, a young woman who is fated to die because of her love for Lancelot. This section, too, is taken from a Tennyson poem, *The Lady of Shallot*, and is more or less a direct description of a painting of the same name by Holman Hunt, another of the Pre-Raphaelites. The Lady of Shallot sets off down the river in a boat and dies. Yet another Pre-Raphaelite, William Waterhouse (1849-1917) also painted this scene. For Sōseki, who had entered the world of pitiful stories so loved by the Pre-Raphaelites with images linking love and death or death and running water, as shown by their use of the Lady of Shallot, it was only natural that he should recollect Millais' 'Ophelia', so much a part of this tradition.

★   ★   ★

Twenty-seven Japanese artists including Matsuoka Eikyū created a scroll painting of *The Three-Cornered World*; it consists of 27 paintings in three scrolls. 'Ophelia in the stream' by Yamamoto Kyujin is painting number 14 in the second scroll. Ophelia in this scroll does not have her hands folded and no robin sits in the branches of the willow. Her features are those of a young peaceful Japanese woman. In Millais' painting, her eyes are slightly open and, with her parted lips and outstretched arms, she seems deep in prayer, almost in a state of rapture, about to embrace heaven's glory. Sōseki must have been struck by the sense that, rather than the expression of one racked with pain, hers is that of one enveloped in the ecstasy of death, passing quietly into God's kingdom. The woman in a green robe floating on the water in the scroll painting is not the tragic heroine of Shakespeare's play. One can imagine Nami, daughter of Nakoi hot spring, giving instructions to the artist to 'show her floating gently in death on the water to which she has committed her body'.[13]

Sōseki was not simply influenced by the Pre-Raphaelites. Sōseki's wife, Kyōko, attempted suicide by drowning, an event which may well have been a factor in his work. The incident took place in June 1898, while Sōseki was working at the Kumamoto 5th High School. They had been married two years. Kyōko was suffering from a nervous breakdown when she threw herself in the Shirakawa river, swollen at the time with the spring rains. Fortunately, she was rescued by some fishermen and was not seriously hurt. The incident appears to have had a significant psychological effect on Sōseki, who used it later in *The Three-Cornered World*.

> Once her fit had subsided and Kyōko had fallen asleep, Kinnosuke (Sōseki) exhausted from caring for her began to doze. The next thing he knew, Kyōko's bed was empty and she was floating down the river like Ophelia. The river was the Shirakawa, but it was as though the river was flowing through the dark recesses of his consciousness and Kyōko was swept along in its jet-black current.[14]

The biographical critic Etō Jun tells us that Sōseki was consistently troubled by these illusions.

I am still researching how the theme of death by drowning by young girls is treated in Japanese literature. However, it is likely that many things contributed to Sōseki's ideas including the *Song of Ophelia* which was translated in Mori Ōgai's *Omokage* (Shadow) (1889) and had a profound impact on literary society. Further powerful stimuli were provided by the images of the Lady of Shallot, Elaine and Ophelia gained from his reading of Tennyson's poems and contact with the paintings of the Pre-Raphaelites. In the classical literary form of *Kairokō* Sōseki succeeded in creating a harmony of East and West. With *The Three-Cornered World* he attempts to go beyond Western art in a search for a Japanese sense of beauty, and presents himself as both narrator and artist. The artist becomes fixed on Ophelia's expression and is dissatisfied, finding it piteous, but his theory of beauty in relation to her countenance succeeds through the discovery of a particularly Japanese sensibility.

THE EXACT LOCATION WHERE MILLAIS PAINTED THE BACKGROUND OF HIS OPHELIA

So where indeed, did Millais paint the scene he used as the background to his Ophelia? Each year over 20 books and more than 200 research papers on Sōseki are published, but though many refer to the link between *The Three-Cornered World* and Ophelia, I have yet to read an attempt to find real proof of this.

In the summer of 1851, Hunt and Millais spent a day at the Hogsmill river in Surrey to paint backgrounds for *The Hireling Shepherd* and *Ophelia in the Stream*. Their choice was determined by the fact that Hunt's grandparents, Mr & Mrs Hobman, lived at Rectory Farm in Ewell and that Hunt, who visited them frequently, was very fond of the rural scenery in the area. There had been a thirteenth century church near Rectory Farm, but this had been pulled down in 1848, so when Hunt and Millais visited in 1851 the new church would just have been completed.

In his work, *Pre-Raphaelitism and the Pre-Raphaelite Brotherhood*, Holman Hunt wrote:

> Millais agreed with me that for the subject of 'Ophelia in the Stream', which he had settled upon, and made a hasty sketch for, and for mine of 'The Hireling Shepherd', there was good probability of finding backgrounds along the banks of the little stream taking its rise and giving its name to our favourite haunt, Ewell; accordingly we gave a day to the exploration. Descending the stream for a mile from its source, I soon found all the material I wanted for my landscape composition...[15]

By coincidence, the Lemprière family, close friends from Millais' childhood in Jersey, also lived in Ewell. Millais was particularly friendly with the two sons, Arthur, later Major-General Lemprière, and Harry. In 1899 Arthur wrote of his friend Millais: 'We always called him "Johnny", and he constantly spent the holidays with us at our home in Ewell, Surrey. My father and mother and all of our family were very fond of him, as well as he of us.'[16] It was, however, only when they were students that Hunt and Millais discovered that they each had friends in Ewell.

'Arriving on a visit to this favourite spot, Millais and myself,' Hunt continues, 'looked in vain during a long tracing of the changing water, walking along beaten lanes, and jumping over ditches and ruts in turn, without lighting upon a point that would suit my companion.'[17] The two men walked some considerable distance searching for a suitable spot:

> Many fresh hopes were shattered, until he well-nigh felt despair, but round a turn in the meadows at Cuddington we pursued the crystal driven weeds with reawakening faith, when suddenly the 'Millais luck' (a phrase which became a proverb) presented him with the exact composition of arboreal and floral richness he had dreamed of, so that he pointed exultantly, saying 'Look! Could anything be so perfect?' And we sat down to enjoy its loveliness, as surely as many thousand other revellers in the beauty of such scenery have since done before the finished picture.[18]

In his work, *The Pre-Raphaelites in Ewell and a Missing Masterpiece*, Charles Abdy writes: 'The precise location is unclear, but it seems to have been somewhere in the vicinity of Worcester Park Road'; it was not possible to locate precisely the background for Ophelia.

Let us now examine carefully, the painting of Ophelia in the Tate Gallery collection. The stream appears to flow at the same time from left to right and from right to left. However, visiting the Hogsmill painted by Millais, it is immediately obvious that it flows from right to left. In other words, Millais was on the west bank facing the river and painted the left side. Millais wrote to Mrs Combe on 2 July 1851: 'I sit tailor-fashion under an umbrella throwing a shadow scarcely larger than a halfpenny for eleven hours, with a child's mug within reach to satisfy my thirst from the running stream beside me.'[19] From the use of the word 'shadow' in this letter, we can deduce that if it was Malden on the opposite side to the Manor House Garden, then he was painting facing the west side.

The bank behind Ophelia is particularly high, but in other places the land is low lying with the river almost reaching the same height as its banks. Visiting the Surrey Record Office with this information and studying the records of Malden Church, I uncovered two particularly useful records of Henry Stapylton, vicar in 1851. On page 197 of one, a large scrapbook, he writes:

> In the early days of the Pre-Raphaelite school of painting Sir John Millais in company with Messrs Hunt and Collins, artists, had lodgings for the Summer season in a farm house that then stood at the end of the Worcester Park Avenue. John Millais then painted his picture 'Ophelia drowning' by the side of the brook below the Manor House.[20]

This allows us to guess at the location, but still does not pinpoint it exactly. But in a file of material, 'Historical Notes' by Henry Stapylton, there are 46 sheets closely covered in small handwriting. A careful reading brings to light a reference to the precise spot where Ophelia was painted. He starts:

> In the summer of 1851 it was occupied by Sir John Millais and Messrs Holman Hunt and Charles Collins . . .? Member of the school of art called Pre-Raphaelite Brethren . . . and the willow about 100 yards above the footbridge across the Hogsmill leading to Surbiton was the background of his Ophelia painted in 1851.[21]

According to these materials, crossing the Hogsmill by a small footbridge below the Manor House and walking about 100 yards, one reaches a dead end. Looking down at the river from the left-hand bank we can still see a large willow tree on the right. This is very likely the spot from where Millais painted the background for Ophelia.

★ ★ ★

3000 volumes belonging to Sōseki are now housed in the Tōhoku University library, because one of his disciples, Komiya Toyotaka, was director there. The collection includes many works on art, but an investigation of the 15 volumes of Newnes Art Library: *National Gallery: A Catalogue of the National Gallery of British Art* (Tate Gallery) reveals no picture of Ophelia. Could it be that another disciple or student had borrowed one of Sōseki's books?

In *The Three-Cornered World*, Sōseki describes 'Ophelia, floating in the river with her hands folden in prayer'. However, Millais' Ophelia does not have her hands folded but lies on the water with her arms outstretched, (more than a shoulder-width apart). It is well known that Sōseki was highly strung but at the same time there was a part of him that was quite *laissez faire*. He is a writer highly esteemed in the Japanese national consciousness; he used many complicated *kanji* characters which needed Japanese readings alongside, yet one is frequently amazed by writings which betray a hazy recollection. Referring to the Noh play *Takasago* in the second chapter of *The Three-Cornered World*, Sōseki writes of an '. . . old man using a broom to sweep as he crosses a bridge'. But Sōseki is mistaken, it is an old woman who uses a broom, the old man uses a rake. So taking these things into careful consideration, it is certain that Sōseki will have seen Millais' Ophelia during his time in London. However, he was unable to find a reproduction of the painting, nor was it featured in any of the books he bought. So Sōseki presented an image of Ophelia dredged up from the hazy recesses of his memory.

Taking a painting of Ophelia as an example, we have seen that Sōseki was impressed by British painting, particularly the Pre-Raphaelites. Himself a water-colourist, he created a Japanese-style Ophelia in keeping with his own sensibility. We can demonstrate that the two years Sōseki spent as a student in London, were of great value to Sōseki the novelist.

16

A Great Ordinary Man: Saitō Makoto (1858-1936) and Anglo-Japanese Relations[1]

TADASHI KURAMATSU

> ... I am definitely not a great man or indeed anyone of
> significance. I am just an ordinary man. I have just tried my
> best in whatever I did; and, before I knew it, people have
> promoted me to lofty positions.

ADMIRAL VISCOUNT SAITŌ MAKOTO is one of the best
known figures in the history of pre-war Japan. Students of modern
Japanese history may not be familiar with his earlier distinguished
career as a naval officer (the only one ever appointed Navy Vice-
Minister while still a mere Captain) or as the longest-serving
Governor-General of Korea (for over ten years). Nevertheless, they
probably remember that he was appointed Prime Minister at the age of
73 after the 1932 15 May Incident, on the advice of Prince Saionji
Kinmochi, putting an end to a brief period of party government in pre-
war Japan; he is also remembered for the fact that he met a tragic death
at the hands of rebel Army officers in the 1936 26 February Incident.

He represented one of those pro-Western moderate Japanese who
remained a friend of Britain throughout their life.[2] Unlike Admiral
Tōgō Heihachirō, who spent over seven years training in Britain or on
board British ships, Saitō's time in Britain amounted to less than nine
months in all. Still he always kept his affection for Britain, which
probably started with his training at the Naval Academy under British
instructors and was strengthened through various contacts he had over
the years, especially at the time of the Russo-Japanese War of 1904-5.

This paper focuses on his earlier life when Japan was emerging as a modern state in the Meiji and Taishō periods under the major influence of, amongst other countries, Britain, and will neglect the period after 1932 when he was catapulted into the centre of Japanese politics.

★ ★ ★

Saitō Makoto was born in Mizusawa, a small city in Iwate prefecture on 27 October 1858. Although small, Mizusawa is notable for having produced three well-known people: Takano Chōei,[3] Gotō Shinpei[4] and Saitō himself. Gotō and Saitō were born in the same street called Kichikoji. Saitō was a year junior to Gotō and medicine, and they were good friends from childhood.

In 1869 with the introduction of the new prefectural system (*hanseki hokan*) by the Meiji government, Gotō and Saitō started to work as *shosei*, private secretaries (or apprentices) to senior officials at the Izawa prefecture office, who were sent from Tokyo and therefore needed people with local knowledge. It was often the case that bright young *shosei* accompanied these officials when they were recalled to Tokyo after a few years, and Saitō was no exception, arriving in Tokyo in April 1872 at the age of thirteen. Without any relatives or a good wealthy patron, Saitō took the exam for the Army Junior Academy (*Rikugun Yōnen Gakkō*) the following February. Although he achieved the required mark, he came twenty-first when the number of government-funded places were limited to twenty. Told that he would be accepted on a privately-funded basis he had to give up. He then applied to the Naval Academy (*Kaigun Heigakkō*)[5] and took the exam in September. A few days later, seventy-two students were asked to spend a two-week probation period at the Academy for further selection and Saitō was one of them. Ironically at the same time, the Army Junior Academy sent for Saitō because somebody had dropped out creating a vacancy. But a couple of weeks at the Naval Academy were enough for Saitō to make up his mind that the Navy was his calling. Luckily, he made it to the final selection and entered the Academy in October 1873.

At this time the Academy was located at Tsukiji in Tokyo and had just welcomed thirty-four British instructors headed by Lieutenant-Commander Archibald Douglas in July. In those days, the entrance examination to the Naval Academy could be taken in Chinese (*kanbun*), English, Mathematics or a combination of these. Having passed it by taking only Chinese, the first major problem awaiting Saitō was that not only were all the textbooks in English but so also were all the instructions! Among his belongings still kept at the Saitō Memorial

Museum is a notebook titled 'English Phrases' from his student days.[6] One notable change in his life happened sometime in 1875 while he was at the Academy. He altered his name from Tomigorō, his birth name, to Makoto, partly because people often told him that Tomigorō sounded like a name of a gangster and also there was at the Academy another Saitō Tomigorō who was a seaman from a training ship. After three years of study at the Academy, and nearly two years on board training ships, which took him from Vladivostok to Singapore, Saitō graduated from the Academy in July 1879. He was third in his class of sixteen, and became a midshipman. After one further year of training he was assigned to HIJMS *Fusō* in May 1880, which was the best ship the Imperial Japanese Navy (IJN) had at the time.[7]

In February 1884 he was promoted to the rank of sub-lieutenant and assigned to the Naval Affairs Bureau. The director of the bureau was Rear-Admiral Nire Kagenori, who was the headmaster of the Naval Academy at the time of Saitō's graduation and also his future father-in-law. This was to be the start of his distinguished career as a naval officer on land rather than at sea. Before settling into his new life on land, however, he was sent to the United States and appointed the first naval attaché in Washington at the age of twenty-five – a remarkable achievement though it was probably more a reflection on the status of the United States as a naval power at the time.[8] Just a week after he was told of his new assignment he was on board the *Oceanic*. He was joined by the party of Prince Yamashina (later Higashi-Fushimi) who was on his way to Europe. Also aboard was Mutsu Munemitsu, who had been released from prison in Sendai the previous year and advised by Itō Hirobumi to broaden his experience overseas. The ship arrived at San Francisco on 12 May and Saitō took a train to New York two days later.[9] After spending some time in New York and having seen off the Prince, Saitō finally arrived at Washington on 22 June.

Saitō stayed in the post for over four-and-a-half years and paid frequent visits to munitions factories, laboratories and navy yards, acquiring information about the latest inventions. He also made acquaintance with naval officers of the US Navy. Probably more important in terms of his career prospects, he often acted as an interpreter and guide to many parties of prominent Japanese, who were on 'Inspection Tours (*shisatsu ryoko*)', which were very popular in those days and whose members usually passed through the United States before proceeding to Europe. In one such tour, Navy Minister Saigō Tsugumichi (half-brother of Takamori) came to the United States in 1885 on his 'world inspection tour' and Saitō, after acting as a guide to the party in the States, accompanied it on its European tour. The party sailed from New York on 4 September on board Cunard's SS *Aurania*.

After a week they arrived in Liverpool. For Saitō, it was the first of three visits to Britain. The party's fifty-day tour of Britain included a visit to the Armstrong factories in Newcastle, various factories in Glasgow, Sheffield and Manchester, naval yards in Chatham, Davenport and Portsmouth, and also the Thames Iron Works to which he was to return ten years later to take over the battleship HIJMS *Fuji*. The party then went on to France and Germany. While in Paris, Saitō was introduced to Hara Takashi, the chargé d'affaires at the Embassy. Being separately funded from the main party, the long sojourn in Europe and – by his own admission – excessive drinking, left Saitō without sufficient resources to sail back to America. Having heard that the embassy usually kept a contingency fund, he asked Hara for a loan of 6,970 francs, which was duly granted. In Berlin, Saitō said farewell to the party and went back to London where he was asked to accompany another inspection party headed by Count Kuroda Kiyotaka[10] to the United States, because there was no one in the party who spoke English! They left Liverpool on 26 February and arrived in New York on 8 March. Saitō's visits to Europe culminated in the so-called 'Saitō report', which included 126 pages on Britain.[11]

After four-and-a-half years overseas, Saitō returned to Japan in October 1888. Having spent six months working at the Naval Staff, he was assigned to the HIJMS *Takao*, to oversee the final stage of its construction at the Yokosuka Naval Yard under the command of (acting) Captain Yamamoto Gonbei. In July 1889 with the creation of the first standing Fleet (*Jobi kantai*)[12] Saitō, now Lieutenant, was appointed staff officer under its C-in-C Rear-Admiral Inoue Yoshika. After two years on board HIJMS *Takachiho*, the flagship, he was back in Tokyo, attached to the Naval Staff.[13] Here he spent just under a year and then, having spent a year-and-a-half as the first officer of HIJMS *Takao*, he was promoted to the rank of Lieutenant-Commander and assigned to the Naval Affairs Bureau of the Navy Ministry in December 1893. It was then that his name started to appear in diplomatic matters concerning Britain.

The first one was the *Chishima* incident of 30 November 1892, when the gunboat, HIJMS *Chishima*, collided with the British ship SS *Ravenna* off Ehime prefecture. Although the damage to *Ravenna* was not serious, *Chishima* sank with the loss of its seventy-four crewmen. The Japanese government brought a lawsuit to the consular court in Yokohama, asking for 850,000 dollars compensation. The owner of the *Ravenna*, the Peninsular & Oriental (P & O) Steamship Company, brought a counter suit for 100,000 dollars but the court ruled that, because the incident took place within Japanese territorial waters, the counter suit was not admissible. The P & O then took the matter to the British High Court in Shanghai which overturned the judgement of the Yokohama court. Then the Japanese government asked for leave to bring the matter to the House of Lords, which was granted on 14 November 1893. It was at this stage that Saitō was assigned to the Navy Ministry and ordered to help the case. Though his involvement was limited and more to do with his reputation as an English expert, it led to another assignment of more serious nature concerning another naval incident with Britain.[14] On 25 July 1894, as the first shots in the Sino-Japanese War had been exchanged, the Japanese cruiser, HIJMS *Naniwa*, commanded by Captain Tōgō Heihachirō, sank the British merchant ship SS *Kowshing* with over a thousand Chinese troops on board.[15]

Concerned with the initially hostile reaction from Britain, the Japanese government immediately appointed an enquiry commission headed by the Director of Legal Bureau, Suematsu Kenchō[16] and the Cabinet named Saitō as its naval member. His appointment probably came from his earlier connection formed in the United States since the Navy Minister at the time was Saigō Tsugumichi, and the Foreign Minister Mutsu Munemitsu.[17] On 29 July the commission left for Sasebo, where the captain and other crew of *Kowshing* were being held, and eleven days later they were back in Tokyo. The next day Suematsu submitted to the Foreign Minister a report, which exonerated Tōgō from any wrongdoing.

On 7 September Saitō was appointed equerry to the Emperor and accompanied him to Hiroshima, where the Imperial Headquarters (Dai-honei) was moved six days later. Having established command of the sea in the battle of the Yalu on 17 September, the Japanese destroyed the rest of the Chinese fleet at Weihaiwei and the Chinese C-in-C Admiral Ting Juch'ang surrendered on 13 February 1895. Now the war was practically over (the Peace Treaty was signed on 16 April), Saitō was back on sea duty, appointed first officer on HIJMS *Izumi* on 20 February, and then staff officer of the Standing Fleet on board its flagship HIJMS *Matsushima* on 17 May.

In October 1897 Saitō was appointed second-in-command of the team in charge of supervising the completion of *Fuji*, being built at the Thames Iron Works, and then of bringing her back safely to Japan. Compared with the then flagship *Matsushima*'s 4,200-ton, *Fuji* displaced 12,500-tons with four 12-inch guns and was the first ironclad of the IJN. It took a long time for the appropriations bill for the building of *Fuji* and *Yashima*, her sister ship, to be approved by the Diet, and on the way it created some disturbance on the Japanese political scene. The Diet itself had just opened in 1890 and in its early days it was common for the members to fight over the budget submitted by the Satsuma-Chōshū clique governments which were directly appointed by the Emperor. The building plan which included two battleships had first been incorporated into a budget submitted by the Matsukata Masayoshi government in 1891 to the Second Imperial Diet, which omitted all the building costs. Matsukata's government dissolved the session and resubmitted its budget to the Third Diet, which again rejected it and the Cabinet resigned.[18] Itō Hirobumi then formed his second Cabinet in August 1892 and submitted its budget to the Fourth Diet, which cut the total expenditure by ten per cent including the building costs. Although the Diet passed this revised bill on 7 February 1893, it threw the Itō government into crisis. This debâcle led to the Meiji Emperor's message (*Sho-choku*) on 10 February 1893, asking for cooperation between the government and Diet. The message also said:

> In the matter of national security, one day's delay might lead to 100-years of regret. I will save 300,000 yen annually for six years from Court Expenses and order civil and military officers, with the exception of those who are under special circumstances, to give up one-tenth of their salary for the same period and this money shall be used to supplement building expenditure.

After receiving Meiji Emperor's message the Diet approved a new budget, which included expenditure for two new battleships, *Fuji* and *Yashima*.

Because Captain Miura Isao, captain-to-be of the *Fuji*, was already in Britain, supervising the work, Saitō led the team of over 230 men, departing from Yokohama on the NYK *Yamaguchi-maru*. Among them was young Sub-Lieutenant Kato Kanji.[19] Saitō's letter to his wife from Singapore included the following description of Hong Kong in those days:

> It has been seventeen or eighteen years since my last visit and therefore it should not be a surprise that I saw such amazing changes. They have built a Cable Car to the top of the so-called 'Victoria Peak' which is the highest mountain on the island. Also at the top there were two or three large 'hotels' and people commute from these 'hotels' to the shops and offices in Hong Kong city and go back to their 'hotels' for lunch. It is an interesting sort of device. ...
> From the water to halfway up the mountain they have built houses wherever it is at all possible to build. Both sides of Hong Kong's vast waterfront were full of warehouses and shops, etc. and it looked as though even inches were not wasted.

After calling at Colombo and sailing through the Suez Canal, the party arrived in London on 30 January and were taken to the Victoria Dock where the *Fuji* was in the process of being rigged. Saitō found his lodging at 80 Gower Street. In his diary there were a few entries of engagements other than supervising the fitting-out work of the ship. On one of these occasions on 30 March, Saitō, accompanied by Minister Katō Takaaki, visited St James Palace for an audience with the Duke of York, later King George V. Also there were a couple of 'open days' of *Fuji* in April, when the ship was opened to the dignitaries. On 19 April when it was opened to the general public, 15,000 people came to see the vessel. Furthermore, Saitō attended a Lord Mayor's lunch on 10 May, and was invited as one of the guests at the annual dinner of the Japan Society at the Metropole Hotel on 25 May, attended by over two hundred people.[20] Because his captain was ill, Saitō stood in to thank Sir Edwin Arnold[21] on behalf of the guests at the dinner:

> I have the honour to belong to a profession which is more one of action than of words, & you will therefore, I know, pardon me if I am so brief in my thanks. For all the kindness we sailors of Japan have received in this friendly country I beg to say; 'Arigato' Thank you! Thank you!

In June there was Queen Victoria's diamond jubilee. For this, Prince Arisugawa (Takehito) came to Britain accompanied by Marquis Itō Hirobumi. On 26 June a naval review was held off Portsmouth with 165 vessels, amounting to 560,000 tons in total. Also present were fourteen foreign ships, including HIJMS *Fuji*, which hoisted the flag of Prince Arisugawa, then Commander of the Standing Fleet with the rank of Rear Admiral. Saitō confided to his wife his impression of the occasion: 'as for the diamond jubilee, I did not feel anything but envy of the splendour of the Royal Navy'.[22] From Portsmouth the *Fuji* sailed for Portland where final tests were carried out and set out on 18 August on her homeward journey during which the battleship made history by becoming the first ship of her class to pass through the Suez Canal safely.[23] She arrived at Yokosuka on 31 October.

With the *Fuji* mission successfully completed, Saitō was promoted on 1 December to the rank of Commander, followed by a further promotion to Captain within a month, and his first command of a ship, the cruiser, HIJMS *Akitsushima*. One notable assignment on *Akitsushima* was a mission to Manila in May 1898, following the outbreak of the Spanish-American War, to protect Japanese residents there. The mission lasted over four months – Manila fell on 13 August – and on his return he was offered another command, the cruiser, HIJMS *Itsukushima*, one of so-called '*sankei-kan*'.[24] However, this assignment was short-lived and after just over a month Saitō's naval career at sea came to an end. In November, after the resignation of the Okuma government, Marquis Yamagata Aritomo formed his second government and appointed Vice-Admiral Yamamoto Gonbei his Navy Minister. Yamamoto in turn chose Saitō as his Vice-Minister.

When Saitō took up his post as No.2 at the Navy Ministry in 1898, Japan was still only an emerging naval power and the strength of IJN was about one third of that of Russia. Therefore his task as vice-minister was the expansion of the fleet and overall development of naval infrastructure. This was to be mainly financed by the indemnity from China, but passing the necessary bills in the Diet required political skills. In constant consultation with successive prime and finance ministers, Saitō became increasingly adept in handling the matter.[25] There were two major diplomatic incidents when he was the vice-minister. From May to August in 1900, he was busy handling the Boxer Rebellion incident. In contrast to the Army, the Navy dealt with the Boxer issue as part of the protection of Japanese nationals overseas, i.e. peacetime operations, and the matter was left in the hands of the Navy Ministry, especially its secretariat under Saitō's direction. Following this, on 30 January 1902, the Anglo-Japanese Alliance was signed in London. This necessitated a consultation between the Royal Navy and IJN and the conference was held on 14 May at the Yokosuka Naval Station. The participants included Admiral Bridge, C-in-C of the China squadron, Sir Claude MacDonald, the British minister in Tokyo, Admiral Yamamoto, General Terauchi, the Army minister, and Saitō himself.[26]

Meanwhile, Japan's relations with Russia went from bad to worse and towards the end of 1903, Saitō was in charge of confidential negotiations for the purchase of two Argentine cruisers, *Rivadavia* and *Moreno*,[27] through Captain Tamari Chikakata, the naval attaché in London. The deal for sale came through, and after these two vessels safely made it to Singapore, Japan broke off its negotiations with Russia and issued an ultimatum on 5 February. The decision was a well-kept secret until the end and Saitō, as the vice-minister and the one designated to see foreign naval and military attachés, who wanted to find out whether Japan was ready for war, was inundated with their calls. The British minister was among them, asking Saitō for a leak 'for the sake of the Alliance'.[28]

The actual course of the war has been dealt with in detail elsewhere and this paper confines itself to Saitō's contribution to the war effort. Since during wartime with the establishment of the Imperial Head-quarters, tactical decisions were in the hands of the Naval General Staff, Saitō's main task was mainly logistical, the coordination of the works at the Navy Ministry. He achieved this brilliantly by concurrently holding the posts of the Chiefs of the Naval Affairs Bureau, the Education Bureau and the Navy Technical Department. Also he attended the vice-ministers' meetings at the prime minister's official residence every

Monday throughout the war. Furthermore, he dealt with most of the meetings with foreign representatives. The most frequent contact was maintained with the British minister, Sir Claude MacDonald. They exchanged visits regularly, including Sundays. One of these visits was on 28 May 1905, the day after the battle of Tsushima. One of the things discussed at these meetings was the question of British observers attached to the Japanese fleet. For this purpose the Royal Navy sent three Captains: Pakenham, Jackson and Hutchison. The war was a great opportunity for Britain to learn the latest aspects of naval warfare first hand and they endeavoured to gather as much information as possible.[30]

Having successfully led the Navy during the war, Admiral Yamamoto resigned as navy minister and the post fell to his natural successor, Vice-Admiral Saitō. He became the minister in January 1906 with the formation of Prince Saionji's first government. It was the beginning of his eight-year tenure as the navy minister, spanning no less than five cabinets. His first duty was to welcome Prince Arthur of Connaught who came to Japan to confer the Garter on the Meiji Emperor in February 1906. The day after the Prince left, the British ambassador – as MacDonald had now become – came to see the navy minister to tell Saitō that he had been made Knight Grand Cross, Order of the Bath.

In the aftermath of the Russo-Japanese War, the Imperial Defence Policy which was formulated in 1907 was adopted which put the United States as its number one hypothetical enemy. In October 1908 the US 'White Fleet' visited Japan, which the Japanese took (rightly) as a demonstration by the Americans. With no indemnity from the Russians, it was a difficult task to build up the strength of the Navy. Saitō did his best over the next few years to secure funding from the Diet. On 5 November 1913 Saitō welcomed the new battle cruiser, HIJMS *Kongō*, at Yokosuka. It was the last battleship built in Britain and signalled that the period of IJN's tutelage under the Royal Navy was almost over. The following year the Siemens scandal dominated the political scene. The scandal deepened with the revelation that Vickers gave a bribe to Vice-Admiral Matsumoto Yawara, the former Chief of the Naval Technical Department in relation to the order for *Kongo*. Ironically, the Prime Minister at the time was Yamamoto, and his naval background added fuel to the critics. The government resigned, and on 16 April Saitō left office. Within a month, he was put on the Reserve List at the age of fifty-five. There followed a relatively quiet five years of his life out of public office, at the end of which Saitō contemplated opening a farm in Hokkaido.

It was about the time when Saitō was planning to leave for Hokkaido that his public career was restored by an old acquaintance from his first visit to Europe. Korea had been formally colonized by Japan in 1910, which was followed by years of disturbance, culminating in the outbreak of 1 March 1919. In August 1919, Prime Minister Hara asked Saitō to become the Governor-General of Korea. Although he was not particularly keen to go back to a burdensome life in public office, Saitō's strong sense of public duty prevailed and he accepted the offer. His ten years in Korea is outside the scope of this paper, but it is perhaps worth mentioning that he adopted conciliatory policies and his tenure was regarded a great success, despite the ominous start on 2 September, when his carriage was bombed on his arrival in Seoul.[31] Specifically, he was successful in pacifying the large contingent of American missionaries in Korea, as testified by the voluminous letters of condolence printed at the end of his official biography.

On 10 February 1927, US President Coolidge invited Britain, France, Italy and Japan to a second naval conference to follow up the Washington conference of 1921/22, which was to be held in Geneva. At the age of sixty-eight, Saitō was appointed the chief delegate of the Japanese delegation to the conference.[32] Following the example at the Washington conference, the Japanese government wanted someone who could carry great authority with the Navy, like Admiral Baron Katō Tomosaburō.[33] British Ambassador John Tilley's information confirmed this: 'I have heard it said that the government believe that his name will cover decisions that the nation might refuse to accept in other circumstances.' He further noted that 'Viscount Saitō has always been friendly to Great Britain'.[34]

Leading a large delegation,[35] Saitō left Kobe on 25 April. He was accompanied by his wife, Haruko. Such was the respect in which Saitō was held that there was no criticism of this, in marked contrast to what happened three years later at the time of the London Naval Conference when Navy Minister Admiral Takarabe Takeshi was severely criticized because he was accompanied by his wife.[36] Among the documents prepared on their way to Europe, there is a memorandum titled '*Tai kaigi-saku koryo* (the essential points for the Conference)' which suggested that they should 'keep as closely in touch with the British as possible' and 'while being wary of Anglo-American collaboration, avoid getting involved in questions which are strictly Anglo-American'.[37] It seems that, despite the abrogation of the Alliance, there was still an 'afterglow' left in the minds of the IJN officers.

Saitō arrived in Geneva on 17 June. There was a rumour that two Koreans were arrested in Geneva for planning an assassination attempt on Saitō. When Hugh Gibson, the US delegate to the conference, mentioned this to Saitō, he replied, 'Oh, I am always [being] assassinated'. We can glimpse a personal side of Saitō from a letter written by the wife of the British First Lord of the Admiralty:

We were entertained at dinner on Saturday night by Sir A & Lady Chamberlain.[38] I sat between ... the Netherlands Foreign Minister & Admiral Viscount Saito the chief of the Japanese Delegation. He is an oldish man, short broad – a yellowish face & white hair. I believe it is not the custom in Japan for the women to talk or seen to be spoken to – & he carried out the latter condition by never addressing me a single remark & [squandering?] my effort to liaise by monosyllables.[39]

The conference was a failure. The British requirement of 70 small cruisers to patrol the Empire and the American strategic need for large cruisers proved irreconcilable. The Japanese delegation led by Saitō for once found themselves in the peculiar position of mediating between the Anglo-Americans, but the task was beyond their ability. Nevertheless, William Bridgeman, the British chief delegate, appreciated Saitō's effort: 'Adm. Saito was a most attractive personality, with plenty of character & considerable naval experience, longing for agreement, and as straight as an arrow.'[40] Saitō's policy was that '... we should not opportunistically attempt a sudden expansion of our navy ... in one conference or two'. Instead, '... we should gradually enhance our national strength – our economic and industrial power – while winning greater respect and understanding from the rest of the world'.[41] Incidentally Admiral Pakenham, who was the naval attaché during the Russo-Japanese War, '... made a great impression at Geneva in 1927 by travelling from England for the sole purpose of calling upon Admiral Viscount Saito'.[42]

After the conference Saitō arrived in London on 10 August for a three-day visit. His diary records that he stayed at Claridge's, did shopping in Oxford Street, had a dinner at the Savoy and saw a musical at the Prince of Wales Theatre. He also renewed old acquaintances, visiting elderly Admirals Moore and Meux.[43] This was to be his last visit to the country he loved so much. After further sightseeing in France, Belgium and Italy, the party left Naples for Kobe on 22 August.

After returning to Tokyo Saitō resumed his post in Korea, but resigned because of ill health in December. His successor, General Yamanashi Hanzō, turned out to be less adept at the job (and less popular among Korean people) and Saitō was called back to Korea in August 1929. He suffered a minor stroke in May 1931 and resigned the following month. Everyone assumed this was the end of his public career.

In 1932 Prime Minister Inukai Tsuyoshi was assassinated in the 15 May incident (ironically carried out by Naval officers). Prince Saionji, the last remaining *Genro*, took an unusually long time to make up his mind, coming up to Tokyo from his residence in Okitsu. After a ten-day deliberation he chose Saitō, calling him back from retirement at the age of seventy-three. He formed a 'national unity (*kyokoku itchi*)' government, putting an end to a brief period of party government in the history of pre-war Japan. The British ambassador to Tokyo, Sir Francis Lindley, reported the appointment to the Foreign Minister Simon:

> The choice had fallen on an ex-naval officer who commanded the respect of all parties and who had given proofs of statesmanship and moderation in many fields. When I saw him a few weeks ago at the Palace on the occasion of the Emperor's birthday, he struck me as a very old man, even for his 74 years, and it is known that he had had a slight stroke from which he recovered. That it should have been considered necessary to choose him, in spite of difficulties, is at once a tribute to his eminence and a confession of the poverty of the land in statesmen of the first class.[44]

Unfortunately, the circumstances were too dire for a man of moderation. Although he did a great deal to restore confidence in public order in the wake of the 15 May incident, he was unable to control the Kwantung army in Manchuria. One of his mistakes was to choose Count Uchida Yasuya as his foreign minister. Although Uchida had great experience in foreign affairs, having been the foreign minister twice in the past, and been regarded as pro-Western up to the 1920s, his tenure as the president of the Manchurian Railway since June 1931 had converted him into a vocal proponent of the Kwantung army. Soon after his appointment he made an infamous (and prophetic) 'scorched earth foreign policy (*shodo gaiko*)' speech in the Diet on the question of recognizing Manchukuo, stating that '. . . there will be no concession on this question and, even if our land is to be scorched, our policy has to be observed'. Therefore against Saitō's inclinations, the government went ahead with recognizing Manchukuo on 15 September 1932. Japan also withdrew from the League of Nations on 28 March the following year. In a way, Saitō, being a consensus-oriented man, waited for a consensus in favour of moderate policy to be gradually formed, but this never materialized. As Shigemitsu Mamoru, who became the vice-minister of the foreign affairs in May 1933, reflected:

> . . . new Prime Minister Saito was not a man of action but of reaction. . . . The government dealt with the Manchurian question as somebody else's affairs. In reality the question of Japan's responsibility which arose out of the Manchurian

question was not somebody else's problem and the action by the military should have been dealt with as an action by Japan for which the Japanese government itself was responsible.[45]

After two years Saitō resigned, nominating Admiral Okada Keisuke as his successor in the hope that the latter would have more success in keeping to moderate policies. Saitō must have thought that this time it was the real end of his public career and took up several less political posts, such as the presidencies of the Japanese Boy Scout Association, the post left vacant since the death of Gotō Shinpei, and the Japan Film Association. However, perhaps Japan's 'poverty' in statesmen was such that he was recalled to public duty once again; and in November 1935 he became the Lord Keeper of the Privy Seal, succeeding Count Makino Nobuaki. The post was an important one as Sir Robert Clive, the British ambassador in Tokyo, noted on Saitō's appointment:

> With the gradual depletion in the ranks of the 'Genro,' or elder statesmen, the political significance of the office of Lord Keeper of the Privy Seal has been greatly enhanced during recent times, for, whereas in former days the office was more or less of a sinecure, the holder has latterly taken a prominent part in important decisions, such as the selection of suitable Premiers and the organisation of Cabinets.[46]

The tragic fact was that this appointment in turn sealed Saitō's fate because by now some young army officers were determined to get rid of those senior statesmen around the Emperor, who, in their view, were manipulating him.

On the evening of 25 February 1936 Saitō was enjoying a film at the US Ambassador's residence, his first experience of a modern sound-film.[47] On returning to his residence just before midnight, Saitō was assassinated in an army coup no more than a few hours later, being shot several dozen times. His wife, Haruko, in trying to protect him by her body, was also hit three times. As she later reflected, '... it was an unfortunate morning, the beginning of the cursed era for Japan'. Three months later, the new Imperial Defence Policy was approved, which included Britain as Japan's hypothetical enemy for the first time.

17

Albert James Penniall: Pioneer of the Japanese Motor Vehicle Industry

C. MADELEY

THOUGH THE CONTRIBUTION of Albert James Penniall to the development of the Japanese motor vehicle industry is documented in Japan, his life and work have received little attention in Britain. Penniall was born in Woolwich Dockyard on 6 May 1872. He spent two years in Japan, leaving Britain in July 1920 and returning in September 1922. During these two years Penniall worked for the Ishikawajima Shipbuilding and Engineering Company Limited of Tokyo, forerunner of Isuzu Motors Limited, on behalf of Wolseley Motors Limited of Adderley Park in Birmingham. He kept a diary during his stay in Japan which, in addition to offering insights into what it was like to work for a Japanese firm in the early 1920s, gives a picture of expatriate life in Japan at that time. It is Penniall's diary which forms the basis of the present chapter.

THE ORIGIN AND DEVELOPMENT OF ISHIKAWAJIMA

The Ishikawajima company can be traced back to 1853. In August of that year the *bakufu* unofficially appointed Hanbei, a scholar of the West from the Mito *han*, as a builder of ships. In November the Mito *han* were officially appointed as shipbuilders, and in December the *bakufu* determined that a piece of imperial land at Ishikawajima should be used to establish a shipyard, putting the Mito *han* in charge of this venture. It was in July of the same year, 1853, that Commodore Matthew C. Perry had reached Uraga with his fleet of ships, thus making the *bakufu* aware of its deficiencies in naval defence. The establishment of the Ishikawajima shipyard may therefore be seen as a direct consequence of the arrival of Perry's fleet.

In 1854 the Ishikawajima shipyard began the construction of a large sailing ship, the *Asahimaru*, which is said to have been the first Western-style ship built in Japan. Staff of the shipyard were sent to Yokohama to examine Perry's fleet of warships which had entered Edo bay in February 1854, and in July of the same year to Nagasaki where they learnt about shipbuilding from the Dutch. The Ishikawajima shipyard was thus established to manufacture Western-style products, and turned to the West to learn how to manufacture them. This learning rapidly bore fruit, the *Asahimaru* was launched in January 1855, completed in May, and presented to the *bakufu* in November of the same year. Ishikawajima were at once ordered to construct four further ships, and produced a number of sailing ships thereafter.

In 1862 Ishikawajima laid down the keel of its first steam-powered warship, the *Chiyodagata*, which was launched in 1863, and in August 1864 Hida Heigorō, who had been responsible for the machinery of the *Chiyodagata*, was sent to Holland both to inspect ship building businesses, and to purchase machine tools. The *Chiyodagata* was completed in 1866. In 1876 the Ishikawajima shipyard became a private company. Ishikawajima did not restrict itself to the production of ships, however. By 1879 it was able to supply boilers and accessories to silk reelers in Gunma and Nagano, and in the same year invited its first foreign employee, Archibald King, to work as a marine engineer, which he did until his death in 1886. In 1881 Ishikawajima acquired the sole right to sell light railway track of the type invented by the Frenchman Decauville, and by 1883 had constructed an iron bridge for Kanagawa prefecture. In 1885 Ishikawajima engaged its second foreign employee, an Englishman named David Blake, as a marine engineer for a period of two years, and subsequently produced mining machinery (1885), Japan's first high-speed steam engine for electric power generation (1892), the first domestically-produced Pelton wheels for Kyoto's hydro-electric power station (1892), railway carriages (1892), and air compressors (1892). In 1893 the company changed its name to 'The Tokyo Ishikawajima Shipbuilding Company', and in the same year purchased twenty-three shell-making machines from the English firm James Archdale, commencing production of Hotchkiss rapid-firing gun shells in the following year. Other products were electric pumps (1895), Japan's first domestically-produced large capacity electricity generators (1896), cranes (1898), Japan's first large-sized submersible (1901), light railway locomotives (1902), gas holders (1907), and pylons for electric power cables (1909).

In 1912 the managing director of Ishikawajima, Uchida Tokurō, went to Britain to inspect machine manufacturing industries, and as the outcome of negotiations with the Sir William Arrol Company of

Glasgow, it was agreed that Ishikawajima would be able to use the latter's designs, and receive supplies of materials, for the production of steel-framed buildings, cranes, and other products. Thus by the eve of the First World War, Ishikawajima had diversified from shipbuilding into manufacturing a wide range of engineering products, and had also gained experience both of employing British engineers and of entering into agreements with British firms.

The outbreak of the First World War brought prosperity to the Japanese economy, and in 1916 the Tokyo Ishikawajima Shipbuilding Company recorded a net profit of one million yen. As it was clear that the war, and the prosperity which it brought to firms such as Ishikawajima, would not continue indefinitely however, how to use these wartime profits became a topic of discussion within the company, and it was decided to enter the car manufacturing industry. Despite its experience in producing a wide range of products, Ishikawajima did not feel able to go it alone in car manufacture, and sought a foreign partner. At that time, only Fiat and Wolseley were represented in Tokyo, and Ishikawajima approached both firms with a view to signing a licensing agreement. In addition, in 1916 Ishikawajima purchased a Fiat car from the Nihon Jidōsha Company Limited and set out to see if it was capable of manufacturing a copy of this vehicle without outside help. This process of 'reverse engineering' was not as easy as had been expected; three months were required just to draw plans of the vehicle, and it was only after one year that the prototype vehicle was capable of running. In the meantime, negotiations with both Fiat and Wolseley had been proceeding. Rights to manufacture and sell vehicles would cost one million yen on the part of Fiat, while Wolseley asked for eighty thousand pounds, approximately eight hundred thousand yen at the prevailing rate of exchange. Not only was Wolseley cheaper, but Ishikawajima was also familiar with the quality of Wolseley products, having used a boat fitted with a Wolseley marine engine. A contract was drawn up between Ishikawajima and Wolseley on 6 November 1918, which was the first agreement made between a Japanese and a non-Japanese firm with a view to production of motor vehicles in Japan.

Under the terms of this agreement, Ishikawajima would pay Wolseley the royalties of eighty thousand pounds in ten annual instalments of eight thousand pounds, irrespective of the number of vehicles produced in Japan. In return, Wolseley would give Ishikawajima the sole rights to manufacture and sell in East Asia three types of Wolseley vehicle; the A9 type car, the E3 type light car, and the CP type one-and-a-half ton truck. Ishikawajima staff were invited to visit the Wolseley factory in Birmingham, and Wolseley undertook to provide support staff in Tokyo. Thus on 30 December 1918 six members of Ishikawajima staff left Yokohama by ship for America, where they visited Ford and other car factories in Detroit before travelling to Birmingham, where they spent about eight months. They returned to Japan via America once again, bringing wooden patterns which they had purchased, machine tools which they had bought in America following guidelines laid down by Wolseley, detailed production plans for the Wolseley A9 type car, and tools required to produce the car. In 1920 Ishikawajima established a car factory at Tomigawa-cho in Fukagawa-ku in Tokyo, and on 9 August 1920 Albert James Penniall landed in Yokohama to take up his post at the factory.

WOLSELEY – FROM SHEEP SHEARS TO MOTOR VEHICLES

Wolseley takes its name from Frederick York Wolseley, born at Golden Bridge House, Dublin in 1837, a descendant of the ancient Wolseley family of Wolseley in Staffordshire, a branch of which had emigrated to Ireland during the eighteenth century. The death of Frederick York Wolseley's father in 1840 left his family impoverished, and Wolseley emigrated to Australia in 1854 at the age of 17. There he began work as an apprentice on a sheep station in New South Wales, rising to the position of manager in 1867, and beginning to purchase land in his own right thereafter.

Wolseley put his mind to the development of a mechanical sheep shearing machine. The number of sheep in Australia had increased rapidly, from 105 in 1792 to over six million in New South Wales alone by 1860, and to thirty five million by 1880. There arose a bottleneck in wool production as hand-shearers were unable to keep pace with the rising number of animals. Wolseley's experiments began in 1868. He was granted two patents in 1877, but did not produce his first successful machine until 1886, when he displayed a sheep shearing machine at the Royal Sydney Show. In the following year the Wolseley Sheep-Shearing Machine Company Limited was established at 19 Philip Street, Sydney to manufacture the mechanical shears, but had difficulty in finding suppliers in Australia who were able to manufacture components of a high enough standard to make the machine a commercial success. One firm that was approached was managed by Herbert Austin, son of a Buckinghamshire farmer, who had emigrated to Australia in 1884. Austin was able to propose so many improvements to the mechanical shears that when it was decided to transfer production to England and establish a factory there, Austin was offered the post of manager, returning to England in 1893.

At first, the business did not go well. Parts bought in were of poor quality, and the firm was obliged to scrap stocks of parts, and replace machines already sold. The company decided in 1895 to undertake all manufacture itself, which though it resulted in an improvement in quality, left the firm with production capacity which needed to be employed to the full. The firm thus began to diversify into the manufacture of machine tools, bicycles and bicycle parts, and Herbert Austin made a trip to Paris to see some of the new horseless carriages which had been produced on the continent. In 1895 Austin completed his first experimental car, and in 1900 a Wolseley car was awarded the first prize in its class in the Thousand Miles Trial organized by the Automobile Club of Great Britain and Ireland. As a result of the favourable publicity which this generated, cars of a similar type were put on sale shortly thereafter.

In addition to the range of products outlined above, Herbert Austin had been approached by Sir Hiram Maxim, of the steel and armaments manufacturers Vickers Sons and Maxim Limited, to help in the construction of an experimental steam-powered flying machine of Maxim's design, and the Wolseley works had designed and manufactured parts for this machine. Though the flying machine was not a success, Maxim was impressed both by Austin's abilities and the success of the Wolseley car in the Thousand Miles Trial. Vickers Son and Maxim Limited were also aware of the military potential of the motor vehicle. The Wolseley Sheep-Shearing Machine Company Limited, for its part, realized that further investment would be needed if the motor car manufacturing activities of the company were to develop, and on 18 February 1901, Vickers registered the Wolseley Tool and Motor Car Company Limited, taking over the motor car operations of the Wolseley Sheep-Shearing Machine Company Limited. The new firm increased its range of models and participated in motor racing trials, though Herbert Austin resigned in 1905 to start his own company. In 1910 Wolseley produced over one thousand cars, rising to almost five thousand in 1913, by which time Wolseley had produced a total of 13,500 vehicles, and was one of the most prolific car manufacturers in Britain. In July 1914 the company changed its name to Wolseley Motors Limited.

The outbreak of the First World War curtailed Wolseley's car manufacturing activities, though the company produced a number of lorries for military use. As a subsidiary of Vickers, the bulk of its wartime output was military. Indeed, when staff of Ishikawajima arrived at Wolseley's Birmingham works in the early part of 1919, the works were still producing aero-engines, and it was not until shortly before their departure eight months later that they were able to see car engines being made. The end of the First World War left Wolseley with expanded but also in some cases inappropriate or worn out facilities and equipment, and seeking to upgrade and then employ these

facilities, the company both took on considerable financial commitments to modernise its production capacity, and sought to expand
overseas demand for its products, appointing resident factory
representatives for South Africa, Australia, New Zealand and South
America. It seems that the agreement with Ishikawajima formed part of
Wolseley's strategy to promote overseas sales.

'MY VISIT TO JAPAN, 1920 TO 1922'

This is the title given by Albert James Penniall to his diary. The diary
offers insights into many aspects of the expatriate's life in Japan, and
here I shall focus on a number of themes that run through the diary,
namely transport and communications, hazards of life in Japan, work,
leisure, and Japan and the Japanese. I hope that the reason for choosing
some of these themes will become apparent in due course, as they have
a bearing on the history of Ishikawajima's motor vehicle manufacturing
section.

Visitors to Japan today probably take for granted the ease and
rapidity of travel to and from the country, but for travellers in the early
1920s, a visit to Japan was an arduous and potentially perilous
undertaking. Penniall left Birmingham on 10 July 1920, and did not
arrive in Yokohama until 9 August, almost one month later. The
Atlantic crossing was rough and calm by turns, and ships exercised
caution in fog, no doubt mindful of the fate which had befallen the
Titanic some eight years earlier:

> July 14th 1920. Evening. Fog showing. Dance at 9-11. Fog
> horns blowing all night. Ship stopped. See Bulletins.
>   July 15th 1920. Still very foggy off Newfoundland. Sea
> calm. Concert tonight in 1st Saloon. Ship stopped twice,
> half speed all day.

The train journey across Canada by Canadian Pacific Railway was
spectacular, but became tedious, and Penniall was glad to reach
Vancouver, where he embarked on the ss *Empress of Russia* on 29 July,
reaching Japan on 9 August after a crossing of ten days:

> August 9th 1920. 5.30 am. Japanese coast in sight. Grand
> morning and very hot. All the ship in whites. I must have
> some on arrival. Expect to land in Yokohama about 3pm.
> Had a very pleasant trip all the way from Vancouver B.C.

Having travelled to Japan via the American continent Penniall was able
to return to Britain via the Middle East, thus completing a round the
world tour. Penniall was impressed by Japan's achievements on the
Asian mainland:

> July 17th 1922. Arrived Dairen 7.15 am. Went ashore. First class city with wide streets. Population mostly Manchu. Coaling ship 18th. Due to leave 20th. This place is in South Manchuria and is the finest city I have seen in the East. Our next port is Tsing-tao.
>
> July 21st 1922. Arrived at Tsing-tao. 21st 8.20 am and went ashore. Motor trip to the ex German forts. Had a lovely day. This port was taken by the Japanese from Germany in the late war. It is a fine city and was heavily fortified.

The return journey was not without incident however:

> July 20th 1922. Left Dairen 2.30 pm. 35 miles out port engine broken down, causing slow passage.
>
> July 27th 1922. Arrived Hong Kong 2 pm one day ahead of schedule. This proves very fortunate. We just got moored when the typhoon started. It has stopped all work so we shall be delayed, further a strike is on. We leave on the 29th for Saigon. Awful rough weather, 3 days typhoon, high seas.
>
> August 5th 1922. 11.30 am leaving Saigon for Singapore. We are a long way behind our sailing schedule.

No doubt Penniall was glad to set foot on home soil again after a journey which began on 11 July and was still not complete on 2 September, the date of the final entry in Penniall's diary, by which time he had reached Port Said.

The mails were a constant source of preoccupation to Penniall, and once again reveal very different standards to those taken for granted today. All mail travelled slowly as there was as yet no air mail service. Moreover, mails did not always get through for a variety of reasons. Robbery was one cause:

> November 22nd 1920. The papers inform me that the mail trains have been held up by robbers in the Rocky Mountains twice this last month. I wonder if my mail has been stolen. I must wait until I hear from England before I can put in a claim if it has been stolen.

Fire was another:

> May 12th 1921. Japan P. Office announces that all English mails between Nov 26 and Dec 6th were destroyed by fire during transit from Seattle to New York.
>
> May 26th 1921. English and American mail burnt at sea. May 2nd off Portland Oregon USA. 6000 pieces.

In 1922 it was the post office itself which was destroyed by fire:

January 13th 1922. Tokyo Central Post Office burnt down. All mails and official papers destroyed. Jan 5, 1922. No wonder I don't get my letters regular. It is now seven weeks since I had my last letters from home.

It seems that fire was a hazard of life in Japan at that time, however. Penniall records a number of fires, including the destruction of several prominent public buildings. On 5 October 1920 the World's Sunday School Convention Hall burnt down. On Tuesday 21 December 1920 Penniall reports a big fire near the Ishikawajima works. On 26 March 1921 six hundred houses were destroyed in a fire in Shinjuku. Then a fire broke out in Asakusa:

April 6th 1921. Another great fire at Asakusa. 1600 houses burnt, 8000 homeless. The Japs have these big fires every spring and they call them 'The Flowers of Yedo'. I can't see anything of a joke in it.

30 October 1921 witnessed the destruction of the Kabukiza Theatre, and 16 April 1922 the Imperial Hotel, at which the Prince of Wales and his retinue were staying:

April 16th 1922. The Prince's band from the 'Renown' played in Hibiya Park. Towards the end of the performance, the Imperial Hotel which is close to the Park, caught fire and in less than an hour was in ruins. The Prince's suite, staying there, as well as the guests lost all their belongings. The decorations which the Prince was to bestow on the Japanese were also burnt.

Of greater potential danger were the recurrent earthquakes that affected the Kantō area at this time, preceding the Great Kantō Earthquake of 1923. Penniall records earthquakes on 3, 5 and 20 December 1920, and 14 February 1921. These were followed by a more serious tremor on 8 December 1921:

December 8th 1921. At 9.30 this evening whilst out for a walk on Ginza, a very bad earthquake (jishin) occurred. I was properly scared, and it fair turned one's inside upside down. It lasted about 5 minutes. I was looking in a large store window, when I was pitched forward and backward, at first I did not realise what was the matter. Everybody was swaying about and shutters were coming down with a bang and clatter, lights going up and down, people screaming, large buildings seemed tumbling all ways. Luckily none fell, or it would have meant no England for poor me.

On 26 April 1922 another earthquake damaged production facilities at

Ishikawajima's car factory:

> April 26th 1922. 10.15 am. Tremendous earthquake. Worst known in Japan since 1904. Altho' the loss of life and damage is not so great, it affected everyone's nerves. Our buildings swayed like a pack of cards and all made for the open. The main shafting broke away under the swaying and machines were lifted bodily.

This was followed by more shocks. On 29 May Penniall reported:

> May 9th 1922. Another bad earthquake. Mr Murakami has mentioned about my return, so things are moving. Let's hurry up and get away from this country before I get caught in the big quake which I believe is coming and which I also believe will exact a heavy toll and loss of life.

Penniall reiterates his prediction on 26 June:

> June 26th 1922. 3. 30 am we have a very big earthquake lasting 2 and a half minutes and altho' it has not caused any serious damage to property it has damaged people's nerves. My old house and bed rocked and shook, it was like being aboard a ship in a light squall. These continued recurrences of earthquakes are, in my opinion, the prelude to a more serious one yet to come and which will alter the whole face of Japan. Let's hope I'm out of it before it happens.

Penniall's predictions proved correct, and though the Great Kantō Earthquake of 1 September 1923 did not alter the whole face of Japan, it did cause serious damage and loss of life in the Tokyo area. In addition, it had an effect both on the work of Ishikawajima's vehicle manufacturing division, and on the subsequent development of the motor vehicle industry in Japan, as will be discussed below.

Penniall was in general most satisfied with the treatment he received by his employer. He was provided with a house which he moved into after staying initially in the Tokyo Station Hotel, and staff to look after him there:

> October 10th 1920. I am going into my house today and trust I shall be comfortable. At any rate I shall have more privacy. The house is Japanese and fitted up European style. I have an Iron bedstead, Oak washstand and chest of drawers. 2 tables, 3 chairs. Combined with sitting rooms and plenty of cupboards. The floors are all covered with carpets and I have to remove my boots every time I come in or go out. It faces the sea and there is also a nice garden. I have a house steward and his wife, who occupy the downstairs rent free for attending me. Electric light and a

gas fire in the bedrooms and sitting room.

He was still able to report favourably after almost a year in Japan:

> June 21st 1921. This completes my first year of service. So far I am perfectly well and happy and have no complaints to make about my treatment by the Company.

Penniall's first impression of the Japanese workforce was very different from the stereotype of hard work and efficiency which is commonplace today, however:

> October 10th 1920. As regards the works, it looks as if it will take 12 months or more to get out one car, as things go very slowly out east, tomorrow will do style of thing.

Nor was he to revise this impression subsequently.

> February 3rd 1921. Things are about the same at the works, no one seems to put themselves out, everyone sits about smoking all day. Workmen all smoke whilst at work.

Penniall's prediction about the amount of time that would be required to complete the first car proved to be correct:

> December 31st 1921. We are making good progress at the works, on the 26th Decr. we took our first car made in Japan on a satisfactory road test.

It was not that Penniall himself felt he was working hard, however:

> Thursday 18th November 1920. I have done more work this week than I have done ever since I left Adderley Park. I have actually designed some tools. This is one continual restful holiday out here.

Subsequently he commented:

> October 17th 1921. What I shall do when I get home to England and have to start 'WORK' again I really don't know.

In addition to being portrayed as efficient and hard-working, the Japanese workforce is frequently portrayed as docile. In post First World War Japan the labour movement was at its height however:

> October 8th 1921. The workmen at the head works have gone on strike for more wages. Management have offered them 10% increase. The men refused this offer. Things look ugly. 1000 police on duty in the shipyard. Mr. Takami is seriously injured by the strikers and is taken to hospital.

The strike then spread to the car manufacturing section of Ishikawajima where Penniall was employed, and was to continue until 15 November 1921. Despite these handicaps production and training continued, though at first relying on parts despatched by Wolseley in Birmingham:

> February 9th 1921. Our first 15 HP chassis is delivered here today.
> February 13th 1921. We have mounted a body on the chassis and been for a run. It is very speedy and in fact too fast for Japan.

Indeed, it seems that eventually Penniall felt he had done his job all too well, for by 10 July 1921, he was writing:

> I am not any too comfortable at the shop either. Now they have the most of the information they treat me as a dummy.

Penniall had high hopes that his period of duty with Ishikawajima in Tokyo would lead to further appointments with the company:

> October 10th 1920. I hope when the job is finished to be appointed British agent for Ishikawajima as regards the purchase of material etc. If I can get a position like that in England my time out here will have been well-spent, as I could then settle down.

If this was not the case in Britain, he would have been prepared to accept an extension of his appointment in Tokyo:

> January 13th 1922. I have sent special enquiry to Wolseley about trucks and lorries. If they reply as I expect them to do, it may change the whole course of our lives. I have written to Alice for her decision in advance so as to be prepared with my answer should the Coy. want me to make another engagement.

As Penniall likens his stay in Japan to one long holiday, let us now examine how he enjoyed his leisure time. Penniall visited many of the sights in and around Tokyo which are familiar to residents today:

> Sunday September 12th 1920. Went to Akusa Park, Neyno (sic – ?Ueno) Park and Hibiya Park. Took the camera with me and got some snap shots. This is my first effort at photography, I wonder what sort of a film I have got.

He also visited the National Chrysanthemum Show at the Wrestling Hall, the Kameido Shrine, 'noted for its "Wisteria" flowers', the 'Narita shrine and to "Sanridsuka" to see the cherry blossoms', "Hori Kiri", the famous Iris gardens of Tokyo', Kamakura, and the Sumidagawa fireworks. Subsequently he travelled further afield to Hakone, and Nikkō. It was the latter which impressed him the most, and to which he returned on several occasions. His first visit moved him to write at length.

> June 24th, 25th, 26th 1921. Visit to Nikko and Chuzenji Lake. See Nikko and then say 'Magnificent'. Beautiful mountains, springs and waterfalls, famous shrines, and lovely pure air. Chuzenji Lake, in the clouds and mountains 4375 feet above sea level. A five hours train journey from Tokyo and then Nikko, 2000 ft above the sea. A visit to its famous temples, admission 90 sen per person. The sacred red bridge over which no person is allowed other than the Imperial family. It is really called God bridge. Inside the shrines and temples which are excellent pieces of work-manship are wood carving, bronze and lacquer work. The praying dragon and sleeping cat, Goldengate. The fire and water gods are all grand, also the roads and lay out of the gardens is the best I have seen in the East. Leaving Nikko for Chuzenji Lake we have a four hours walk in front of us. Up, Up, Up. Climbing the mountainside, over river beds and rock. The road is impassable except for footpassengers and rickshaws and packhorses. Going up the waterfalls were enclouded with mist, but on our return the sun had burst through and we had a grand sight. I intend to go again to both these places if I can possibly manage it.

Penniall did indeed return to Nikkō on three occasions during his stay in Japan; during the summer of 1921, again during the autumn strikes in the same year, and at New Year in 1922. Before the end of Penniall's contract, and his return to England, Ishikawajima arranged for him to visit some of the sights in western Japan, a trip which he also enjoyed, visiting Ise, Nara, Osaka, Kobe, Miyajima, and Kyoto before returning by train to Tokyo.

Some aspects of Penniall's impressions of Japanese customs and people in Japan that he recorded were very different to today:

> August 22nd 1920. You can walk through all the stores here and none will ask you to buy. As you go in you either take your boots off or have them covered. They relieve you of your umbrella and parcels (if any) and return them when you leave. This necessitates a large staff and one exit.

Others, however, were very similar:

> August 22nd 1920. Travelling in the tram cars is most objectionable. They crowd all they can in them, no limit, so long as you can hang on it's all right.

Penniall seems to have been impressed by the Ginza, subject of a lengthy description which is reproduced in part below:

> March 31st 1921. An evening's stroll down the Ginza, Tokyo's main street and shopping centre. The street is wide, wider than Corporation Street, B'ham, double tram lines, motor buses, ricksha's, some large shops. Shops all along each side, willow trees every 25 or 30 yards, at night time booths on the sidewalks, electric light for these being obtained from standards erected for the purpose by the Corporation. Click-Click-Click-Click-Click-Clack-Click. All down Ginza... When the winter evenings come, and the lights are lit, shewing thro' the boughs of the willows that droop over the pavements, where, without a break the 'geta' (Japanese footwear) babble, babble, like a brook over pebbles, clicking, clacking, clicking, and the shop fronts' glare with the gorgeous bright shades and colors of 'obi' (Worn by ladies as a sash), and heaps of crumpled silk and cotton and merino in most startling patterns, and fruit makes splendours, of spots in brass, and gold and copper. And you see dried squid (fish) for sale and other curious edibles (such as seaweed) next door to brilliant silverware and lacquer and ivories. While inside sitting, or squatting on green baize, round hibachi (charcoal fires in earthenware or copper urns) clerks in brown kimonos bend over abacuses (sorobans) (Japanese counting frames) and make out your accounts with brushes dipped in pots of India ink.

Penniall did not approve of what he perceived as excessive drinking on the part of the Japanese, however. He first comments on this in connection with the New Year festivities in 1921:

> January 1st 1921. The Japanese have started their regular annual holiday. This seems to consist of making themselves a nuisance by imbibing great quantities of 'Sake', playing shuttlecock, and bawling about the streets. This is to go on for 3 weeks I am informed.

The arrival of the cherry blossom viewing season four months late served only to heighten Penniall's revulsion:

> April 17th 1921. I have seen more drunkenness today than I have seen in 10 years in England. Flower viewing is no pleasure to a white man, the way the Japs go on. I had a decent opinion of them until today. After seeing them in their element they have dropped 99% in my estimation.

Penniall's response was to attend the Company's social events less frequently:

> January 1st 1922 I am spending at home by myself very quietly. I did not go to the Coy's dinner and reception today. I saw quite enough of the style last year. Tomorrow Mr. Cartwright and myself are going up to Nikko for a few days to escape the Japanese festivities in Tokyo.

The account given by Penniall in his diary generally coincides with the account given in both the Ishikawajima and Isuzu company histories. There is, however, one noteworthy difference. Penniall states that the first car made in Japan was taken on a road test on 26 December 1921. Both the Ishikawajima and Isuzu texts state that the first car was completed on 31 December 1921. The staff of Ishikawajima, according to the latter accounts, wanted to test this car at all costs before the end of the year, and set off on a test drive to Miura Misaki, to the south of Tokyo. It being New Year's Eve, and as the car was running well, they stopped for a rest, lunch, and a drink when they reached Uraga. It seems the drink was alcoholic for, shortly after setting off from Uraga, the driver lost control of the car on a bend, crashed into a police department telegraph pole, and severely damaged the radiator. The car was able to proceed to Miura Misaki, and back to Tokyo again after emergency repairs, but did not return to the factory in Fukagawa until nine o'clock in the morning on New Year's Day. If Penniall had been present, it is unlikely that this incident would have escaped his attention, and comment in his diary, particularly if he had known the cause of the accident. Nor would his Japanese colleagues have escaped his wrath! It seems, therefore, that the Ishikawajima and Isuzu accounts refer to the first car completed by a purely Japanese team without Penniall's assistance.

SUBSEQUENT DEVELOPMENTS, ISHIKAWAJIMA, WOLSELEY, AND ALBERT JAMES PENNIALL

Though Ishikawajima were able to manufacture cars of Wolseley design, these were unable to compete on cost and reputation with imported American cars such as Buicks or Hudsons, and a stock of unsold cars accumulated. Ishikawajima thus turned its attention to the manufacture of trucks which would qualify for the subsidies offered under the Military Vehicle Subsidy Law enacted by the Japanese government in 1918. In October 1922 a Mr Murakami of Ishikawajima was despatched to Birmingham both to attempt the negotiation of a reduction in the royalty payments, which Wolseley financial records suggest Ishikawajima had been unable to meet in any case, and to gather information about the Wolseley CP type truck which Ishikawajima had purchased the rights to under the licensing agreement of 1918.

Murakami returned to Tokyo in March 1923 with plans for the truck, and two trucks which Ishikawajima had purchased from Wolseley. Ishikawajima set about the manufacture of a truck with a view to submitting it for the qualifying trials for the subsidy, but production received a setback when the Great Kantō Earthquake of 1 September 1923 severely damaged the company's production facilities, and destroyed the stock of A9 type cars which had been manufactured in Japan. (Ishikawajima did not manufacture the E3 type car, but imported it with a view to sales in Japan).

The earthquake also damaged Tokyo's rail and tramway system, and as this was slow in being repaired, the Tokyo municipal authorities sought to buy a fleet of vehicles to use as buses in its place. Neither Japanese nor European manufacturers were able to supply suitable vehicles in the quantity required at short notice, so an order was won by Ford for two thousand Model T truck chassis to be fitted with bus bodies in Japan. The use of these vehicles made both the Japanese public and authorities more aware of the potential of motor transport, but it also made American manufacturers aware of the potential of the Japanese market, and as a result both Ford and General Motors established assembly plants in Japan, whose products dominated the Japanese motor vehicle market in the pre-war period.

Nonetheless, Ishikawajima was able to complete a truck which satisfied the qualifying trials for the subsidy in March 1924, and manufactured a total of approximately 560 of the CP type one and a half ton truck, and a smaller CG type one ton truck, both built to Wolseley's designs, up to 1927. The original truck submitted for the qualifying trials is now restored to running order and on display in Isuzu's Head Office in Tokyo, one of only two Wolseley trucks to have survived to this day, the other being in preservation in the UK. In 1927 managing director Shibusawa Masao of Ishikawajima was able to negotiate the annulment of the agreement with Wolseley one year before it was due to expire, and in the same year the motor vehicle division of Ishikawajima adopted the trade name 'Sumida' after the river in Tokyo on which the factory was located, and continued to manufacture trucks which were based on Wolseley's design with various improvements under this name.

In May 1929 the vehicle manufacturing division of Ishikawajima was made a separate company, the 'Ishikawajima Jidōsha Seisakusha Kabushiki Kaisha'. Subsequently, in March 1933 it merged with the 'DAT Jidōsha Seizō Kabushiki Kaisha', becoming the 'Jidōsha Kōgyo Kabushiki Kaisha', and became involved in the Government-inspired programme to produce the 'Isuzu' standardized truck in 1934, named after the Isuzu River which flows near the Ise Shrine in Mie prefecture. In April 1937 the 'Jidōsha Kogyō Kabushiki Kaisha' merged with the 'Tokyo Gas Denki Kogyō Kabushiki Kaisha's vehicle manufacturing section, becoming the 'Tōkyō Jidōsha Kogyō Kabushiki Kaisha'. In April 1941 this company changed its name to the 'Diesel Jidōsha Kogyō Kabushiki Kaisha', and in July 1949 was renamed 'Isuzu Jidōsha Kabushiki Kaisha'.

'Isuzu Motors Limited' renewed its ties with the British motor industry when in February 1953 it made an agreement with Rootes Motors of England to produce Hillman cars under license, and subsequently entered an agreement with General Motors of America in July 1971. Production of commercial vehicles in a joint venture with General Motors began at Luton in 1989. A discussion of these developments is beyond the scope of this chapter however.

Wolseley Motors Limited found itself in difficulty after the First World War as demand for expensive luxury vehicles of the type it produced fell and demand for cheap utilitarian vehicles arose. Wolseley was unable to honour financial commitments undertaken to finance the re-equipping of its works after the First World War, and was declared bankrupt in 1926, being purchased by William Morris in the face of competition from former Wolseley employee Herbert Austin, and General Motors. The Wolseley brand continued as part of the Morris group of companies, which merged with Austin in 1952 to form the British Motor Corporation. The last car to carry the Wolseley badge was produced in 1975.

As for Penniall, it is said that he was dismissed by Wolseley shortly after his return from Japan, though whether this was due to Wolseley's general financial difficulties, or stemmed from some dissatisfaction with Penniall's performance in Tokyo is not known. Penniall was now fifty years old, and it is said that he had difficulty finding regular employment thereafter. By 1938 he was living in Sutton Coldfield with his wife Alice, where he passed away on 1 August 1949 aged 77. His occupation at death is listed as 'Foreman tool-maker retired (motor car manufacture)'. Penniall did not live to hear of Isuzu's agreement with the Rootes Group therefore, nor did he live to see the appearance of Japanese-made cars on British roads, including those manufactured by his former employer in Tokyo, and the establishment of Japanese motor vehicle plants in Britain. It is likely that he would have been very surprised had he witnessed such developments. In any case, as Ishikawajima's car manufacturing division had changed its name, it is unlikely that Penniall would have recognized Isuzu vehicles as products of a company which he had helped to bring into being almost thirty years before.

The author gratefully acknowledges the kindness of Bridget Furst and Ann Causer, granddaughters of Albert James Penniall, in making his diary available for this paper.

Bibliography

English language

Baldwin, N. 1995. *The Wolseley*. Princes Risborough: Shire Publications.

Beasley, W. G. 1990. *The Rise of Modern Japan: Political, Economic and Social Change Since 1850*. London: Weidenfeld and Nicolson.

Chang, C. S. 1981. *The Japanese Auto Industry and the US Market*. New York: Praeger.

Cook, J. 1996. 'Horse Clipper or Sheep Shearer', in *Farm and Horticultural Equipment Collector*, July/August 1996. Cudham, Kent: Kelsey Publishing Limited.

Genther, P. A. 1990. *A History of Japan's Government-Business Relationship: The Passenger Car Industry*. Ann Arbor: University of Michigan.

Isuzu Motors Limited Public Relations Department. 1998. *This is Isuzu: Data Book 1997*. Tokyo: Isuzu Motors Limited.

Madeley, C. 1995. 'Oriental Wolseley', in *Old Glory*, October 1995. Cranleigh, Surrey: CMS Publishing.

Nixon, St. John C. 1949. *Wolseley: A Saga of the Motor Industry*. London: Foulis.

O'Toole, J. 1995. *Frederick York Wolseley*. Carlow: Jimmy O'Toole.

Penniall, Albert. *My Visit to Japan, 1920 to 1922*. I am grateful to Ms Bridget Furst, and Ms Ann Causer, Albert Penniall's granddaughters, for allowing me to use this unpublished diary as the basis of this chapter.

Shimokawa, Koichi. 1994. *The Japanese Automobile Industry: A Business History*. London: Athlone.

Wolseley Motors Limited Ledger General Number 4. British Motor Industry Heritage Trust Archives.

Wolseley Motors Limited Ledger General Number 5. British Motor Industry Heritage Trust Archives.

Japanese language

Ishikawajima Jukogyō Kabushiki Kaisha Shashi Hensan Iinkai. 1961. *Ishikawajima Jukogyō Kabushiki Kaisha 108 Nenshi*. (The 108 Year History of Ishikawajima Heavy Industries Company Limited). Tokyo: Ishikawajima-Harima Jukogyō Kabushiki Kaisha.

Isuzu Jidōshashi Hensan Iinkai. 1957. *Isuzu Jidōshashi*. (The History of Isuzu Motors). Tokyo: Isuzu Jidōsha Kabushiki Kaisha.

18

Hisaakira Kano (1886-1963): International Banker from a Daimyo Family

KEIKO ITOH

INTERNATIONAL BANKER, Viscount Hisaakira Kano,[1] established his reputation as an ardent supporter of Anglo-Japanese friendship during his life in London as the general manager of the Yokohama Specie Bank from 1934 to 1942. In those turbulent years leading up to the outbreak of the Pacific War, he had used all the influence he could in his contacts with leading figures in both Britain and Japan to prevent war between the two countries. As we now know, his efforts had little effect on the course of history, and what remains of Kano's international legacy are memories of a charming and generous, but rather opinionated, eccentric Japanese aristocrat, who was a true friend of Britain. It was Kano's ideas, as much as his actions, that made him unique.

Hisaakira was born in Tokyo in 1886. He was the oldest surviving son and one of eight siblings born to Viscount Kanō Hisayoshi, former daimyo of Ichinomiya *han* in Chiba. Hisaakira's career path was very much a reflection of the opportunities open to him coming from a ruling samurai background in the middle to late Meiji period: he studied at the Peers' Middle School and High School (Gakushuin), graduated from Tokyo Imperial University with a degree in Law in 1911 and then joined the Yokohama Specie Bank. What set Hisaakira apart from his many distinguished fellow Japanese bankers was his outspokenness and determination to make a difference, not only in the world of banking but in the world at large. He was assigned to various overseas postings with the bank, including Dairen, New York, London

212

twice and Calcutta, and travelled extensively. He was proud and grateful for the 34 years with the Yokohama Specie Bank during which he was able to travel 250,000 kilometres by aeroplane and visit 43 countries.[2] His directorships at the Bank of International Settlement in Basle, and the International Chamber of Commerce gave him further opportunities to 'become friends with some of the world's greatest financiers and entrepreneurs' and exchange ideas with them. Compared to Japanese bankers whom he found dull, Hisaakira enjoyed the company of European and American financiers who 'greet one with human warmth, statesmanship and diplomacy'. When Hisaakira was the general manager in London, the Yokohama Specie Bank ensured that Hisaakira had two very competent deputies who ran the business. For his strength by then was acknowledged as diplomat and spokesman for a Japan whose international reputation was fast sinking as a result of her actions in China.

This essay is as much an exploration of Kano's upbringing as the oldest son of a former daimyo which made him the man he was, as it is about his life in London. For, significant as many of Kano's achievements were, his place in history, I believe, belongs as a case study of an individual within a family that rode the tide of a rapidly changing Japan, being open to Western ways and modern thinking, but responding always with the sense of public vocation and responsibility that came from his traditional samurai background.

Hisaakira's first assignment to London was from 1921 to 1924, when he was in his mid-thirties with a young and growing family. In those days, only the heads of offices were entitled to bring their families with them abroad, and in the case of the Kanos, it was Hisayoshi, Hisaakira's father who was paying for all the extra expenses involved with taking the family along to the overseas postings. Although he was still a relatively young banker, Hisaakira's anticipated arrival in London was reported in the *Nichi-Ei Shinshi*, the Japanese community newspaper which was published in London between 1915 and 1938. The general manager of the London Branch of the Yokohama Specie Bank at the time was Ōkubo Toshitaka (son of Count Ōkubo Toshimichi, one of the Meiji oligarchs) who lived in the Master Lodge, the official residence of the general manager in Streatham, and the Kanos lived in a house nearby. Hisaakira's life in London in this earlier period was still free of public responsibilities and his activities revolved around his family, the Bank, the Japanese community in London and pursing his personal interests. Within the family, he was a somewhat short-tempered, strict and education-minded father, who would scold his sons for being rowdy on the one hand, and on the other hand would explain business matters to them and practise his speeches in front of them so that they could correct his English. This is when his sons were in primary school!

Hisaakira set out to be an active participant among the Japanese community in London, which numbered about 1,500 at the time. Although he was relatively junior in rank at the Yokohama Specie Bank, he was part of the elite among the Japanese community and, true to form, he made his presence known. Records show that he gave a lecture at the *Budō Kwai* in December 1922 on 'The Social and Economic Situation in Japan',[3] and joined the *Nihonjin-kai*, a club for Japanese 'gentlemen' created in the mode of English clubs, in May 1923.[4] The *Budō Kwai* was the Japanese martial arts club, started in 1917 by Gunji Koizumi. For Hisaakira, who was brought up by a father who was a master horseman and who viewed sports as an essential component of physical well-being and character building, the *Budō Kwai* was a natural institution to support, for encouraging Japanese martial arts among the British, and also to enlighten both British and Japanese through the lectures. Hisaakira was also a patron of the Mutual Aid Society, the *Kyōsai Kai*, which was established in 1919 to provide assistance to the less well off Japanese among the community. It was a time when many Japanese seamen who had worked on British merchant ships during the First World War were losing their jobs as the British returned from military service.

Hisaakira also pursued his personal interests, which included going to Fabian Society lectures, collecting and reading the books of H. G. Wells, and taking a soap box to Hyde Park to make speeches on whatever topic that was foremost in his mind at the time. Hisaakira's socialistic leanings were in fact very much a product of his generation. When he was at the Tokyo Imperial University from 1907 to 1911, he had been deeply influenced by Uchimura Kanzō, the famous Japanese Christian reformer. Uchimura's church was at the time a principal sponsor of the pioneer labour organization, the *Yuaikai*, which was modelled after the British friendly societies.[5] What was unusual in Hisaakira's case is that he passionately advocated his progressive views while at the same time being a member of both the old and the new Japanese establishment, working for a government-related bank. He recalled having been scolded about his open support for birth control by the head office during one of his business trips back to Tokyo.[6] 'But as far as I was concerned, so long as I was not neglecting my job, I could engage in anything I wished. After all, birth control is an extremely important matter.'[7]

Hisaakira's confidence and eccentricity were firmly embedded, I believe, in his family background and upbringing. For this reason, I propose to look back one generation to Hisaakira's father.

KANŌ HISAYOSHI

Hisaakira's father, Kanō Hisayoshi was born in Edo on 19 March 1848 as a lesser relative of the daimyo, or lord, of Tachibana Yanagikawa *han*.[8] After becoming orphaned at the age of eight by losing both parents overnight during the Ansei earthquake of 1855, he was taken in to live with his much older brother, who by then was adopted into the main Tachibana family as the lord, and was a senior member of the Tokugawa *bakufu*. Lord Tachibana spent as much time as he could with his little brother and took over his education. In addition to reading and calligraphy, he taught him archery, and sent him to study under a grand master in horsemanship.

The Japanese political scene then was in great turmoil following Commodore Perry's arrival in Edo bay in 1854. Lord Tachibana was responsible for overseeing military reform which was considered crucial at a time when the *bakufu* realized that Japan was militarily too weak to oppose Western pressure to end its policy of seclusion. Influenced by his brother, Hisayoshi became interested in French military strategy. As a teenager, he was given a company of farmer soldiers to lead, and participated in joint military practice with other *han* troops. Then Hisayoshi himself became a *bakufu* daimyo in August 1866, at the age of 19. Hisayoshi had always been a favourite of Lord Kanō Hisatsune of Kazusa Ichinomiya *han* (in Chiba), and upon his death, Hisayoshi was adopted into the family to inherit the title and domain. The Kanōs were a traditional family who were not at all interested in Western military strategy, but Hisayoshi, upon entering his new domain, reportedly assembled all the samurai and made them undergo Western military practice.

Then within two years came the Meiji Restoration, ending 300 years of Tokugawa rule. In the ensuing radical political transition, Hisayoshi remained calm and collected. He was quick to accept the changed circumstances, and was first among the Kantō daimyo to return his domain to the Emperor, and was given the title of Viscount. Relieved of his feudal duties, his greatest desire was to study French and law in France. However, the conservative Kanō family saw study abroad as an abandonment of family duties. From 1872 onwards he became a government employee, first in the Ministry of Education, then with the Ministry of Justice. In 1895, he was appointed as governor of Kagoshima, a position he held for seven years and for which he was best known.[9] Kagoshima at that time was split into two political factions and the prefectural bureaucracy was embroiled in political infighting. However, Hisayoshi managed to stay out of politics and devoted all his energies to promoting industry in the prefecture. In order to demonstrate ways to engage in productive industry, he even converted the garden in the governor's residence into an experimental agricultural laboratory, keeping different kinds of hens and bees, growing various fruit and vegetable crops and constructing a special out-building for making compost.[10] In the house, Hisayoshi's wife would be giving lessons in raising silkworms, flower arrangement and cooking. In the course of implementing all his ideas, Hisayoshi poured in vast sums of his personal funds, ending up with huge debts. His family and retainers back in Tokyo finally had to hold a family conference and concluded that Hisayoshi must resign, or the family assets would be depleted.

Had he not been forced to resign, he probably would have remained as governor of Kagoshima for a longer period. After returning to Tokyo, Hisayoshi was elected to the House of Peers and held several positions, including chairman of the Imperial Agriculture Committee, vice chairman of the Central Industrial Union Committee, and chairman of the Agriculture Study Group which comprised of members from both houses of parliament. In his later years, Hisayoshi returned to Ichinomiya, the seat of his former domain, to become its mayor. He made the town famous, not only for its model administration, but also by providing it with a very unusual 'aristocrat mayor'.

Hisayoshi was one of the early Meiji public-spirited intellectuals, concerned with the philosophical questions of creating 'a new Japanese for the modern age'. He was in his early twenties during the heady days of the immediate post-Restoration period, when the educated classes were absorbed by the presence of the West – its power, science, achievements and progressive thoughts. And he shared with many of his contemporaries an enthusiasm for the adventure of modernization. On the one hand, his Confucian education had instilled in him a high sense of public vocation based on the virtues of 'benevolent rule' by which the wise ruler looked after his subjects' interests. His moral code was bushido, the way of the warrior, which called for selfless devotion and an ascetic and frugal lifestyle. Personal consumption was seen as wasteful expenditures, and profitable expenditures were those spent in fulfilment of one's obligations to lord, family or country, or in his case, Kagoshima. On the other hand, he was open to new ideas, and believed that new approaches and new ways of thinking was the way forward for the next generation of Japanese leaders. This belief he demonstrated in how he brought up his children.

THE UPBRINGING OF THE KANŌ CHILDREN

Being a superior horseman and competent in the martial arts, Hisayoshi encouraged sports for both his two sons and six daughters. He was strict with their upbringing, but at the same time, was unusually progressive. In Kagoshima he sent the children to a Western missionary who had opened a church nearby to receive instruction in Christianity and English. He also invited Catholic and Protestant missionaries to his house to give the children Bible readings in English. There was an organ in the dining-room, and Itsuko, Hisayoshi's wife, took music lessons. Some of the daughters also learned to play the organ and sing hymns.[11]

After returning to Tokyo from Kagoshima, the girls went to the Peers' Girls School. Their classmates were mainly also from aristocratic families, and they wore long sleeved elegant kimonos and commuted to school in horse carriages or rickshaws. The Kanō girls, however, under the influence of Hisayoshi, who was strictly against extravagance, were made to wear a special outfit which was known as the 'Kanō improved dress' – kimono-like outfits with straight narrow sleeves. Hisayoshi was a great believer in practicality, and this attire was aimed at giving greater mobility to the wearer.[12] The Kanō girls were also made to commute to school by train, walking quite a long distance between the station and the school. They became well known by the residents along the route.

Hisayoshi believed that a new Japan needed to educate a new breed of women. He thought that women should be able to take decisions and initiatives on their own. To instil independence in his daughters, by the time they were in their mid-teens, he made them plan and execute a short trip on their own during the spring holidays. The girls would plan the itinerary, work out the budget, and then show their plans to their oldest brother, Hisaakira, for his input. Once the plan was finalized and approved by Hisayoshi, off they went on their adventure. With the oldest being about 15 or 16, the troupe of four sisters were expected to manage everything on their own from transportation to accommodation, and were given Hisayoshi's name card to use only in the case of an emergency. The girls, however, never once had to use the card, and always completed their trips without mishap.

Another unusual custom in the Kanō household was the Saturday evening family speech events. Hisayoshi believed that in a modern Japan, it was important to be able to clearly and confidently speak one's own opinion in public. Everyone in the household, including the servants, was required to attend the Saturday event. Speakers for each week would be designated beforehand, and were expected to speak about what was on their mind, or give a report. These speech events became known outside the family, and the Kanōs were often asked if observers could attend. Hisayoshi thought that the bigger the audience, the better the experience, and encouraged and welcomed visitors.

TATSUKO KANŌ

For Hisaakira, who often chaired the family speech events and oversaw his younger sisters' education, finding a wife who would share his progressive views could have been a problem. In fact, Hisaakira was influenced by the theory of racial improvement through mixed marriage and he even contemplated marrying a Western woman in order to improve the Japanese race. Apparently, Hisayoshi did not object, but his mother pleaded against such radical action, and in the end, they went to the headmistress of the Ochanomizu Women's College and asked to be introduced to the brightest and most physically attractive and well-built graduate. This is how Hisaakira came to meet Itō Tatsuko, who became his wife.

Tatsuko was born in 1893 to Itō Suketaka and Shō, and married Hisaakira when she was 18 years old. It could not have been easy for her in the beginning for she had married the eldest son of a former daimyo, and as such, despite her tender years, was expected to take charge of the household, which at the time consisted not only of her parents-in-law, but also Hisaakira's four younger, unmarried sisters. As soon as she married into the family, Tatsuko was given the responsibility of managing the household budget and organizing all the family meals. Hisaakira's transfer to Dairen, in Manchuria in 1915 must have been a welcome relief, giving her for the first time a chance to lead an independent life as Hisaakira's wife.

By all accounts, Tatsuko was a remarkably forward-looking modern woman. She was, in her own right, an activist, who participated in the activities of the *Nihon Kirisutokyō Fujin Kyōfukai* (Japanese Women's Christian Temperance Union) which fought to end Japan's licensed prostitution. It was also a movement that agitated for the right of women to participate in political activities and called for equality in gender relations.[13] Tatsuko certainly seems to have merited the high recommendation placed on her by her headmistress for she is remembered as having been competent in everything she did.[14] When in New York, around 1918, she learned how to drive a car and was better at it than Hisaakira. Even her English was better than his, although Hisaakira had been studying English since his teenage years. One of their sons recalls that Hisaakira had an inferiority complex towards her, but perhaps another way to look at it is that Hisaakira readily accepted and respected her abilities. For, Hisaakira had been brought up in a household where the women were trained to be independent. And he was a firm believer in the equality of women, as manifested in his attendance at the Fabian Society lectures, his support for family planning, and his voracious reading of H. G. Wells. It is difficult to say whether it was Tatsuko who influenced Hisaakira in this regard, or the other way round, but the couple were well-matched in their abilities and beliefs and enjoyed a progressive relationship based on equality, which was hardly typical at the time.

Tatsuko was indeed a new breed of Japanese woman who lived up to the challenges of adapting to the requirements of a rapidly modernising Japan. However, as in the case of Hisaakira, her forward-looking attitude and courage were products not only of the modern education that she received, but also of the traditional samurai values that were inculcated in her during her upbringing. For Tatsuko came from a family of spirited samurai, and was brought up under the samurai code for women which preached that '... a woman must be ever on the alert and keep a strict watch over her own conduct... In her capacity of wife, she must keep her husband's household in proper order. If the wife be evil and profligate, the house is ruined.'[15] The irony is that the very same samurai values that made Tatsuko a modern woman perfectly comfortable in Western surroundings, had led her grandfather, Itō Gunbei to take drastic action against Westerners in the tumultuous years preceding the Meiji Restoration.

For Gunbei was the samurai who, in 1862, attacked the British legation at the Takanawa Tozenji Temple in Edo in an attempt to assasinate Sir Rutherford Alcock, the first British minister to Japan.[16] Gunbei's assassination attempt was the third major incident against foreigners and the second attack on the British legation. His solitary act was committed to resolve what to him was an insurmountable dilemma. For, following the first attack, the *bakufu* had assigned Matsumoto *han*, to which Gunbei belonged, to guard the British compound despite the fact that many of its samurai including Gunbei were *sonnō jōi* supporters who believed that the course for Japan was to unite under the emperor and expel the barbarians. If Gunbei did not protect the British legation, he would be disobeying *bakufu* orders. On the other hand, if he did his duties, he would be fighting his own *jōi* comrades and acting against his principles. Gunbei decided that the only course of action was to sacrifice his own life: by murdering the British minister, he would fulfil his principles, and as a result of his act, the *bakufu* would surely release Matsumoto *han* from the intolerable duty of protecting the British legation. He himself would commit suicide once his mission was accomplished.

In the event, Gunbei ended up killing two British guards and fleeing as soon as the Japanese guards were alerted of the commotion for he did not want to have a confrontation with his own clan samurai. He reported back immediately to the Matsumoto *han* residence, informed them of his action and took his own life with his sword. Anticipating the shame he was to incur on his family, he had stipulated in his will that his marriage was to be dissolved. Gunbei was 23 years of age at the time with a young wife and two little daughters. As he had planned, the *bakufu* reprimanded and relieved Matsumoto *han* of its guard duties. In face of British demands for severe punishment, Gunbei's remains were discarded in a prison yard (although many years later he was properly buried in a cemetery) and the Lord of Matsumoto *han* ordered that his family name and his samurai status be taken away. The following year, however, under a general pardon within the *han*, the family was reinstated and Gunbei's former widow once again became a member of the Itō family.

Tatsuko Kanō's mother, Itō Shō, was the older of the two daughters left behind by Gunbei. When living in London, Tatsuko would often marvel about the changed times since her grandfather's days. Whereas he had given up his life to expel the barbarians, there she was, speaking English fluently and entertaining at her home in Kensington many members of the British establishment, acting as a bridge between Japan and Britain.

HIRAM HISANORI KANŌ

If Tatsuko was an example of a modern Japanese woman whose progressiveness was rooted in her samurai upbringing, yet a different example is provided by the life of Hisanori Kanō, Hisaakira's younger brother by four years.

While all the Kanō children had been strongly influenced by their early exposure to Christianity, Hisanori, who had returned to Kagoshima to study at the Number Seven High School after graduation from the Peers' Middle School in 1907, became heavily involved with the Japan Christian Church. Although he was not baptized at the time, together with two Christian classmates, they held morning prayers each day, took turns reading the Bible and sang hymns. In his second year, Hisanori ran a high fever which turned out to be paratyphoid. Whilst in hospital, he also came down with appendicitis and peritonitis, and was so weakened that he could not even open his eyes. The doctors contacted the Kanō family in Tokyo, and Hisanori himself was prepared for death.[17] It was then that he found God. He could not describe the experience in words, but felt complete peace and even physical strength. Miraculously, the infection in his stomach healed from that moment. This experience became the very core of Hisanori's faith and the basis of his religion for the rest of his life. He was baptized in 1909.

Partly because of his long illness and partly because he became more interested in missionary work than his studies, he was failing at school and was ashamed of himself knowing that his parents were paying for his schooling and providing him with everything he needed, and yet he had failed to fulfil his responsibilities. When he went home for the summer holidays, he found that Hisayoshi had received a long letter from the headmaster, who had written that Hisanori's absorption in religion had led to his failed studies. Hisanori was called to his father's study, and asked to explain the situation. He immediately responded that, due to weakness of character, he had failed, and asked Hisayoshi to take any measure against him as he saw fit. Hisayoshi simply said that it was not a matter of weakness of character. All Hisanori needed to do was study harder. Nothing was mentioned about religion even once.

Hisanori obtained a degree in agriculture from the University of Tokyo in 1916. Upon graduation, Hisayoshi asked him what his future plans were, for he had an offer from a certain baron in Shinshu asking for Hisanori to marry into the family to become heir. This came about just when Hisanori himself had wanted to discuss his future with his parents. He had studied the problems of Japan's land, food and population situation and was interested in Japan's colonial and immigration policies. He believed that it was God's wish for him to go abroad as an immigrant. His desire would be to emigrate rather than marry into a baronetcy. Upon hearing this, Hisayoshi immediately decided to cancel the marriage offer and encouraged Hisanori to seek advice from a prominent geography expert on where best to emigrate. Upon this professor's recommendation, Hisanori decided on America, where the immigration restrictions imposed against the Japanese would present him with a true challenge. His mission was not simply to make a living as an immigrant, but to dedicate his life to improving the conditions of Japanese immigrants in America and working towards a solution to the immigration issue. With an introduction from his father to former Secretary of State W. J. Bryan to be his sponsor, Hisanori, student visa in hand, set off on the *Siberia Maru* on 8 October 1916.

Hisanori obtained his Masters degree in Agriculture from the University of Nebraska in 1918, and in 1919, Nagai Aiko, daughter of a loyal Kanō former retainer, travelled alone from Japan to marry Hisanori, whom she had never met. In the same year, Hisanori purchased a 300-acre farm, which he ran with Aiko and called Humble Cottage Farm. It was also in 1919 that Hisayoshi died at the age of 75. Hisanori continued to receive both moral and financial support when in need from his mother and the 'family conference' back in Japan. While managing the farm, he became the chairman of the Japanese Enlightenment Society, devoting much energy to the education of fellow Japanese. In 1925, however, responding to an ardent plea from Bishop Beecher of the Anglican Church in Nebraska, he agreed to give up his farm and become a lay preacher to devote his life to spreading the gospel and working for the Japanese American community. He moved his residence every few years so that he could reach all Japanese

American communities throughout Nebraska and, after 32 years of missionary work, he became Rector Emeritus upon his retirement in 1957. During World War II, as one of the leaders of the Japanese community, Hisanori spent two years behind bars and a further three years under parole in internment camps, having no contact with his family for four years. His faith never failed him however, and he was loved and respected by other internees and even by some of his captors during his internment. After he gained freedom in 1946, Hisanori continued his role as loved priest and leader among the Japanese American community both in Nebraska and later in Colorado. Although in a totally different context, Hisanori in fact had followed in his father's footsteps: he had dedicated his life to the betterment of his fellow Japanese Americans in the manner of a humble daimyo. Hisanori died in 1989 at the age of 99.

HISAAKIRA'S SECOND TERM IN LONDON

While Hisanori was spreading the gospel in Nebraska, Hisaakira's career with the Yokohama Specie Bank had taken him to assignments in Calcutta, Japan, China and back again to London. When he returned to London in 1934, Hisaakira's personal circumstances were different from his previous stay: he was now head of the London Branch of the Yokohama Specie Bank, and as such, was officially one of the leaders of the Japanese community. His older children had grown and he returned only with Tatsuko, youngest child, Rosa, and a Japanese servant, Masa.

The most significant change, however, was Japan's image in Britain. By then, Japan's reputation within the international community had rapidly deteriorated. The Manchurian Incident of 1931 followed by Japan's occupation of Manchuria, the report of the Lytton Commission of Inquiry on behalf of the League of Nations and Japan's withdrawal from the League in 1933, had tarnished Japan's image in British public opinion. Moreover, Japan's increasing trade with China and Southeast Asia was seen as a threat to British markets. When the Kanōs returned to London, the atmosphere was no longer the same as it had been in the early 1920s. Whereas in the earlier decade Britain saw Japan as an aspiring nation and Japan sought to learn from Britain, by the mid-1930s Japan had become a fully-fledged competing power.

Hisaakira's activities during his second term in Britain were very much dictated by these changed circumstances both on a personal level and publicly. At home, the Kanō lifestyle now reflected his more prominent social standing, and while day to day family activities remained relatively simple, there were grander social occasions. Hisaakira's public activities were inevitably focussed on efforts to repair Japan's reputation and international standing. He saw it as his duty to be a bridge between Britain and Japan: he believed that with better mutual understanding of each other's circumstances, the unravelling friendship between the two countries could be repaired. And he used his position and connections to the full to advocate his opinions and negotiate peace measures. As the representative of one of the biggest foreign exchange banks in the world which was government backed, he had access to the major international financial leaders, as well as British statesmen, and they were his counterparts in his diplomatic efforts.

At home, the Kanōs entertained at least one in every three evenings, and Hisaakira also travelled widely to other European capitals. Hisaakira's lifestyle was seemingly grand: he had moved the general manager's residence from Streatham to Kensington and all their groceries were ordered and delivered from Harrods. Hisaakira also made sure that his youngest daughter, Rosa Hideko, was presented to court as a debutante. In Hisaakira's thinking, maintaining the lifestyle and standards of what was expected of a viscount in Britain was a necessity. He selflessly devoted himself to Japan's cause, and used as his means his social standing which he made sure was matched by appearance as well as substance. In doing so, he, like his father in Kagoshima, did not hesitate to spend his personal funds.

An additional responsibility for Hisaakira as general manager of the Yokohama Specie Bank was to be a director of the Bank for International Settlements in Basle, as the Japanese representative in commerce, industry, and finance. From May 1934, Hisaakira went to Basle every month to attend the directors' meetings. These meetings with the world's major financiers were to him important opportunities to explain Japan's international situation, and he also travelled extensively, both to feed his natural curiosity and to engage in conversations to help Japan be better understood.

It was during one of his monthly trips to Basle in May 1935 when tragedy struck at home.[18] Without any forewarning, Tatsuko suddenly died. The day before, she had as usual had her riding lesson with her daughter, Rosa, in Hyde Park and then gone for an afternoon of tennis at the Yokohama Specie Bank tennis courts in Lower Sydenham. On the Sunday of her death, she had read the Bible and sung hymns with Rosa as was the custom, and was spending a quiet afternoon knitting when she collapsed. Her death was so sudden that Hisaakira did not make it back to London in time. She had been a great source of strength to him, and also an invaluable partner in his diplomatic efforts for she was the gracious hostess who presided over his social events. Her death at the age of 42 came at the height of Hisaakira's career with the Yokohama Specie Bank. For those who knew her, she is always remembered as the modern, accomplished, and vibrant woman in her very prime.

From then on, Hisaakira increasingly relied on Rosa to take over household management and act as his hostess although she was only 14 years old. He continued to entertain extensively at home, and although the cooking was done by Winnie, the cook, Rosa was responsible for deciding the menu. She was also his travelling companion on many of his trips. During a trip to Scandinavia, just as they reached Norway, Hisaakira picked up a newspaper and learned of the China Incident. He was terribly upset, and returned immediately to London.

The Japanese ambassador in London from 1936-38 was Shigeru Yoshida, whose family was very close to the Kanōs. They were often invited to embassy functions and also visited the Yoshidas at their summer place near Henley. As Ambassador Yoshida was doing all he could on the diplomatic front to keep Japan closely tied to Britain and against her strengthening ties with Germany, Hisaakira, as a banker, was pursuing his channels towards the same end.[19] They both believed strongly that Britain and Japan should and could cooperate, especially vis-à-vis China. At the Japan Society dinner to welcome Ambassador and Madame Yoshida in October 1936, Hisaakira took the floor in response to the toast given by the Earl of Cromer:

> 'I am not a politician – I am just a poor banker, handling other people's money and calculating other people's interest,' he said. When in Japan he had admonished leading industrialists, especially in textiles, that they lacked sympathy for and understanding of their fellow capitalists in Lancashire who were facing competition from them. 'On the other hand, however, there is much which I might say to my British friends with regard to Japan's position and grievances and the underlying causes of commercial and industrial competition. It is my own firm opinion that there is no real reason why the two countries cannot reach a happy adjustment of commercial relations. So many immense uncultivated markets exist in the world. Capitalists of both countries know all too well that unnecessary and unhealthy competition simply kills their own business. What is needed is collaboration, not competition, co-ordination, not antagonism.'[20]

In his efforts to promote dialogue among British and Japanese businessmen, Hisaakira initiated the Japan Society monthly business-men's lunch discussion groups. As the international situation deteriorated in the late 1930s, he became increasingly involved in various diplomatic negotiations which went beyond banking and business circles to save Anglo-Japanese friendship. His British contacts included Prime Minister Baldwin, Foreign Secretary Eden, Montagu Norman, Governor of the Bank of England, Lord Hankey, Lord Lloyd, Chairman of the British Council, General Piggott, George Sale and various influential friends from the Japan Society.[21] On the Japanese side, he was in regular telegram and letter correspondence with Count Makino, Prime Minister Konoe, Kido Kōichi and Harada Kumao.[22]

Up until the 6 December 1941, he was in contact with those among the British establishment who shared his view that war between Britain and Japan should be avoided.[23] However, all his efforts came to nought on 8 December.

In a little pamphlet entitled 'My London Records', dated February 1942, Hisaakira wrote:

> Monday, December 8th, 1941, was a tragic day. The war broke out between Great Britain and Japan. I left Princes Gate Court at 7 o'clock on that morning and took No.9 Bus to the city. As soon as I arrived at my office, the London Branch of the Yokohama Specie Bank, I called in ten Japanese colleagues to my room, and told each one of them the most important thing at this time were "Health and Character". I told all British colleagues and messengers – about 60 in all them – (about 30 were already in military service) that the extremely sad situation had developed entirely contrarily to what I had worked and wished for, and thanked them for their friendship and assistance in the past, and prayed for the early return of happy days.[24]

With war declared, most of the senior Japanese businessmen and many others were immediately interned on the Isle of Man. Hisaakira was spared internment until March 1942 due to the intervention of the Foreign Office, which was concerned that his internment might lead to retaliatory treatment to British officials in Tokyo.[25] An exchange repatriation was being negotiated. In March, however, the newspapers reported that he had refuted Mr Eden's statement about Japanese atrocities in Hong Kong as Chinese propaganda. Pressure mounted for his internment and he was arrested by Home Office officials on 12 March.

For Hisaakira, the reported Japanese atrocities were inconceivable simply because he fundamentally believed in the morality of men. Even the most Anglophile of Japanese was a true nationalist at heart, and apart from believing in Japan's legitimate rights in China, he was becoming increasingly exasperated by what he saw as British pettiness and dishonour ever since the freezing of Japanese assets in July 1941. Although he loved Britain and the British, once war had been declared between the two countries, his allegiance inevitably had to be towards

Japan. Because he had worked so hard to avoid such a development, the situation brought him all the more sorrow.

EPILOGUE

Hisaakira's brief internment ended in the summer of 1942 with an exchange repatriation. During the few months in the Isle of Man, Hisaakira was a natural leader amongst the Japanese internees, and helped organize the group to occupy themselves productively through educational and sports activities. He also injected a sense of fun while doing routine chores. When on floor-cleaning duty, he would use his mop as a calligraphy brush and swoop around writing giant letters on the floor.

War brought about the end of Hisaakira's life in Britain as well as his career as a banker. In the immediate post-war years, the Yokohama Specie Bank, which was viewed by the Allied Occupation as having played a significant role in Japan's war efforts, was restructured and privatized to become the Bank of Tokyo. Hisaakira, as one of the directors of the Bank, was purged from holding public office until 1950 and then held a number of posts in both the private and public sector. He remained deeply attached to Britain, and was a member of the council of the Japan-British Society in Tokyo throughout his post-war life. Forever a man with progressive, sometimes far-fetched ideas, he is best known in Japan as the first president of the Japan Housing Agency, and finally as the governor of Chiba prefecture. Just as his father had ended his life as mayor of Ichinomiya, Hisaakira also returned to his family's former domain so that he could put all his innovative ideas to practice in the land from which he came. Sadly, however, only three months into his governorship, he died suddenly of a stroke on 21 February 1963. He was 76 years old.

Hisaakira, his father Hisayoshi, and his brother Hisanori, each led very different lives, but all were united in their strong sense of public duty and commitment to the welfare of others which came from their upbringing as ruling samurai. Those traditional values, combined with their enormous curiosity, openness to new ideas and courage to act on their beliefs made them unique in a society dominated by convention.

19

'That Loyal British Subject'?: Arthur Edwardes and Anglo-Japanese Relations, 1932–41

ANTONY BEST

ONE OF THE IRONIES of history is that the reputation of any individual rests so substantially on circumstance. If history had been different, and if by some means the Pacific War had been avoided and a rapprochement reached between Britain and Japan, it is possible that an essay on the figure of Arthur Edwardes, the British-born adviser to the Manchukuo government in the 1930s and later adviser on world affairs to the Japanese embassy in London, might have appeared earlier in this series of volumes on the personalities who have helped to develop and enrich Anglo-Japanese relations. As it is, the fact that conflict did break out means that Edwardes, on the rare occasions when he is mentioned in history books, emerges as a shadowy and slightly sinister figure working on the boundary where a naive devotion to friendship between states borders on treachery.

★ ★ ★

Arthur Edwardes was born in 1885. He came from an upper-class background, his father was Lt-Colonel C.E. Edwardes, a son of the third Lord Kensington, while his mother was Lady Blanche Butler, the daughter of the second Marquess of Ormonde. He was educated at Haileybury and in 1903 entered the Chinese Maritime Customs Service (CMC). By all accounts he was generally a sociable individual, but 'never displayed great abilities or any aptitude for hard work'.[1] These latter failings did not, however, act as a bar to promotion, as he soon became a trusted protégé of Sir Francis Aglen, the Inspector-General of Customs.[2]

His eventual appearance as a key figure in Anglo-Japanese relations in the 1930s came about through a circuitous route, related to his troubled time in the CMC in the 1920s. Aglen in the middle of this decade began to cultivate Edwardes as his successor, and when on 31 January 1927 the former was suddenly dismissed by the government in Peking, the latter was quickly appointed as acting Inspector-General to take his place.[3] Edwardes could hardly have taken over the reins of power at a worse time, for the whole future of the CMC was now becoming a battleground between the KMT (Nationalist) government in Hankow, and Chang Tso-lin's government in Peking. From the first Edwardes was compromised in the eyes of the KMT by his links with Chang's administration and his inherent conservatism. His cause was also not helped by the fact that the ambitious CMC Commissioner in Shanghai, Frederick Maze, was all too happy to conciliate the KMT in order to outflank Edwardes and steadily erode his authority. On 31 December 1928, after a fruitless attempt to have the victorious KMT appoint him as the permanent Inspector-General, an exasperated Edwardes resigned his post and was replaced by Maze.[4]

Edwardes left China in February 1929 boiling with resentment at the treatment that had been meted out to him by Maze and the Nationalist government. His mood was not improved by Nanking's reluctance to reimburse him for a year's annual leave to which he claimed to be entitled. The Chinese rejected his claim on the grounds that he had overpaid himself while in the post of acting Inspector-General, an accusation which he fervently denied.[5]

Edwardes was, however, on the verge of another very lucrative career. His new employer was to be the Japanese puppet-state of Manchukuo. His link with Japan arose out of his doomed attempt to be made the permanent Inspector-General. During this contest the one state that had provided Edwardes with apparently unqualified support was Japan.[6] In addition, during his time in China Edwardes had made a number of Japanese friends, including up-and-coming figures in the China service of the Gaimushō, such as Yoshida Shigeru, the consul-general in Tientsin, and Shigemitsu Mamoru, the first secretary at the Japanese legation in Peking.[7] Edwardes was thus sympathetic towards Japan, and might also, as some pointed out at the time, have taken delight in working for the Japanese as a flagrant act of revenge against Nanking. The Japanese government in turn seem to have seen him, with his professional and personal links to the British business world and the conservative élite, as a useful channel to those still friendly towards Japan.

The post that Edwardes was offered and which he accepted in the autumn of 1932 was that of financial adviser and London agent to the Manchukuo government with a salary of an astonishing £5,000 per annum. Edwardes's primary task was to act as a 'propagandist' for Manchukuo in Britain and to interest British business in investing there, an exercise that was intended to bring both economic and political benefits to the new state.[8] Edwardes first appeared in his new role at Geneva in December 1932 when he acted as an adviser to the Japanese delegates at the League of Nations, Matsuoka Yōsuke and Matsudaira Tsuneo.[9] At around the same time he began his business activities by having lunch in London with Sir William Clare Lees, a leading figure in the Manchester Chamber of Commerce. The intermediary who arranged the meeting was Edwardes's friend H.A. Gwynne, the editor of Britain's most Conservative daily newspaper, the *Morning Post*, who was himself a fervent believer in the need for Anglo-Japanese friendship.[10]

After this initial burst of activity, in March 1933 Edwardes left Britain for a visit to Manchukuo and Japan in order to study the prospects for British trade. By this time the Foreign Office was aware of his new role, in part because of complaints from Maze but, in addition, because just before his trip to the East he met Sir Edward Crowe, the Comptroller-General of the Department of Overseas Trade, at a lunch at the Japanese embassy.[11] Opinion on Edwardes's new role was divided. In Peking Sir Miles Lampson, the British minister, urged caution in dealing with him, even though Edwardes was a family friend. Lampson noted to Crowe on 15 May 1933 that even if Edwardes was in a position to help British trade in Manchuria, his presence could jeopardize Britain's position in China proper:

> His name remains mud in China, particularly as he is returning to the stage in the employment of Manchukuo maybe with the intention of getting his own back on T.V. Soong and company.[12]

Lampson's suspicions were raised even further when it became clear later in the year that Edwardes appeared keen to act as a facilitator of British recognition of Manchukuo.[13]

These suspicions were not widely shared in the Foreign Office, the Department of Overseas Trade or the British embassy in Tokyo, all of whom believed that Edwardes could prove useful as a means of directing contracts from the Manchukuo government to British firms. This was of particular importance as through both press and intelligence sources, Whitehall was aware that a Japanese-French syndicate was in the process of being formed in order to exploit Manchukuo's potential.[14] When in Tokyo in July 1933 Edwardes directly addressed the prospect of French investment in a conversation with Alvary Gascoigne, a first secretary at the Tokyo embassy, and hinted at his desire to use his position to help British companies bid for contracts.[15] Armed with this intimation of his desire to help, the line finally agreed in Whitehall was that while there could be no official dealings with Edwardes, as this would be tantamount to *de facto* recognition of Manchukuo, there was, as the Foreign Office noted, '... no reason why he should not be received and called into private consultation or even unofficially put in touch with British firms seeking business in Manchuria'.[16]

This hope that Edwardes could be kept at arm's length and that he would operate solely within the realm of trade was, however, to be frustrated. Lampson's fear that Edwardes would act as much in the political as the economic sphere in the end proved not to be too wide of the mark. Using the bait of contracts from the Manchukuo government, Edwardes did indeed act to create a climate within which right-wing opinion in Britain would move towards the espousal of *de facto* or even *de jure* recognition of Manchukuo. He was aided in this task in 1934 by the growing consensus in the Treasury, centred around Neville Chamberlain, the Chancellor of the Exchequer, and Sir Warren Fisher, the Permanent Secretary at the Treasury, that Britain should improve its relations with Japan in order to limit the scope of British rearmament in order that Britain might concentrate its arms expenditure against the German threat.

Edwardes had a channel to Fisher through H.A.Gwynne. In the winter of 1934 Gwynne, with Edwardes's knowledge, held a series of meetings with Fisher in which he warned that the United States might be close to recognizing Manchukuo.[17] Fisher was at first suspicious, but Edwardes acted to reinforce Gwynne's contention by supplying reports that supported this impression and demonstrated American business interest in Manchuria. Fisher passed this disturbing information to Chamberlain, who in turn asked Sir Walter Runciman, the President of the Board of Trade, to see Edwardes in order to discuss the Manchukuo question.[18]

At the same time that he was approaching the Treasury, Edwardes was also in contact with Guy Locock, the Director of the Federation of British Industries (FBI), about the possibility of a FBI-sponsored mission to Manchuria to investigate the potential for British trade and investment. This was a clever and welcome proposal, as its unofficial status would avoid any diplomatic difficulties while still benefiting Britain in the field of trade, and with Edwardes having already smoothed his path at the Treasury, it received warm backing from all the relevant ministries in Whitehall as well as the FBI itself.

Nevertheless, it soon transpired that the mission also had a political angle. Edwardes arranged that he would accompany the mission in order to smooth its way. However, he also had an ulterior motive. Sometime in the summer of 1934 it was decided by Fisher and Matsudaira Tsuneo, the Japanese ambassador in London, that while Edwardes was in Japan he should act as a secret conduit of the Treasury's thinking on Anglo-Japanese relations to the heads of the Gaimushō and other significant Japanese policy-makers.

The FBI mission arrived in Japan in late September 1934 and made a short visit to Manchuria in mid-October. It received an enthusiastic if choreographed reception. Behind the scenes Edwardes met with a number of Japanese officials, including his old friend Shigemitsu, who was now the vice-minister at the Gaimushō, the Foreign Minister, Hirota Kōki, the Navy Minister, Admiral Ōsumi Mineo, the Army Minister, General Hayashi Senjūrō, and his recently retired prede-cessor, General Araki Sadao. To each Edwardes presented a letter which contained a plan for a Gentleman's Agreement between Britain and Japan, which would establish a channel for private consultations over issues of common concern including China. He received a warm response. Shigemitsu, in particular, was keen to use Edwardes as a channel to Fisher and Chamberlain in order to pave the way for Japan's abrogation of the Washington and London naval treaties. The vice-minister noted to Baron Harada, the secretary to Prince Saionji, that Edwardes was useful as he '... has personal friends in the British Government, and hopes that the relations of Japan and Britain would revert to those of the old days'.[19] Edwardes returned to Britain in November armed with expressions of goodwill from Shigemitsu. On 26 November he sent a letter to Fisher detailing the discussions he had had with the vice-minister, in which Shigemitsu had stated that Japan would never go to war with Britain and had agreed to the conclusion of a Gentleman's Agreement between the two states.[20]

Edwardes's naïve foray into diplomacy was, however, to be thwarted by the actions of his own paymasters. At the same time as he was in East Asia, a crisis had broken out over the decision by the Manchukuo government to establish a state oil monopoly, an act which hardly suggested that Manchuria was to be a conducive environment for British commercial activities or that Japan sincerely believed in good relations with Britain. In addition, Edwardes's activities were blunted by a series of forthright letters from Sir George Sansom, the commercial counsellor at the Tokyo Embassy, who argued that the Japanese were trying to fabricate an Anglo-Japanese friendship without offering any real concessions to British interests. This proved to be useful ammunition for the Foreign Office who saw the Treasury's drive to achieve a *rapprochement* as misguided, as it failed to deal with the issue of China and would clearly be unacceptable to the United States.[21]

The idea of a *rapprochement* based on trade in Manchuria and a Gentleman's Agreement was, however, soon to be put to one side, for in November 1934 Yoshida Shigeru arrived in London as a 'touring ambassador' and brought with him a new plan for Anglo-Japanese cooperation centred upon the rehabilitation of the Chinese economy. This provided a new potentially useful avenue and Edwardes once again acted as a channel of communication between the embassy and the British Treasury.[22] On 14 January 1935 Edwardes provided Fisher with an unsigned memorandum that stressed the dangers of Britain not helping Japan, noting of the latter:

> It was to England that she looked in the past for friendly guidance and it is to England that she is turning now for a repetition of the guidance. If England refuses to co-operate, and if that refusal results in Japan taking the bit between the teeth in the Far East, we could not hold ourselves entirely guiltless.[23]

On the positive side, however, he recorded that Japan was willing to cooperate with Britain and the United States in the reconstruction of China, and evinced that this would also be acceptable to the Chinese financial and trading communities. He also emphasized that any '... constructive policy for settling for settling Far Eastern problems should not ignore the question of Manchukuo'. These ideas were close to the Treasury's own thinking on China, and in the coming months were to evolve into the famous mission to East Asia led by Sir Frederick Leith-Ross, Chief Economic Adviser to the British government, in 1935. Here, too, however, Edwardes's efforts to build a framework for closer relations came to nothing.

After this initial flurry of eventually fruitless endeavours, Edwardes retreated more into the background in the forthcoming years. In particular, he found that his activities directly related to Manchukuo began to tail off, as the government there failed to follow up on any of the offers made to the FBI mission, leaving the impression that a British presence in Manchuria would not be welcome. Increasingly Edwardes's activities concentrated upon propaganda on behalf of Japan, such as liaising with the British press, and arranging lunch and dinner parties where visiting Japanese diplomats and politicians could meet the upper echelons of British society.

He also still acted as a political channel to Whitehall for the Japanese embassy and in particular developed a good working relationship with Sir Horace Wilson, Chief Industrial Adviser to the British Government, who was even closer to Chamberlain than Fisher.[24] In the summer of 1936 Edwardes was the recipient of a letter from Shigemitsu calling for an improvement of Anglo-Japanese relations in the commercial field. After consulting with Gwynne, he dutifully forwarded this communication to what he referred to as the 'Select Few', and thus helped to lay the foundations for Yoshida's arrival as the new ambassador.[25] In addition, as Hosoya Chihiro has noted, it is more than likely that Edwardes played a role in drawing up the proposals that Yoshida presented to Chamberlain in October 1936 laying the basis for the Eden-Yoshida talks.[26]

By this time, however, the Foreign Office, with Anthony Eden at its head, was sceptical about the prospect of improved relations with Japan and treated Edwardes with due suspicion. Such was the state of affairs that when in May 1937 Leith-Ross met in private with Edwardes to discuss the Japanese view of the China consortium, the former sent a note of his conversation to Waley in the Treasury with a warning that he was not to mention this to anyone else as '... the FO would have fits if they thought I talked to Edwardes about the consortium'.[27] Edwardes reciprocated the Foreign Office's animosity and in particular was highly critical in conversations with Malcolm Kennedy, the former Reuter's correspondent in Japan, of Eden and of the then ambassador to Japan, Sir Robert Clive.[28]

The opening of the Sino-Japanese War only increased Edwardes's difficulties. He was now responsible for putting over Japan's point of view in a country which, influenced by reports of Japanese bombing of civilians in China and the infringement of British interests, was becoming increasingly hostile. One particular problem that Edwardes faced was that there were few newspapers in Britain still willing to carry pro-Japanese articles or leaders. The *Morning Post*, to Edwardes's great regret, ceased publication in August 1937 on being merged with the *Daily Telegraph*, and Gwynne settled into retirement. Even worse was that *The Times*, which was seen by many as the mouth-piece of the British government, was taking an extremely vocal anti-Japanese stance. In January 1938 Edwardes wrote to Amau Eiji, the Japanese minister to Switzerland, on the subject of the British press and noted:

> The charge that the British press has been pro-Chinese and anti-Japanese is unfortunately true. Under the leadership of *The Times* which is American-owned and which is tainted with American dictation over its policy, the trend of the Press has been hostile to Japan to a degree which has been as dangerous as it is unfair. Unfortunately we live in the days of Press sensationalism and the Head-lines which our newspapers have produced have done infinite harm in misleading the public.[29]

Edwardes was, however, also critical of Japan itself for failing to make peace in China. In another letter to Amau in December 1937 he noted that the Japanese elder statesman, Viscount Ishii, had recently come to Britain to meet Chamberlain, who was by now the Prime Minister. During his stay Ishii declared in an interview with the *Sunday Times* that the Japanese Army would call a halt to its activities after the fall of Nanking, only to be dismissively contradicted by a Gaimushō spokesman the following day. Edwardes observed mournfully that he had been arranging a 'luncheon party of considerable importance' for Ishii to further express his views, but that '. . . naturally the pronouncement from Tokyo cut the ground from under his feet and he was unable to say anything more'.[30] He also noted that Japan's friends could simply not understand why it continued fighting.

As the war in China dragged on, a debate began in Japanese circles about the best way of utilizing Edwardes. The Manchukuo government which paid his salary was, due to the conditions in London, receiving little for its money and began to suggest that he might make a suitable inspector-general of customs for the Japanese-dominated Peking provisional government. Rumours to this effect reached the Foreign Office from the London office of Jardine Matheson in July 1939, and surprisingly met with little objection from the Far Eastern Department.[31] Shigemitsu, however, who had from October 1938 become the Japanese Ambassador in London, had different ideas. He wished to keep Edwardes on his staff and to once again use him as an unofficial diplomatic channel in order to facilitate negotiations. In order to do this and to allow Edwardes for the first time to have access to the Foreign Office, Shigemitsu changed his title to 'Adviser to the Japanese on World Affairs'. Edwardes was now in a position where he could make use of a very good contact, for R.A. Butler, the parliamentary under-secretary at the Foreign Office, who appeared to be sympathetic to Japan, was distantly related to Edwardes's wife, Lilah.[32]

Edwardes's chance to make his mark came in late August 1939 after the signing of the Nazi-Soviet Pact. The German deal with the Russians was a profound shock to the Japanese government, which had from the autumn of 1938 been seeking an alliance with Germany and drifting ever further apart from Britain. Indeed, in the summer of 1939 Britain and Japan had almost come to blows in the Tientsin crisis, and only two days before the Nazi-Soviet Pact was signed, talks in Tokyo over Tientsin had broken down in deadlock. Shigemitsu and Edwardes saw the dramatic change in international conditions as a great opportunity for an improvement of Anglo-Japanese relations.

On 25 August Edwardes met with Butler to ask whether if Shigemitsu made overtures to the Foreign Office he would be snubbed. In addition, he put forward what he said was his own proposal for a settlement of the financial issues outstanding at Tientsin.[33] Butler's reaction was positive, as was that of the Far Eastern Department, and within a few days Shigemitsu was discussing his ideas with Butler and the Foreign Secretary, Lord Halifax.[34]

Building on this basis, Edwardes began to hold a series of talks with Butler in the autumn of 1939, became a frequent correspondent, and supplied him with a number of memoranda on various aspects of Anglo-Japanese relations. In one of these dated 22 September Edwardes argued that 'a judicial mind' looking at Japanese activities in China would recognize that Japan did not intend to overthrow Western interests as this would deny it access to the capital needed to develop China and expose it to the possibility of economic sanctions. He argued that Japan had behaved as an honourable ally in the Great War and was willing to help once again in the new war against Germany, particularly in the area of trade.[35] While Butler appeared to be enthusiastic about his new contact, the Far Eastern Department steadily grew more sceptical. One of its number, Esler Dening, noted of the above memorandum:

> I hope it will be remembered that Mr Edwardes is a *paid* Japanese propagandist and that his views are suspect, apart from the fact that his facts are not facts, and that he has no first-hand knowledge of Japan or the Japanese.[36]

The Department was not averse to studying the possibility of an easing of tensions with Japan, but it did feel that this should be approached in a realistic way, and certainly not with any sentimental notions about Japan's loyalty in the First World War.

Despite the suspicions of the bureaucrats, Butler remained in contact with Edwardes, sometimes sharing the latter's communications with the Far Eastern Department but at times keeping them to himself. The correspondence between them reached new heights with the Burma Road crisis in the summer of 1940. In June Japan demanded that Britain close the Burma Road as a supply route to China. Halifax's initial impulse was to resist but with the situation in Europe so precarious after the fall of France, Churchill decided that it was necessary to appease Japan. On 17 July Sir Robert Craigie, the British ambassador to Japan, committed Britain to close the Burma Road for three months in return for a Japanese promise to pursue a negotiated truce with Chiang Kai-shek's government. The hope of the Japanese embassy was that this move by Britain marked a turning point in relations and Shigemitsu and Edwardes began to put pressure on Butler to continue the momentum. They argued that the new Foreign Minister, Matsuoka Yōsuke, would be receptive to any further conciliatory moves and, in particular, they pushed the idea that Britain should send a mission to Japan to help celebrate its forthcoming 2,600th anniversary.[37]

Their assurances were, however, soon revealed to be worthless. From 27 July there was a wave of arrests of British subjects in Japan and Korea on spying charges, and one, the Reuter's correspondent Melville Cox, committed suicide in police custody. Both Shigemitsu and Edwardes were aghast at this news, and in an effort to rescue something from the wreckage, the latter took to emphasizing to Butler the ambassador's horror at the turn of events. On 31 July he noted to Butler:

> The inner atmosphere of the Embassy staff is very different and the word resignation has passed several lips. H[is] E[xcellency], however, refuses to accept defeat and he is determined to fight on. His bitter comments to me on his Government are not such as he could make to the S[ecretary] of S[tate].[38]

In addition, he observed that the arrests were the result of German machinations and intended to weaken the position of both Shigemitsu and Matsuoka.

What was interesting about this letter and indeed others of the time was that Edwardes was now apparently far more revealing about the state of affairs within Japanese circles than he had been at the start of his correspondence with Butler the year before. This raises a number of questions about the nature of his activities in this period. Clearly Edwardes would have been aware by the summer of 1940 that he would be a prime target for internment under Article 18b of the Defence of the Realm Act should a war with Britain and Japan break out. After all, the arrival of the Churchill administration had quickly led to the imprisonment of Oswald Mosley, Captain Ramsey and other sympathizers with Nazism. In addition, Edwardes himself was worried about the prevailing trends in Japan and feared they would affect relations with Britain. For example, on 17 June 1940 he had noted confidentially to another prominent Japanophile, Major-General F.S.G. Piggott, the former British military attaché in Tokyo, that he was '. . . developing a serious anxiety as to the situation in Japan itself', as the Axis victories in Europe had strengthened the 'wrong elements', and he feared that Japan was about to change from being a benevolent to a hostile neutral.[39] It is therefore logical to imagine that he realized the need to use his link with Butler in order to stress that he was more than just a Japanese propagandist and that he retained a sense of loyalty to Britain. The best way to prove this was to go beyond his normal duties and provide 'information' to Butler in the form of insights into Japanese thinking and reports on the rumours circulating within the embassy.

Whether Shigemitsu was aware of this aspect of Edwardes's activities is unclear. What is certain is that as Anglo-Japanese relations worsened Edwardes revealed more and more. On 2 September Edwardes sent a further letter to Butler. This time, as well as his usual special pleading for gestures from Britain to Japan, he revealed that Shigemitsu was facing new obstacles due to the recall of the pro-Axis diplomat Shiratori Toshio to the Gaimushō and that rumours were circulating that Japan intended to establish military bases in Thailand.[40]

The Foreign Office diplomats were not sure if Butler was wise to allow this correspondence to continue. In early August after Butler had discussed with Edwardes an idea that had been put to him that the King should send a message to the Emperor, Dening had minuted his fears:

> I venture once more to record the opinion that Mr Edwardes is very dangerous as an intermediary between this Office and the Japanese Ambassador. He is a paid agent of the Japanese Government, and does not get £5,000 a year for nothing. On several occasions recently his influence has been really pernicious, and it is known in this Dept. that M.I.5 are now watching his activities.[41]

At this stage the new head of the Far Eastern Department, John Sterndale Bennett, hesitated from joining in the chorus of alarm. When, however, Edwardes's letter of 2 September was shown to him he did indicate his concern. Butler's response was robust, minuting back to Sterndale Bennett that:

> I find this type of information, as does the S[ecretary]/ S[tate], really quite valuable. I am taking the utmost care with this contact, but I refuse to be turned into a robot by our Gestapo.[42]

Ironically, however, Butler himself was just on the cusp of changing from his previously benign attitude towards Japan towards the espousal of a policy of containment. With the signing of the Tripartite Pact between Japan, Germany and Italy on 27 September, the Edwardes-Butler correspondence appears to have more or less come to an end.

In the coming months it would be Piggott rather than the tarnished Edwardes who would act as the mouthpiece for improving Anglo-Japanese relations. Edwardes once more retreated into the background, although he remained an object of intelligence surveillance. In February 1941 the caustic permanent under-secretary at the Foreign Office, Sir Alexander Cadogan, was shown the record of a conversation between Edwardes and Lord Sempill, another Japanophile who worked at the Admiralty, about the recent war scare between

Britain and Japan. Cadogan duly noted in his diary: 'It's amusing watching the smug futility of these ridiculous busybody dupes! Edwardes ought to be jugged & Sempill crucified.'[43]

Cadogan was given another chance to gloat about Edwardes's misfortunes as Britain and Japan drifted ever further towards war. In July 1941, following the American lead, Britain froze all of Japan's assets, which meant not only that trade could no longer be financed but also that the salaries of the Japanese embassy's employees could not be paid. In September the Japanese chargé d'affaires, Kamimura Shinichi, visited Cadogan to plead fruitlessly for a loosening of the restrictions. Cadogan noted with glee in his diary that '. . . he [Kamimura](and that loyal British subject Mr. Edwardes, and that patriotic nobleman Lord Sempill) see their salaries dwindling!'[44]

At around the same time the activities of Edwardes and the other Japanophiles were coming to the attention of the Prime Minister. On 13 September an intercepted telegram from Kamimura to the Gaimushō, which indicated that the former was 'well informed' about the situation within Britain, was shown to Churchill who demanded to know from the Foreign Secretary, Anthony Eden, the identity of the chargé d'affaires's sources.[45] Eden replied with a list of names that included Edwardes, Piggott and Sempill, and this information was supplemented by a letter to Churchill from the Minister of Home Security, Lord Swinton.[46] It was clear that Edwardes was in fact not the most worrying source as his status was well known, it was rather Sempill who was the chief cause of concern which led him to be transferred from the Admiralty to a remote naval station in northern Scotland. However, in Swinton's report on all of the protagonists it is interesting to note that some of the small section on Edwardes has been retained by the Cabinet Office.[47]

What happened to Edwardes after 8 December 1941 is not clear. The Home Office state that there is no record that he was detained under Article 18b.[48] Perhaps the information that he passed to Butler had in the end proved useful? What is clear is that in the remaining years of his life he decided to expunge from his *Who's Who* entry all mention of his career during the 1930s. Edwardes died in July 1951 at the age of sixty-six. In 1953 Shigemitsu paid tribute to his friend 'Teddy' Edwardes in his memoirs, *Gaikō Kaisōroku*, noting the latter's unceasing efforts to improve Anglo-Japanese relations and also recording that in the hard years from 1938-41 they had had many arguments over Japanese policy and the need for Japan to compromise with Britain, indicating that at least in Shigemitsu's eyes Edwardes had been loyal to his country.[49] It is also interesting to observe that many of Shigemitsu's comments on Britain in the 1930s, such as his accusation that *The Times* was pro-American and admiring Chamberlain and his acolytes for their rejection of the League of Nations, echo the views Edwardes expressed to Amau in December 1937.

In the end Edwardes is not an easy figure to assess as so many of his activities went unrecorded. It is probable, however, that one has to conclude that he was a baleful influence on Anglo-Japanese relations in this crucial period. In regard to his effect on British opinion, he was too keen to emphasize Japan's desire for moderation if only Britain would be reasonable. He seemed to be unaware that he was being manipulated by factions within Japan and engaged in naive diplomacy which only helped to encourage the hopes of Fisher and Chamberlain. As for his effect on the Japanese, it seems that here, too, he put across the views of the Treasury and of the right-wing Conservatives as if they were the opinions of the country as a whole, raising expectations that would only be dashed. In a more conducive atmosphere his amateur diplomacy may have been useful, but in the decade that led to war such activity could bring little good and much harm.

20

Takayuki Eguchi

EDNA READ NEAL

MY FATHER, Takayuki Eguchi, was possibly Britain's longest-held prisoner of the last war. He was detained without charge or trial for two thousand, one hundred and seventy-five days – almost six years. He was arrested and taken to Pentonville prison on 14 July 1940, seventeen months before Pearl Harbour. Why? I do not think he ever knew the reason. My mother, Winifred, believed it was because of certain undesirable friendships he had with Mosley and other National Socialists. Many friends, and certainly my school fellows thought he must have been a spy. Until I began researching the life of my parents, I did not know the answer, indeed as an Anglo- Japanese child born and brought up here, losing my father at an early age, my knowledge of him and his country of origin was abysmal.

Takayuki was born on 22 April 1895, the first child of Komaichi Eguchi, a wealthy landowner listed in the *Teikoku Kōshinjo Directory* as a highly successful businessman, a millionaire, who inherited from his father, Hisaemon Eguchi, property in the province of Owari, adjacent to Mino in Chuba. The family wealth came from forests and land let to tenant farmers. However the earthquake which destroyed Nagoya in 1891 changed this traditional business as Komaichi's father began to sell some of his country properties and invest in the rebuilding of Nagoya City twelve miles away. Here he gradually acquired estates and houses for letting and Komaichi followed his example, so that by 1914 he owned some forty properties in Nagoya's best commercial street, and built the first cinema and an arcade of shops, similar to London's Burlington Arcade.

Nagoya was a thriving city, exporting textiles from its weaving and dyeing factories, chemicals, porcelain (a great speciality), watches and clocks, lacquerware, fans, glassware and cement. Its rapid development was due to investment by men like those of the Eguchi family who had the vision to see the potential of its location, its natural assets and fine harbour which made Nagoya the fourth greatest seaport in the country. Komaichi's brother was twice elected to the Aichi prefectural assembly and in 1914 was its speaker. Through this uncle's visits to Tokyo, representing the Aichi prefecture, the family were well aware of the growing relationship between Japan and the West, and had seen the government adopting and assimilating Western systems of law, taxation, coinage, railways, post offices, newspapers, lighthouses and dockyards. Western clothing was adopted and in 1872, two years after the birth of Komaichi, the most ambitious programme of universal education was launched with the building of over 53,000 elementary schools, one for every six hundred inhabitants, resulting in one of, if not the most highly literate people in the world. He even reported on the shocking activities in the *Rokumeikan*, the Hall of the Baying Stag, built by an English architect, where Japanese women were laced into Edwardian corsets and bustles and waltzed in the arms of Western visitors.

Takayuki spent his first years on the country estate at Kashiwamori, but when he was five years old, Komaichi moved his family into a modern house he had built in Nagoya, designed to withstand earthquake and fire, in order to more conveniently manage his business and property interests. A year after the move, when Takayuki was six years old, his mother Shigeno died and his father's remarriage within a year was the catalyst which set in motion the events which influenced the course of his life. The second wife was no replacement for Takayuki's lost mother and he led a lonely existance. His father gave him great attention, especially to building his health through sporting activities such as fencing, archery and ju-jitsu. All the clothing and equipment had to be specially made for the small boy. Komaichi even bought two of the first bicycles to be seen in Japan and the father and son created a sensation pedalling around Kochino and Nagoya. People would come out of their houses and stare in open-mouthed astonishment at this most extraordinary sight.

Takayuki entered the Aichi Prefectural Middle School and, as the eldest son, was already receiving training in his father's business, being a shareholder in a number of companies and entrusted with collecting rents (a chore he disliked). His place at table was beside his father and no-one else sat there. Even when he was at school and left for England his place continued to be set. At twelve years of age he spent a holiday with an uncle who had a fleet of tankers importing coal and oil, based at Taketoya port, and for the first time heard English spoken. This immediately interested Takayuki who learned as many words as he

241

could and, proud of this new knowledge, returned to his father with some excitement.

At the age of thirteen, Takayuki became a boarder in a school located an hour's train journey away from Nagoya. He was accommodated with two hundred-and-fifty fellow students in a two-storey Western-type dormitory. It seems to have been run on lines similar to an English public school with plenty of physical activity and cold showers in the morning. From his second year to his graduation he was always one of the top twenty-five students and excelled at ju-jitsu; he was the youngest to achieve a seven-hour swimming endurance test. He also climbed Mt Fuji. On leave at weekends he spent as little time as possible at home, visiting his father's cinema and having extra coaching in English in preparation for his objective of completing his education in Britain. After graduation, he spent several months having intensive coaching in English at the Eastlake English School in Tokyo. It was probably at the suggestion of his English tutor that he wrote to the *Chums* magazine in London, asking for penfriends. All these communications from England I recently found in a box in the family home in Nagoya. A fascinating detail of these touching mementos is the brevity of the address to which they were sent:- Mr T. Eguchi, Aichi-Ken Japan, or Mr T. Eguchi, Nagoya, Japan. This was about 1910, and only twenty years later the population of Nagoya would be nearly one million, and an envelope thus addressed would have had a small chance of finding him.

When Takayuki was due to leave, he suddenly realized that saying goodbye to his family and friends would be hard and he was afraid he might break down if they came to the station, and so it was with his father alone that he set out. They spent a few days sightseeing together, sitting quietly in contemplation of the twin waterfalls at Nunobiki, before boarding his ship, the SS *Miyazaki Maru* in Kobe on the 15 January 1914. Here his father disappeared into the crowd, like his son, unable to face that final moment of departure. The seven-week voyage was an opportunity for Takayuki, who was a good sailor, to adjust to Western food, plumbing and beds. The hardest thing for him was doing without Japanese baths because he always considered the way the British sat in their dirty water very unpleasant.

It is difficult to imagine the effect on Takayuki of his arrival in London, the goal to which he had been striving for so long. The huge city, heart of great British Empire filled him with awe. The magnificent buildings of brick and stone, the wide roads full of traffic, the parks, and the huge variety of its populace from every part of the world overwhelmed him. He lodged with kind landladies who mothered the shy young man; indeed he sadly compared the affectionate ways of his first English family with the coldness of his stepmother. They took him to church, to places of interest, and to watch the Oxford and Cambridge boat race. Takayuki wrote long letters to his father, in one of which he said, 'This country is not only Great, it is truly Glorious!'. He managed to travel unaided on the underground to report his progress at Clark's College, Romford, at weekly meals with Mr Itō, the first secretary of the Japanese embassy who was acting as his guardian, and he, together with Mr Yoshida, the manager of the London branch of the NYK Shipping line, made arrangements for Takayuki's education.

On 4 August, only five months after his arrival in London, Britain declared war upon Germany, His anxious father conferred with Mr Itō and Mr Yoshida as to the advisability of Takayuki remaining in England. However there was a general feeling that the war would be over by Christmas and it was agreed that it would be best if he continued his plan to complete his education. In October 1914 he moved to the West Ham Technical Institute in Romford Road where he enrolled on the matriculation course which was considerably more difficult for him. Takayuki needed a new vocabulary, so his father went to great trouble to search out and send by sea mail, (not easy in the conditions of war) suitable English/Japanese dictionaries and reference books to help him.

The war became an inescapable reality. The euphoria of early August evaporated as the Germans swept over most of Belguim, forcing the French retreat to the Somme, the last barrier before Paris. The British Expeditionary Force of 70,000 men landed secretly in France on the 17 August to relieve Mons. It was an appalling disaster, the retreat became a rout and on 23 August the Emperor of Japan declared war on Germany. Takayuki was astonished when strangers stopped him in the street to shake his hand and he was even borne off to a public house and treated to beer by complete strangers, impressed by Japan's stand alongside Britain, honouring the terms of the Anglo-Japanese Alliance. The winter closed in with the blackout, meatless days and the terrible sight of the returning soldiers, exhausted and broken, who had set out so jauntily and bravely. Due to raids from Zeppelins, Takayuki was moved to lodgings further west, staying at addresses in Turnham Green and Richmond. Once, when leaving a student meeting, bombs fell nearby and he saw the horrible result of the dead and injured in the wreckage of their homes.

In September 1915, Takayuki enrolled at the the London School of Economics and Political Science and the three and a half following years were probably the most influential of his life. He was stimulated by his fellow students and the social and political issues which were their concern. He felt greatly privileged to have so many distinguished professors and he kept a list of them, including Sidney Webb, the founder. He also remembered the occasional lecturers, George Bernard Shaw, Lee Smith, Hugh Dalton, Norman Angel, Arnold Laski and Clement Atlee. This was strange company for a descendant of the samurai, but he wholeheartedly embraced the precepts of the Fabians. He translated Ramsey Macdonald's *Contemporary Socialism* and sent it to be printed in instalments in *Shin-Aichi,* Nagoya's daily newspaper. These articles, bearing his name, greatly upset his father who wrote to Takayuki expressing his displeasure at the radical views he was promoting. Takayuki failed to gain a degree, due perhaps to his lack of French or German, but he nevertheless felt well trained for a career in business. He became a life member of the School and treasured his blazer pocket badge which I found in a frame on his study wall.

At this point, the purpose of completing his education had been achieved and his father expected him to return and assume the duties of managing the family estate and investment properties. But Takayuki had no wish to do so and the final breach with his father came when he wrote with the news that he wished to marry an Englishwoman, Winifred Thompson. Komaichi's patience was at an end. Takayuki was summoned home, and when he refused to do so, his hitherto very generous allowance ceased. Previously this had enabled Takayuki to live the life of a wealthy playboy, a member of Crockfords and other clubs; he knew many of the rich and famous, including the Siamese Princes Chula and his nephew Bira, the racing driver who married an English wife, members of the Rothschild family and Diana, the Countess of Westmorland whose name was written in his 1946 diary in Japan. Takayuki solved this crisis by setting up home with Winifred and taking employment as secretary of the Bank of Taiwan in Old Street in the City of London. He extended his stay in London by several years and he and Winifred already had a six-year-old daughter, Alma, when they finally married two months before I was born.

Because by this time he was well established in London, Takayuki was an invaluable resource for visiting Japanese or for diplomats and businessmen arriving for their tours of duty. I recently met the daughters of Mr Matsuda revisiting London after an absence of sixty years. Their father came to a post in the Bank of Taiwan, and they remembered my father's assistance in finding the family a house and taking their parents to buy furniture for it. In other ways, too, he became useful, acting as a spokesman for Japan when various organizations made requests for a speaker on issues concerning Japan's foreign policy. An example of the engagements Takayuki fulfilled was a debate in March 1931 organized by the Central Association of Indian Students on the subject of the Sino-Japanese conflict which was attended by 60-70 people. On the same subject at the City of London College in May 1932, he proposed a resolution that 'There will be no peace in the East unless Japanese privilege in the economic matters in Manchuria has been accepted'. After the debate the resolution was passed 60–40 in favour. At another meeting in February 1933, he was the only Japanese invited to a meeting at the Memorial Hall, Farmington Street, to request an arms export ban to Japan. He is reported as 'vigorously refuting charges made against Japan' (The Editor of the newspaper, *Nichi-Ei Shinshi* added, 'the meeting was very noisy. During Mr Eguchi's speech someone shouted "You are a liar!" Mr Eguchi stressed the irrational destruction of lands and goods and obtained big cheers'.)

At another meeting organized by the Japanese Students' Association for the employees of City banks and companies in April 1932, *Nichi-Ei Shinsi* reported that 'the majority of the audience seem to have been socialists who were very much impressed by Mr Eguchi who gave an impassioned speech and about eighty per cent looked likely to agree with the cause of Japan'. The same newspaper quotes Takayuki addressing a birth control conference at the London School of Hygiene and Tropical Medicine in 1933 with a speech on politics and the economy and in February the following year he spoke on the same subject to the Rotary Club of Golders Green. That he was a persuasive speaker seems demonstrated by a meeting organized by the *Daily Express* where he spoke about Japan's population problem. A young man in the audience was so moved by his presentation that he proposed a motion that Japan should share part of Australia and this was approved unanimously by the meeting. In 1937, he was busy explaining the Japanese position in the Sino-Japanese conflict addressing eight public meetings between September and November alone. Between January and March 1938 he spoke at six meetings.

The mid-Thirties were politically difficult for Japanese Anglophiles and Takayuki was busy as a member of the Foreign Press Association writing articles for a number of newspapers, among them the *Shin Aichi Daily News, Nagoya and Kokumi Daily News*, the *Asahi Shimbun* and *Nichi Shimbun*. The decade had begun badly personally for Takayuki and Winifred when their much loved first child, Alma, died of meningitis at the age of nine. This tragedy set in motion profound changes in their way of life and the relationships within the family. In an attempt to improve their health, Takyuki bought a small house at the seaside in Sussex and Winifred, myself and a new baby brother moved out of London and never returned to live in the family home in Kensington.

Komaichi Eguchi responded to his son's bereavement with a shipment of some valuable items from his art collection. These included paintings and calligraphy by many well known masters including the artists Shunsui Miyakawa, Gantai, Buncho, Buson, Baiitsu, and Jyakuchu. Scrolls from this collection were selected and exhibited by Laurence Binyon, Keeper of Oriental Art at the British Museum, and later when they were seized from the strong room of the Bank of Taiwan by the Custodian of Enemy Property and auctioned, the British Museum acquired the best of them and the whereabouts of sixty other missing items is unknown. The most important thing for Takayuki, however, was his father's forgiveness and invitation to bring his wife and family to Japan. This took place in 1934, the return journey by sea taking six weeks each way and three months were spent sightseeing and visiting relatives in Kobe and Nagoya.The reconciliation was complete.

Meanwhile, international tension deepened and whereas the British had been approving of Japan's conflict with Russia (indeed, many of the battleships which contributed to the victory had been built in the north of England and their crews trained by Royal Navy officers), the new incursions into neighbouring countries was causing a hostile shift in public opinion. The Japanese found criticism of their policy of expansion difficult to understand since their role model was the British Empire. Like the colonial administrators in India, they laid down railways, roads and bridges in Manchuria and set up an education system and built schools where none had existed. They felt that they had benefited the people by bringing law and order to a country previously at the mercy of rapacious warlords. In London, Takayuki watched as the clouds of war gathered over the peoples of Europe and shared with many of his associates deep uneasiness about the fact that the country which had won the war seemed to have lost the peace. The grievous social and economic problems of the country were painfully demonstrated by the 1936 Jarrow march of unemployed miners. He was not alone in his search for answers and solutions and like many of his friends he found much of interest in the restoration of totally defeated Germany into a powerful nation.

These friends included men and women who were drawn to radical new political parties which claimed to be forging new policies which would save this country from another war with Germany. They came from some of the most aristocratic old families, men with distinguished careers in the services and from many professions and walks of life and Takayuki knew many of them, including Sir Oswald Mosley. These fascist organizations identified the Jews as the cause of the country's economic problems and admired the strength of Germany. As a member of the Press Association, Takayuki attended more than one of Hitler's Nurenberg Rallies and there is no doubt that his concern for the well-being of Britain led him down this dangerous path. The Special Branch of Scotland Yard infiltrated meetings of the National Socialist Party and the Nordic League, an umbrella organization for the most rabid anti-semitic groups. Takayuki's presence as a newspaper correspondent was also recorded by them.

The Coronation of King George V1 in 1937 was an occasion of national celebration and happiness, a relief from all the news of rearmament, conscription and atrocities such as the bombing of the Spanish town of Guernica. The Japanese in London were delighted by the visit and reception of the Crown Prince and Princess Chichibu who as representatives of the world's oldest royal family preceded all the other Kings and Queens as they entered Westminster Abbey. Both Takayuki and Winifred attended events in their honour, and there is a photograph showing Takayuki standing with other bank officials at a Garden Party given at the Hurlingham Club.

War was declared against Germany in September 1939, and six months later as the Germans swept through Holland and Belguim, Takayuki sent his wife and children away from the vulnerable South Coast to the Cotswold village of Painswick. It was here on 22 May 1940 that he arrived with a set of Dickens' books for my birthday and although I did not know it, I would never see my father again.

On 14 July Winifred got a telegram requesting her immediate return to London. Takayuki had disappeared and embassy officials had failed to locate him. They hoped his English wife might be more successful. I remember my brother and I accompanying our mother as she tried to find him, and the shock of seeing our father's photograph in someone's evening newspaper as we travelled on the underground after another frustrating day. Winifred eventually discovered him in Pentonville detained under Article 12 (6c) and (5a) of the Aliens Order 1920.

Takayuki was held in a number of different prisons and he kept a unique diary recording his experiences on sheets of 'Bronco' toilet paper. On one thin 6x4-inch sheet, using his fountain-pen with its fine nib, he could inscribe four to five hundred words in English. There are twelve pages describing events in his daily life and nine pages of lists and notes relating to his fellow internees. Takayuki spent the next four months in Pentonville, distressed and depressed, while London became the front line of the war. Despite the brevity of his notes one senses his shock at the grim atmosphere in the prison one morning, when an Indian, described by my father as a patriot, was executed. Takayuki heard him shouting and all the other prisoners banging their cell doors until 9.00 am, when a terrible silence ensued and he knew that the man was dead. On that day the prisoners were taken out of their cells after tea from 6-8.00 pm for extra exercise.

Takayuki was allowed newspapers at the end of July and was amazed to find that his arrest was front page news, accompanied in some papers by his photograph. He was trying to find some reasons for his imprisonment. He learned that on 27 July the Japanese, in reprisal, had arrested eleven British diplomats and businessmen in Japan and on the 3 August, counter reprisals continued with the arrest of four other leading members of the Japanese community in London including Satori Makihara, manager of Mitsubishi Commercial Company, Shunsuke Tanabe, manager of Mitsui Bussan Kaisha Ltd, and a Mr Judo and a Mr Tani who were taken to Brixton. The diplomatic reprisals continued and in the Foreign Office files one can follow the method which was applied when selecting Japanese for arrest – it had little to do with any misconduct of the person. Ashley Clarke wrote on 31 July 1940:

> It is of first importance that very early action should be taken. On this Sir R. Craigie [British Ambassador to Japan] is in agreement with us. One point however arises. Sir R. Craigie speaks of the arrest of suspected Japanese and in his telegram No. 1384 recommended the detention of Japanese nationals 'against whom there is *prima facie* evidence of having been engaged in espionage or intelligence work'. The difficulty is that if in selecting Japanese for arrest, we adhere strictly to this criterion, we shall only be able to apprehend persons of no importance whose arrest would in no way disturb the Japanese or deter them from further arrests of British subjects.
>
> The Japanese have themselves arrested on trumped-up charges mostly of a trifling nature, the leaders and most respected members of the British community in Japan. It is therefore most desirable that the list of Japanese to be arrested should include some important members of the Japanese community, whether here or in other parts of the Empire, who have a certain standing, even if there is not evidence in every case of espionage activities. It is essential also to take in the chief representative of the Japanese News Agency as a *quid pro quo* for Mr Cox, who was representative of Reuters in Japan. This principle has been applied in selecting candidates for arrest submitted in a separate paper.
>
> Ashley Clarke, 31 July 1940
> (Foreign Office Records, Public Record Office, FO371/ 24738)

Perhaps the tone of this directive had been considerably affected by the suicide two days before of Mr Cox, Reuters correspondent in Tokyo, who (it is claimed) threw himself from the window of the room where he was being interrogated by Japanese police.

On 14 August Takayuki and a number of other Japanese citizens, were transferred to Brixton prison where he was locked into a tiny cell where the air was so bad he nearly fainted. Next day, when released for an hour's silent walking in single file around the excercise yard, he met his old friend, Mr Tanabe, who stealthily managed to pass Takayuki some white bread, sweets, a banana and an orange, none of which he had seen since his arrest. However, when Takayuki returned to his cell he was told to pack and was taken under military escort to a camp at Ham Common on the west side of Richmond Park, an interrogation centre run by the army for Category A aliens, those considered dangerous, and imprisoned. (When at war with Japan Winifred was classed as Category B, under police supervision and not allowed to travel more than five miles from her home without a permit).

Life here was even harder than in Pentonville; there were no newspapers, no visits, no communication allowed between prisoners and all books, letters and personal belongings were searched. Except when out for exercise, guarded by soldiers with loaded pistols, he was held in solitary confinement. The food was inadequate for healthy men and the exhausting interrogations badly affected many of them. Takayuki records a young Briton and an Italian broken in health and spirit and the insults he suffered from 'Stephen' during a cross-examination. On 22 August a particularly unpleasant incident occurred but Tayayuki does not specify the nature of it – only the statement that '... death is better than this shameful treatment...' He needed attention from a doctor. He was also forced to mend one of the soldiers' dirty socks. However, it was not all humiliation; some kind-hearted soldiers gave him food from their mess and a few forbidden cigarettes. He even heard a sergeant reprimanding a cruel soldier by shouting 'remember, you are a soldier'!

On 31 August the unrelenting interrogation ended and he was returned to Brixton prison where he was to remain for the next six months. Again he felt faint when locked in a tiny airless cell, so he complained to the prison governor who, perhaps suprisingly, saw that he had better conditions, but the grinding routine of scrubbing and cleaning continued in the company of all kinds of criminals including prisoners on remand, army deserters, looters and thieves.

In mid October 1940 he was moved to 'F' Wing where he met members of the National Socialists, the Nordic League and the Right Club including Mosley, Admiral Domville, and the anthropologist Pitt-Rivers. He comments on the improved conversation with men of their intellect and education. He spent a lonely Christmas and New Year, his thoughts inevitably with his children, wondering how Winifred would manage to make it a happy time for us. He himself took his daily excercise, 125 steps on the outer circle, 85 steps on the inner circle, one hour in the morning and one in the afternoon. At 4.00 pm the day was finished and he was locked in his cell until morning. The only words addressed to him were 'Close the door', 'Hurry up', 'Keep walking', and 'Empty slops'.

On 13 January 1941, Takayuki was taken from Brixton prison to a camp for internees at Lingfield racecourse near Crawley where, in bitter weather, he was accommodated in a dirty, cold stable surrounded by mud and lacking the most basic amenities (the only way of keeping clean was to shower outdoors in the yard). However here, for the first time in six months, he was addressed as 'Mister' by an officer and found a great improvement in the interviews conducted by the camp commander, Major Tillman, whom he had previously known in the City. After 10 days in the stable, he was moved to a better camp close by. Here he rejoined men whom he had known in Pentonville and was shocked to see their physical deterioration. The inmates felt particularly isolated as incoming letters took not three days as at Pentonville but three weeks; one letter posted by Winifred on 26 January reached him on 3 March – with a number of lines deleted by the censor's black crayon. The dining-room was shared with three hundred fellow prisoners representing twenty five different nationalities. It was a hellish noisy Babel which he found intolerable.

No sooner had Takayuki adapted to the regime at Lingfield than he was moved yet again. On 4 March 1941 he was marched between soldiers to the railway station for transfer to York. He describes suffering from the utter shame and humiliation of this. Some of the men were in tears. Worse was to come when they finally arrived at their ultimate destination to find themselves accommodated underneath the mouldering race stand. No beds were provided. He was given only four damp blankets and a steel bowl for his food. There were only two meagre lights, one cold-water tap to share with twenty-five other people and two cracked cooking stoves. He complains of standing in the bitter cold queuing for food, holding his steel bowl in his freezing fingers. A nineteen-year-old Dutch boy tried to commit suicide. He acknowledges being bathed by kind Dutch naval officers which surely means he was unable through sickness or ill treatment to look after himself. An unexpected toothache necessitated Takayuki visiting a dentist, his first release from the routine of prison life. He was shocked to notice signs of food shortage in the bakers' shops he passed and writes of what a good feeling it was, when, after his treatment, he rested in an armchair with a carpet under his feet.

On 27 May 1941, Takayuki left York and was taken to the Isle of Man with 823 other internees on the Belgium cross-Channel vessel, the *Princess Josephine Charlotte*. To Takayuki's amazement, the officer, whose task it was to get the prisoners transported to various camps, did not yell 'Quick march', but ordered in a reasonable tone of voice, 'Now, *please* get going!' Takayuki arrived at Peveril Camp, Peel, where he found that he was the only Japanese among 739 inmates, and was accommodated in House 31, a private seaside boarding house with its own garden and flowers. He shared a room with a very pleasant Danish cook who broke down and wept as he told Takayuki his experiences in the prison at Durham, where he had been savagely kicked by soldiers and his food thrown on the floor.

By 18 July the authorities must have realized Takayuki was not potentially dangerous and separated him from the Fascists by transferring him from Peel to the Camp at Ramsey. By leaving behind all the hardline Fascists, Takayuki was to avoid several notable events at Peveril including a riot and escapes. His diary makes no comment about the entry of Japan into the war, but records his contempt for the men who held positions of power in civilian life who broke down in the camp and his admiration for officers, their uniforms now in rags, who worked for a few shillings a week as cooks, cleaners or even raising rabbits. Prisoners were allowed one parcel a week, but it could not contain any goods rationed in England, or food in jars or tins. Sweets were unwrapped and shortbread biscuits cut into three pieces. Books and newspapers could not be sent by a private person, only by a publisher. Scissors were taken away and everyone issued with a razor, tooth and hairbrush, five blankets and a towel, but no sheets or pillowcases. Takayuki who was 45 years old was not able to go on the walks three times a week, again an indication of some physical disability.

My father, whose previous life had been lived in such very different circumstances, seemed to bear the privations and stress of his imprisonment with a calm demeanor and stoic acceptance, but it is very noticeable that his diary changes quite dramatically, particularly after the time when all the other Japanese had been repatriated in 1942. Although he goes on writing in the same style, the chaotic content of the latter pages suggest that he is no longer able to concentrate and it surely indicates a deterioration of his mental state caused by his long detention. Takayuki's mind must have worn out wondering why he was kept behind when all the other Japanese were repatriated. Was he to be charged with some offence? Was there to be a trial? If so, on what grounds? Why wait so long before taking action? Or would he be released because of his English family and had he been held back for their sake? When would he be told his fate? Why was he now the only Japanese prisoner remaining on the Isle of Man?

After over fifty years of ignorance, my researches at the Public Record Office, Kew, and access to files allowed me by the Home Office, enable these questions to be answered. It all began in January 1940. In Kobe the Japanese arrested a certain Vincent Oswald Woodfield Peters born 24 August 1893, who lived in Yamamotodori, as he was about to leave for Shanghai on the SS *Taiyō Maru*. He had arrived in Japan on 7 October 1936 as a British businessman, but evidence produced connected him with espionage of sensitive naval and economic details. He had obtained statistics on the nature, quantity and routes of shipments being made to Germany and had been under surveillance for a long time for relaying messages between Kobe and Hong Kong using British Blue Funnel line boats. Peters was held in prison under the Law for the Protection of Military Secrets. There seems little doubt that there was a case against him and that the British were very anxious to recover him. Consequently, the British authorities in London decided, even before any directive was issued on 31 December 1940 to arrest a prominent Japanese to use in bargaining for the release of Peters.

Takayuki, a well-known member of London's Japanese community, having lived in Britain since 1914 and being, conveniently, of non-diplomatic status, was considered eminently suitable for this purpose. He was arrested on 14 July and shortly afterwards his name appears for the first time in this exchange between London and Tokyo.

> Foreign Office telno. 1327 to Sir R.Craigie (Tokyo)
> British Ambassador
> 27th July 1940 5.5 p.m. No 1327 (R)
> 24 July 1940 R.3.10 p.m.
> Your Telegram no 691. (F3065/653/23)
>
> There has been no change in position. (Peters)
> Consul has applied at intervals for interview but has invariably been informed that the case is not concluded. Written request of examining judge on July 17th elicited oral reply that examination would finish within a week and consul reports there are indications investigations are nearly concluded.
> I have again urged at Ministry for Foreign Affairs that proceedings be expedited.

At the bottom of this page and occupying a further half sheet is the following, written in the bold hand of Mr Ashley Clark.

> I gave Mr Okamoto a copy of the memo within marked X and asked if he could help. He had just suggested that we should allow Mr Eguchi, arrested in this country to be sent back to Japan. As a personal suggestion, I wondered whether Mr Peters could not be sent back to England?

On 6 August, the arrest of Takayuki Eguchi eventually made the newspapers and prompted a telegram from Sir Robert Craigie, Britain's ambassador in Tokyo, asking if the fact of his arrest before that of the

Britons in Japan might be useful, and a handwritten note from A.W.Scott at the Foreign Office agrees:-

> This is certainly useful ammunition. As regards Mr Eguchi, we are hoping to arrange an exchange with Mr Peters (who has been detained since the middle of January).

And on the same day, Mr J.C.Sterndale Bennett signs a typewritten minute that:

> Mr Okamoto referred today to a recent conversation which he had had with Mr Ashley Clarke about the detention of Mr Eguchi. Mr Ashley Clarke asked him in conversation to look into the case of Mr Peters and try to get it expedited. A telegram had accordingly been sent to Tokyo.
> (FO371/24737)

Despite the impression given by these notes that every effort would now be made to effect the achievement of this objective, there is nothing more on the matter for the rest of August, the whole of September and half of October.

But perhaps the long-awaited trial of Vincent Peters in September was the reason, and the severity of his sentence of eight years penal servitude, without stay of execution, followed by his appeal halted their endeavours. The Japanese were clearly not prepared to do a deal swapping a convicted spy with Takayuki, although they made several unsuccessful representations to the Foreign Office, trying to get his release to join boats that were taking Japanese home. (The embassy had Winifred on standby for repatriation.)

★ ★ ★

In 1943 Takayuki was sent to India and Winifred believed that through the International Red Cross, an exchange was set up to take place there. New evidence from the Foreign Office has revealed that if this was the case, their hope of effecting the exchange at last was extinguished by the news of Vincent Peter's death from pneumonia in May 1943 while in prison serving his sentence. After an appeal this had been reduced from eight years to five. Included in the new evidence is an uncorroborated suggestion that Peters himself was 'framed' in which case his part in this story is tragic indeed.

This circumstance kept Takayuki in a large British internment camp in Deoli in a Rajasthan, 150 miles northeast of Bhopal and 80 miles north of the Tropic of Cancer for three years. It was very hot. It housed about 3,000 prisoners of whom 2,600 were Japanese, mainly soldiers or fishermen who had previously been interned in Malaya;

Takayuki regretted that before his arrival all people of status and education who might have been interesting company had gone back to Japan. The camp seems to have been very well run with meticulous annual inspections by officials from the International Red Cross. Their reports describe three brick-built barracks with shady verandahs, one for men and two for families, their furniture and occupants. They list 200 children and the books in the libraries. There were thirteen teachers among many illiterate people. Takayuki taught English, book-keeping and economic theory to adults who requested that they take the examinations of the British Institute of Commerce and Accountancy in Bombay. Others occupied themselves growing vegetables.

It seems likely that Takayuki's command of English made him very useful to the British commandant, and that the role of communicating instructions may have carried with it an aura of complicity with their jailers. It may have been for his protection that Takayuki was accommodated with the families.

After Japan's surrender, the commandant told the inmates and said that regulations would be relaxed, allowing them to leave the camp for a day each week, providing they did not go into the villages. The prisoners did not believe what they were told; it was impossible for Japan to be defeated and they took the easing of restrictions as a sign of Japanese victory. In order to get the message across, two eminent Japanese visited the camp to speak to the prisoners, one of the visitors, Mr Henzo Sawada, was well known to Takayuki, and among other camp leaders he was able to see them. From them the prisoners heard of the devastation of their country, not only from the atomic bombs, but also by the saturation firebombing of Japanese cities by the American Air Force. They were told that in Japan people were dying of starvation, and that there had been no way except for the Emperor to surrender. On the following day Takayuki was asked by his fellow prisoners if Mr Sawada was the real Sawada or an imposter and he became aware that there were a large number of hardliners who still believed Japan had won the war, and regarded those (like himself) who accepted the truth as traitors. His pupils were intimidated and failed to attend their classes; the other teachers were similarly affected.

On the morning of 25 February, the anniversary of a famous military massacre, a Formosan pupil told him that there was a plan to attack all the 'defeatists' and he and his wife tried to help Takayuki to escape through the barbed wire using some planks they had concealed for the purpose. He waited for them in a lavatory, but was discovered by three men armed with home-made knives. They told him they would cut his throat in front of the whole camp in the morning. His knowledge of judo enabled him to escape the beatings which were being inflicted on the other teachers and his friends, a bucketful of urine tipped over him was all he suffered. The commandant had previously tried to move Takayuki into the camp hospital for his safety but he had refused because he knew he was not the only one who was vulnerable if there was trouble. Now he came to his room and insisted that Takayuki joined forty severely wounded colleagues in the hospital. This riot was finally quelled only by the intervention of the Indian army who had to open fire on the insurgents, killing fourteen of them, including two innocent women. In all three hundred and fifty people were segregated for their protection and Takayuki was elected their camp leader. But after only a week or two, he resigned, not well enough to carry out his duties.

At last in May 1946 he was repatriated, and was given a first-class cabin on a British liner to Singapore. One wonders if this was an act of kindness by the camp commander, Lt.Col R.F.Craster who must have got to know Takayuki well over a period of three years. On the return journey he met the very men who had attacked him, their demeanor very changed as they begged his forgiveness, having finally accepted Japan's defeat.

★ ★ ★

Takayuki was a journalist and wrote accounts of the fanatics' riot and also chronicled his return to Nagoya, passing one devastated city after another on the long journey to Nagoya. He described how from the train, across a sea of rubble, in distance similar to that from Holland Park tube station to Elgin Crescent, he could clearly see the copper roof of his father's house. Indeed, in Surugamachi only five small houses beside this large modern one survived of the one hundred and seventy residences in the street. He wrote movingly of the suffering of the homeless, hungry people, the shameful profiteering by black-marketeers and the hopeless lack of government initiative. Without American aid many thousands would have died. He occupied one floor in his family home which had been looted of its furniture, but it is his overwhelming joy at being a free man at last which illumines this journal.

He gradually began to put together a new life in Japan, which, because he was so thoroughly Westernised, replicated what he missed of England. He built a new house in the garden of his father's house, agonising over the cutting down of a tree, but incorporating part of it in the *tokonoma*. In 1953, when all was finished, he met Winifred in Paris, their extraordinary reunion after thirteen years was described by my mother in the autobiography she wrote in her seventies. Takayuki tried to persuade her to spend the rest of her life with him in Japan, but she refused, feeling that my brother and I still needed her here.

He worked for the Tōhō Rayon Company, mainly travelling to trade fairs in various countries until his retirement, when he took private pupils for English conversation. He remarried and had a daughter, Takako, who was a great joy in his final years, almost as though he had been given again the two daughters he had lost. To the end of his life he expressed admiration for British political and personal standards, extolling democratic and Christian principles as a proper foundation for public and family life.

I am grateful that an extraordinary circumstance led me to write to my father in 1962, twenty-two years after his arrest and that we corresponded until he died in February 1967. Through these precious letters I learned about our family and, most important the kind of man he was. Remarkably, he was not bitter and still loved this country above all others. On his study wall were his drawings of Winifred and Queen Elizabeth.

21

John Morris, George Orwell, the BBC and Wartime Japan

NEIL PEDLAR

THE SAKÉ CUP glowed symbolically as the tall solitary figure of John Morris bent down to retrieve it from the ashes of his former Tokyo home. He named it 'The Phoenix Cup' and gave his fifth book that title. He was alone in Shibuya amongst the terrible devastation of war with no neighbours, no old friends – not even a stray cat or dog to keep him company – and the cherry tree under which he had relaxed just five years previously with cups of hot saké brought to him by his old housekeeper was now a charred stump of dead wood. Happy memories of his Shibuya home briefly flooded his mind, but then he began wondering if his housekeeper had been prosecuted for her loyalty to a so-called 'British enemy alien'. Soon the awful desolation of the place, the filth, the skeletons of the once busy structures he had known and lived amongst began to depress him, so he walked briskly away on that cold January afternoon in 1946.[1]

Morris had first arrived in Japan at Kobe in the autumn of 1937 on his way home to Britain after spending 15 years in India. The adventurer visited most of the usual tourist attractions, mostly historical sites, but in doing so felt a strange familiarity with the places he saw. He experienced an inexplicable feeling that he had seen them all before even though it was his first visit to Japan. The only possible explanation was that during the previous six months he had been isolated in a lonely Himalayan village, where the only book he had was a translation of *The Tale of Genji* which he had read several times.[2]

While in Tokyo on that first visit he was invited to speak to a few university mountaineering clubs because of his participation in the 1922 and 1936 Mount Everest expeditions. Contacts made during

257

these talks led to him accepting the post of Professor of English Literature at Keiō University the following year. This appointment also involved lecturing at the Tokyo Imperial University College of Literature, and advising the Ministry of Foreign Affairs on the English language. Morris made no deliberate attempts to obtain these positions, for his intention was to return to London now that he was 42 years old, and write more about his experiences in the East.

Born in Gravesend, Kent, in 1895, his love of music at home and school attracted him to a career as a pianist but as World War I intensified, he joined the Army, despite poor eyesight, and in 1915 served with the Leicestershire Regiment. He saw action in the Somme and was wounded both physically and mentally. In 1918 he joined the Gurkha Rifles as a regular in the Indian Army which took him to Palestine, Afghanistan, Waziristan and the NW frontier of India. However, during 1921-24 his travels in Tibet, Nepal, Sikkim and Bhutan made the greatest impression on him where he felt at home with the peoples, learning their languages, especially Nepali.[3] Hence his value to the Everest expeditions. His *Times* obituary states that 'he felt at home with these peoples'. His final work for the Indian Army was a pioneering survey in Chinese Turkestan (Xinjiang) for which he was awarded the Murcheson Memorial of the Royal Geographical Society, just before he was invalided out of the Army.

Returning to Britain, Morris, now in his 30s, looked to further education and, ahead of his time in his attitude to education, he eventually graduated from King's College, Cambridge, where he achieved an MA and MSc as well as a Diploma in Anthropology having held the William Wyse studentship. He developed a deep curiosity, interest and passion for peoples of different cultures, and his experience in Nepal and neighbouring countries helped him in his studies. He knew that he could have remained in British India, but felt that he had to leave because his position in the Army had frustrated him from meeting Indian people on equal terms. On the other side, the British subjection of the Indian people resulted in a cowed and subservient population which added to his disgust. 'Long years of servility and a lack of educational facilities make any sort of equal intercourse impossible', he wrote. He felt that he had to reject the seduction of the European life there – the numerous servants, the large salaries with the minimum of work – in order to 'remain a civilised being'.[4] His decision to leave India at three day's notice proved to be a traumatic experience for Morris, yet it also gave him a born-again feeling.

TOKYO 1938

By this time Morris had had a good foundation both academically and experientially of living with people of different races with different, strange but rational customs. He had also become politically aware in his own way. Aware of the relationship between economics and power, and aware that a sense of humour was vital for survival for living among people in a new culture.

During the few weeks of planning before Morris had to start lecturing at Keiō University, he settled into his house in Shibuya. He was delighted with many aspects of living in a compact Japanese house, but surprised to find that in the centre of Tokyo there was no mains' sewage disposal system. A commercial company regularly, for a fee, cleaned out the lavatories in each household, the contents of which were used to fertilize the rice fields in the suburbs. Rice was the most important commodity in the Japanese economy then, and as one French commentator wrote at the time: 'La base de l'economie japonaise, c'est la merde!'[5]

Morris had found it easy to obtain a telephone in his home because of his connection with the Japanese Foreign Office, but for ordinary citizens it entailed a complex and expensive procedure. The telephone system had become a government department although originally the capital had been raised for it by public subscription. Most of the shareholders were government officials who did not take up stock but took telephones and exchange numbers instead, and then hired them out at extortionate rates. So it would appear the Morris was a highly privileged individual having his own telephone; not surprisingly, his friendly neighbours were soon forming orderly queues in his small study in order to use it. One of them even had Morris' number printed on his *meishi* (name card).[6]

When Morris began his lecturing work at Keiō University, he found that there was no real contact between teachers and students. The atmosphere was impersonal and the classes so large in some departments that teachers found it impossible to know the names of all their students. Morris remembered the great value he obtained from attending tutorials where a teacher invited a small number of his students at a time to his private study for intimate discussions when he was at King's College, Cambridge, and tried to change the system by introducing tutorial sessions for his students, but without success. Like all the others, his students were so overloaded with the sheer mass of the syllabi that they had to cover in a set time that they merely stayed away from tutorials in order to catch up with their other studies.

Morris was also deeply upset by the poor living conditions of some of his students, most of whom were lodged in one-roomed accommodation in extreme discomfort. The Sino-Japanese War that began in 1937 necessitated austerity measures which meant that no classrooms could be heated in the winter, resulting in about 10% of students leaving their studies due to ill health. Most had contacted tuberculosis. The compulsory military training also affected their progress, for every educational institution in Japan had army officers attached to it who supervized route marches and various military exercises along with special lectures on discipline and the great merit in dying on the battlefield for one's country. These lectures meant that the foreign teachers' instruction was often cancelled. Field training occurred once every year for a week, and all the students hated the exhausting programme they were forced to endure. 'But', as Morris recorded, 'the army controls everything in Japan and there is nothing anyone can do... The only interest the Japanese army has in education is to get it over as quickly as possible in order to swell the flow of recruits'.[7] This disgust came from an ex-soldier!

Two of his students committed suicide by jumping in front of a fast-moving train just before they were due to report for service in the army. This action, said Morris, did not reflect their fear of military training but was a protest against the army's domination of affairs in Japan. The mental confusion of this generation, he concluded, was caused by the liberalism of their youth being suddenly replaced by a rigid system of militarily-enforced nationalism where the expression of 'unorthodox' thought was punished by imprisonment and possible beatings and torture. Thousands of members of the Communist Party were already in jail, while the number of people joining the '*Kempei*' (military security police) was increasing and imposing a reign of terror throughout society in Japan.

Morris wrote:

> Every school and university in Japan has a photograph of the Emperor, and in a fire or any other calamity this portrait must at all costs be saved. There are cases[8] on record where a school principal has lost his life in attempting to save the Imperial photograph; or, having failed in his attempt, had committed suicide.

Such control through mere symbols by the military authorities is, if true, terrifying from today's perspective. Morris described his environment while teaching at the first university he was employed at in Japan before his Keiō days: 'The building was suggestive of a prison rather than a university ... not cleaned since the day it was built ... Windows thick with grime ... broken sash left unmended...'[9]

Japan had been continually at war with China since 1931 and such outcomes were a natural result of this. Morris was obviously frustrated as a teacher due to the restrictions, but philosophical and on a learning curve which his books expressed.

As the months went by Morris investigated and reported on many aspects of Japanese life and institutions – food, dress, marriage, the press, sports, the stage, radio broadcasting, prostitution and music – and he was perceptive enough to note how the new political atmosphere was affecting each one. Food became increasingly scarce and eventually, with the outbreak of war, there were long queues at foodshops where his housekeeper was constantly reviled for looking after an enemy person. Changes in fashion became apparent to Morris as to everyone, including women of all ages, was encouraged to wear utility clothes of a military cut and colour. When the Pacific War began it became illegal for women to have their hair permed as it reflected both Western culture and money wasted. Even chorus girls from shows were required to march through the streets in short skirts with rifles on their shoulders![10]

In the foreign community in Tokyo, divisions arose between people from the Allied nations and those aligned with Nazi Germany. Censorship in the English-language press became intense and one by one these newspapers and magazines were squeezed out as advertisers were instructed by the military government not to support them, and eventually each one was bought out by the Foreign Office. The last paper to go this way was the *Japan News Week*, owned by the American W.R. Wills, for whom Morris wrote a weekly review column. The books he reviewed, he claims, were chosen carefully so that he could write some thinly disguised ant-Nazi propaganda. But even though the German embassy complained about this, the authorities found it impossible to censor a Briton who criticised Japan's then closest ally because he was working for the Japanese Foreign Office! Afterwards, Morris began receiving a weekly parcel of Nazi literature from the German embassy in Tokyo which was intended to make him alter his views. Later, Morris found out that his name was placed on the official Gestapo 'Black List'.

DIFFICULTIES INCREASE

As war became imminent, so Morris' teaching of English Literature at Keiō University became increasingly difficult. There was no decrease in the number of students opting for English, nor any increase in the number choosing German, but the ban on the importation of books in English caused problems for the teachers. The proscription of certain authors, such as Aldous Huxley, was followed by the police buying all available copies of such works in English. Even Basil Hall Chamberlain's *Things Japanese* (sixth edition 1939) was censored.

Words used in sport were also affected, with young students playing baseball being admonished for shouting *sturaiku!* (strike) and *auto!* (out) and instructed to utter *ii tama!* and *damme* by their military attachés![11]

Food-rationing was another consequence of war that affected Morris. He relates the shortage of '. . . coffee, of which the Japanese are extremely fond. Its place was taken by a revolting Ersatz liquid, made, I believe from soya beans'.[12]

As the Pacific War gained increasing momentum, Morris noticed with trepidation that bilingual signs in both *kanji* (Chinese characters) and *rōmaji* (phonetics using the ABC Western alphabet) on streets and railway stations were replaced by monolingual (*kanji*) ones. But however inconvenient for Morris whose knowledge of Japanese *kanji* symbols was limited, more positive campaigns began to make life more uncomfortable for him. Anti-spy posters began to be displayed on every hoarding, and this resulted in young boys calling 'Spy!' to him in the street; one even daubed the character for 'spy' on his front door, which a friend translated for him. There was only one occasion when he met with really rude treatment in wartime Japan and that involved an unknown army officer who pushed Morris into the gutter with his sword scabbard and swore at him.

After 7 December 1941, Morris' life and that of many of his Western friends in Japan began to be radically disrupted. After a lazy few hours on (Sunday) 7 December, he began to write an article about the English authoress Virginia Woolf whose recent suicide had saddened many fellow writers. The article he was writing was for the *Japan News Week* and, as usual later that evening, the editorial staff met at the house of Paul Rusch to discuss the forthcoming publication. Rusch had first come to Japan in 1923 as a YMCA volunteer to help Japanese people traumatized after the Great Kantō Earthquake. He decided to stay on as an educational missionary to create, through his own determined efforts, a fine social service camp for boys. The war was about to end Rusch's activities, but he is still remembered today as the man who introduced American Football there.

The meeting at Rusch's house was attended by Wills, Phyllis Argall, the managing editor, and Air Commodore Bryant, the British air attaché. Bryant, being a member of the diplomatic corps, had access to a supply of petrol and was able to take the other members home late at night. But anyone associating with British diplomats was immediately under suspicion; unbeknown to Morris, the *kempei* were watching from the shadows. The next day he was eating breakfast with the radio on as usual, but instead of the regular music programme an excited commentator was repeating a sentence over and over again. Morris was able to make out the phrase: 'Japan and America now at war!' He called his housekeeper and she confirmed the statement, but she added that he should not worry about it and she told him to hurry or he would be late for his work.

That day his students reacted normally during his lectures, but when he had finished he was instructed not to give any more until further orders were received from the authorities. On his way home he went to see his friend Frank Hawley, the director of the British Council library that had been recently set up, but found that Hawley and his Japanese wife had both been arrested at dawn.[13] He was not allowed to visit them, and some months later he learned of the cruel police methods and obscene prison conditions the Hawleys were subjected to for eight months.

On arriving home that night, he found eight policemen at his house and all his personal property in disorder. Books, clothes and bedding were scattered across the floor, and the police had decided to confiscate a few books – all with red covers – some old newspapers and four X-ray photographs of his lungs. 'Do you have a shortwave radio transmitter?' they asked him, 'Or perhaps a machine-gun or rifle?' After further questioning they left, only to return a few days later demanding that he explain in Japanese the contents of each of his remaining books!

Because of his position as an employee of a Japanese university Morris was never arrested, but he suffered intense loneliness and severe mental strain as all his foreign friends were one by one interned or imprisoned. His old Japanese friends remained true, however, and continued to visit him and supply him with food, sometimes going short themselves. Many openly criticized the Japanese military adventures, but Morris was wary of expressing his own thoughts knowing the underhand and devious methods of the *kempei*.

AUSTERITY AND AIR RAIDS

Rationing was immediately introduced with the outbreak of war, and food was distributed through the old 'neighbourhood association' (*chikukai*) system. Petrol was unobtainable for civilian use and taxis were converted to run on charcoal. Alcohol consumption increased, but as drinks were now made from chemicals instead of natural ingredients, stomach complaints increased among beer drinkers. Some small snack-bars, unable to obtain proper whiskey, refilled their bottles with a concoction based on methanol![14] Air-raid precautions were supervised by the '*chikukai*', and a central office instructed that every household display one bucket of water and three sandbags in case of fire. This was utterly useless and merely acted to reassure people, making it appear that the government knew what to expect, but Morris had to comply. There were no public air-raid shelters in

Tokyo, and, unlike London, the subway system had not been built deep enough to afford any protection against bombs.[15]

* * *

When General James Doolittle led the first air-raid on Tokyo at noon on 18 April 1942, Morris was strolling down the Ginza. He glanced up and saw the planes flying low and he noticed that no-one made any attempt to shelter despite the howling sirens. Soon afterwards barrage balloons appeared over Tokyo, but the surprise raid had had its effect as civilians began to lose faith in the army's ability to even defend the homeland. This only caused the authorities to become even more chauvinistic: education at school level became more nationalistic and Morris noted that he '. . . saw in the press articles claiming that the aeroplane was a Japanese invention, and that the Japanese were responsible for most of the major discoveries of modern science'.[16] History in Japan, it seemed, was being rewritten once more.

In that same month Morris was summoned to the Foreign Office and was introduced to the chief of the foreign section of the Japan Broadcasting Corporation who, after a preamble, offered him employment as a broadcaster. When it became clear that he was expected to take the role of Japan's Lord Haw Haw and broadcast propaganda in order to dishearten the Allies, he lost his temper, refused categorically to undertake the work and stormed out of the room; in so doing he fully expected to be arrested and interned, but to his surprise nothing happened.[17]

Towards the end of May 1942, the word was circulated by some ex-students that the interned Americans were being allowed to leave Japan by ship from Yokohama. Many had been languishing in Sugamo prison for months. Their friends could see them off, they were told, and about 200 Japanese friends gathered at the railway station to say farewell. However, despite this seemingly generous gesture, the friends were stopped from talking to the Americans by the police, and some were questioned and a few arrested. Morris was there, and had to return to his house feeling even more sad, lonely and insecure. In July the sailing of the British internees and diplomats was arranged, but Morris' name was not on the list as issued by the neutral Swiss Embassy. He despaired, and applied for permission to travel to Karuizawa to escape the summer heat of Tokyo. The police phoned him back with the message that he was free to leave with the British ship! He was informed that he had 48 hours to prepare for the journey and was forbidden from taking any books, manuscripts or letters, and could only take a small amount of money.

Frantically Morris made preparations, transferred most of his money to a Japanese friend, copied his address book onto thin paper and concealed it in a hat and was just ready to depart as customs men arrived to inspect his possessions before they transferred them directly to the ship. When all was done and he was on the point of leaving, an income tax inspector arrived to see him to demand payment. A year's tax in advance was required despite the fact that Morris' income from Japan was about to cease! It was an old confidence trick to play against someone nervous about escaping from a horrific situation. Morris showed the inspector the tiny amount of cash that he was told he was permitted to take out of the country, and finally, at midnight, he signed away all his furniture to the income tax department. At dawn, on 26 July 1942, he left to board the ship at Yokohama.

ENGLAND AND THE BBC

Morris' feelings on arriving back in England are not recorded. But in retirement he confessed that: 'I have felt true contentment only when surrounded by people of an alien culture.'[18] In the same 1960 book, he admitted his homosexuality, which for the time was brave and progressive.

In February 1943, Morris had been offered a job with the BBC as Head of Broadcasting in the Japanese section, part of the Far Eastern Service. Here he met Eric Blair – better known as George Orwell – who was also a broadcaster and writer; both men occupied adjacent small rooms at the BBC's 200 Oxford Street premises.[19] The two men were involved in similar work at the BBC, and because of their close working and living quarters must have socialized to a certain extent, both being creative writers and seekers after truth. The BBC offices, in fact, occupied the open space of a whole floor of an Oxford Street department store, each separated by thin nine-foot-high partitions.[20] It is recorded that Orwell was rude to Morris[21] on various occasions, although it may have been that Morris was over-sensitive to Orwell's remarks, or perhaps somewhat naïve following his loss of touch with British social culture through being abroad for so many years. It may have been that Orwell was in awe or jealous of Morris' publishing success, for *Traveller from Tokyo* sold over a quarter of a million copies as it went into Penguin paperback.

When Orwell's novel *Nineteen Eighty-Four* was issued in 1948, the latter's writing success was assured. Orwell as early as 1943 had prepared a detailed outline for the book under the title 'The Last Man in Europe'.[22] In the pages of this futuristic novel of fiction that has had so much influence on artistic and political thought, we find many possible references to Morris' wartime experiences in Japan, as recorded in his book. In fact the basic structure of the novel was the same as Morris': main character (Winston Smith or Morris himself) who seeks truth by writing in a secret diary finds himself in a frustrating and frightening environment which is described in detail and over which he has little control. Morris must have seen the morning callisthenics, still performed to military music by every employee in Japanese companies and organizations. 'Arms bending and stretching!' she rapped out. 'Take your time by me. One, two, three, four! One, two, three, four! Come on comrades put a bit of life into it!'[23]

Japan may not be the only nation that is flexible or even mendacious in the recording and reporting of its own history, but it has a reputation for it. Winston Smith had an official post in the fictional Ministry of Truth, abbreviated to 'Minitrue', where he was responsible for destroying old records and writing new ones to replace them so that Big Brother's and The Party's predictions are always found to be true. His job, along with hundreds of others, was to rewrite history. 'The reason is that the Party member, like the proletarian, . . . must be cut off from the past, just as he must be cut off from foreign countries, because it is necessary for him to believe that he is better off than his ancestors.' But more importantly 'is the need to safeguard the infallibility of the Party'.[24]

There is a propensity in Japan to shorten or abbreviate long words and expressions, especially new foreign words, and to invent new ones for new ideas. Morris seems to have been aware that the Japanese Emperor's 'divine status is of comparative recent invention. The myth has been built up gradually by the army for its own ends'.[25] His information probably came from either the short pamphlet by the Japanese language expert, Basil Hall Chamberlain, in his 1912 *The Invention of a New Religion – on Mikado Worship*,[26] or its reprint as an article in the sixth edition of his *Things Japanese* in 1939. This posthumous edition, although written in English, was banned in Japan.[27]

'History is so taught to the young (of Japan) as to focus everything upon Imperialism, and to diminish as far as possible the contrast between ancient and modern conditions,'[28] wrote Chamberlain, who continues:

> As for Bushido, so modern a thing is it that neither Kaempfer, Siebold, Satow, nor Rein – all men knowing their Japan by heart – ever once allude to it in their voluminous writings. . . Bushido was unknown until a decade or two ago! The very word appears in no dictionary, native or foreign, before the year 1900. . . Bushido as an institution or a code of rules, has never existed. The accounts given of it have been fabricated . . . for foreign consumption.[29]

266

Here we have the creation of a new word for political reasons, and perhaps the seed for Orwell's 'Newspeak'? Chamberlain observed that 'Meanwhile a generation is growing up which does not so much as suspect that its cherished beliefs are inventions of yesterday.'[30] This is a major theme in Orwell's *Nineteen Eighty-Four* in which a Comrade Withers was 'awarded a decoration, the Order of Conspicuous Merit, Second Class'.[31] Winston Smith searching his memory knew that it was a lie 'as was claimed in the Party history books, that the Party had invented aeroplanes'.[32] He disliked children who were always 'watching for symptoms of unorthodoxy . . . and by means of such organizations as the Spies. . . denounced parents to the Thought Police'.[33] Because of continual war, many things were rationed and poorly made like 'coffee filthy-tasting, cigarettes insufficient – nothing cheap and plentiful except synthetic gin'.[34] The parallels with Morris' book continue. In the final scene, Winston after torture with the rat, finally succumbs and decides 'everything was all right, the struggle was finished. He had won the victory over himself. He loved Big Brother'.[35] Similarly, Chamberlain ends his tract with: 'People can always believe that which it is greatly to their interest to believe. . . Accordingly, they (members of the Japanese ruling class) achieve the apparently impossible. "We believe in it", said one of them to us recently – "We believe in it, although we know it is not true".'[36]

JAPAN'S PASSING LANE

By 1972, the word 'Orwellian' had been long established worldwide. During that year the Japanese journalist Kamata Satoshi worked for six months as a migrant worker on the production line of the Toyota Motor Company Ltd. at Nagoya. After a very thorough and humiliating medical examination, the new recruits watch a film showing 'the "official" history of the Toyota Motor Company up to the present date'. The opening, with its long line of trucks along a muddy road (in China, it seems) during World War II, is a shocking reminder that Toyota owes much of its expansion to military production.'[37]

Like Winston, as well as morning callisthenics and chanting the company song, Kamata describes how young workers starting off full of potential 'slowly but surely, they enter a permanently closed society. "Rationalization" of production changes even their personality . . . Ultimately it's a kind of lobotomy.'[38] Kamata also kept a secret diary on which his book is based, and in the Introduction, Ronald Dore deplores '. . . the tight surveillance, the claustrophobic requirement of conformity in word, deed, and thought. . . even a man's biorhythms and what time he goes to bed are a matter of the firm's concern if they are likely to have any bearing on his productive efficiency or his proneness to accidents'.[39]

George Orwell worked from late 1940 to 1943 as a Talks Assistant, and later as a Producer, with the BBC. As already mentioned John Morris had a room next to Orwell in Oxford Street, and the former was Head of the Japanese Section with the BBC Far Eastern Service from February 1943 on arriving from Japan until 1952. He was then promoted to become the Controller of the Third Programme until his retirement in 1958. The poet William Empson (1906-84) was also part of the BBC team, and he had been Professor of English Literature at Tokyo University (Bunrika Daigaku) from 1931-34 and had seen the Japanese military machine gather pace. He would have related his experiences to Orwell too.

RETURN VISIT

In January 1946 Morris was lent to the BBC's News Division in order to travel back to Japan and send back a series of weekly talks based on his observations.[40] After the nostalgic trip to the ruins of his former home in Shibuya where he found his 'Phoenix Cup', he travelled to many parts of Japan during the course of that year. In Hiroshima he found 'a determination to recover such as I sensed nowhere else in Japan'. He reported that the local newspaper *Chūgoku Shimbun*, had gone to press just six weeks after the A-bomb explosion even though the monotype machines had been ruined by the heat. Young boys had used tweezers to delicately pick out the *kanji* type and then set them by hand.[41] Morris reported on the lack of food for ordinary people in Tokyo, and how many had died of starvation, especially the elderly; on the humane conditions of the 'War Criminals' at Sugamo prison; on the first democratic elections held on 10 April 1946, where women could vote for the first time ever. He watched the repatriation of 6.5 million Japanese soldiers at Otake port, one of the 12 reception camps around the country at which several thousand arrived daily in all manner of floating craft.

The men, who were all then officially prisoners-of-war, looked ill and dejected as they landed back on their homeland with no sign of any emotional feeling. Their kit was first inspected for drugs and contraband, and then, regardless of rank, they were lined up to be sprayed with DDT. Finally, in apathetic silence, they were inspected by an occupation officer and all badges of rank taken from them and immediately destroyed. They then became civilians and were free to go. Many were confused and did not move, waiting for further orders. Nothing in the military rule book had prepared them for this, years of receiving and giving orders within the rigid military hierarchy made them freeze with fear of freedom.

Their next fear was that their families would not accept them back, for they had committed the crime of coming back alive and felt guilty and disgraced at being taken prisoner. Some of them had officially been reported dead. A great number remained in the reception camps for several days, traumatized, until they began to inspect the large-scale maps that covered the barrack walls and that showed every part of Japan, with devastated areas marked in. When they eventually found the courage to travel back to their home town, many found a friend or acquaintance to act as a go-between to break the news of their arrival to their family. Some refused to accept them back, and the ex-soldiers had to depart from their own homes and families permanently.[42]

Morris met one who had thankfully been welcomed back by his aging mother in Tokyo. He told him the story of how his ship was sunk by enemy air attacks and thousands of his comrades drowned. He spent six days clinging to a raft before drifting to an Australian occupied island where he was taken prisoner. The remainder of the war he spent in confinement, but was surprised and impressed by the comfort and humanity offered by his captors who treated him for the malaria he had caught. He could not understand why he had not been brutally killed and this had caused him much mental stress. Indeed, he had contemplated killing himself for, it had been impressed on him continually, that was the way that war should be conducted. 'Once I was an out-and-out militarist', he confessed to Morris in his home, 'Now I wish we could have true fraternization, it is the only way we Japanese can learn to become democratic. We must, first of all, respect each others' rights.'[43]

Soon after, Morris left the desolation of Japan and visited other countries in the Far East to assess the impact of the war on each one. But the tangle of national interests was such that he could only conclude, as an Englishman: 'There are many tasks still left for us to do in the Orient; but they cannot be usefully done unless we are prepared to carry them out in a spirit of helpfulness and cooperation with the local peoples.'[44] His 'we' no doubt referred to those who administered the British Empire whose rapid decline was imminent. Both Morris and Orwell had held minor governmental 'Imperial' posts in India and Burma respectively in their younger days, and both became aware of 'the equivocal moral position of Britain, with its democratic phrases and its coolie empire' and also of 'the sinister development of Soviet Russia, the squalid farce of left-wing politics – (but) all this fades away' declared Orwell 'and one sees only the struggle of the gradually awakening common people against the lords of property and their hired liars and bumsuckers'.[45]

Morris retired from the BBC in 1958, shortly after he had persuaded playwright Samuel Beckett to contribute several famous radio dramas, he moved to Henley-on-Thames and wrote three more books. He died in December 1980.

22

Sir John Figgess KBE, CMG
(1909-97)

SIR HUGH CORTAZZI

JOHN FIGGESS made a significant conribution to better understanding between Britain and Japan. His life had many facets –
businessman, army intelligence officer, military attaché in Tokyo,
diplomat who served as information counsellor in the British embassy,
British Commissioner General at Expo 70 in Osaka, once again
businessman and for much of his life expert in oriental art and
Japanologist.

Figgess was a big man both physically and intellectually. Once met
he was not easily forgotten. In stature tall, he had a balding head, florid
face and prominent nose. He had a booming voice and strongly-held
views. The warmth of his personality, his enthusiasm for the best in
Japan and his charm were obvious to all who met him. His height and
voice and his ill-disguised contempt for those who did not share his
enthusiasms may have put off a few small-minded people, but no-one
who got to know him doubted his genuine kindness, especially to his
juniors, his loyalty to his friends and the depth of his sympathies. He
did not speak ill of others and was charitable in the best sense of the
word. He was invariably courteous and sensitive about the feelings of
others. He did not flaunt his religious beliefs but, especially in his later
years, he was a conscientious member of the Church of England.

★　★　★

John George Figgess was born into a family of Ulster Protestants from
Enniskillen in 1909. His father was killed in the First World War and
his mother was left in straightened circumstnces. He was educated at

271

Whitgift Middle School in Croydon. He would have liked to go on to university and had his eyes on Cambridge, but family funds did not permit this. He always regretted that he had not had a university education and this may have been one reason why he was reticent about his education.

I have been unable to discover what he did between school (the school records simply state that he was unplaced) and going to Japan in 1933 when he was 23. Perhaps he worked in business in London. In Japan he worked for Strong and Company who had an import/export business in Yokohama and presumably they sent him out there. He became in due course head of their sundry goods section. He was a robust young man and was an active member of the Yokohama Cricket and Athletic Club (the YC and AC) where, according to his friend Alf Bennett who was then an RAF language student (later Group Captain, RAF and post-war air attaché), he was captain of the Rugby XV. John and Alf Bennett, who first met in 1935, became good friends. John would invite Alf to 'crew for him racing his dinghy', and would occasionally drive up to Hakone where Alf took a summer house and they sailed a much smaller dinghy on the lake.

John found that, to quote Bennett, his British contemporaries, who 'lived their British life – eggs and bacon, steak, evening beers all round at a few boozy bars', 'limited their ability to do business with the Japanese, while some foreigners learned Japanese and enlarged their competitiveness. Seeing this John managed to live with a Japanese family for some two years, so acquiring fluency in speech and customs'. Once he had attained this fluency he 'reverted to the young ex-pat practice of living in messes of six or eight. . .but John never joined the beery round even after a muddy scramble of Rugby or a soaker in his dinghy'). He did not learn to read Japanese at this time and had to struggle hard later in life to teach himself *kanji*. Alf Bennett commented that John's main characteristic at this stage was his self-confidence.

On 9 December 1936 a marriage was solemnized at the British consulate general in Yokohama between John Figgess aged 27 and Lesley Valli Parsons, described as spinster and her age quoted as 'full'. The address for both of them was recorded as 38A Bluff, Yokohama. John's father's name was given as Percival Watts Figgess and his profession as accountant (deceased). Her father's name was given as Leslie Edward Parsons, insurance executive. They had apparently met on a boat to Australia. I do not know when it became clear to John that they were not suited to one another. Perhaps this was during the war when they were parted by his absence in India. At any rate the marriage eventually ended in a divorce in 1947. A decree nisi was issued on 22 July 1947 and made absolute on 7 January 1948. One James Ross Parratt was named as co-respondent.

John's family always understood that he had been involved in secret intelligence work before the war. But a careful check on the records have not shown any trace. There is equally no trace in War Office records of his being employed by military intelligence. John Figgess apparently first offered his services to the War Office in a letter dated 21 December 1938. He wrote from 7 Britten House, Chelsea and said that he was then working for Graham Brothers of Bradford Avenue EC (I have been unable to trace this firm). He claimed that he travelled extensively in Europe and the Far East. His letter attracted the attention of Gerald Templar, then a colonel in military intelligence (later Field Marshall), who minuted on it on 18 January 1939, but it was not until 1939, after the outbreak of the war with Germany, that Figgess was accepted for the army. He named his father-in-law Leslie Parsons, then working at 10 St Mary Axe, as a reference. Those who should have known are certain that John was not in intelligence before the war. Why then did the suspicion arise? Perhaps it was the fact that he never liked to talk about his pre-war days in Japan and would clam up if asked about this period of his life. This silence may have been due to his regrets about his lack of a university education and a desire not to upset his second wife Alette who was sensitive on the subject of his first marriage, not least because his mother would never acknowlege her. This was a great sadness to them both.

John was commissioned in the intelligence corps and in July 1940 he was sent as a GSO3 (General Staff Officer grade 3) to 61 Division. In 1941 he graduated from the Army Staff College and in 1942 he was posted to India to join the 'Wireless Experimental Station' (i.e.Signals Intelligence or SIGINT) travelling out by air via Kenya. According to William Watson who worked with him in Delhi, John, who had been rapidly promoted to lieutenant colonel, was in charge of the unit studying the Japanese order of battle. Watson described John at this time as maintaining a good soldierly bearing and having an open Irish and bonhomous temperament. His spoken Japanese was very good, although he had little knowledge then of the written language. When they discussed what they might do after the war John ofered to help him through his father-in-law to get a reasonable job in insurance and implied that he (Figgess) would go back into business. (Watson later had a distinguished career at the British Museum). Slogging away in the summer heat of New Delhi working on wireless intelligence must have been unexciting work but his job took him from time to time to Burma where he could observe the battle with Japan more closely than at Headquarters in Delhi.

When the war ended in August 1945 he was summoned to appear before the Brigadier General Staff (Intelligence) at the Headquarters of the Supreme Allied Commander in South East Asia in Kandy. General

Gairdner, the newly-appointed personal representative of the prime minister to General MacArthur, wanted a senior Japanese-speaking assistant. Figgess, having returned to Delhi to pack up, left Calcutta on 23 September 1945 with General Gairdner and his other aides. They flew via Kunming and Manila to Tokyo arriving on 26 September. In his account of this period of his life (*Proceedings of the Japan Society*, Spring 1993) John describes his return to a Japan which he had left in early 1939. He would never forget the ride into Yokohama from Atsugi airbase. 'The landscape on all sides was flattened and black.' 'We bumped our way through the unending scene of devastation that had been the city of Yokohama.'

The party proceeded through the ruins to the British embassy, then an RN shore-station named HMS *Return*. A Foreign Office representative Dermot MacDermott, formerly of the Japan consular service had already arrived. John described MacDermott as 'a man of few words', although John Pilcher, later ambassador to Japan, used to say of MacDermott that he was the only man he ever met who could 'discourse coherently about transsubstantiation while drunk'. Figgess was billeted in no. 4 house in the compound. Their immediate task was to make contact with the office of the Supreme Commander for the Allied Powers (SCAP i.e. General MacArthur) and to liaise with the Japanese on problems such as the repatriation of Japanese forces from overseas.

John recorded that 'Contact with the Japanese population while not forbidden by SCAP was not exactly encouraged', but he managed to get in touch with some of his old friends. 'There was little food to be had in the towns, money was all but worthless; people survived by journeying to the countryside in search of almost anything edible.' 'This was a society shattered by its defeat in the war and torn from its roots.' He noted that '. . . the nation as a whole seems to have concluded that the best course was unquestioning and ready compliance with the demands of SCAP'.

In his note for the Japan Society, John recorded a number of interesting episodes in these early post-war days. There was inevitably a tendency on the part of British leaders to be less than friendly to senior Japanese. The Chief of the Imperial General Staff (the CIGS), Field Marshal Alan Brooke, was an exception when he visited Japan. He wanted to meet Prince Takatsukasa with whom he shared an interest in ornithology. Prince Takatsukasa was then the Keeper of the Meiji Shrine. John arranged the visit expecting to have to interpret at a rather formal meeting. In fact the CIGS and the Prince '. . . seemed to be communicating perfectly well, mostly in Latin. Soon they were both on the floor engrossed in discussion'.

In the absence of a British consular representative, John found himself having to keep an eye on the Indian community in Japan who during the war had taken a critical line towards Britain in an effort to avoid internment. Subhas Chandra Bose, who had been responsible for raising the anti-British Indian National Army, had been in Japan but at the end of the war had tried to escape and had reportedly died in an air crash at Taipei. It fell to John to get confirmation of this fact from his Indian contacts. This he succeeded in doing. He was also involved in the surrender to the occupation authorities of Ba Maw, the Japanese war-time puppet prime minister of Burma.

★ ★ ★

When Sir Alvary Gascoigne came out as head of the United Kingdom Liaison Mission to SCAP (UKLM) with the rank of ambassdor, John became assistant military adviser to the mission and so remained until the Peace Treaty came into force in April 1952. He then became assistant military attaché. His knowledge of Japanese, his ablity to get on with Japanese in all walks of life, and his contacts with the military side of the occupation forces made him a very valuable member of the mission. John was much better informed and in touch than his immediate boss, the regular army brigadier who was the military adviser and later military attaché, but John was always loyal and did not try to upstage his superior.

Among the many people John met in military circles were three young Dutch girls with the Dutch mission. At first they had the rank of corporal, but as this limited them to NCO messes they were promoted to second lieutenant which meant that they wore a single star like that of an American brigadier general. As a result they came to be called the 'baby-generals'. John's favourite was a girl called Alette Ildenburg. Elizabeth Borgman-Brouwer, who was with Alette as another of the 'baby-generals', referred to her friend

> ... as pretty dreamy Alette. Life was pleasant and carefree and we often spent week-ends at Hayama where John had rented a small Japanese house right on the sea with the hills in the back. Their mutual interest grew into a lasting love. After a fairly short courtship Alette decided a year after her arrival in Japan to return to her parents in Indonesia. Not long afterwards the marriage took place in Holland.

They were married in the Reformed Church at the Hague on 5 February 1948.

Alette Ildenburg was born on 21 June 1925 in Bogor (then Buitenzorg) in Java. Her father was a senior civil servant in the government of the Netherlands East Indies. Her mother had been born in South Africa. In 1938 Alette and her elder brother returned to Holland to continue their education. During the war they had a very difficult time. Her brother, who tried to escape to Britain, was arrested by the Germans and sent to Dachau concentration camp. Alette's mother in Java was imprisoned for three months after being tortured by the Japanese *kempeitai* (secret police) and later interned with the rest of the family. Alette managed to get out to Djakarta in 1946 and from there was recruited to go to Japan as a secretary to the Netherland Military Mission in Japan.

John and Alette were devoted to one another and had a very happy marriage. They had two daughters, Sandra and Michaela.

I do not know exactly when John Figgess began to collect oriental ceramics and other art objects, but it seems probable that his interest was stimulated during the occupation when many Japanese collectors had to dispose of items from their collections to pay taxes and to live. Alette, according to her sister, had had in her early youth a real interest in Chinese and Japanese porcelain and had started a small collection. She and John, with his increasing knowledge of the subject, made 'a unique combination'. John was what the Japanese call *me-kiki* literally 'the effective eye', which means having an instinctive understanding of what is artistically oustanding and in good taste. John's preference in accordance with Japanese cannons was for the *shibui*, literally astringent, but which essentially means restrained and simple.

I first met John and Alette in 1951 when I joined the UKLM as a third (later second) secretary in the chancery (political section) of the embassy. John used to bring his black labrador 'Jimmy' to the office and it was difficult to envisage him without his beloved dog.

In late 1952 John was transferred from Tokyo to serve as a GSO 1 in the War Office in London. I do not think he greatly enjoyed his time in this post but he managed to develop his relations with members of the Japanese Self-Defence Forces who came on visits or training assignments in Britain. General Kurisu Hiromi remembered how John had helped him when as a lieutenant colonel he had been sent to Britain for over three months in 1955. In those days Japan was very short of foreign currency and the Japanese embassy in London had booked him and his fellow officers into cheap accommodation. John, as soon as he saw where they were staying, declared that the place was not suitable for Japanese officers and moved them into a better hotel. Kurisu thought that the guards at the War Office must have been astonished to see the towering figure of John Figgess followed by such a tiny Japanese officer. John had been very attentive accompanying them on their visits and explaining carefully in Japanese what they were shown. He had also invited them to his home for a meal. Kurisu was introduced to Sandra with whom he played. Although their paths did not cross frequently they kept in touch until John died in 1997.

In 1956 John was appointed military attaché in Tokyo with the rank of full colonel and remained there until his retirement from the army in 1961. He was a conscientious military attaché and maintained a good working relationship with members of the Self-Defence Forces, visiting Japanese units whenever he could. General Yamada Masao who had been chief of staff of the Ground Self-Defence Forces recalled that after making an inspection trip to Japanese forces in Hokkaido, John had commented that the establishments of the Japanese GSDF units seemed to him 'too small and tight. When a battle begins casualties arise inevitably' and Japanese units had no replacements. In Japanese units the commanding officer did not like to take leave. In British regiments the officer commanding took leave from time to time and his deputy took over and learnt by experience.

John was in these years more than just the military attaché. He gave active support to the Japan-British Society and continued to widen his circle of Japanese friends. The British ambassador Sir Oscar Morland found his advice of great value. When Sir Vere Redman, the idiosyncratic information counsellor (see my portrait in *Biographical Portraits* Volume II) was due to retire, Oscar Morland managed to persuade the Foreign Office to appoint John, (who was due to be replaced as military attaché) as a temporary member of the foreign service to fill Redman's vacant post.

John had learnt a great deal about the work of the embassy and the change was not as much of a cultural shock as it would have been to most other serving officers. Indeed, he adapted himself with enthusiasm to his new role. He developed good relations with the media including jounalists on the main newspapers such as the *Asahi*. His best friend in the media who shared his enthusiasm for art was Enjōji Jirō who became president of the *Nihon Keizai Shimbun*. But he soon realized that the emphasis hitherto placed on explaining British world policies had to be modified to reflect Britain's changing role in the world and he worked hard to develop new priorities.

In 1966 when I came back to the British embassy as commercial and economic counsellor the work of the Information Department under John Figgess's guidance was increasingly geared to promoting British products in the Japanese market. John also continued to back the Japan-British Society. He maintained his close relations with Aso Kazuko, daughter of Yoshida Shigeru, and the Aso family, and also with Princess Chichibu who was the honorary patron of the Society.

John Field, who worked for John in the Information Department from 1966-68, recorded that his main memory was

> ... of his exuberance: he was one of those people who always made one feel that everything was possible... One

277

of our fondest memories is of the dinner evenings, when some of his Japanese friends would come and, when the port came round, out would come beautiful *furoshiki*, which guests had hidden under their chairs. When unfurled they would reveal all sorts of treasures – pots, scrolls, lacquer. These were lovingly handed round the table and admired by all the guests. Of course John always had some of the best pieces, which he would discuss with his guests. What a civilized evening! Being new to the Service I thought all diplomatic dinners would be like these.

Takagi Mariko, who was John's secretary from 1963-67, was rather worried when she started work for him. He had been so serious at the interview and had not revealed that he spoke Japanese. She soon found that his Japanese was very good, and that he had

> ... a very caring, warm heart behind those sharp looking eyes. He was always energetic and very strict at work. I remember whenever we heard his strong footsteps and booming voice marching down the corridor a bracing air filled the office.

She and John Field recalled that Jimmy, John's black Labrador, personified him. 'The same bouncy enthusiasm and the same inability to take no for an answer.' Mariko continued to keep in touch with the Figgeses and regarded John as '... not only like a father who had a big warm heart but also a great mentor as he always gave us some good advice'.

One story about John's time as information counsellor was recalled by Lees Mayall in his autobiography *Fireflies in Amber*. John had a serious motor accident. Fortunately, no-one was hurt. He was driving up a one-way street with his lights on and met a three-wheeled truck coming down the street in the wrong direction without lights. There was a head-on crash. John's car was badly damaged and the van was a write-off. John persuaded the ambassador to waive his diplomatic immunity in the interests of the insurers. The Japanese judge summing up said that the Japanese driver was '... to be severely censured for driving inebriated, without lights, the wrong way down a one-way street and we take a very grave view of this matter and he would do well to eschew such behaviour in future. However, if the foreign barabarian had not been in the street at the time there would probably have been no accident. So we will call it fifty-fifty'. The Japanese van driver was penniless and uninsured. Somebody had to pay something. It had to be the foreigner and his insurance company.

By 1969 the Foreign and Commonwealth Office were getting restless about a temporary diplomat filling a counsellor's post and John was in any case 60 that year. Sir John Pilcher who had arrived as ambassador in 1967, was an old friend, who shared John's love of Japan and Japanese art. He did not want to lose Figgess and recommended that he should be the British Commissioner General at the international exposition in Osaka in 1970 (Expo 70) at which there was to be a British pavilion. Pilcher's views prevailed and John was appointed. He was made a KBE (he had been awarded a CMG in 1960 and an OBE in 1949).

Bill Bentley (later Sir William Bentley) who had been a language student in Japan was appointed as Deputy Commissioner General. Neither John nor he were greatly impressed by the rather uninspired pavilion which had been designed under the auspices of the Central Office of Information (COI), but they and the ambassador were determined to make the best of it on behalf of Britain. There were strict rules about what could be sold in the pavilion, but John and Bill were disappointed by the lack of enterprise shown by British firms in exploiting the limited opportunities available. The Figgess/Bentley combination worked well and they knew that they had the support of the ambassador and his staff in Tokyo.

On taking up his new appointment John, to quote Bill Bentley, '... went to great lengths to set himself up there in a traditional Japanese-style house and life-style. I think this had been one of his life's ambitions and he achieved it with a thorough-going attention to detail (though not without some regard also for Western-style comforts)'. He '... had recognized long before Expo began that entertaining would be a key to getting the most out of what was far from an inspiring exhibit...Entertaining he saw as one way of compensating for this; another was the idea of bilingual hostesses, roughly half British and Japanese'.

Their entertaining budget was limited by Britain's straightened circumstances and was far less than that of many other participating countries. They also knew that to be effective their entertaining had to be of a high standard to satisfy Japanese expectations. They decided that the only way to find the necessary means was to make some money through pavilion sales. The concession for medals had been snapped up but no-one had thought about badges. As Bill expllained: '... we hit on a design, found – with difficulty – someone to make them for us and set up our stall. For good measure we also set up an ice-cream kiosk'. The money earned enabled them not only to entertain 'at full blast' throughout Expo, but they were able to make a contribution of £50,000 to the UK treasury. So no awkward questions were asked.

Most of the entertaining was aimed at Japanese not least because Expo was 'essentially for home consumption'. 'So we had a steady stream of political, economic, academic and cultural Japanese leaders to our dining room and I was astonished by John's range of contacts and knowledge of matters of interest to them.'

Of course foreign dignitaries visiting Expo had to be given appropriate VIP treatment. One of these was Prince Charles, the Prince of Wales, who managed to visit 25 pavilions in one day. The Emperor of Ethiopia '. . . who arrived late on one day and sagging visibly. . .struggled manfully round what turned out to be his 22nd pavilion that day' was rather disappointed to learn that his record had been beaten by the Prince of Wales, but considering the difference in age this was hardly surprising.

When John left Osaka he was still only 61 and as an active man he had no wish to retire. During the run-up to British Week in Tokyo in 1969 John had had a number of meetings with George White of Maples Leblanc who had taken the opportunity of promoting sales of British antiques, objets d'art and, it must be said, bric-a-brac. George was an entrepreneur, and invited John to become a director of Maples which John accepted. But John did not find George White's methods of operating agreeable and the arrangement was soon terminated. Following this John became a major shareholder in Blanchards with Aldbrook as managing director, who had been an associate of George White. This firm was also involved in the antiques trade. John sold most of his shares in Blanchards in 1988. His main work after his retirement was, however, for Christie's, the auctioneers which he joined initially as adviser in 1972. He later became a director of the firm. He finally retired in 1982 although he continued thereafter to give occasional advice and help. As a director of Christie's he was responsible for organizing Christie's attempt to put on a Western-style auction in Japan. This experiment was not repeated because of Japanese regulations on auction sales and the closed shop of the Japanese antique trade.

★ ★ ★

At Christie's John Figgess was able to continue with his devotion to oriental art and particularly oriental ceramics. Colin Sheaf who worked with him at Christie's, has commented on John's 'natural charm, sense of humour and ability to mix easily with Asians'. Sheaf noted '. . . the way in which the rituals and conventions of Japanese connoisseurship had come to influence the way in which he [John] looked at objects; both intellectually in the way in which he assessed them, and physically in the way he handled and stored them'. John could put Japanese buyers at their ease and '. . . was as much at home in a low-key (but fiendishly expensive) restaurant in Tokyo, hosting a top dealer to encourage a consignment to be sent to Christie's London, or chatting fluently with guests at a wedding reception in Osaka, as he was at lunch in Christie's boardroom or dining with an eccentric Lord in Gloucestershire'. 'His most famous discovery' arose out of a visit to the home of 'a distinguished Duke for a routine valuation, north of London'.

> 'After a leisurely morning, everyone adjourned for lunch, and John went to wash his hands after handling the standard accoutrements of a country house... He returned to a stunned dining room, announcing that in the loo was standing an unrecorded, museum quality massive four-teenth century Chinese jar, painted in the rarest of all fourteenth century palettes, underglaze copper. Plenty of claret and port circulated to celebrate this discovery.'

The jar was sold at Christie's for nearly £100,000 and is now in the Matsuoka Museum in Tokyo.

Colin Sheaf noted that John's '... particular affections were for lacquer and ceramics, especially Chinese lacquer which had entered Japanese collections at an early date...He was one of the first to help distinguish Yuan lacquers with mother-of-pearl inlay'. 'He enoyed Chinese ceramics, particularly those of the Song, Yuan and Ming periods, though he had no time (like almost all Japanese collectors!) for the refined elegance of Qing Imperial wares. A veteran of many tea ceremonies, he enjoyed rustic simplicity in ceramics as much as the outstanding qualities of early Chinese blue and white.' He knew a great deal about *mingei* and about Korean wares. 'His knowledge lay within fairly defined parameters; he had no interest in the meretricious (in his opinion) wares of nineteenth century Japan, or categories like *netsuke* and *inro* which for him were accessories, not main-stream art... Japanese dealers and collectors respected his advice and were prepared to commission him over the telephone to buy objects in London sales which he recommended; a rare accolade.'

While he was at Christie's, John one day interviewed Toshi Hatanaka for the post of Christie's representative in Tokyo. Hatanaka recorded that '... the interview was very brief. Sir John asked me in Japanese if I was married. When I told him I was not, he asked me if I would appoint him as *nakodo* when I got married. He told me that he gave numerous speeches at Japanese weddings as a guest, but he had never been asked to be the *nakodo* and he was longing to be one'. John kept his promise. He '... was specially happy to know that I was marrying Yuriko who was a neice of his close friend Mrs Yuriko Yasuda beside the fact that he employed her as a secretary for Christie's Tokyo'. He was thus more than a nominal *nakodo*.

John Figgess had become a member of the Oriental Ceramic Society

(OCS) in Britain in 1955. He served on the council of the Society from 1975 and was elected President in 1987. During his period of office he presided over the outstanding and very successful joint OCS/British Museum exhibition 'Porcelain for Palaces'. John was a member of the advisory council of the Percival David Foundation and did much to help the Victoria and Albert Museum. He was, for instance, chairman of the advisory team preparing the Samsung Gallery of Korean Art in 1990-92. He was also a generous donor to the museum. Among the splendid objects which he and Alette donated were a rare Japanese lacquered *Amida Nyorai* sculpture dating from the Kamakura period, and a beautiful sixteenth century Korean lacquer box inlaid with mother of pearl.

John was a friend of the Japanese art critic Koyama Fujio who lived in Kamakura. I recall visiting Koyama-sensei with John one hot summer's evening in the late summer of, I think, 1968. After a bath we looked at the moon, drank saké and talked about art and ceramics. John had cooperated with Koyama in 1960 on *Two Thousand Years of Oriental Ceramics*. He translated and adapted Koyama's book *Nihon Tōji no Dentō* (Traditions of Japanese Ceramics). John gave his adaption the title *The Heritage of Japanese Ceramics*. (Weatherhill, 1973). The book had an introduction by Alexander Pope whose comments on Japanese pottery seem to reflect John's own views: 'Seeing. . .is not enough. The pieces must be handled. . . and discussed with Japanese who are at home with the lore. Even then the student must not expect to get straightforward answers to direct questions. He must watch and listen and gradually, little by little, begin to approach comprehension. . .' On the title page John quotes the following remark by the famous art critic Sir Herbert Read:'The art of pottery is of all the arts the one that fuses together in indestructible unity earth and heaven, matter and spirit.'

John Figgess's expertise was respected and quoted by art historians such as Sir Harry Garner (*Chinese Lacquer*, London, 1979) and G.S.G.Gompertz (*Celadon Wares*, London, 1968). He also contributed occasional articles to journals such *Arts of Asia* on aspects of oriental art.

Figgess was much in demand as a lecturer on Japan, China and Asian art. He spoke to the Japan Society on 7 November 1972 on 'Japan's Relations with China from Earliest Times to Meiji' On 27 September 1973 he spoke with authority and enthusiasm on 'Treasures of the Shosoin'. On 20 October 1981, in the context of 'The Great Japan Exhibition' at the Royal Academy, he spoke to the Royal Society of Asian Affairs on 'Japan's Foreign Contacts in the Sixteenth and Seventeenth Centuries.'

Japan and Alette Figgess spent their final years largely at Burghfield near Reading. They had many local friends and enjoyed an active life until almost the end. John continued to take his dog for long walks and enjoyed working in his garden, becoming an expert on various shrubs. He corresponded with the Forestry Commission on lime trees and presented a *Sansho (Xanthoxylum Piperitum)* to the Japanese ambassador's renovated residence garden in 1994. John and Alette gave active support to their local church They enjoyed playing bridge and entertaining their old friends. John did not disguise his admiration for Japan's economic and technological successes or his regrets at the failure of Britain to come to terms with its reduced status in the world. In November 1986, in recognition of his outstanding contribution to Anglo-Japanese understanding, Sir John Figgess was awarded The Order of the Sacred Treasure, Gold and Silver Star'.

Note. I am indebted to many friends who generously contributed their recollections of John Figgess.

23

Kazuko Asō DBE (Hon.) (1915–96)

PHILLIDA PURVIS

TO KAZUKO ASŌ Britain and British friends were, throughout her life, of central importance. She could not have failed to have been influenced in this by the experiences of her own family. These went back, on her mother's side, to the arrival in Britain in 1872 of her great grandfather, Toshimichi Ōkubo, as part of the historic Meiji Iwakura mission. Before coming on to Europe he had left his sons to be educated in America. The younger Nobuaki, then aged nine, Kazuko's grandfather, was later adopted into the family of Makino. His distinguished diplomatic career, which culminated in his serving as foreign minister from 1913–14 and included a three-year posting to the Japanese legation in London. During this time he gained a love of Britain which he transmitted to his daughter, Yukiko, so that when she herself first arrived to live in London in 1909, newly married to the young diplomat Shigeru Yoshida, she '. . . fell in love with England and her people and never recovered it from it. . .'.[1] Although she never met him, Kazuko's paternal grandfather had also enjoyed a London posting, and maintained many British friendships in his subsequent connections with the Scottish trading firm, Jardine Matheson. He died a wealthy man, after setting up his own trading firm. Yoshida, his family believe, drew on this inheritance, to finance the considerable costs of renovating and refurbishing the embassies, in Rome and London, to a standard with which he was satisfied, rather than passing them on to the Foreign Ministry.

Kazuko's inherited predisposition to like Britain was reinforced by her own first-hand experiences of living in London, from 1920–22, and later from 1936–38. These presaged a lifetime commitment to Anglo-Japanese causes, for which she was eventually given recognition with the award in 1975 of an honorary Dame Commander of the British Empire.

★ ★ ★

Kazuko was born in 1915, the third of the four children of Shigeru and Yukiko Yoshida. Shigeru Yoshida had been adopted by the childless Kenzō Yoshida from the family of businessman Tsuna Takenouchi, whose fifth son he was. Although Kazuko was born in Antung in China, many of her earliest memories were of London where her father was posted as first secretary at the Japanese embasssy in 1920 and the family lived in a large house in Streatham Hill. Kazuko's older sister, Sakurako, at that time ten years old, and brother, Kenichi, then eight, attended English schools and Kazuko went to a local kindergarten. Baby Masao, at three years old, can remember being pushed about in his pram by the English nursemaid. Here the children began to speak English and were almost always to do so between each other. Their English was encouraged by their parents, who themselves invariably conversed in English, Yukiko having become fluent in English and German during her own diplomatic childhood. It was maintained by their English governess, Miss West, during their stay in Tientsin (Tianjin), where Yoshida moved as consul-general. This was his second posting in China. The first, to Antung, on the Korean border, where Kazuko was born, had shown that he 'enjoyed no favours from his father-in-law, then Foreign Minister', his son Masao has commented. In Tientsin the Japanese consulate was in the British concession and the children went to the Tientsin Grammar School where all classes were taught in English. Yoshida was transferred in 1926 to Mukden but for the sake of their education the children did not accompany him but returned, with their mother, to Tokyo. Kazuko joined the international Catholic Sacred Heart School, her brothers, Gyosei. Her mother, who had become a Catholic, and brought up her younger three children as Catholics, was later to be closely involved in the establishment of another Catholic school, Seisen. Yoshida was reunited with his family on taking up the post of vice-minister for foreign affairs in 1928.

By the time that Yoshida was posted abroad again, this time to Italy as ambassador, Kazuko had graduated from school and was able to join in her parents' active lives in Rome. Sakurako married a young diplomat and had begun her own diplomatic postings, first to Manchuria and then to Portland, Oregon. In 1940 she was widowed at the young age of thirty when her husband died of pneumonia. Kenichi did not accompany his parents to Italy but went to study English literature at Cambridge which lead him into a distinguished career as a writer and critic. Among other work he translated his father's memoirs into English and *Brideshead Revisited* into Japanese.[2] The younger Masao attended the Lycée Chateaubriand in Rome where he added fluency in French and Italian to his English ability. Yukiko was very much at home in Rome, having been born there, living there as a child, from the ages of eight to ten, and returning there early in her married life. Her own first child, Sakurako, was also born there. With her father frequently away, spending much of his time attending sessions of the League of Nations, and on an official tour of inspection of Japanese diplomatic missions, Kazuko was company and support for her mother.

That by this time young Kazuko had already developed a Yoshida firmness of character there can be no doubt. She displayed her decisiveness and bravery in the legendary part she played in helping her grandfather, Count Makino, escape from his would-be assassins, during the Incident of 26 February 1936, in which a small faction in the army organized a *coup d'état* in which they hoped to eliminate a number of key political figures. This incident was not unconnected with Yoshida's appointment as ambassador to London. As a result of the mutiny, the cabinet had fallen and Yoshida had been asked by Prince Fumimaro Konoe, President of the House of Peers, '... to prevail upon Kōki Hirota to accept the Premiership and, under those circumstances, (he) could not very well decline to assist to some extent in the selection of candidates for the various posts in the new Cabinet'.[3] There was also some talk of his becoming foreign minister and it was to this that senior members of the Army General Staff strongly objected, because of his liberal pro-British and pro-American opposition to 'the extremist policies they advocated' and also, no doubt, because of his connections with Makino. Yoshida himself suggested that '... perhaps by way of some compensation for my having failed to obtain the post of Foreign Minister, Premier Hirota nominated me for the post of Ambassador to Great Britain'.[4] The current ambassador, Tsuneo Matsudaira, then on leave in Japan, had just been appointed to serve in the imperial household. Alone of their children Kazuko joined her parents on their departure for London in April 1936. Kenichi, was back in Tokyo, now married and Masao stayed on to complete his high school education at the Tokyo High School, where science was his principal focus but he continued his studies in French, English and now German which he was to use extensively throughout his engineering career.

Because of the many lifelong friendships she made and the special relationship she shared with both of her parents, Kazuko always recalled her time in London with pleasure, despite its tensions for the Anglophile Japanese living there. These have been movingly recorded by her mother in her autobiographical account *Whispering Leaves in Grosvenor Square*.

Yukiko lists many of their friends in that memoir and where they had sons and daughters of Kazuko's age, they became her friends and swept her up in all the excitements they enjoyed in the London of the thirties. One of them can recall how captivating were her beauty and vivacity. She for her part clearly loved her English friends especially her '... English sisters. Their frank open-heartedness, broad-mindedness and unfailing sense of humour have enriched our lives'.[5] Many of the friends she made at that time remained friends for life. She regularly met with them later on in her life on her frequent visits to Britain and they, and their families, were sure to be entertained at memorable dinner parties at her family home in Kamiyama-cho and guided around Tokyo, when they in their turn visited Japan. She became godmother to several of the children of her British friends, and they became godparents to her own, cementing some of those closest friendships.

Kazuko obviously enjoyed her days in London to the full. One of her own accounts had her returning home at dawn walking on the walls of the Embankment, carrying her party shoes! One of the highlights of the Yoshida's time in London was the visit of Prince and Princess Chichibu, and the coronation of King George VI on 12 May 1937 as well as the first Court which preceded it, at which Yukiko describes Kazuko as looking 'like a fairy child'.[6] Another historical event was the record-breaking flight from Japan to Britain, by Iinuma and Tsugakoshi in the Asahi plane *Kamikaze*, in April 1937. On arrival it was Kazuko who gave the pilots flowers of congratulation.

One of Kazuko's favourite pursuits was riding and this she sometimes did in Hyde Park with her father, and often walked there with her mother, 'in Nature's company'[7]. She also enjoyed playing golf. In *Whispering Leaves* Yukiko describes her pleasure in the travels of 'the three of us'[8] around the country, to Scotland, Wales, Devon and Cornwall and favourite spots such as Brighton, Tonbridge Wells and Bournemouth. Masao visited his family from Tokyo and toured the length and breadth of Britain. Kazuko sometimes joined her friends on trips to the continent, flying over on Imperial Airways from Croydon. Once she flew with her mother to Brussels to stay with Ambassador Kurusu there. In the summer of 1937 the family took a house, 'Little Fishery', at Maidenhead, and here enjoyed boating on the Thames and long walks and rides along the river and through the countryside. It was here that Yukiko, whose health was never robust, fell ill and had to be operated on for a hernia. Her own account of her convalescence in hospital confirms the closeness of mother and daughter. Kazuko visited her mother every day and stayed with her for the best part of it. Yukiko recalled '. . . I was impatient to see her whose company I enjoy the best. She is my dearest friend'.[9]

★ ★ ★

The pleasure of their time in Britain was marred by the growing number of newspaper reports criticising Japanese intentions in China. Kazuko would certainly have joined her mother in her wish 'that nothing disagreeable would happen between our two nations'.[10] She naturally supported her father's principal mission in Britain – to win back British good opinion of Japan. This he endeavoured to do as soon as he arrived, without reverting to Tokyo where the push for Japan to join forces with the Axis powers was gaining momentum. Yoshida was strongly opposed to this, despite every effort to make him change his mind, but nevertheless Japan went ahead and, in November 1936, signed the Anti-Comintern Pact which became the Triple Alliance. Yoshida continued his efforts to influence the British government (these were very often through private channels) until the Japanese army's march into Shanghai, in July 1937, with the consequent irretrievable damage to British interests, proved them vain. Gradually, like Yukiko, Kazuko will also have felt 'the difference of atmosphere of the public towards us' although the attitude of their 'personal friends did not change'.[11]

Kazuko and her mother left London in August 1938, to prepare for her wedding to Takakichi Asō. She had met Takakichi when he had stopped off in London, as part of a round the world trip with his widowed mother Natsuko and siblings, to stay with her brother, Viscount Hisaakira Kano, General Manager of the Yokohama Specie Bank in London, himself a widower. His daughter Rosa, at a young age, had become her father's hostess and accompanied him on many of the engagements he was required to perform as a leading member of the Japanese community. Although several years her junior, Rosa had become a close friend of Kazuko. Viscount Kano acted as *nakodo*, go-between, in the marriage that was subsequently arranged between the twenty-three-year old Kazuko and his twenty-seven-year old nephew.

Before leaving London, Kazuko gave her debut lecture, on 26 May 1938, on 'The Japanese Woman'.[12] She agreed to give this talk, her first recorded public-speaking engagement, to the Japan Society 'which has always been so helpful and kind through the most difficult times' so that she could feel that she had at least 'tried to do something' for it. She also wished to do her 'bit for the cause so dear to my father's heart that of better friendship between our two countries'. In the lecture, two of Kazuko's comments are particularly worth remembering. She explains to her audience that Japanese women have a '. . . history of unfailing gentleness and fidelity, wisdom and silent strength' and that there is '. . . beauty in the delicacy and gentle strength of the women of Japan'. As Professor Ian Nish, in his historical introduction to *Whispering Leaves*, suggests '. . . we may imagine that in this speech Kazuko was reflecting some of the views of her mother'.[13] Perhaps also Kazuko was actually thinking of her mother and in the end the tribute could have been applied to herself.

Yoshida returned to Japan in October 1938, in time for Kazuko's wedding in November, and resigned from the Foreign Ministry in March 1939. From that time, for six-and-a-half years, Yoshida was without any official position of any kind. He wrote in his memoirs:

> People might reasonably have thought of me as a retired diplomat enjoying his leisure years in the same way as others whose careers had ended. The reality was somewhat different. The international situation was steadily worsening from day to day; the state of affairs within Japan was no more encouraging. And since it was not possible to remain out of touch with the world or ignore the way things were developing, I was forced, whether I liked it or not, to play my part in events to the best of my power'.[14]

Although only newly married, Kazuko spent a great deal of her time, before the birth of her first son Tarō, in September 1940, with her parents, as her mother's health suffered with worsening cancer of the larynx. Finally, Yukiko died in October 1941, leaving a void in the family. Although she and her husband could hardly have been more unalike in character they clearly held each other in deep respect and Yoshida dedicated his memoirs to her '. . . whose constant faith in her country and her people strengthened and inspired me during the years of crisis'.[15]

At this same time Prince Konoe resigned as Japanese Prime Minister in protest at the marching of Japanese army units into French Indo-China and was succeeded by General Tōjō Hideki. Yoshida tried to help the new Foreign Minister, Tōgo Shigenori, in his endeavours for peace by addressing the China issue. He met on various occasions Sir Robert Craigie, British ambassador to Japan, but by November it became obvious that Churchill and the British government were prepared to do almost anything to draw the United States into the war. Japan declared war on the United States on 8 December. Even when it was evidently dangerous for him to do so Yoshida, sometimes accompanied by Kazuko, continued to call on the British and the American embassies, whose diplomats and families were interned. Before members of the British embassy were repatriated, Kazuko contrived to meet them when they visited the medical clinic, the only occasions they were allowed out of the embassy compound, and bravely passed on supplies and encouragement. In the spring of 1942 Singapore fell to the Japanese troops who had penetrated down through Malaya. Yoshida's hopes that this would provide the excuse for Japan to make peace overtures came to nothing.

Young Masao completed his studies in mechanical engineering at Tōhoku University and returned to Tokyo, to do research at a Navy Research Institute in Meguro and to live with his father, who meanwhile showed little inclination for family life and remained immersed in his books. At one point during this time Kenichi and his family came to live with them, as their own house had burned down. Kazuko had moved down with Takakichi to the Aso family home in Kyushu and passed the war years raising her growing family and farming. Occasionally she braved the tiring and difficult journey to visit her father who depended on her more and more, now that he was widowed. She describes the journey in her memoirs of her father.[16] The train stopped at almost every station from her home in Fukuoka to Tokyo and was so crowded with people, dressed in odd, ill-matching assortments of *mompei* and other clothes, that the windows could not shut and passengers within were blackened with soot after passing through tunnels.

In April 1945, Yoshida was arrested, and held for forty days, by the *kempeitai*, the Japanese secret police, for supporting the advice to the Emperor of elder statesmen, Prince Konoe and Count Makino, that, more than surrender, Japan should fear the possibility of a Communist revolution, following the defeat which then seemed to him sure. When the war finally ended, Yoshida was confined to his house in Oiso with an illness, and played no part in it. In September he was appointed foreign minister in the cabinet of Prince Higashikuni and was retained in that post by Baron Kijirō Shidehara, his successor from October. In reality there was no Foreign Office and Yoshida's work was restricted to communicating with the Occupation Forces' GHQ on important matters connected with the Japanese government.

The Aso family moved up to Tokyo and Kazuko worked almost constantly with her father at his official residence in Azabu. From her room on the second floor, she acted as his secretary, assistant, companion and general right hand. She helped him with the heavy correspondence from the people he knew. He had other help with the flood of letters which came in from all quarters expressing every sort of view, right wing and left. In helping him in this work, Kazuko recognized in her father a natural love of politics, although diplomacy was his calling. She wrote of him that he had always insisted that no diplomat should represent his country who could not also understand its politics and recalled how he had often gone to listen to debates in the House of Commons, while he was ambassador in Britain, commenting in detail on the views of the different politicians he met.[17] She knew that he also believed that a diplomat could not, therefore, be a spokesman for a policy he could not approve and for this reason had turned down an appointment to Washington. Rather than entering into his passion for politics, Kazuko felt it her duty to support him as her father, as he needed her. When she was not with him, he would write her plaintive letters saying he did not know what to do about this or that and she resolved to be with him to help him in any way she could. She accepted his passion for politics but feared for him. He depended on her.

Pressure was put on Yoshida to become president of the Liberal Party, by Shidehara and by Hatoyama, who had been purged at the insistence of the Soviet Union (but was eventually, as president of the Japan Democratic Party, to form a government in 1954 succeeding Yoshida). Yoshida said at the time that he could not take up the post without consulting his daughter. He finally agreed, when he realized there was no other way out of the political gridlock and in May 1946 formed his first cabinet. Kazuko worried greatly that he might be assassinated. He was small in stature and, from his residence, he frequently went out walking around the ruins of Tokyo, accompanied by only one bodyguard whom he instructed to run away should any trouble occur. There were frequent demonstrations on the streets of Tokyo and red flags waved everywhere. Inflation raged and stabilization of the economy was the government's most important task. Regardless, the trades unions, encouraged by the Communists, called a general strike. The Occupation authorities prohibited it and Yoshida was compelled to dissolve the Diet.

Kazuko helped her father campaign and win a seat for the first time in the House of Representatives. A new Socialist government came to power, in a coalition with the Democratic party. Those that refused to support a coalition which contained Communists broke away to join the liberals in a new Democratic Liberal Party of which Yoshida became president. This coalition was successful in the following election but without a majority were forced to go to the country again. Their victory in January 1949 was overwhelming and Yoshida was set to be prime minister of Japan for the following six years.

★ ★ ★

During these years, Kazuko was hardly able to spend any time with her young children but she always encouraged them to think of Kyushu as their home and returned with them to spend the long summer holidays there. Grandmother Natsuko, too, lived with them. They can never recall suffering from their mother's absence and know that she was very careful about all the arrangements which concerned them so that they should not. Takakichi encouraged Kazuko in her support of her father and also played his part at home, to prevent her absences causing disruption. He himself was lured by his father-in-law into the political arena to stand for election in the House of Representatives for his home constituency, and was easily elected. He remained a member of the House of Representatives until his father-in-law retired as prime minister. It was not, however, his natural home and he was happiest in the field in which he particularly excelled, pioneering the development of coal-mining in his home area in Kyushu and in the philanthropic work to which he and Kazuko gave so much.

It may not have been politics which stirred Kazuko's own passion but she occasionally took up an issue with her father as prime minister. One such instance was his plan for agricultural reform, which she objected to, knowing that it would be harmful for her own Aso family. Her father was able to convince her that the greater the chance there was for ordinary people to own however small an amount of their own land, the less was the likelihood of their being persuaded into communal land-holding which the Communists, whom he deeply opposed, were urging on the people.[18] During these experiences Kazuko displayed her strength of personality and was always clear about the people she came across. Her ability to assess character she developed as a skill which she was able to put to good use throughout her life. She did not shy from making judgements, and was sometimes chided by her husband for so readily airing them. She herself disliked MacArthur, although admiring his wife, who was the same height as her. She was, however, amazed at the miracle which allowed the two powerful characters of MacArthur, representing the victors of war, and her father, representing the vanquished, to work together so well.[19] Had he not had this sort of relationship with MacArthur, Yoshida would have resigned, but he held him in great respect as a politician and as a 'good public servant', his highest accolade about anyone.

Kazuko shared with her father a lively sense of humour. She enjoyed recounting the story of MacArthur, patronisingly to her mind, offering her father the treat of a cigar from Manila and his declining it on the basis that he only smoked Havana cigars. She often laughed with her old friend Jirō Shirasu, whom she had come to know in England, where he had studied at Cambridge. He had helped introduce her to Takakichi and was, after the war, Yoshida's most invaluable intermediary with GHQ. Kazuko loved the story of his first meeting the Texan General Page at GHQ and being complimented by him on his English speaking ability. 'With a little practice you could speak like this too', had responded Shirasu whose Cambridge-accented English was impeccable.

The most highly publicised support Kazuko gave to her father was accompanying him to the San Francisco Peace Conference in September 1951. Film footage of the time shows her in the midst of the Japanese delegation of the leaders of the Democratic Party, the Ryokufukai Group in the Upper House, the Governor of the Bank of Japan and the Minister of Finance. The conference, which was attended by representatives of fifty-two countries, was conducted in a friendly atmosphere, and opened by President Truman with his famous speech which began: 'Let us be free of malice and hate, to the end that from here on there shall be neither victors nor vanquished among us, but only equals in the partnership of peace.'[20] Yoshida believed that the terms of peace had gradually been made clear throughout the duration of the Occupation '... so that our daily negotiations with GHQ were so many negotiations for peace'.[21] In being alongside her father throughout the meetings, and with him at that culmination, Kazuko had played an historic part. What she gained from meeting, throughout this period, every political and industrial figure in Japan of significance was not a desire herself to join the world of politics and influence the world of the élite, but to use those connections to benefit the most needy in Japanese society.

★　★　★

A chance meeting at a busy crossroads in Tokyo brought Kazuko into contact with a home for orphaned children. She took up their case with businessmen who could support them and found that she was easily able to win them round. Her native charm and engaging smile, her conviction in her cause and innate sympathy, which she inherited from her mother, her knowledge of how to persuade and familiarity with the influential, which she gained from her father, and an understanding of the philosophy of charity which she may perhaps have learned in Britain, combined to make this Kazuko's natural calling. Her fundraising work over many years with *Akenohoshikai* and other charitable organizations is unrivalled in Japan. She continued to give her support to the Seishōnenfukushi Centre. She took over from Takakichi, when he died, the Chair of the Japan Animal Welfare Society (JAWS) and presided, until her own death in 1995, over its immensely successful fundraising activities.

In 1959, together with Dorothy Britton (Lady Bouchier), she founded, and chaired for the rest of her life, the women's association of the Japan-British Society, the Elizabeth-Kai, which continues to flourish under the chairmanship of her oldest daughter, Yukiko

Sohma, who has inherited her mantle of charitable work in a number of different organizations. Kazuko was immensely supportive of the Japan-British Society and served as its vice chairman for seventeen years. She gave a talk to it the month before she died, on 28 February 1996, in memory of the late Princess Chichibu, who was herself daughter of a former Japanese ambassador to Britain and had long been the Society's Patron. Kazuko was joined in these 'Recollections' by her son-in-law, Prince Tomohito of Mikasa and the late Masako Shirasu, renowned writer, widow of Kazuko's long-time friend Jirō Shirasu, and herself a close friend since childhood of the Princess. Kazuko had often been called upon by the imperial household to accompany Princess Chichibu, as a lady-in-waiting, on many of her travels and had shared many experiences with her.

Kazuko was constantly asked to support causes and did so as far as she possibly could with her characteristic, single-minded determination. Many of these causes, because of old friendships, were British. Pleas for her intercession increased commensurate with the boom in the Japanese economy. Once called upon by Lord Drogheda to raise funds for the Royal Opera House, she delayed admitting herself to hospital, as her doctors requested, until her mission was successful. She was often to be met going in and out of the offices of chairmen and presidents of Japan's leading companies, putting the most charming pressure on them to support some cause or other. This charitable work brought Kazuko enormous pleasure. Her last charitable event was for JAWS, on 1 March 1996, just a fortnight before she died. The following day she told Sachi Yasuda, one of the organizers: 'Isn't it a wonderful feeling to be able to help others!'

Kazuko had a close circle of devoted friends around her all her life. Many of them had similar family backgrounds and were widely travelled, well-read and international in outlook. In addition, she was courted, throughout her life, by the diplomatic community. She was friends with all the British ambassadors and their wives in particular – the Elizabeth-Kai, and all her old friends, creating special connections. Kazuko made a point of extending hospitality to many visiting foreigners. In this private-sector diplomacy, she was joined by her cousin Yuri Yasuda, and one of her closest friends from her childhood days in London.

Most important to Kazuko was her family – her father, who died in 1965, her husband and her six children, all of whom inherited in large part her vitality and drive. The family were not unspared by tragedy. Kazuko's beloved second son, the popular, vivacious, dynamic Jirō, was tragically killed in a boating accident while he was a student at Gakushuin University. This brought the family ever closer together. After Takakichi died, surviving long enough to see their youngest daughter Nobuko become HIH Princess Tomohito of Mikasa, Kazuko became their mainstay. Their oldest son, Taro, became a member of the House of Representatives in the Liberal Democratic Party. Younger son Yutaka became president of the family business, Asō Cement. Their middle daughter, Asako, married a diplomat and travelled frequently overseas with her family. Between them they have eleven children, all adoring of their grandmother.

The wider family of siblings and cousins was also close and always deeply respectful of and devoted to their 'Auntie'. She instilled in them an appreciation of art, literature and music, and of the importance of doing one's duty, behaving with good manners and providing generous hospitality. She and Takakichi entertained their young relations, children's friends, friends' children and other young people, over four decades, at their lovely Kamiyamacho home, with its reminders of past eras. These regular get-togethers at which Kazuko gently and with enormous good humour imparted her wisdom, and what she regarded as the important principles of life, came to be known as the Kamiyama Junior Club. She often gave a dinner on Christmas Eve for these young people so that they might accompany her to Midnight Mass and pause to think about the importance of the spiritual side of life. Many club graduates still discuss amongst their alumni what Kazuko might have said or done in particular situations. In her giving of hospitality Kazuko surpassed herself on the occasion of her seventy-fifth birthday in 1990 with a huge marquee in her beautiful rose-filled garden.

Kazuko derived a great deal of pleasure later in life from her travels abroad, when she became free of the many commitments at home which she felt it her duty to observe. She often came to London to see old friends. Her final trip was for the unveiling of the latest statue at Madame Tussaud's, of her father Shigeru Yoshida, for whom she brought one of his old silk *hakama*, Japanese traditional men's formal dress. Gradually, her illness gained hold and she died, peacefully on 15 March 1996, after a fortnight of unconsciousness following a day out with her daughter Yuki. Her funeral was held at St Mary's Cathedral in Tokyo on 18 March. Three thousand people attended the service at which she was given the name Maria Dorothea. Kazuko's religion had always been of importance to her, she had brought up all her children as Catholics and Takakichi himself became a Catholic shortly before he died, as had her father Shigeru Yoshida too. In October a memorial service was held for her in London, at the Church of the Immaculate Conception, which she had so often visited with her mother. The turnout at this memorial service, and the tributes paid to Kazuko at it, were the evidence of the affection which all who knew her well felt for her and the significance and uniqueness of the place she occupied in Anglo-Japanese relations.

24

Sir John Pilcher GCMG (1912-90)

SIR HUGH CORTAZZI

JOHN PILCHER, British ambassador in Japan between 1967 and 1972, helped to revive Anglo-Japanese friendship after the Second World War and was long remembered with affection both in Japan and by his friends and colleagues.

John was short and rotund with a balding head. He was witty and amusing with a fund of stories. He was also very well read, an accomplished linguist and a man of broad culture. He was modest, courteous and hospitable. A convert to Catholicism, he was sincerely religious, but he was tolerant and understanding of those who did not share his beliefs. He took a particular interest in Buddhism and appreciated the Buddhist and Shintō elements in Japanese culture. He was an amused observer of Japanese idiosyncracies and his love of Japan was rarely tinged with annoyance at the unpleasant elements which can be encountered there. His second name was Arthur, but in Japan he did not use all three initials, reading JAP, as he knew how sensitive Japanese had become about this abbreviation.

John Pilcher was born in Quetta (now Pakistan) in 1912 where his father, a Royal Engineer, was at that time a lecturer at the Staff College. He was the only child of elderly parents who were very musical. He came to England in 1921. His parents, who lived in Bath in Georgian comfort, encouraged his interest in music and wanted him to become a good linguist. So as a small boy he often stayed with relations in Normandy and spent some time in Italy and Austria. As a result he soon became fluent in French, Italian and German.

His school days were spent at Shrewsbury where he found the regime barbaric and was delighted when he could escape to the civilized atmosphere of Clare College, Cambridge. John had become fascinated by the classical architecture of Bath and he at first wanted to study architecture, but doubted whether he would ever find a sufficiently wealthy patron to pursue what was for him more a hobby than a means of earning his living. He therefore decided to study Spanish and perfect his Italian. Somewhat surprisingly one of his hobbies at Cambridge was beagling.

One of the first Japanese he met at Cambridge was Yoshida Kenichi, the eccentric son of Yoshida Shigeru, Japan's first prime minister after the war. Another Cambridge acquaintance who later became a good friend was Itoh Eikichi later chairman of Itohchu, the large Japanese trading house. At this stage, John had no idea that Japan would play such a major role in his life.

It was suggested to him that he should join the diplomatic or consular service where his knowledge of languages would stand him in good stead. Although he failed to turn up for the economics paper John was accepted for the Japan consular service.

Together with another language student Tom Bromley, who became a good friend, John made the usual sea journey to Japan, arriving in February 1936 in time to witness the revolt of young turks in the army on 26 February in what came to be called the *Ni-ni-roku jiken*. John later told Peter Martin, who was British Council representative in Kyoto at the time he became ambassador, that he had waded ashore on to a beach from a ship's cutter because the ship would not or could not enter Yokohama. In a lecture entitled 'A Perspective on Religion' delivered at the Nissan Institute on 4 May 1984, John said that the incident in which 'the young military showed their conviction that they alone could properly understand and interpret the will of the revered Emperor' confronted him at once 'by Japanese religious beliefs and their contemporary expression'.

John and Tom Bromley shared the language students' flat which was above the offices but which now forms part of the chancery. They had a maid of all work who had several children by one of the embassy's drivers. When they found their bills escalating they remonstrated with her. In dudgeon she walked out after locking the doors and throwing the keys down the lavatory. Jimmy-san who was later the butler at the residence when John Pilcher became ambassador recalled seeing John climbing up the drain pipe to get into the flat through a window.

John was given the task of acting as private secretary to Sir Robert Clive who was then British ambassador. He found Clive 'a rather pompous old bird' who was getting deaf. Clive was reputed to be having an affair with the wife of the French military attaché. Lady Clive, in a desire to annoy her husband, was said by John to have filled the ambassador's study with birds at whom Clive in frustration would from time to time hurl books.

John Pilcher did not at first take to Japan but his interest in the country was encouraged by George Sansom, the eminent scholar of Japan, at that time commercial counsellor, and his wife Katherine who befriended him. He also became a close friend of Ashley Clarke, who was head of chancery at the time and who later became a distinguished ambassador in Rome. They used to enjoy amateur dramatics and played duets together. His growing interest in Japanese civilization led him back to his European roots and he bagan to take instruction in the Catholic faith.

After Sir Robert Craigie came out as ambassador to Japan, John, who had at one time wondered whether he should ask for a transfer from Japan, persuaded the authorities in the embassy to allow him to go to Kyoto to study away from the distracting pressures of the embassy.

John '. . . was completely bowled over by the beauty of the great Buddhist temples of Nara and Kyoto'. He

> . . . studied Japanese at the feet of a Zen priest (of Shokokuji, one of the great Zen temple complexes of Kyoto, who was occasionally prevailed upon by the authorities to leave with me thoughts of the National polity, of Shinto inspiration and then much in vogue. The great Suzuki Daisetsu inspired studies in Zen. I had therefore to try to understand the dual principles behind Japanese Life: Shinto and Buddhism and the influence on Confucianism on civic structure.

John had a small Japanese-style house with a tiny Japanese garden near Nanzenji. In his lecture of 4 May 1984 John commented that during his two years in Kyoto he lived '. . . in the grounds of a *Ryobu Shintō*, establishment, separated from its Buddhist element after the Meiji Restoration. Behind my house was a waterfall under which it was meretorious to stand and pray. I could, therefore, feel the omnipresence of Shintō around me.'

He enjoyed working in the garden and was able to employ a cook who could produce Japanese and Western cuisine and a young maid called O-Haru-san who looked after him very well. He became thoroughly '*tatamise*' to adapt a Japanese word in the French way. He bought a bicycle and explored Kyoto's temples and gardens. He did not play golf or bridge and was able to concentrate on Japanese culture. He became fascinated by aspects of Japanese language. He particularly enjoyed learning abstruse and grandiloquent terms of address which amused his acquaintances.

His interest in Japanese art was encouraged by the friendship which he developed with Kawai Kanjirō – the famous potter and leading figure in the *Mingei* movement who lived in Kyoto. Through Kawai and the English potter, Bernard Leach, with whom he had a distant family connection, he got to know Yanagi Soetsu and Hamada Shōji who had founded the movement.

One Japanese scholar whom he saw frequently was Professor Jugaku Bunshō who was translating Dante's *Inferno* and *Paradiso* into Japanese and who was very interested in William Blake. John who could recite long passages of Dante was able to help the Professor.

Jugaku Bunshō's daughter recalls how when she returned from school she would often find John ensconced sitting crosslegged on a cushion. He would join the family for meals and much enjoyed Mrs Jugaku's home cooking and simple Japanese fare. She describes him as going around in a greenish suit and brown soft hat.

Despite the growing militarism in Japan, the Jugaku household remained a haven of free speech and pacifism. Professor Jugaku had an imperial connection and this may have helped to ensure that when John visited them he was not generally troubled by the police or the *Kempeitai* who were highly suspicious of all foreigners in Japan at this time. But John's other Japanese friends who feared that their telephone calls were being tapped were increasingly reluctant to receive visits from him although at times, in order to avoid embarrassment to his friends, he used to leave his bicycle around the corner when making calls.

Professor Jugaku's daughter recalls John's sense of humour and his ability as a mimic. When imitating a Japanese Shintō priest, for instance, he would do an exact copy of the priest's walk. On hot summer days John, when he came to their house, would strip off and wallow in a cool bath. Afterwards he would put on the *yukata* which the household kept for him and then sit on the verandah enjoying the cool of evening.

John was worried that the Jugakus might be in need and kept in touch with them. He managed to visit them in Kyoto in 1948 when he was on an official tour of the Far East despite the difficulties of travelling in Japan at that time. Miss Jugaku was delighted to see him again when he returned as British ambassador in 1967. She found that he had not changed and still retained his sense of humour and his knowledge of the language of Kyoto.

★   ★   ★

John had known the Ponsonby Fane family in Somerset at their estate at Brympton d'Evercy near Yeovil, and naturally renewed his acquaintance in Kyoto with the eccentric Richard Arthur Brabazon Ponsonby Fane, who always wore '... *haori hakama*, surmounted by a decayed woollen scarf with the ravages of moth in evidence on it. It had been knitted for him by the Dowager Empress, widow of the Taishō Emperor'. Ponsonby Fane who 'imbued' John 'with his sense of the fascination of Shintō was '... a convinced Anglican and led a dual life as a sage studying Shintō in Kamigamo outside Kyoto and as a cricket-loving country squire in Somerset'.

Peter Martin recalls John's account of Ponsonby Fane's funeral. This was apparently a bizarre affair which was attended by Ponsonby Fane's sister who was described by John as a 'hearty extravert daughter of the shires' who comported herself in nonchalant style throughout her stay in Kyoto. When she visited her brother's house she could not find a chair on which to sit: so she plonked herself down on the *tokonoma* and proceeded to eat a banana from the elegant display set out on a precious dish where she was sitting.

Subsequently, Ponsonby Fane's nephew and niece who came out to wind up his affairs discovered that he had a huge sum in his Kyoto bank account. They tried unsuccessfully to transfer this sum to England. So they drew the money out in cash. The niece then alleged that she was pregnant and was in such a delicate state that she would have to be carried onto the NYK vessel which was to convey them to America. Arrangements were accordingly made, no doubt with John Pilcher's connivance, for her to be taken to the ship lying on a mattress stuffed with yen. As soon as the ship reached US territorial waters she had a miraculous recovery from her pregnancy and managed to convert the yen into dollars with the help of the ship's purser.

All good things have to come to an end and in 1939 John was instructed to report to the British consular post at Tsingtao initially for six weeks although in the event he had to stay for over a year. His job was to act as a link between the consulate general, which was normally staffed by members of the China consular service, and the Japanese military authorities who were making life difficult for the British there. Pilcher did not enjoy his time in Tsingtao. The consul general had fortified himself within the compound and John found him an unsympathetic boss. John had been horrified on arriving in Shanghai to see a British woman kick a Chinese rickshaw puller and to discover that the average British resident in China at that time had only learnt enough Chinese to tell their servants to get out. The British residents in Tsingtao who objected to doffing their hats to portraits of the Emperor did not understand the value of politeness. John was accused by the consul general and some residents of being pro-Japanese, but having seen the best of Japan in Kyoto he now saw some of the worst features of Japanese behaviour outside their own country. In 1940 while serving in Tsingtao he was received into the Catholic Church with a German priest officiating.

In 1941, before the war with Japan began, John was transferred to

London. He travelled home via Manila and the USA. From there he managed to get a place on a flying boat to Lisbon where he made the acquaintance of Norman Douglas, the author and authority on Italy. On his arrival at Bristol from Lisbon the customs officers were very suspicious of John's address-book in Japanese and refused to let him enter Britain until they had confirmed his bona fides with the Foreign Office. The ship on which he was originally to have travelled from the USA was sunk with all his effects on board.

In London John met Delia Margaret Taylor, the Irish Catholic daughter of a retired army officer. John did not participate in the pastimes of the landed gentry such as riding, hunting, shooting or fishing and Delia's family did not approve of the match. So Delia who had been acting as a land girl for the war effort left home and John and she were married privately.

While John worked at the Ministry of Information, Delia joined the Council for Music and the Arts, the forerunner of the Arts Council. One of John's tasks at the ministry was to help cheer up the young students of Japanese from the forces studying at the School of Oriental and African Studies, some of whom were reported to be suffering from stress as a result of the pressures of learning quickly such a difficult language. I was not stressed out but I shall always recall the talk which he gave us in late 1943. He enlivened our day with his humour and his mimicry sitting down on the floor and doing his Kabuki act.

★　★　★

The Pilchers found a house in Chelsea. In the immediate post-war period the pressure of work in the information department at the Foreign Office in which John was then working declined and John was able on most days to get home for lunch and a snooze. One day, there was a telephone call from the Foreign Office who were worried because the ceiling in John's office had fallen down and they could not find him! In 1948 I called on John in his office in Carlton House Terrace to discuss a letter which Ron Dore and I had jointly written to *The Times* complaining about the ban imposed by the American occupation authorities in Japan on the sending of books to Japan. In the same year, John was posted to Rome as first secretary information. His excellent Italian and extravert personality made him an ideal choice for the job and the Pilchers greatly enjoyed life in Italy.

In 1951 he was promoted to counsellor and made head of 'Japan and Pacific Department' in the Foreign Office. He thus became responsible for seeing through the ratificaton of the Peace Treaty with Japan, concluded at San Francisco in 1951 (the Treaty came into force in April 1952). This was a difficult period in Anglo-Japanese relations.

There was still strong resentment against Japan not least because of the maltreatment of British prisoners-of-war but also because of widespread fears of unfair competition from cheap imports of Japanese-made textiles and sundry goods, allegedly made by sweated labour. John did his best to get ministers to take a more objective view of Japan but it was an uphill task. He used to say that whenever he put up a memorandum on policy towards Japan Anthony Eden, then Foreign Secretary, would simply write on the submission: 'I do not like the Japanese. A.E.'

I was at that time a second secretary in Tokyo and had to spend a great deal of time on negotiations with the Japanese authorities on a United Nations Status of Forces Agreement. This was required to cover bases for UN forces operating in Korea who until the Peace Treaty with Japan came into force had been provided with facilities by the occupation authorities. We received repeated instructions which were increasingly unrealistic to ensure that UN Forces continued to operate 'under the American umbrella'. One day I managed to get a telegram to London approved which inadvertently contained a startling mixed metaphor. 'Surely it is time that we gave up flogging the dead horse of the American umbrella'! This caused ribald mirth in London and John Pilcher sent Arthur de la Mare, then head of chancery in Tokyo, a four-page letter in long hand in which there was a mixed metaphor in every sentence. Sadly the letter has not survived.

John's next post was as minister in Madrid, first under Jock Balfour, and then under Ivo Mallet, 'an old acid drop'. John and Delia much enjoyed their five years in Madrid. As Franco was still in charge in those days and his government was generally ostracized, they did not have a single ministerial visit. John did, however, have to deal on one occasion with George Brown who was a Labour MP, later to become Foreign Secretary when John was in Tokyo as ambassador. John was in charge of the embassy which was at San Sebastian where the Spanish government in those days spent the summer months. George Brown demanded an audience with Franco. This was not at all easy to arrange at any time least of all for a 'socialist'. But John knew Franco's confessor and managed to fix the appointment. He felt it desirable to brief George before the audience and asked the Browns to lunch at a famous fish restaurant. Brown commented:'I suppose any old fish restaurant is good enough for an out-of-office socialist.' John pointed out that the restaurant was very exclusive and expensive. George arrived for the lunch rather the worse for wear, but John managed to sober him up in time for the meeting which went reasonably well.

From Madrid John was posted as ambassador in Manila which he had thought from his first visit in 1941 was 'the bottom' in the Far East. In fact, however, he and Delia who were determined to like wherever they went greatly enjoyed the Philippines. They travelled widely in the air attaché's De Havilland Dove and developed a liking for the people and their culture. Their ability in Spanish and the fact that they were both Catholics no doubt helped. They were very hospitable and John coined the phrase (only to be used in strict privacy!) that the recipe for a good party was a mixture of 'Flips and Brits, Dips and shits' (Inevitably this was adapted when John eventually became ambassador in Japan.)

From Manila John returned to London as assistant under secretary in charge of information and culture. This should have been just the job for him, but he found it a frustrating experience as there was never enough money to do anything worthwhile especially in cultural relations. He asked to be appointed as minister to the Vatican but was told that no Catholic could fill this post at the Holy See. Instead in 1965 he was appointed ambassador to Austria. Harold Caccia, then Permanent Under-Secretary, had become fed up with ambassadors who did not enjoy Vienna and wanted someone like John, with his capacity for getting on with people and enjoying life, to go there. Moreover John spoke Austrian German. Once again John and Delia were in their element. They were amused by Viennese society and snobbery and they both adored music. But in 1967 he was told that he was being appointed to Tokyo on promotion to replace Tony (Sir Francis) Rundall who was retiring early owing to ill health. Pilcher managed to postpone his departure until after the Salzburg Festival.

John and Delia arrived in Tokyo in October 1967 and he remained ambassador to Japan until his retirement in the summer of 1972. For John, although he was immersed in European culture, it was great fun to be back in Japan. They soon made an impact on the Tokyo social scene. They entertained widely and became well known for their cultural interests especially their enthusiasm for music. They developed particularly good relations with members of the Japanese Imperial Family, especially Princess Chichibu, and with their diplomatic colleagues. But their circle of friends which included intellectuals, artists, potters and priests, was much wider than that of the normal diplomatic merry-go-round.

They took every opportunity to travel especially to John's beloved Kyoto. They usually stayed at the Miyako Hotel where according to Peter Martin, John had great fun addressing the maids '. . . in ornately old-fashioned Japanese with a wealth of subjunctives, largely incomprehensible to them'.

By his informality and his clear liking for the Japanese and Japanese culture, John Pilcher added a new dimension to Britain's relations with Japan. It would be unfair to his predecesors to imply that they had not worked hard to improve relations but they had generally lacked the personal warmth he displayed. Certainly he helped to interest British ministers in Japan and to improve understanding in Britain of Japan.

★ ★ ★

John did whatever was necessary as ambassador. He enjoyed his work and was conscientious, but he was not a workaholic. He realized that commercial and economic work was becoming increasingly important and as his commercial and economic counsellor I found him always ready to support our efforts even if, as he readily admitted, he did not understand economics (John never made up for the fact that he missed his economics paper when he joined the consular service before the war. Ben Thorne remembers him asking one day, no doubt with his tongue in his cheek, 'What is an economic?') He teased me frequently about the flood of trade missions which we had to look after referring to them as 'Hugh's peddlers and meddlers', but he greatly enjoyed briefing them about Japan. They were usually enthralled as he explained to them the intricacies of the Japanese language and aspects of Japanese culture. The groups usually called on him before coming on to a reception which I was giving for them and would often arrive late because John would not or (could not) cut short his performance. I would ring through to his study to remind him that my guests were arriving, but John soon got wise to this and simply picked up and put down the telephone receiver. In the end I had no alternative but to arrange the briefings at a different time.

John was also always ready to support our representations for trade-related concessions. One day, I had persuaded him to give a lunch for Raymond Bell, a dour senior official from the UK Treasury whom John found difficult as did we all. The lunch had gone well not least because John had hit it off with, for a Japanese Ministry of Finance official, an unusually cultured individual. At the end having said goodbye to the Japanese guests John turned to Raymond Bell and declared: 'Do you know what Hugh is making me do this afternoon? I have to go with him to see the Minister of the Agriculture to discuss the tariff on biscuits!' He said the word 'biscuits' with much emphasis and contumely. I wondered if John would explode when Raymond Bell replied: 'Well, Ambassador, that is what you are paid for!'

The culmination of our trade promotion efforts was 'British Week in Tokyo' in the autumn of 1969. Every Japanese department store in Tokyo agreed to put on a promotion of British goods at the same time. We had a major exhibition of Britain in the Budōkan and a scientific instrument exhibition at the Science Museum. John was at first rather doubtful about the plans, but when he had grasped fully what was intended and realized the scope for the combination of commerce and culture, he was enthusiastic and active in promoting the success of the week. He insisted on joining many of the planning sessions. Ben Thorne who was in charge of the British Week Office, remembers one occasion when a meeting was called in the ambassador's study in the residence at 9 o'clock in the morning, but the chief information officer from the Department of Trade and Industry, Arthur Savage, had not turned up. Eventually, he arrived clearly under the weather. John determined to adminsiter his favourite remedy. The butler was summoned to bring a glass of dark liquid. This was John's cure-all, Fernet Branca. Arthur was made to drink this foul-tasting potion. He manged to get it down before dashing for the door.

British Week attracted many VIPs from Britain. Princess Margaret accompanied by Lord Snowdon, was invited to Japan to open the Week and visit the various exhibition sites. John and Delia were in their element although having the Princess and her entourage for a lengthy stay could not have been restful. All went well including the ball which the Pilchers gave when the Princess would not go to bed. Prince William of Gloucester had been sent to work in the embassy and John had allocated him to work under me in the commercial department. Commercial work was not his metier and I gave him the task of organizing his cousin's programme. This caused many problems and I had to have frequent recourse to John Pilcher to sort out royalty!

Another of our VIP visitors for British Week was the then Lord Mayor of London who was one of the more pompous city gents. He determined to wear his robes and thought himself at least the equal of the Governor of Tokyo even though his 'domain' was a mere square mile. One evening, at a reception at the embassy, the Lord Mayor, finding Pilcher on his right, declared: 'No one stands on my right except the Queen.' John who had suffered much from the man's pomposity stormed back: 'I am the Queen' which, in so far as he was the Queen's representative, was correct.

Shortly after British Week on 28 October 1969, John signed a despatch which had been long in gestation entitled 'The Merry Wives of Ginza: Women's status in Japan'. In the opening paragraph he acknowledged his debt to John Morley, an embassy counsellor, in the drafting of this despatch, but it had all the hallmarks of a genuine Pilcher piece. The despatch begins: 'Japan for the foreigner is a land abounding in optical illusions. One of its most deceptive phenomena is the Japanese woman.' After noting that Japanese men were not good at sex Pilcher asked: '. . . would it be a calumny to add that the congenital inability of the Japanese male to improvize, if projected into the bedchamber, may well deprive his advances of that spontaneous elan which elicits, so they say, the most heartfelt response?' He commented that '. . . there is still about Japanese girls trying to be sexy in public an embarrassingly amateur quality which conjures up the image of some nubile but callow Roedean sixth-former playing Salome'. In conclusion he asked: 'Are they really merry, those wives of Ginza? They still have a profound sense of the sadness of things and of the transience of existence, but at least they would always have agreed with Piers Plowman that "chastity without charity shall be chained in hell".'

Among the many visitors to Tokyo the Pilchers had to look after was George Brown, now Foreign Secretary, and his wife. I realized, when John rang me up on the Sunday evening after they had arrived and asked us to help them over dinner, that despite the episode in San Sebastian recorded above, George was being difficult. He had arrived not in the best of spirits (perhaps because he had already had too much of the liquid sort). George was argumentative and cantankerous. It soon became clear that the only way to deal with him was to stand up to him and not allow him to get away with his bullying.

One visitor who charmed us all was Harold Macmillan. Senior staff were invited to listen to him for an hour or so. He was a great raconteur. He recalled that after the Great Earthquake in Yokohama in 1923 Macmillans, the publishers, had been generous to Maruzen, the Japanese booksellers, allowing them extended credit. Maruzen remembered this generosity and had received Harold Macmillan with great courtesy. John Pilcher also liked another visitor, Arnold Toynbee, whom he took to an audience with the Emperor, with whom he had an extended discussion considerably overstaying the time allowed.

Expo 70 in Osaka was another major event in John's time as ambassador. He had recommended the appointment of John Figgess, whom he had known since before the war, as British Commissioner General. They got on well and had many cultural interests in common. Unfortunately, this could not be said of Pilcher's relations with Robert John, the consul general in Osaka, who had an unerring capacity for rubbing people up the wrong way. In particular Robert John refused to acknowledge the prime significance of Kyoto!

The most important British visitor to Expo 70 was Prince Charles. The Prince of Wales was still a young man in his last year at Cambridge. This was his first official visit abroad. John Pilcher took the Prince round his favourite sites in Kyoto and expounded about Japanese Buddhism and culture. The Prince, who was very impressed by what he was shown, remembered John Pilcher with affection and respect.

The highlight of his time as ambassador in Japan was the State Visit by the Emperor Hirohito (Showa) and the Empress to London in the autumn of 1971. The Showa Emperor, although he was barely 70, walked and talked like an old man and conversation with him was difficult. The Emperor was not received with any warm acclaim in

Britain, and the tree which he planted at Kew was pulled up in protest at Japanese treatment of prisoners-of-war; nevertheless, there was none of the rude and intemperate protests which marred the visit of the Emperor Akihito in May 1998. The Showa Emperor was particularly pleased by the restoration of his banner as a Knight of the Garter and by his appointment as an honorary Fellow of the Royal Society. John Pilcher for his part was awarded the Grand Cordon of the Rising Sun as a member of the Emperor's suite

In advance of the State Visit John sent home a despatch dated 3 March 1971 on the theme 'The Emperor of Japan; Human or Divine?' He answered this question in the following words:

> Officially he is human; in practice his divinity such as it was – and not to be confused with the Christian (or Islamic) concept of one transcendental Godhead – remains. He reports to his heavenly ancestors at Ise and communes with them there. He prays to his deified grandfather at the Meiji shrine, the most popular place of worship in Japan. He carries out in private innumerable rites and ceremonies in his priestly role, traditionally concealed from outside observers. He remains the living link with the past, the unbroken thread in Japanese history (adoption notwithstanding).' [...] 'Thus the Emperor is the symbol of what is best in the Japanese character and of what is the worst. He inspires the nation to feats of loyalty and self-sacrifice, but he also sums up their racial, cultural and religious exclusivity which cuts them off from others and makes them so disliked. With no recognition of any scale of values other than their own; with no sense of the divine outside and above the world; with no feeling that their exertions can only be an approximation to that which is right, to that which is perfect, the Japanese are odd men out in the world.

He concluded that the Japanese '... have a greater aptitude than the White Queen for believing impossible things, even before breakfast: they positively revel in ambiguity. Hilaire Belloc might have written especially for them the refrain:

'Oh never, never let us doubt what
Nobody is sure about.'

John's sense of humour rarely deserted him. He also had a quick wit and was an expert in repartee. Few of us can remember for very long witty remarks we have heard, but Brian Hitch, who was head of chancery in Tokyo, recalls one good example. John Pilcher was in the Rolls with the Governor of Hong Kong whom he had just collected from the airport. As they passed the parliament building in Tokyo the

Governor asked what it was. John replied 'The Diet'. The Governor commented that he thought that was a way of eating to which John riposted: 'Like the Diet of Worms.'

John liked to shock the prim and there was an element of prep-school humour in him. He used to have fun writing his name in characters which could be read *pe-ru-cha* where *pe* was the character for fart, *ru* meant stop and *cha* meant tea. If he was leaving early in the morning it was always said to be at 'sparrow fart'. He liked to recall, too, the reply of the keeper at the zoo to a question from the Showa Emperor on his visit to London in 1971 about why the pandas had failed to mate: 'He mistook the orifice, sir.'

John's child like-qualities appeared in his desire to win at scrabble which he and his guests played at the embassy villa at Chuzenji. Jimmy Abraham, the naval attaché, remembers how John would cheat shamelessly at the game, looking over his opponents shoulders.

He certainly did not believe that 'silence is golden'. Carmen Blacker recalls that '. . . once when invited to Chuzenji for the weekend with Joan Martin they left the Ambassador's residence at 4.30 am and John treated them to an unquenchable flow of anecdotes from then until dusk. He was particularly memorable on the subject of the "long, long scarf" worn [in Kyoto before the war] by old Mr Ponsonby Fane day and night.'

John stayed in Tokyo until after the Queen's birthday party in June 1972 and left with a flourish on Concorde which was on a proving flight in the Far East. (It was destined never to come into commercial service other than over the Atlantic.)

On 4 April 1972 shortly before his retirement he wrote a summing-up despatch on the theme of 'Basic Japan and the Shifting Mood 1967-1972'. He began by commenting on Shintō and on the influence of Confucian morality on Japan. He noted the way militarism had deformed the Japanese but thought that the occupation had redressed the balance. Economic man had become the foundation of the new order but the excesses of economic success had brought their own nemesis. A new realism had forced the Japanese to understand the need to curb the upward surge of their exports and adopt orderly marketing. It had also led them to see the need for social expenditure. In his concluding paragraphs he suggested that '. . . we should offer them the benefits of our experience of the welfare state'. He did not anticipate the errors and excessives of the last Labour administration in the 1970s or the need for cutting back on the welfare state, but he was undoubtedly right in urging the Japanese to relax, to take life less seriously and pay attention to the amenities of living.

Turning to foreign affairs he noted that in South East Asia the image was of 'the ugly Japanese'. China, he thought, exercised an excessive fascination for the Japanese. Above all they needed to become more international.

The following are a few key quotations:'Being a Japanese was – and is – a religion in itself.' '"My country right or wrong" is the very essence of their outlook.' 'In Japanese terms: right is what profits Japan: wrong the reverse. The military had proved themselves to be wrong.' 'Perhaps Japan had succeeded where others had failed in finding a middle way (so dear to Far Eastern minds) between Communist planning and capitalist competition.' 'The old aesthetic is nearly no more and no new set of values has replaced it. Taste itself, which traditionally in Japan governed so much, has nearly vanished.' But he ended on a more optimistic note: 'Before the war they were blissfully ignorant of their defects; now they are aware of them and will try to correct them.'

★ ★ ★

After his retirement John took on a number of jobs in the city which enabled him to travel widely including to Japan and South America. He particularly enjoyed taking his friends and business associates to Kyoto where he could expound to them on his pet themes and charm them with his wit and erudition. But he was not a bit conceited or pompous. He just wanted everyone to enjoy themselves. He did his duty conscientiously for the societies connected with the countries where he had served. For the Japan Society he did two separate three-year stints as chairman of the council and did whatever he could to further Anglo-Japanese understanding. Unfortunately the *Proceedings* of the Society do not include the texts of his two lectures to the Society as he did not prepare anything in writing. The only piece by him in the *Proceedings* is one which he prepared for visitors to Japan entitled 'Conservation, East and West' (*Japan Society Proceedings* No. 115, March 1990, pp. 7-12). The flavour of this piece is conveyed by his opening sentence: 'I suspect that we are all brought up on La Rochefoucauld's dictum that "the sole excuse for copying is to show up the faults of the original"'. He concludes by relating how he took some Japanese architectural students to Thaxted: 'Their only comment was that we were primarily concerned with the exteriors and were relatively disinterested in what went on inside. They would tend to view the matter, they said, from the inside out. You may think that there is some validity in their view.'

Sadly John Pilcher never wrote his memoirs. He could not see why anyone should be interested in what he had done or thought. I hope that in this short piece I have at least proved him wrong in this respect. When he died in 1990, having suffered from Parkinson's disease and a

stroke, Japan and John's colleagues lost a good, charming, understanding and amusing friend.

25

Ariyoshi Yoshiya, KBE (Hon) (1901-82)

SIR HUGH CORTAZZI

IN HIS LATER years Ariyoshi Yoshiya was to many of his friends 'The Grand Old Man of Japanese shipping'. But he was much more than this. He was an unforgettable figure, a big man in every sense of the word. He had a delightful sense of humour, a ready wit and was rarely without a twinkle in his eye. He seemed to have an almost inexhaustible fund of amusing stories and experiences and was quite ready to poke fun at himself. He had a zest for life and was determined to enjoy whatever came his way. He could be tough, and was no doubt a hard taskmaster, but he had great human sympathies and was very kind to his foreign friends.

He was an Anglophile who had hugely enjoyed his stay in Britain before the Second World War and had retained an affection for Britain and its people. He spoke good English and was outspoken in a way which made him seem more English than Japanese, but he had absorbed Japanese traditions and ethos and many of his attitudes were very Japanese. He was proud to be Japanese and stood up for Japanese interests. His ability to straddle Japanese and European cultures enabled him to explain each to the other.

Ariyoshi was a great devotee of sport. He was a good swimmer. As a young man he rowed, played rugby and enjoyed skiing, but his main sport was baseball in which he was known as a good pitcher. Like so many Japanese businessmen he was an enthusiastic golfer throughout his life. He was also an aficionado of the world of the geisha and enjoyed Japanese saké, beer, wine and whisky although he was in no sense an alcoholic.

★ ★ ★

Whenever I think of NYK (Nippon Yusen Kaisha), the premier Japanese shipping company, I think first of Ariyoshi who became president of the company in 1965 and chairman in 1971. In 1978 he retired to become *Sodanyaku* (Counsellor to the board of directors).

NYK was established in 1885. It followed the merger of Yūbin Kisen Mitsubishi Kaisha and Kyōdō Unyu Kaisha. Mitsubishi Kaisha had been founded by Iwasaki Yatarō who can be regarded as the progenitor of the Mitsubishi group of companies. Iwasaki had started the business in 1870 by buying three steamers to operate in Japanee coastal waters. When it was formed in 1885, NYK had 58 ships with a gross tonnage of some 65,000 tons. It grew steadily, developing services to Europe and the USA. In 1926 NYK absorbed Tōyō Kisen Kaisha and as a result became the largest passenger and freight carrier on the North Pacific route. At the beginning of the Second World War, NYK had 133 ships with a total tonnage of 872,000. At the end of the war, NYK had only 37 ships left with a gross tonnage of some 155,000. When NYK was allowed to resume operations it had to borrow heavily to reconstruct its fleet, but by 1973 it owned 168 ships with a gross tonnage 4.6 million. It had begun in 1959 to add tankers and bulk carriers to its fleet of cargo liners, and in 1968, its first container ship sailed across the North Pacific. NYK became one of the leading Japanese companies in the shipping conference system which regulated competition on the main shipping routes.

Ariyoshi was the son of a Japanese civil servant who had been baptized as a Christian. This led to many contacts with missionaries and other foreigners. He was brought up in Yokohama where he learnt to swim and to row. From his father's house he could look out on to the port and the sight of the ships entering and leaving the harbour spurred his interest in shipping. His grandfather lived outside Kyoto and his frequent visits there helped to develop his understanding of Japanese history and culture.

At the Kanagawa Middle School in Yokohama he was taught English by an Englishman who had taken Japanese nationality. His teacher had a unique method of teaching English. Each pupil was called in rotation to make a short speech in English on a subject of their own choosing. The teacher '... would correct not only our English, but the way of posing on the podium, our gestures, and our selection of subjects.' Ariyoshi one day decided to speak about Japanese haiku and wanted to refer to the great haiku poet Bashō whose name means a Japanese banana tree. When he began 'Once upon a time there was a famous poet whose name was Banana' the class dissolved into laughter. His teacher taught them many English and Scottish songs including 'It's

312

a long way to Tipperary'. Ariyoshi, unlike many of his British friends, remembered not only the words and the refrain but also the preamble, starting with the words 'Up to mighty London came an Irishman one day...'

He went on to High School in Matsuyama. He entered Tokyo (Imperial) University in 1922 where he said that the only subject tested in those days was English. In 1925 he graduated from the English Law Course and joined NYK. 'The entrance test was nothing rigid.' 'Someone asked me, "Why do you want to join NYK?" I replied, "Because I think shipping is the most important field of business to our Japanese Empire, Sir," and he said, "Fine." That was all.'

Ariyoshi was duly appointed as an assistant purser or *Kaikei-san*. He was given a week's training which was designed '... to teach me good table manners, including the proper use of knives and forks to eat Western food'. He was then assigned to a 5,000-ton cargo/passenger ship named *Nikkō Maru*, '... a small, but stylish ship. What embarrassed me was sloppy manifests and galley accounts.'

All sorts of tasks fell to him as an assistant purser: 'Sometimes I fell sea-sick in rough weather but I usually enjoyed my life aboard ship and learned much... It was really pleasant to drink after a day's work on the Indian Ocean glowing with the setting sun.' He learnt 'what young seamen thought and wanted'. On one ship in 1925 the captain of his vessel summoned him and told him that the ship was to carry a kangaroo to Bombay and its pen would be near Ariyoshi's cabin. So it would be his job to look after the animal. At first the kangaroo was very bad-tempered and punched and kicked, but after a bit of cajoling and coaxing Ariyoshi managed to make friends with the animal. That same year he bought a baby crocodile in Singapore, hoping it would grow big enough to turn into a lady's handbag. One day the captain asked him to show the baby crocodile to the passengers in the lounge. At first it was docile but suddenly '... started running around with great speed. The ladies screamed and the gentlemen kicked and all left the room in a great hurry. The captain got furious although he was the one who asked me to bring the creature.'

After a year at sea Ariyoshi worked ashore. In 1934 he was transferred to NYK's London office. Although he was by then 33 years old he 'was considered still young for overseas duties'. 'NYK's allowance for overseas duties was miserably small indeed. You couldn't afford to make merry with it.' But it seems from his account of episodes in his London life that he nonetheless managed to have a jolly time.

He declared that he had been a 'Chonger' in London. This meant that he was a temporary bachelor or, as they say in Japan today, he was there *tanshin funin*. His funds were low and he had to be content wth the cheapest possible furniture which '... happened to be all blue in

313

colour. The carpet was blue, wall papers were blue, chairs and sofas were all covered with blue cloth, and even the lamp shades were blue. The first guest invited aptly quipped, '"We feel as if we were at the bottom of the sea."' In other accommodation: 'To save the trouble of making meals myself, I subsisted on beer for 45 days before my wife's ship arrived at London. My wife was flabbergasted to see nothing but beer in the larder and a mountain of empty beer bottles in the backyard.'

He found that the local staff in the London office handled all the regular business and the Japanese staff were left to deal with

> . . . the accounting and the administrative work. We asked them at least to let the Japanese handle the collection of cargo of Japanese trading companies. But, no. Having nothing better to do, I spent a lot of time inspecting the new ships of companies of all countries and shipyards and machinery plants. Thanks to the name NYK, most places allowed me freely to see whatever I wanted.

He tried at first vainly to find a club where he could play golf, but wherever he went he saw the sign 'Members Only'. One day at Dulwich at the entrance to a golf club a man asked him if he wanted to play and took him into the club where he paid a modest fee and played a round with a member of the club. One club where he often played later was the Knole Park Club near Sevenoaks where there were many deer. A number of them were in front of the first tee. This worried Ariyoshi and his friends, but 'a typical retired colonel' with a very red face and white moustache told them that deer were never hit by golf balls. 'Deer, he said, could see from the stance you took at driving where the ball was heading.' Ariyoshi was furious at seeing the deer grazing calmly on the fairway '. . . judging that I could not hit the ball in the middle'. He swung vigorously '. . . and sure enough my ball sliced far into the rough'.

Ariyoshi recalled playing golf with some young Japanese naval officers in 1936 at Sandwich. They had stayed the night at an old inn where they had begun to drink English warm beer. They were joined by the locals, mainly fishermen and the singing started till '. . . a gruffy salty chorus reverberated in the usually quiet streets of the town'. Next day at the course they found that their singing friends moonlighted as caddies.

1 October 1935 was NYK's 50th anniversary. After the morning ceremony, alcohol was served and 'the staff got very jubilant'. Ariyoshi and a friend went out for some fresh air. When they were zigzagging down the street they heard sirens sounding and his friend was picked up by an ambulance. They then

... came after me. I had to run like a rabbit and duck into the tube station of 'Bank'. I thought I was saved. I felt very relieved and started singing when I got out of the tube staion at Piccadilly Circus. It was in broad daylight and I straight away attracted the attention of a policeman. True to the British police reputation, he was very polite, but his grip was very strong. 'This way, please, Sir,' and instantly I was in the police court of Vine Street, facing the magistrate, who fined me one pound for disorderly conduct, told me to pay the cashier, and banged the gavel on the table. (Ariysoshi told Kerry St Johnston (later Sir Kerry) that he had given a false name on being arrested and the call had gone out for 'Prisoner Saito'.) The cashier was all smiles and with a cordial 'Thank you, Sir,' gave me the receipt. The policeman at the entrance asked me 'Taxi, Sir?' When I said 'Yes,' he whistled for a taxi and put me in it and shut the door with utmost courtesy, saying 'Good day, Sir.'

In an essay entitled 'Ichi for Michi' (or 'one for the road') Ariyoshi recorded:

When I was young and gay, full of zeal to learn everything English, being fresh from Japan, there was no lack of volunteers to tutor me on this ambitious project. They came out in droves every evening after office hours. The lesson started at a pub off Leadenhall Street, as the fee for my tutoring was paid in beer. After a language lesson or two, we went driving around the countryside. The gang (of tutors) insisted that the English history could not be learnt unless we visited places of historical interest. How amazing it was that the places of historical interest of England exclusively consisted of bars, pubs and inns... After many 'ichis' under our belt, we set out to Michi for another place for more historical lessons... One of the gang owned a dilapidated Morris four-seater without a top, so we all piled in and and drove around. We took turns in driving, usually the one most drunk insisted on taking the wheel. The evenings ended up invariably with music lessons.

Ariyoshi also recorded how he had enjoyed strip shows such as those at the Windmill Theatre although doubtless he was disappointed that full nudity was only allowed as 'a tableau'.

If a naked girl moved, it was illegal and the girl would be fined or suspended. Once...a mouse scampered on the stage and a frighened girl ran. She was immediately arrested by the police and fined. I followed with great interest the

315

hue and cry of the newspapers of the day covering the incident, mostly sympathizing with the girl and blaming the police. The papers were treating the matter so seriously as if it were an affair of national importance. [Shortly after he was invited by an English friend to the Raymond Revue Bar, off Regent Street.] In the course of the evening, there was a number in which a girl took off her garments one by one as she sang and danced. The show itself was not too hot, at least for men from Tokyo...When the girl took off her last piece of her foundation, a gentleman in the front row collapsed and fainted, and eventually was carried away on a stretcher. In amazement I asked my English friend, 'Was he that excited?' He replied dryly, 'No, he must have been disappointed.'

These are no doubt stories recollected through rose-coloured glass, but they underline what a good time Ariyoshi had in London before the Second World War.

★ ★ ★

In 1937 he was transferred to Berlin. He took his wife and son with him and from 1937 to 1939 he was the only NYK staff member stationed on the European continent. He thought that he was transferred because he had been 'complaining about having little to do in cargo business' in London. But the real reason seems to have been that the Japanese military did not think it wise to leave all the handling of precious cargoes to local agents. On arrival in Germany, he found that there were many cargoes destined for Japan. In addition to war supplies such as rolling mills and hydraulic presses to make 18-inch guns and 18-inch armour, Japan was buying from Germany almost all her machinery needs because Britain and America would no longer supply such items to Japan. All these items were covered by the shipping pooling arangements but NYK's London office was reluctant to allocate space out of NYK's share in the pool to carry such cargoes. 'I felt that it was impermissible that, at such a critical moment for the nation, NYK was prevented by the British-dominated conference from carrying Japan's urgent needs, and I became an outright opponent of the conference system.' (After the war Ariyoshi changed into an ardent supporter of the system.)

He became an expert in the stowage of heavy cargoes and the carrying of dangerous cargoes. 'On one voyage, thousands of one-ton bombs were transported' through the Suez canal in lots of a thousand tons although the rules specified a maximum of three tons of explosive per ship. As the representative of NYK he was '... often entrusted by

316

the military and naval attachés with official consignments to their ministries'. These had to be carried personally. 'It was hard work carrying two or three suitcase-sized packs by myself from Berlin to Hamburg – first by taxi, then train and then by taxi again before I could take them on board a ship at anchor.' One day, someone dropped the hint in front of the attachés that not all consignments were worthy of such treatment as some attachés included personal items. After this he found that the number and size of the packets he was expected to carry were reduced significantly.

After the '. . . flooding of China's Yellow River had destroyed the army's bombers en masse' the Japanese army sent a mission to buy bombers in Europe. They managed to purchase some bombers from Fiat and Ariysohi was involved in arranging shipment from Turin via Pisa and Leghorn. He was 'amazed at the enormous power of a dictator' such as Mussolini who ensured that all obstacles were removed from the path taken by the trucks transporting the bombers.

Ariyoshi was determined to enjoy himself in Germany as he had in Britain. He arranged for a pint of beer to be delivered every morning with the milk.

> Believe it or not, I was very slim until then, and since I started taking German beer at every breakfast, I began to put on weight. The German beer halls were, and still are, very congenial drinking places.

Once he was taken to a beer-drinking contest. The contestants lay on the ground under beer cylinders with rubber tubes attached which the champions put in their mouths. 'The winner finished guzzling 30 liters in 30 minutes.'

During his years in Germany Ariyoshi had to look after hordes of Japanese visitors. He decided to seek the assistance of *tanzerinnen*. 'Although they were called dancers, they were actually female entertainers, not unlike Japanese geisha, active at. . .restaurants-cum-cabarets, which dotted the famous Kurfurstendam of good old prewar days of Berlin.' Ariyoshi wanted to organize them in the way that Japanese geisha are at the *Kenban*, a central geisha office. He managed to do this and to

> . . . assign clients as they came in, in rotation. The *tanzerinnen*'s job was to take the clients around town and entertain them with lunch and/or dinner. The fees for sightseeing, attendance and entertainment were to be billed to him. 'Further arrangement was entirely up to their . . . skill and charm.'

This took a great work-load off his shoulders.

In 1939 Lt General Ōshima, the Japanese ambassador to Germany, ordered the evacuation of Japanese nationals from Europe to Japan. After the war had started in Europe and German ports were blockaded, Japanese purchases from Germany had to be sent through to Genoa for shipment to Japan. Ariyoshi himself returned to Japan via Italy and the USA reaching Tokyo in January 1940.

At no point in his account of these years did Ariyoshi suggest that he had any doubts about the ethics of what he was doing or about Japanese aggression in China. Like most Japanese at the time, he seems to have been very proud of Japan's military strength.

He found that Japan had changed greatly in the six years he had been away. He had left during the depth of the depression. He had had some sympathy with the masses who were suffering and were fed up '. . . with the incompetence and corruption of the government and political parties. [referring to the 26 Feb. 1936 incident] It was no wonder that many found something refreshing in the uprisings of young soldiers'. When he had been asked in Germany about the outbreak of war in China he had taken the official line and had declared: 'This is only a local incident. With our military srength we can finish it in a very short period.' He realized later how wrong he had been. When he thought later of Japanese pride in their 'big military power', it made him nervous about Japanese '. . . thoughtlessly bragging about our "economic big power"'.

On his return to Tokyo, Ariyoshi noted that '. . . the common trend of the NYK staff in those days seemed to be rather passive and unenterprising'. NYK's leading shareholder was the imperial household and '. . . NYK was therefore immune from bankruptcy – both the management and employees were convinced'. They became 'opportunists and red-tapists'.

He was appointed chief of the 'general affairs' and 'ship assignment' subsections in the cargo section of NYK. 'Ship assignment was a very busy task. The war had created enormous confusion on many shipping routes.' After Italy joined the war, NYK sent their ships round South Africa to Europe, but their liners were harrassed by the British and the French because they carried cargo destined for Germany and neutral countries. The shipping service to Europe had to be suspended in October 1940. There were fewer problems on Pacific routes, but the Americans closed the Panama Canal to all foreign ships in July 1941.

Ariyoshi's subsection was responsible for handling ships requisitioned by the Japanese army and navy. In the War Ministry responsibility for dealing with such ships fell to the architectural section. He surmised that 'It was perhaps because they thought ships were a kind of architecture, like houses and bridges.' He became increasingly irritated by the arrogance and high-handed behaviour of the military who would summon top leaders of private companies and keep them waiting for long periods in the cold and rain. He was also frustrated by the jealousy between the two services, but he decided that the army was smarter than the navy.

* * *

After the Japanese attack on Pearl Harbour in December 1941, Ariyoshi was loaned to the newly established Ministry of Communications to help develop the legal framework for the Ministry's regulation of Japan's shipping industry. Although he had graduated in law, he thought legalese was a lot of nonsense. In March 1942 he joined the *Senpaku Uneikai* (the ship operation group) as head of the documents department. He found the atmosphere was much more informal than at NYK and straightforward colloquial language was used whereas NYK had stuck to the classical style, but he was frustrated by the frequent reorganizations and by the way in which 'operating agents' for ships under the control of the Ministry were appointed. He thought the system inconsistent and the government's control of the Japanese merchant marine 'incomplete, lukewarm and shortsighted'. He was 'irritated' by the almost complete absence of escorts for merchant ships' which were being lost at an alarming rate. The 'wartime standard ships' which were built as replacements 'were really miserable tubs'. The government officials in charge of the programme seemed to be mainly concerned about the number of ships built not their quality, and repairs were neglected.

When it was decided at the end of April 1945 to move the organization of marine transport to Ujina near Hiroshima, Ariyoshi moved with it. He was 'soon annoyed by poor communication' and by bureaucratic rules. He also found the 'admonitory speeches and lectures' took too much of their insufficient time and '. . . by the forced waste of time in practising military salutes'. Inspections also caused further time-wasting and conferences were pointless as '. . . nobody could object to the opinion of somebody having one more star on his epaulet'. He soon managed to return to Tokyo where he found that his house in Shibuya had been burnt down.

After the war ended in August 1945, Ariyoshi, with his knowledge of English and his ability to type in English, was soon at work again. He was once more frustrated by the quarrels between the Japanese army and navy and by their efforts to conceal Japanese cargo ships from the occupation authorities. He decided that this would be a mistake and revealed all Japanese ship schedules to Rear Admiral Ballentine representing the occupation authorities. The Admiral appreciated his frankness and they quickly managed to establish a good working relationship.

The main emphasis had to be on providing ships for the repatriation of Japanese forces and civilians, amounting to some 6.6 million people, from overseas. The Americans assigned some 'Liberty' ships (quickly and simply contructed war-time cargo ships) to help, and Ariyoshi and his colleagues worked hard to accelerate repatriation. Despite all the difficulties they encountered over supplies most Japanee overseas, other than those in Soviet camps, had been repatriated by December 1946.

While working with the organization controlling Japanese shipping during the occupation, he became involved with the shipment of an elephant presented to Japan by Prime Minister Nehru of India. The elephant unfortunately became sea-sick; so the ship was diverted at great cost to calmer waters to allow it to recover. On arrival it walked from the docks in Yokohama to Ueno zoo after dark.

On 25 June 1950, the day the Korean war broke out, Ariyoshi was at home '... drinking saké with carpenters and scaffolding men to celebrate the framework raising of my little house' (replacing the house which had been burnt down in 1945). He did not then realize that the Korean war would give such a significant boost to the Japanese economy as a result of the special procurement measures which the Americans were forced to adopt. It also gave a new lease of life to Japanese shipping which had gradually resumed operations as the Americans realized that if Japan was to survive it had to have an effective merchant marine.

The Peace Treaty signed at San Francisco in 1951 came into force at the end of April 1952, but it was not until May 1953 that Ariyoshi was able to return to NYK. 'In March that year, freight conferences of Far East/US routes had adopted an open rate system, and liner services were in utter chaos.' His opposition to the conference system which had, he thought, worked against NYK's interests, now crumbled. Japan '... could not afford to be condemned as unqualified for membership in conferences. 'Particularly when we were weak, we should rely on conferences. There was nothing else for us to count on than the trust and understanding of fellow conference members'.

Ariyoshi revisited Britain for the first time in November 1953. He was shocked by the anti-Japanese feeling he encountered, but when he revealed that he was from NYK, he was warmly welcomed by everyone involved with shipping. At the meeting of the freight conference for which he had come, he was assured that '... NYK would be naturally reinstated to its old status upon formal restoration of peace'.

One of the first problems he faced was the decision of Mitsui Line to enter the Far East/Europe liner trade. The Far East/Europe conference '... was a closed organization...no newcomer could readily obtain a sailing right in its framework. The profit per voyage was accordingly greater, and membership in this conference was far more valuable than one in a US conference'. Tariffs had to be cut to 'to fight this invasion'. NYK was particularly hard hit. The Mitsui Line problem was eventually solved after the Japanese Ministry of Transport set up a mediation committee and the Far Eastern Freight Conference sent three top members to Japan, including Sir John Nicholson, chairman of Alfred Holt and Co. (Blue Funnel Line), to discuss the problem. Sir John had been in Yokohama before the war and remembered the kindness shown to him by NYK; he and Ariyoshi soon became good friends. Later Mitsui and OSK amalgamated to form Mitsui-OSK

Ariyoshi was also involved with the Far East/Australia route,'But Australians' antipathy toward the Japanese was even severer than Britons', and visiting the country was in itself an unpleasant experience for us. . .Their grudge stemmed at least in part from the ill treatment of many Australian prisoners-of-war.'

He managed to build up a friendly relationship with American shippers by patient cultivation of personal relations. One problem with which he had to deal was the American shippers' suspicion that someone was trying to 'steal a march on others'. He accordingly devised 'an umpire system' which was the forerunner of the 'neutral body' formula eventually adopted. But he was always highly critical of US anti-trust laws. He took the view that stability in the shipping industry was 'not just necessary but a good thing'. He was always a consistent advocate of Japanese national interests. If other countries subsidised their merchant marine, Japan should do so too. If other countries reserved a part of their trade to their own ships, Japan should follow suit.

Ariyoshi and his fellow directors at NYK reconstructed the company and set about diversifying its activities. They set their 'eyes on tankers'. The emphasis on tankers was at least in part inspired by his meetings during his regular visits to London. He was often entertained in the dining rooms of P & O and Blue Funnel and found the informal exchange of views which these occasions provided very valuable. Among those whom he got to know well, in addition to Sir John Nicholson, were Sir Donald Anderson and Lord Geddes of P & O. From the latter, he learnt about P & O's tanker plans.

NYK's *keiretsu* relations with Mitsubishi group companies ensured that in the development of tankers and later of ore carriers NYK was able to establish profitable businesses. He was anxious to ensure that NYK had '. . . a well-balanced fleet combining different types of vessels in the right proportions'.

In 1957 the possibility of restarting passenger services was considered and plans were made to build two passenger liners of 26,000 tons for the North Pacific route, but government funds originally earmarked for this project were used for reconstruction following the Ise Bay typhoon. In 1960, NYK decided that it would not even carry any passengers on its cargo ships. There was no demand in Japan at this time for cruise ships and Ariyoshi concluded that the days of passenger services was over.

The British lines were the first to recognize that the old cargo liner trades would have to be replaced, urgently and on a massive scale, by container ships. Yet Ariyoshi at once recognized the inevitability of this, and led both NYK and Mitsui-OSK into a serious alliance with the British and German lines in the Europe trades under the banner of the Trio Consortium. This endured, profitably, for many years. NYK's first container ship 'was built all the way from design to completion in only 10 months in spite of her being an entirely new type'. NYK's container ships quickly became profitable.

He welcomed the official decision to promote mergers in the shipping industry in the early 1970s. He believed that '... the international competitiveness of the Japanese merchant marine sharply increased after the reorganization'.

Ariyoshi spent a great deal of his time negotiating with foreign shipping companies. He had to travel extensively to Europe and the USA in the days before modern jet services were available. He had a particularly gruelling schedule but he continued to maintain patience and his usual good humour despite his fatigue, and, on one occasion, having to undertake a very long and tiring journey soon after an operation for appendicitis. In these lengthy negotiating sessions his patience, practical wisdom and sense of humour stood him in good stead. Even if they disagreed with him, his foreign counterparts liked and respected him. He knew that 'Artifice is of little avail in a truly complex situation.' There was 'no room for cheap tricks'. As a result of his open and frank behaviour Ariyoshi won and kept the trust of his fellow shipping conference members. Kerry (later Sir) St Johnston has recorded that Ariyoshi

> ... had the uncanny knack of knowing where a concession had to be made and where to interrupt a tense negotiation with a note of levity or a shaft of humour. Often this would take the form of matching a Japanese proverb to a particular feature of our negotiations which provoked laughter and relief at the time ... More importantly, one always felt that Ariyoshi-san would give one a sympathetic and balanced ear when negotiations reached some particular impasse or when one of our number was being peculaiarly stubborn. In short, he provided that subtle inspiration which is the true hallmark of a great man.

Ariyoshi never forgot the importance of personal relationships and knew that kindness to the young and to the newcomer was likely to be more appreciated than similar acts towards contemporaries in age and status. Among the many recipients of such kindnesses was Kerry St Johnston. Ariyoshi greatly enjoyed introducing him to his geisha friends and seeing that he had a thoroughly good time when he was a young man in Japan working with Swires for Alfred Holt and Company and Ariyoshi was President of NYK. On one visit to London, Ariyoshi sent Kerry his own translation in long hand of a Japanese poem about a seaman parting from his lover. The last verse in Ariyoshi's translation reads: 'If only I'd known that the ship will stay one more day waiting tide, I regret very badly that we parted too soon.' Kerry was '... never conscious of Ariyoshi's age nor the difference beween his age and mine, since he had the amazing gift of thinking like a young man and projecting his thoughts to to others as a young man'. His '... youthful exuberance and drive in negotiations...' were '... infectious and hence forcefully persuausive. The same enthusiasm and exuberance flooded his family and personal life, bringing colour and laughter to all around him'.

Sir John Nicholson wrote of Ariyoshi:

> His was a vivid and universally attractive personality, distinguished by warm and perceptive sympathy, a quick and inquisitive intelligence and an unique and irrepressible turn of humour. But behind lay a character of rare depth and strength with firm convictions about all important issues ... He had no patience with vainglorious pretensions.

Ariyoshi was a very hospitable man and an excellent host. The azalea parties which he and his wife gave each spring in his garden in Shibuya in his later years were always remembered by his friends. As the Tokyo spring weather is very fickle, it was difficult to choose the right date. Sometimes it was said that Ariyoshi would be out with a hair dryer trying to bring on the flowers.

He received many honours but he was particularly proud of the award of the Japanese First Class Order of the Sacred Treasure, and greatly apreciated his appointment in 1981 as an honorary Knight Commander of the Order of the British Empire (KBE) which I had the honour as British ambassador to Japan at that time to hand to him.

Ariyoshi was a Japanese nationalist but understood the importance for Japan of international relations. Writing towards the end of his life he affirmed that '... as long as we Japanese retain our vitality, we shall manage to overcome every hardship.' He looked '... forward to the next fifty years with great expectations'.

26

Ninagawa Yukio (b. 1935)

DANIEL GALLIMORE

IN 1954 the director Fukuda Tsuneari (1912-94) visited London in search of inspiration. He found what he was looking for in Michael Benthall's production of *Hamlet* at the Old Vic Theatre, starring Richard Burton in the title role. Fukuda's own production of the play the following year was deeply influenced by the Benthall production and (according to the Shakespeare scholar Anzai Tetsuo) itself marked the beginning of a new phase in the history of Shakespeare in Japan.[1] Forty-four years after Fukuda's epiphanal experience, another Japanese director, Ninagawa Yukio, brought another production of *Hamlet* to a very different London theatre, the Barbican. Ninagawa's *Hamlet* was not as well received as his Eighties' tours of *Macbeth* and *Medea* had been but then no one seemed surprised that he should have coped with this long and demanding tragedy with his usual apparent ease.

Within the Japanese theatre, Ninagawa and Fukuda are as different as chalk from cheese: Fukuda the conservative academic and translator; Ninagawa the quintessential theatrical personality and glad that he never went to university. Yet it might be observed that Ninagawa 1998 was in a sense returning the favour granted Fukuda all those years ago. The Benthall production enabled Fukuda to produce a Shakespeare with a clear and accessible message, albeit one still heavily dependent on the British theatre for both style and content. This was the kind of Shakespeare dominant during Ninagawa's youth and against which he reacted to produce Shakespeare that was still accessible but now a recognizably independent creation: Japanized or internationalized perhaps, but definitely his own.

EARLY CAREER

Ninagawa Yukio was born on 15 October 1935 in the city of Kawaguchi just north of Tokyo in Saitama prefecture. *Sen no naifu, sen no me* ('1000 Knives, 1000 Eyes'), the collection of reminiscences he published in 1993, is reticent about his formative years, shying away from any formal analysis of his life, but a number of early influences are apparent. Kawaguchi was originally a staging post on the road north out of Edo (famous for the manufacture of temple bells) but with the onset of industrialization in the Meiji Era developed into one of those many unremarkable cities that have been critical to economic growth in modern Japan. Ninagawa's early memories are of a rough but honest people who had to make their feelings known in order to survive[2] and had little time for the niceties of educated Tokyo society across the Ara River from Kawaguchi.

It was a time of hardship and (with the onset of war) danger – Kawaguchi provided the perfect vantage point for the Tokyo firebombings of 23 March 1945 – and Tokyo was a colourful place in a yet more personal way for the young Ninagawa, since from an early age his mother took him there to see not only performances of kabuki and *bunraku* but also concerts of Western classical music.[3] If the sights and sounds of working-class Kawaguchi gave him the raw material that fuels his vision[4] then his early cultural excursions gave him a lens through which to interpret that experience. His productions make frequent use of Western music, both classical and popular – like many Japanese of his generation he is a fan of Mick Jagger – and are rich with references to the classical theatre of Japan. From an early age, Tokyo had become established in his mind as the centre of cultural activity, the place where he had to make his mark.

At Kaisei High School in the early 1950s, Ninagawa rebelled against a restrictive and didactic education, often playing truant, and graduated somewhat later than usual at the age of 19. He remarks in his autobiography that his teachers singularly failed to show him why he should do as they told him to.[5] As a director, Ninagawa has compared academics and critics to 'hyenas':[6] ever ready with a facile comment and lacking in that essentially Japanese quality of sincerity that characterizes his own work. He is also impatient with bad acting and once had a reputation for throwing shoes and ashtrays at actors who failed to meet his high standards.

Ninagawa's path from school to stardom was not without struggle. Like Alan Rickman, who starred in Ninagawa's British tour of *Last Tango at the End of Winter*, Ninagawa's first ambition was to be a painter but he failed the entrance examination for the Tokyo National University of Fine Arts and Music. He often sketched as a teenager and, although he does not design his sets, his visual sense has obvious implications for his role as a director. Ninagawa's interest was soon drawn to the theatre when he saw a production of Abe Kobo's first play *Seifuku* ('Uniform') by the Seihai theatre company. Like *Hamlet*, this is a play about the pursuit of meaning in a hostile world, and so it is significant that it was this homegrown production rather than the Fukuda *Hamlet* of the same year that inspired Ninagawa to enter the theatre.

Aged 21, Ninagawa joined Seihai as an apprentice actor and remained there until 1967 when he formed his own company. During those years, Ninagawa achieved a slight reputation for himself as a stage actor and also for his appearances in films and television dramas but was too self-conscious ever to be a star. He writes that his feelings of inadequacy were redeemed by a pride in his craft, a loyalty to Seihai and a deep motivation.[7] He remembers announcing to a group of fellow actors one day:[8]

> I don't want to write the story of my life. I want to transform my creativity and impressions into living experience. That's the kind of actor I will be.

These qualities are certainly apparent in the contemporary Ninagawa. Two recent British interns at the Ninagawa Company remarked on the orderliness of rehearsals, the sense of vision instilled and the degree of self-discipline.[9]

SPEAKING TO THE GODS (1)

Ninagawa became an actor at a critical moment in the history of Japanese drama. The *shingeki* (literally 'modern drama'), which had emerged in the 1920s as a force to challenge traditional forms and ideologies, had by the late 1950s itself become a part of the traditional mainstream and thus, in the eyes of many of its younger exponents as well as critics, a vehicle of cultural oppression.[10] These feelings were crystallized in 1960 with the decision of the Japanese government to renew the US-Japan Security Treaty, which guaranteed Japan's political dependence on the United States and signalled the continued dependance of mainstream culture as well. Alongside the student and worker demonstrations grew a movement of small 'underground' (or *angura*) theatres in which Ninagawa was deeply involved and which captured the radical agenda from the *shingeki*.

Ironically for its antagonism to Western culture, the movement echoed the more or less contemporaneous Theatre of the Absurd and its unofficial manifesto in the plot of Beckett's *Waiting for Godot*, first produced in English in 1955. A shared concern with theatricality and nihilism[11] paved the way for Ninagawa's own experiments with Western drama and besides, it was not so much that the *angura* rejected Western drama outright but rather the unimaginative way in which it had come to be presented on the *shingeki* stage.[12] To rediscover the substance of that drama, it was necessary first to work with the safer material of native playwrights. The plays of writers such as Kara Jurō (b. 1940) and Satō Makoto (b. 1943) located the framework of infinite discovery within a strictly Japanese setting. The Christian God of Western Imperialism was rejected as an abstract and determinate entity in favour of the much more slippery gods of Japanese mythology who were interesting not so much for their supernatural credibility, which was hardly taken seriously, but as elusive objects of the eternal quest: as sources of inspiration and creative power. In other words, the gods made good stories.

Cut off from the mainstream (and from any kind of sponsorship[13]), the ambience of the *angura* was makeshift and experimental. It had to discover for itself the meanings of traditional forms and also to create some new ones along the way. Ninagawa's earliest productions were put on late at night in a cinema in Shinjuku after the final showing; there was no question of affording a permanent venue. With his very first production, the drama was heightened by the sudden appearance of actors dressed as riot police[14] at a time when such intrusions were not uncommon in the streets outside. Drama was a dangerous activity that continged on real life.

In June 1968, the year of *les événements* in Paris and of student riots in Tokyo, Ninagawa at last formed his own company, the Gendainin Gekijō (Contemporary People's Theatre), and some months later married the actress Mayama Tomoko. As the name of the company suggests, Ninagawa's appeal was initially to the younger generation for whom fashions matter as a means of discovering who they really are. He is a pioneer in the sense that he is closer to the heartbeat of Japanese youth than any of his contemporaries, while it is contemporaries such as Suzuki Tadashi (b. 1939) who have chosen to distil the past thirty-five years of experimentation into something approaching a theory of drama. Ninagawa insists that he has no theory of drama and, despite his radical roots, seems suspicious of ideological structures. His 1972 production of Shimizu Kunio's *Bokura ga hijō no taiga wo kudaru toki* ('When We Travel Down the Great River of Callousness') was a powerful critique of the Japanese Red Army incident of the same year, when student members of this radical sect were murdered by their own members for 'ideological deviation'.

The reputations of both Ninagawa and Shimizu (b. 1936) had already been established by *Shinjō ni afururu keihakusa* ('Sincere Frivolity', 1969), a play that presented the demonstrators outside not

327

as two-dimensional radicals but as real people, and not just students but also people with actual jobs. The most striking feature of the production was Ninagawa's use of the famous zig-zag line into which the demonstrators used to form themselves against the riot police. To put it literally, the aggressively straight lines of the riot police (seen also in their batons and the cut of their uniforms) was vividly contrasted with a line that was soft and elusive yet united in spirit. As his blocking plans make clear, Ninagawa exploited the zig-zag on both the horizontal and the vertical planes, giving his very ordinary characters a shifting perspective, creating real people.[15]

Ninagawa was learning how to speak to the gods. The concept of the mythic had been made famous in the West through the writings of Antonin Artaud in the 1930s. Ninagawa himself would have known more about Brecht, whose thinking dominated the *shingeki* through to the 1960s, but it is quite likely that he may have heard of Artaud through university-educated friends such as Shimizu. As for Shakespeare and the British theatre, Artaud's ideas were revived by Peter Brook but Brook was not to visit Japan until 1973 (where his production of *A Midsummer Night's Dream* was to have a profound impact on Shakespeare production in Japan). What is clear from this example of the Shimizu play is how Ninagawa has sought to recreate the physical patterns of human behaviour within the confined space of the theatre.

SPEAKING TO THE GODS (2)

Talk of 'the gods' would seem most obviously to refer to Artaud's 'mythic dimension' or else Brook's 'holy theatre' yet in Ninagawa's case, it may mean nothing more than the very practical problem of projecting the drama to the area furthest from the stage: 'the gods'. Yet doing so is not easy. Ninagawa always tries his productions out in the small theatre or experimental studio before taking on the larger auditorium. The fact of his success in large auditoria in Europe and North America, and among non-Japanese audiences, suggests that he is able to reach somewhere quite profound within the individual and communal psyche.

Three-dimensional theatre implies an open relationship with the audience. The meandering zig-zag is always open to truly interested observers, if they dare to get so close. It can also be resisted, and Ninagawa has not been without his critics. Criticism of his work, which has come solely from within the Japanese theatre and not from overseas, has been levelled at his use of Japanese references in his productions of non-Japanese drama. To an educated eye, these can seem to detract from both their original context (often noh or kabuki) and the new one: all the worse that they should be exploited before foreign audiences who are even less likely to understand the sources. In a recent production of *Twelfth Night*, Ninagawa turned the comic figure of Sir Andrew Aguecheek into a parody of a Heian court lady. More than just being very funny and a perfect adjunct to Sir Andrew's effeminate personality, it was one of a range of cultural references that combined to contrast the illusoriness of Malvolio's fantasies with the actual love plots developing at a higher level. It did not matter that none of the actors had been trained in the classical theatre[16] – they were only acting after all – and indeed their very theatricality reinforced an underlying tension that could only be resolved by the humiliation of Malvolio and the couplings at the end. One sensed that Ninagawa was speaking to the gods of the Japanese theatre, past, present and future.

Ninagawa is a visceral director, and so perhaps the deepest response that he has drawn from his critics is in actual fact a sadness at the commercialization of the theatre movement (traditionally left-wing) to which Ninagawa would surely reply that while his is a flexible theatre, he has never abandoned the principles of his early productions with Shimizu, which implies a responsibility to reach out to every seat within the auditorium, whatever the politics of its occupant. Brechtian realism is hardly absent from the mature Ninagawa but is always subordinate to an overriding interpretation that may equally embrace the stylization of kabuki. It has been his commercial success that has allowed such artistic forays.

Ninagawa collaborated with Shimizu on a further five plays up to 1974, when the Sakura-sha company which he had founded in 1972 with Shimizu and others (to succeed the Gendainin Gekijō) was dissolved, and he went freelance in the commercial theatre. The small theatre had become too small for him and the majority of his productions since 1974 have been large-scale; the production of *Romeo and Juliet* required a cast of 2,000. He continues to collaborate with Shimizu from time to time, most notably on the play *Tango – fuyu no owari ni* ('Last Tango at the End of Winter'), first produced in Tokyo in 1984 and later to make a successful tour of London and Edinburgh with Alan Rickman in the leading role of Sei.[17]

Sei is actually a retired actor in his forties who has been forced to retire young due to a Japanese predilection for novelty and youth, yet the play can be read more generally as a sympathetic portrayal of the middle-aged *angst* experienced by many Japanese males who had been involved in the student resistance movements of the 1960s but then graduated into salaried jobs in big business and the bureaucracy. Staged in London as part of the Japan Festival of 1991, the play struck a chord among a British public just getting used to the idea of working for a

Japanese company (and many of whom were middle-aged themselves).
Under Ninagawa's direction it drew a palpable connection between
the Tokyo of the 1960s and the London of the 1990s, at the same time
promoting the name of Ninagawa's old friend Shimizu Kunio among a
wider public.

NINAGAWA THE SHAKESPEAREAN

Ninagawa is best known in Britain as a director of Shakespeare, having
brought four of the plays to theatres in London and Edinburgh:
Macbeth (1985), *The Tempest* (1988), *A Midsummer Night's Dream*
(1995)[18] and *Hamlet* (1998). A bilingual production at the National
Theatre of *King Lear* is planned for 1999 (starring Nigel Hawthorne as
Lear). Unlike his early work with Japanese playwrights, Ninagawa's
productions of Shakespeare have always been in the commercial
theatre, and indeed his first foray into Shakespeare was also his first
experience of that theatre: a production of *Romeo and Juliet* for the
Tōhō Company in 1974. In 1987 the Tōhō executive Nakane Tadao
formed his own production company called Point Tokyo, and this has
produced most of Ninagawa's work ever since.[19]

It is a mark of his role as pioneer that Tōhō should have trusted this
product of the underground theatre to produce a box office success
long before such liaisons between the commercial and avant garde had
become common. Similar to Romeo trying out his book learning on a
far more ambitious prize, Tōhō relied on Ninagawa to transfer the
techniques he had developed in the small theatre to a larger, more
critical audience. Ninagawa had already risked much by dissolving
Sakura-sha and putting on Shakespeare at a time when the Japanese
economy was experiencing severe recession. Yet the country had had
enough of political squabbles and demanded unity, which is the theme
of *Romeo and Juliet* if ever there was one.

He is not a Shakespearean in the tradition of Tsubouchi Shōyō
(1859-1935), who was the first Japanese to translate the Complete
Works, or even of Nakano Yoshio (1902-85), the Tōdai professor who
(with Fukuda and others) did so much to propagate the myth of
Shakespeare's humanism following the War. He is too much interested
in theatre for its own sake to make Shakespeare his unique concern,
and he is reluctant to use Shakespeare as a vehicle for any overtly
ideological message. Rather, he sees his role as that of transforming
literature into drama: of extending the imagery and meanings he
discovers in his reading of the texts into the living experience of live
theatre.[20] For this reason, he distrusts the more literal or academic
translations of Shakespeare for their tendency to obfuscate the natural
expression of underlying meanings, and has used first the stylish

Odashima Yushi (b. 1930) and more recently the first female translator, Matsuoka Kazuko (b. 1942). As retirement looms, however, Ninagawa looks set for a more traditional role. He has taken on the roles of artistic producer and joint director of a production of the Complete Works that began in 1998 with *Romeo and Juliet* and will end in around 2010, when Ninagawa will be 75. Non-Japanese directors and theatre companies will be invited to participate.

One of the first of the plays that he is likely to direct will be *The Merry Wives of Windsor*, which was the first of Shakespeare's plays that Ninagawa ever saw. He recently recounted that his long-submerged memory of the impression that it made on him as a teenager was revived on re-reading the play.[21] Perhaps, as with other rebellious teenagers, he saw a role model in the boozy but harmless Falstaff. More probably, it was the direction of the leading Brechtian of the *shingeki* movement, Senda Koreya (1904-94). In 1944, Senda founded the Actors' Theatre (Haiyu-za) which trained a number of actors and directors later to be prominent in *angura*, in addition to producing Shakespeare in collaboration with the translator Mikami Isao. Ninagawa's political sympathies, such as they are, are most likely to be towards the socialist Senda.

NINAGAWA THE INTERNATIONAL DIRECTOR

Ninagawa's career after 1974 can be divided into two main phases. The first phase tackles the big themes of big drama and is predominantly tragic: *Medea* (1978), *Chikamatsu shinjū monogatari* (1979) and *Ninagawa Macbeth* (1980). Towards the end of the 1980s, he suffered a creative block which prevented him from attempting any new productions on a large scale, but by 1987 he had evidently recovered his confidence to direct *The Tempest* for Tōhō.[22] In an interview in 1996, he admitted that he had become 'less like Prospero' and 'more relaxed':[23] no more flying ashtrays and he had quit a heavy smoking habit. This is the period of Ninagawa the mentor. Like so many successful Japanese directors, he has sought to pass on his skills to young actors. In 1984 (when he was 49), he founded an experimental group of young actors called Gekisha Ninagawa Studio, which is now known as the Ninagawa Company.[24] These actors provide the core of the large casts required for his large-scale productions. He has recently been appointed consultant director at Bunkamura Theatre Cocoon in Shibuya and teaches drama once a week at Tōmei Gakuen Junior College.

Ninagawa's first phase (1974-87) explores the often horrible suffering of individuals pitted against the norms of their society. This is a theme of much of the kabuki and, in its way, of the *angura* as well but it becomes something bigger, less suppressed in the hands of Ninagawa, partly because of Ninagawa's determination to make it so and partly because of the material he was now using. As already mentioned, Ninagawa insists that his main inspiration for directing Shakespeare comes from the texts themselves: Shakespeare's flood of imagery demands expression. The tragedy of Macbeth is not some exquisite exposition of feeling such as one might experience in the kabuki but a tragedy that begins pretty much in the first scene. Setting his production in medieval Japan, Ninagawa's Macbeth has been sucked outside the normal constraints of time and space and into hell not heaven; he has lost all capacity for self-mastery and indeed pleasure. The interpretation is not so very different from that of Kurosawa Akira (1910-98) whose film adaptation of the play, *Kumonosujō* ('Throne of Blood', 1957), was also set in the period of the warring samurai.

The difference between the two treatments lies in the medium. Kurosawa's Washizu is a man on the run who seldom manages to escape from the cold eye of the camera,[25] nor eventually from his opponents. Ninagawa's Macbeth is already trapped within the parameters of the stage. In a lesser situation, he might have been able to act his way out of his predicament but the nature of his crime, above all the oppressive guilt, deprives him of any real communication with his subjects, and his world becomes one of complete self-absorption, a fearful stillness. The brusque and manly samurai of Ninagawa's characterization is well suited to the role but, to paraphrase Macbeth himself, those fierce monologues and denunciations 'signify nothing'.[26]

In the Ninagawa production, that nothing is dramatized in a beautiful but eery soundtrack alternating Barber's *Adagio for Strings* with the Fauré *Requiem*, through the gentle descent of cherry blossoms, and most prominently the massive facade of a Buddhist temple. Ninagawa has sometimes staged the production using the actual facades of shrines and temples in various locations around Japan. The blend of Western music and Japanese historical and cultural references universalizes the truth that Macbeth comes to realize only too late: the transience of life.

A year before *Ninagawa Macbeth*, Ninagawa had directed a play that, although in an original script by a living playwright, Akimoto Matsuyo (b. 1911),[27] derives both its style and content from the classical tradition. This was *Chikamatsu shinju monogatari* ('Suicide for Love'), which takes its theme from the classic plays by the greatest of all *bunraku* playwrights, Chikamatsu Monzaemon (1653-1725). *Shinju* is the double suicide of two young lovers who, whether for reasons of adultery or social prohibition, choose to kill themselves and be united in the Western paradise of Buddhist belief rather than submit to the agony of separation. The reality of suicide therefore transforms an everyday affair into a passion that is timeless, beautiful and wholly sincere, and so the success of these plays depends on the degree of pathos which they elicit from their tragic situation.

Under the Ninagawa treatment, it is not so much society that is dark but the world around. The stage is barely lit (just enough to illuminate the action); the main source of light comes from within the tea houses of the pleasure-quarters and spotlights on the leading characters. Ninagawa draws a vivid contrast between the corruption of the floating world and the sincerity of the lovers meandering their way away from a world of security (where everyone knows their place) towards something else.[28] Like the stars themselves, they exude a dim but distinctive light. The 'floating world', by contrast, spins around from day to night, from one fashion to the next. This tale of stardom would seem equally applicable to a modern world equally obsessed with fame and fashion: a very Japanese play but one with universal implications.

In 1981 *Chikamatsu shinju monogatari* won for Ninagawa the coveted Japan Arts Festival Prize and was a daring venture for a freelance director in the commercial theatre. The commercial theatre has a variegated and demanding audience, while the specialized audiences of the kabuki are generally middle-aged and female, and the main kabuki theatres owned by Tōhō's rival, Shōchiku. Ninagawa conquered these potential barriers by choosing a theme that was popular and accessible and above all by catering for a demand for excess. He had already acquired experience of the kabuki genre from his 1971 production of the ghoulish *Yotsuya kaidan* ('Yotsuya Ghost Story') by the early nineteenth century dramatist Tsuruya Nanboku. Typically, this production had been for the small theatre (the Yotsuya Public Hall) so that for *Chikamatsu shinju monogatari*, he was able to combine a basic expertise with his later experience of large casts and auditoria to produce a theatrical sensation. In 1989, he took the production to London to the Lyttleton Theatre, where although not as immediatelly accessible as his previous *Macbeth* and *Medea*, it was warmly received.

As a freelance director, Ninagawa is more or less free to choose the plays he is going to direct. The title of 'international director' would seem the most appropriate label and it would seem to be a title won on the back of his confidence with the traditional Japanese genres. Following the success of *Chikamatsu shinju monogatari*, he collaborated again with Akimoto Matsuyo to direct *Nanboku koi monogatari* ('Nanboku Love Story') in 1982, *Genroku minato uta* ('A Seaport Song of the Prosperous Genroku Era') in 1984, and *Shichinin misaki* ('The Seven Spirits') in 1991. A more successful venture has been Horii Yasuaki's 1988 adaptation of the most famous of kabuki plays, *Kanadehon chushingura* ('The Revenge of the Forty-Seven Samurai'), which was revived in 1991. *Chikamatsu shinju monogatari* vies with *Macbeth* and *Medea* for frequency of performance, and so its success casts some doubt on the assumption that Ninagawa is primarily a director for young audiences. All three plays came at a highly productive stage in Ninagawa's career, when he was on the verge of middle age himself.

Medea (1978, when Ninagawa was 42) was the first in this unofficial trilogy. As with his experience with kabuki, he had had some experience of directing Greek tragedy before he came to *Medea* with a modern version of Sophocles' *Oedipus* in 1975. His production of the Euripides play remains his most popular overseas, having been performed throughout Europe (most appropriately in an ancient Greek theatre in Athens), in North America and in East Asia. It seems to bring together the best of Oriental acting traditions with a fundamentally Occidental myth. Where the two lovers in *Chikamatsu shinju monogatari* are equal and united in their fate (and the patriarchal society the villain that cannot tolerate such equality), where Macbeth and his lady are equal but divided (by a nature they cannot resist), Medea and Jason are both unequal and divided. Medea is free to choose her destiny but it is the chorus who help her to make up her mind, who draw her towards apotheosis.

These three plays posit different kinds of encounter with the supernatural forces of myth. Macbeth's early encounter with the three witches conditions the rest of the play. For the kabuki lovers, the gods exist outside the play; they are the audience, the mirror-image of the society on stage, cruel and sympathetic in equal measure. Medea too, dishonoured by her husband's adultery, is equally a figure of shame and of sympathy. Corinth cannot take away her shame but it can at least project on her a vision of redemption. The divine is formed in the human imagination: Medea (together with the children she has murdered) is drawn up into the heavens in a dragon-winged chariot. Elsewhere, the play's striking fusion of human and divine gave Ninagawa licence for some of his most striking costumes and special effects. This mythic dimension has also made it appropriate for production in a range of sacred and ancient settings in Japan and overseas, most of them outdoors.

Only twelve years into his career as a director, this most meticulous of stylists had already presented before his public three fundamental archetypes of human community: one conditioned by the divine (*Macbeth*), one conditioned by society (*Chikamatsu shinju monogatari*), and a third conditioned by both (*Medea*). They are each of them tragic visions and so it is hardly surprising that – these challenges successfully tackled – he should have turned to lighter fare: *The Tempest* (1987), *Peer Gynt* (1990), *A Midsummer Night's Dream* (1994), and a number of other smaller and occasional ventures, such as a 1992 production of Wagner's opera *The Flying Dutchman* (conducted by Ozawa Seiji) and *Waiting for Godot* in 1994. His production of *Shintoku maru* (1997) was a daring and provocative exploration of familial relationships that revealed a side to modern Japan that was of greater interest to a British public now looking beyond the cherry blossoms and samurai. Ninagawa can be said to have contributed more than most Japanese to this process of educating Westerners about his country.

NINAGAWA THE MENTOR

The role of educator is one that has fallen increasingly on Ninagawa's slight shoulders. The significance of Ninagawa (and others of his generation) within Japan's culture is as one qualified to connect an older, insecure generation, desperate to learn from the West, with one that is monied and self-confident, that does not know what it means to be poor and hungry, does not to a great degree appreciate the value of learning and literature. As a leading figure of the generation that came of age in the 1960s, Ninagawa is especially qualified to speak to young, old and middle-aged alike. In an interview with Michael Billington, he discusses how theatrical training has changed since when he was learning how to act in the 1950s:[29]

> ... in my generation, the theatre education that was, we studied the subtext in the way they do [in England], so to me it is no hardship to come to these English actors today. But today's Japanese actors are not my generation. They have not been given that kind of training, so if things are ambiguous or vague they don't get this subtext in their mind in the training. So it seems that today's actors are not very serious about trying to learn different cultures and they are not very serious about challenging those cultures.

In such an environment, Ninagawa's style remains authoritarian (although less so when working with British actors). The subtexts are learnt and absorbed over the course of time such that long-term members of his company can be expected to know as much about Shakespeare as their counterparts in Britain, but until Japan's education system changes – in particular, until sensitivity to subtext be promoted as much as the deciphering of surface meaning – it seems that the potential for a freer, more combative style of rehearsal will remain restricted. This is not to say that Ninagawa ignores whatever insights (spoken or unspoken) his actors bring to the rehearsal space. It is just that they are subordinate to his overall vision.

Ninagawa's *Tempest* (1987) drew parallels with the life and work of the great *noh* dramatist Zeami (1363-1443). In 1434, Zeami was exiled from court to the island of Sado by the Ashikaga shogun for reasons unknown but quite possibly for the envy and fear which his great talent must have aroused. Ninagawa's production was set on Sado, the characters entered the stage by a noh *hashigakari* (bridgeway), noh chanting and dance were in evidence throughout and to particular effect in the marriage of Ferdinand and Miranda. It was an enchanting and enchanted production that seemed to have given Ninagawa the director a solution to the problem of personal advancement posed by Kurosawa in 1957: to show how the magic of authority could be used for the common good. His production seven years later of *A Midsummer Night's Dream* espoused yet greater confidence in the legitimacy of authority, since Oberon and Titania never even question their right to tamper in human affairs. Yet its visual semiotics suggested a production more concerned with time than power. The court of Theseus is set in a traditional Japanese rock garden rather than in Athens,[30] but in the past nonetheless. The wood where the lovers flee is free yet uncertain: the present. These two spheres are united by the device of sand falling in illuminated pillars and representing the flow of time. The future is (if anywhere) inhabited by Oberon and Titania. It is Oberon and Puck who facilitate the eventual pairings of the four lovers (a situation which could have easily resulted in tragedy) and it is the imagination that motivates human behaviour. Ninagawa's production seems to me a statement about vision and aspiration.[31]

CONCLUSION

Perhaps the most serious criticism that can be made of Ninagawa's achievement is that he has rather monopolized the international production of Japanese-language drama to the exclusion of others. The only director that comes near him is Suzuki Tadashi, who unlike the Tokyo-based Ninagawa[32] works mainly in rural locations. Ninagawa's career has shown a remarkable consistency, a careful nurture of creative energy that exploded on to the international stage with *Medea* and *Ninagawa Macbeth*. As he approaches 65, the energy has no doubt been waning for some time and so his main concern must be that his wisdom is properly transferred to the younger generation. The Ninagawa magic may itself solidify into something cramped and respectable.

Ninagawa once suggested rather gingerly that his ultimate goal and motivation is nothing more than pleasure:[33]

> ... perhaps the truth is that I want to create for myself a time when and place where I can lose myself, where I can enjoy myself, where I can please and delight myself.

Prior to Ninagawa, the most famous of Japanese cultural figures in Britain was another Yukio, Mishima Yukio (1925-70). Mishima, who also witnessed the red skies above Tokyo, also gave tremendous pleasure to his Western admirers but it was of a different hue. The beauty of his novels is borne from a fierce private anguish, above all sensitivity to his country's recent humiliation. Mishima's Japan was always an exotic creation whose very beauty prohibited intrusion. Cherry blossoms are a trademark of Ninagawa's as well but are used to bring his audiences into a deeper involvement with the drama rather than as ends in themselves. His theatre is a communal experience that has drawn loyal followings in the West. It is not a theatre of isolation, nor one that celebrates death.

The reasons for Mishima's dramatic suicide by *harakiri* are still not fully understood but it must have been presaged in part by the intense beauty with which that act is evoked in his novels and short stories.[34] *Harakiri* may seem beautiful to a British audience too but is fundamentally foreign to British culture. The Ninagawan celebration of life is grotesque at times but is actually more palatable and less elitist than our earlier encounters with Japanese culture. Ninagawa speaks a language of the body that we all can understand:[35]

> I want my productions of Shakespeare to help people appreciate the world of their own feelings. If they can achieve that kind of universality, that's what makes me most happy.

27

Britain's Contribution to the Development of Rugby Football in Japan 1874–1998

ALISON NISH

THE JAPAN YEARBOOK for 1933 reported on rugby as follows: 'Imported from England, this winter sport has gained much popularity in Japan during the past decade. Leading universities in Japan have a league and their matches draw huge crowds.'[1]

The British contribution to Japanese rugby is natural. The game started at Rugby School in November 1823, and by the end of the nineteenth century it was being 'exported' to various parts of the world. In Japan it had been played since 1874 by clubs in the treaty port communities of Yokohama and Kobe. From the 1880s onwards, it was important for the history of rugby that a number of Japanese students, often from influential families, went to study at universities in Britain. Many of the young Japanese developed a great enthusiasm for Western sports during their time abroad and became critical of the Japanese education policy which had no sport in the curriculum.

CLARKE, TANAKA AND EDUCATION

Prominent in the movement for the introduction of Western sports to Japanese students were Edward Bramwell Clarke and Tanaka Ginnosuke who are often described as the two founders of rugby in Japan. Clarke was born in 1875 in Yokohama. His father was a baker who supplied the needs of the foreign residents of Yokohama. After receiving his basic schooling in Yokohama, Clarke studied at the University of Jamaica. He then went to Britain to study literature and

338

law at Corpus Christi College, Cambridge. During his time at Cambridge he enjoyed outdoor sports such as cricket and rugby. After graduating in 1899 he returned to Japan to take up an appointment as language instructor at Keiō University. During his eleven years at Keiō, he also acted as instructor at Daiichi Kōkō (Ichikō), the prestigious First High School in Tokyo. After that he became an instructor at Tokyo Metropolitan University which is now called Tsukuba University. In 1913 he moved to Daisan Kōkō (Sankō) in Kyoto before becoming Professor of English at Kyoto Imperial University in 1916, a post which he held until his death on 28 April 1934 at the age of 61. Apart from rugby, he was famous as a scholar of English literature and was extremely friendly with Lafcadio Hearn. He presented to Kyoto University countless manuscripts about Hearn which are in the Clarke archive collection in the university library.[2]

In the promotion of rugby, Clarke was associated with Tanaka Ginnosuke. Tanaka's adoptive father had developed business interests in the 1850s and become rather prosperous. Ginnosuke was born on 20 January 1874. At the age of 14 he was sent to the Leys School in Cambridge. From public school he went on to study at Cambridge University, where in 1896 he was reunited with Clarke whom he had not seen since school. Tanaka Ginnosuke returned to Japan after eight years in the UK and busied himself with the family business as an entrepreneur. He devoted his private fortune to developing a physical education club in Akasaka and exerted himself to promote sports apart from rugby.

A 'high collar' gentleman, Tanaka was asked by Clarke, to persuade his alma mater, Keiō University, to adopt rugby. The standard history of rugby takes up the story:

> Under the leadership of these two men, a group of ten students joined the club and rugby began to blossom at Keiō. On 7 December 1901 the members of the Keiō Rugby Club, selected by Tanaka and Clarke, took part in the first rugby game with foreigners at Yokohama. Of course this being the first historic game in Japan, it was recorded in Japanese newspapers. The game took place in Yokohama Park and the final score was Yokohama foreigners – 35, Keiō – 5. Clarke was at full-back and Tanaka stand-off. Keiō wore shorts, which were actually made from normal trousers cut at the knee, and red leather boots. For a year they had to use a second-hand ball lent to them by the Yokohama foreigners. While the Physical Education Society at Keiō had been founded in 1892, the introduction of rugby as an official 'undobu' (athletic club) only took place in 1903. The rugby club was however founded earlier than soccer.[3]

Clarke admitted that he had introduced rugby to his students at Keiō Gijuku because they '... loitered around wasting the hours and the lovely autumn weather'.[4] His essay entitled 'The Cult of the Body', shows his personal philosophy and is typical of his approach to sports:

> The student classes are the worst developed physically of any in Japan. This clearly proves that the attention paid to their physical development is insignificant. Military drill is indeed obligatory, but as a means of physical culture it is insufficient and vastly inferior to games. It brings into play only the lower portion of the body; the chest, shoulders and arms are left comparatively unexercised.[5]

The philosophy which he had learnt at Cambridge was that:

> The strength of the British Empire lies in the strength of character of the individual Englishman, and that strength, I am persuaded, is perennially nourished and kept up by nothing so much as by the national worship in which all classes meet, of athletic, outdoor life and sport.[6]

His recommendation was that the Japanese government should emphasise games in schools:

> The time has not yet come when every school has a spacious grass-covered playground where a number of games may be indulged in. It is, however, high time that the Educational Department devoted its attention to this all-important subject. I should like to see a system of inter-school or inter-collegiate sports, like those in England and America, established in Japan. This would be effective socially, as it would bring into friendly relations students of different institutions; foster school or college loyalty and also fix some standard for the various games and sports.[7]

Clarke is speaking both of individual physical fitness and of team games in general rather than rugby in particular, but his message is clear enough. We do not know what impact Clarke's essay had, but it is likely that through writings such as these, the Third High School's administration first introduced rugby to the school in 1910, three years before Clarke moved there.[8] Moreover, one may assume that the matches between Keiō and the Third High School owed something to his influence. Clarke died in 1934. His grave is in the foreigners' cemetery in Futatabi, Kobe, where his tombstone carries the words: Life's race well run/ Life's work well done/ Life's victory won/ Then cometh rest.[9]

By the 1920s, varsity sports in general flourished and other universities soon followed the lead of Keiō. Dōshisha established a rugby club in 1911, Waseda in 1918, Kansai in 1919, Kantō ARC in 1920, Kansai Gakuin and Tokyo Imperial in 1921, Tokyo Sandai in 1922, Kyoto Imperial in 1923, and Meiji and Rikkyō in 1924, the same year that the Kantō rugby association was established. The Seibu (Western) Rugby Association followed in 1925. An All-Kyūshū team was established in 1926, but it was not until after World War Two that the Kyūshū Association established its independence from the Western Association.

By 1928, the universities which had established teams and competed regularly in the Kantō region were Keiō, Waseda, Tokyo Imperial, Meiji, Rikkyō and Hōsei. Matches involving Waseda, Keiō and Meiji Universities attracted huge crowds in excess of 20,000. In Kansai, Dōshisha, Kyoto Imperial, Osaka Higher Commercial School, Osaka Kōkō, and Kansai Gakuin all had established rugby teams at that time.

Why was Keiō the first university to adopt rugby? It seems that Clarke's persuasive arguments and Tanaka's efforts were part of the reason, but equally that Keiō's founder, Fukuzawa Yukichi, was enlightened enough to try to promote western learning by hiring foreign teachers. Moreover Keiō was private, and private universities tended to be more flexible and innovative and have more money to spend on foreign teachers than the public ones which were answerable to the government. The fact that the first three universities to form rugby clubs, Keiō, Dōshisha, and Waseda were indeed private, seems to support this view.

Once rugby had been adopted at university level, it also penetrated to prestige schools. An early observer of rugby in schools was Lord Davies of Llandinam, who visited Japan in 1904-5 and as a Welshman was naturally interested in rugby. He visited the Peers School (now Gakushuin) and watched the sport at the invitation of the president, Baron Kikuchi Dairoku who had himself been educated at Cambridge. Davies recorded in his diary on Saturday 10 December 1904:

> After lunch to the Peers School. Baron Kikuchi meets us but does not take us over the buildings which are rather dirty, and were partially destroyed some time ago by an earthquake. There are about 800 boys at the school, two-thirds are of noble birth. Prince Tokugawa's son is head of the school at present. It is the Eton of Japan. The school is a court institution and is controlled by the Household department. There is an extensive playground in front, and we watch the boys at drill and gymnastics – jumping and walking along a plank, 20 feet from the ground, riding horses over miniature fences. Then we see some single stick and jujitsu, which are very interesting, especially the young boys. Mr Tanaka, an old Leys and Cambridge man, comes

to give the boys a lesson in Rugby, and they play well for beginners. They have plenty of dash, but not enough weight. The ground is very hard.[10]

In 1911 the rugby club at the Third High School (Sankō) in Kyoto was formed. There is no evidence of rugby matches being played at the First High School, Ichikō in Tokyo until 1925 although Clarke had been an instructor there around 1904. These élite institutions which prepared their students for entry to the Imperial Universities in Kyoto and Tokyo hoped to produce 'English gentlemen,' and English teachers with sporting qualifications were welcome. The importance of sport and exercise was also stressed in the curriculum.

In the case of rugby, as Clarke had predicted, playing games against expatriate groups like Kobe Rowing and Athletic Club and Yokohama Cricket and Athletic Club and Universities such as Keiō and Dōshisha, helped the prestige high schools broaden their frontiers. Indeed the fact that rugby had developed in the treaty ports of Japan in expatriate communities may have made it more attractive to these schools. As one history says, the regular triangular contests (sankōteikisen) between the three schools, Keiō, Dōshisha and Sankō were a pioneering effort.[11]

From 1900 to 1920, secondary schools nationwide engaged in a mixture of traditional Japanese and Western sports, including kendo, judo, archery, track and field, rugby and baseball. It may have been because traditional samurai training had stressed the martial arts and the idea of competition, as well as scholarship, that Western team sports like rugby and baseball were readily accepted as part of the general education programme.

Rugby, however, faced certain disadvantages. In stature, the Japanese were smaller and of slighter build than the average Westerner. But team games were good for student morale. Universities like Oxford and Cambridge, which were their model, stressed sports and outdoor activity as part of a character-building, all-round education. The mastery of Western sports was seen as an important step in gaining international prestige. Moreover, rugby in Britain had public school connections and was seen as a sport suitable for English gentlemen. A further boost to this élitest image was the attendance of the Prince of Wales at the Sankō versus KRAC rugby match in April 1922.

What rugby needed at this stage of its development was a royal patron. Prince Chichibu, second son of the Taishō Emperor, came to be regarded as the 'sporting prince' and became connected with rugby in May 1923. Chichibu was president of the Sixth Far Eastern Olympics (now known as the Asian Games) which were held at a sports ground on reclaimed land in Osaka. The games started with a rugby match in which Keiō University defeated Waseda University 11-

6. Since this was the first time that the Prince had seen a rugby match, he had to have it explained to him.[12]

RUGBY IN THE ARMED FORCES

In the late nineteenth century the Japanese modelled many of their state and governmental institutions on the West, and it was natural that in seeking to inaugurate a Japanese navy they should look for their inspiration to Britain. On 26 March 1873, Captain Archibald Lucius Douglas (see Ch.13) was appointed director and commander of the British naval mission to Japan which was dispatched to Tokyo at the request of the Japanese Government. The mission of 34 officers under Douglas's command, arrived in 1873 and remained a number of years. They were to supervise the development of the Etajima Kaigun Heigakkō or Naval College (situated between Miyajima and Kure), established for the training of officers. The Japanese government invited the British to lend their experience and knowledge, and to 'open out the path of naval studies, both practical and theoretical'. 'The British love of sport was also to be inculcated in the young Japanese.'[13] Apparently, thanks to Douglas, who was himself a good sportsman, games were encouraged among the students at the college and they entered wholeheartedly into the recreations provided for them. Indeed, some writers have credited Douglas with introducing rugby, cricket and billiards to Japan.[14] Western sports such as rugby, soccer, basketball, baseball and tennis complemented the programme of physical training at the naval college which was largely dominated by Japanese sports, such as kendo, judo and sumo.

After the British naval mission had left, the Japanese naval authorities continued to employ British teachers. And since there had been British English teachers at the naval college who were often employed for their interest in sport, there is reason to believe that rugby continued to be played by the cadets.

Cecil Bullock, the last in a long line of British civilians employed as English instructor at Etajima Naval College, wrote a book describing how he taught the cadets what an English gentleman was and how he should behave. His description of college life at Etajima between 1932 and 1935 gives an interesting insight into the physical side of the officers' training. By the 1930s, traditional Japanese sports occupied 'pride of place in the scheme of physical training at the college' with Western sports introduced as a balance. Rugby, soccer and basketball were played daily during the short rugby season, which was a month in the autumn and spring. On Sundays cadets were free to choose which sport they wanted to play during general exercise, and it was usually rugby, soccer, tennis or baseball that got their vote.[15] Because facilities consisted of one rugby pitch, one soccer pitch, and one basketball court, Bullock writes, the average cadet played only one game a week and an occasional extra one on Sunday morning, which made perhaps a total of thirty games in his college life. Moreover, because the average cadet had never played these team games before he entered Etajima, Bullock explained that the standard of play was 'very low', adding that,

> Rugger is played with a good deal of fighting spirit but very little skill. At first, like most of my predecessors, I did my best to improve the standard of play by strict refereeing, talks in the English classroom, having copies of the rules printed and given to each cadet, and of course coaching on the field. But with so little time given to the game during the year, the effect was slight. Later I felt that the cadets appreciated this rare opportunity to break away from the stiff formality of their usual form of exercise into the spontaneity of a game of rugger, and that what they wanted was to play and not be coached. Usually, therefore, I let them get on with the game, and confined my attentions to refereeing. The opening formalities were typical of Etajima; the two teams would march on to the field with parade-ground smartness, proceed to bow to the referee, and then on with the game! It ended in the same way, more bowing, more exercises, and the smart march off the field to the changing rooms.[16]

It is not known whether similar developments took place among army cadets whose training had been started under the influence of German instructors. However, in the Imperial army, there is evidence of rugby being played in garrisons in Korea and Manchuria in the 1930s.

The emphasis on team sports in the military, the universities and schools contributed to the popularization of Western sports and the idea of competition. During the 1920s more than fourteen amateur sports organizations each dealing with an individual sport were established with offices in Kantō and Kansai. In the case of rugby, the need for some measure of organization and structure had become paramount, so the clubs formed the Japanese Rugby Football Union (JRFU) at the Kishi Memorial Physical Education Hall in Shibuya ward in Tokyo in 1926. The founding of the JRFU came after the first university match had been established between Dōshisha and Waseda in 1923. This was significant because at this stage of its history the strength of the game was to come from the university clubs.

KAYAMA AND PRINCE CHICHIBU

One of the key figures at this stage of rugby's development was Kayama Shigeru who was coach of Tokyo University rugby team in the 1920s and was later to become coach at Kyoto University. Kayama published a book on rugby in 1924 and the English poet Edmund Blunden offered a poem on that subject in order to congratulate him on its publication. Blunden, who had a high reputation for writings on the First World War, came to Japan as teacher of English literature at Tokyo Imperial University. He wrote:

> I hear from winters long ago
> Resounding to the frosty sky
> The shouts of 'Feet, feet, feet!' 'Go Low!'
> The splendid roar that hailed the try

> I hear from winters yet to come
> Those old glad cries from new throats hurled,
> And feel, when you and I are dumb,
> Still Rugby will refresh the world.

> Friend, may this book of yours advance
> This noble sport in old Japan
> Till your disciples take on France,
> England, New Zealand; when they can,

> May we be there to swell the cheers
> That loud and brilliant will proclaim
> 'Japan's first try!' In after-years,
> Could your heart wish a happier fame?[17]

In 1927 Kayama became president of the Japanese Rugby Football Union before going on a year's course in London. There he played for Harlequins and Richmond, both of which were important teams in the 1920s, and returned to Japan with considerable understanding of administrative affairs. He appreciated the need for schools and universities to be involved, and such was his groundwork that schools and universities are still the foundation on which the success of the sport within the country rests.

According to a biography of Kayama, Prince Chichibu and Kayama, who had first been introduced at the Asian Games in November 1923, met again in May 1925, this time at a Tokyo University athletic meeting. It emerged in conversation that both were about to travel to England: Prince Chichibu, to study at Oxford University, Kayama for his rugby training tour. The Prince asked whether they could travel together, but protocol would not allow it, so the Prince sailed by the cruiser *Izumo*, while Kayama went by the NYK *Hakozaki Maru*. They

345

joined up in Hong Kong, and travelled onwards together in the *Hakozaki Maru*.

They reached London in July and Prince Chichibu went to live with General Laurence Drummond in Kenley House on Richmond Hill. According to the account in Kayama's memoirs, Chichibu and Kayama met at a reception at the Japanese embassy on 31 October. It being a Saturday, the prince wanted to be taken to a rugby match. They consulted the newspaper and attended the match at Richmond Rugby Ground between Cambridge University and London Scottish. After that, they went to see rugby together many times. They attended both the 50th Oxford-Cambridge University match which, he writes, 'maintains the highest traditions of English rugby' on 10 December and the England trials on 2 January. These took place, he tells us, at Twickenham in the outskirts of London, which is known as the 'mecca of rugby'.[18]

The Taishō Emperor died on 25 December 1925 and the prince had to return to Tokyo immediately after only one term at Magdalen College, Oxford. Although his experience of college life was short, he always said that it had impressed him greatly. At college he had learnt to appreciate sports, and among these rugby was his favourite. But because he had to wear glasses he could not play himself.

By the time Chichibu returned to Japan, the Japanese Rugby Football Union, had been officially formed on 30 November 1926, with Takagi as first president. The prince began his patronage of Japanese rugby and thereafter was prominent by his attendance at matches. In the autumn of 1927, an East-West (Kansai-Kantō) contest took place and the prince donated a cup for the winners.

On 29 January 1927, he attended a match at the Shrine Ground in Tokyo, (*Jingu kyogi jo*) between the Welsh regiment from the British defence force at that time stationed in the Shanghai International Settlement and Keiō University. Since he was at the time a lieutenant in the Japanese army, he took the whole of the sixth company of the third infantry regiment to see the match and proceeded to explain the game to his men. Since they remained seated for the British national anthem, he had to tell them to stand up, while, when Wales scored a try, he had to tell them to applaud. 'He was a true leader of men in the real spirit of rugby.'[19]

In 1928, the Prince married Setsuko, the daughter of Matsudaira Tsuneo, the ambassador to London. In 1937 they visited England to attend the coronation of King George VI. In his wife's autobiography *The Silver Drum*, she writes: 'After we had moved from Hove to London, I accompanied the Prince to see some of his favourite rugby, and we also went for walks in the area around Kenley House where he had lived with the Drummonds.'[20]

His interest in rugby football was shown by his continuing as president (*sōsai*) of the JRFU until his death in 1953. He did not live to see the completion that same year of the Prince Chichibu Rugby Stadium in Tokyo which commemorates for posterity his love for the game and his services to it in Japan.

University rugby was becoming ambitious by organizing foreign tours. Keiō went to Shanghai in 1922, Waseda went to Australia, while Meiji went to Shanghai in 1927. The same year Oxford University sent a team to Japan. Japan also hosted international touring sides; after an All-Japan team visited Canada in 1930, the JRFU arranged visits by the Canadian national team in the three seasons 1932, 1933 and 1934. They beat Canada and pleased a growing number of fans. Though Canada cannot be treated as a major rugby nation, the victories gave the JRFU confidence. Australia came to Japan in 1934 and New Zealand schoolboys in 1936. It was a period when 'so many exchange games were played by touring All-Japan and High School teams'. However, because Britain was so remote it was less easy to have exchange visits than for other Commonwealth countries. Japan also exported her rugby in the 1930s. In Korea it was largely organized by the Imperial army. In Manchuria where it was played from 1923, the Manchuria Rugby Association called *Manshū Shūkyū* (literally football) *Kyōkai* was set up in 1928. The Association published a handbook on the game in 1935.[21] One account describes the overall picture of Japanese rugby in the 1930s as the 'golden age' of the sport.

In the days preceding World War Two, Western sports were discouraged in schools, and traditional martial arts received official support. By the late thirties the pre-war militarist government was condemning anything 'un-Japanese'. Golf and tennis were criticized as luxuries; and pastimes deemed 'immoral and Western' like ballroom-dancing were discouraged. The government wanted to unite every sector of society behind the war effort and saw that some sports could be an important element in the physical training of the people. Moreover, sport could fulfil very patriotic and military roles in wartime Japan and there was no thought of abolishing games like rugby and baseball which were considered 'manly' and good for building up physical fitness. However, under the influence of nationalism a new vocabulary was created. Rugby became known as '*tokyu*' (fighting ball), while baseball became '*yakyu*', (field ball). Both remained popular and we have evidence from the history of Keiō RC that it played a match as late as 1943.[22]

At school level, according to *Kindai ragubi 100 nen*, rugby at Sankō in Kyoto continued throughout the war, though the last games in the war period appear to have been in January 1943, at the 25th All-Japan secondary school rugby tournament which had been sponsored by

Mombushō 'for promoting physical education in wartime'. Korea, Taiwan and Manchuria could not send teams to compete in these games. But Tennōji beat Fukuoka 6-0.[23]

This modifies some of our understanding of the war. The usual account of the war years is that the military dominated the life of schools and universities, even private schools and universities. While the army line was that Western sports were to be discouraged, they appear to have made exceptions. Or it could be that the 'rugby establishment' convinced the army of the merits of continuing the sport. Possibly because of the aggressive nature of the game, rugby did not suffer a blank period like some other sports and while it was renamed, it was permitted to continue. However, the general picture seems to have been that, while top teams continued to play, lower down it was more difficult. By about 1943 the military had seized control of many of the pitches for its own use, young men were away and the whole country was disrupted, with the result that regular competition was terminated.

RUGBY'S POSTWAR RECOVERY

When General Douglas MacArthur landed in Japan on 2 September 1945 to accept Japan's surrender, he had the authority as Supreme Commander Allied Powers (SCAP) to introduce a comprehensive programme of reform. One aspect of this was reform of the education system, of which sport was an important part. The Allies ended the regime of militaristic sports which had been predominant in schools since 1937, and during the occupation years sport was brought under SCAP's control. Those which suffered were the martial arts (kendo, judo, sumo etc), although the ban was gradually relaxed over the occupation years. It was also SCAP's intention to encourage team games; and a baseball craze took root throughout Japan. Indeed, American team games, most notably baseball, began to develop under American influence and have thus established themselves as professional sports. Many pre-war rugby players were thus lost to professional baseball.

The British Commonwealth Occupation Force (BCOF) did not have an educational function. There were however rugby enthusiasts among the BCOF and, despite the poor facilities, rugby was played by the troops and sometimes with Japanese sides. It is likely that rugby continued to be played by the British troops who remained in the Kure area well into the 1950s because of the Korean War.

Japan's involvement in World War Two had cost rugby dearly, and after peace was declared it became clear what a state of disrepair the country was in, in terms of facilities like pitches, and interest in the sport. It is surprising, then, to discover that within only three weeks of the surrender, Japanese rugby players, through newspaper advertisements, had assembled and resumed playing. There is photographic evidence of the first rugby game to be played in the post-war period which took place on 23 September 1945.

The first game in the Kantō region was over a month later than in Kansai and took place on 2 November 1945. The Keiō Rugby Club history reports their first game being on 1 January 1946 against Kyoto University. It is remarkable that rugby should have resumed so soon after the war. I assume that it was the work of a group of enthusiasts. While we know the facts, we would like to know the reasons. With Japanese men presumably demoralized, it may have been for the purpose of morale-boosting that games were arranged so soon.

As Japan recovered from wartime destruction large corporations emerged as major patrons of Japanese sport, and rugby was no exception. The system of corporate support of club rugby has been a distinctive aspect of the game in Japan. Increasingly prosperous companies were anxious to establish international connections through sport. By 1952, the Japan Travel Bureau in their official guide could report that, '... at present Japan has three excellent Rugby Football grounds, at Aoyama in Tokyo, Hanazono in Osaka and Mizuho in Nagoya where universities since the war have played many big games'.

September 1952 saw the resumption of foreign tours to Japan with the visit of the Oxford University Rugby Team. The Oxford captain, Giles Bullard, in a lecture to London's Japan Society gave the background:

> The idea (of a tour to Japan) was first suggested in a letter which was sent to Ian Gloag, the Cambridge captain, and myself, in the winter of 1951, by the Japanese Rugby Union. The Japanese authorities offered to pay all our fares and expenses, and proposed a tour of about a month, during which six or seven games should be played all over the country. Both Cambridge and ourselves had to turn down the original proposal which was for the Easter of 1952, because of term dates. But we (Oxford) accepted for September and early October, and throughout the summer negotiations went on with Embassies, health authorities, B.O.A.C., and of course the Japanese themselves. In London a great many people lent their help to the idea, notably Mr Pilcher of the Foreign Office, Mr Abe of Nippon Yusen Kaisha, Mrs Clarke of the BBC, Mr Shimada and Mr Shiino of the Asahi Shinbun.[25]

Playing against representative sides and the stronger university teams, Oxford won all but a close match against Waseda easily, yet the

Japanese teams 'never stopped trying whatever the score'.[26] The Oxford students were surprised to play in front of as many as 30,000 spectators from Tokyo to Fukuoka. After each match, both teams would analyse the game and the Oxford players in effect acted as coaches for their Japanese counterparts. As Bullard pointed out:

> One of the most rewarding parts of the tour were the meetings we had with the rival team the morning after each game. There we would discuss, with the aid of an interpreter, the points which either side wanted to raise, and we augmented these discussions with occasional demonstrations and lectures to the teams on the playing-field.[27]

The Japanese were keen to learn and this post-match analysis was an integral part of the tours. In some ways, the early tours could almost be seen as 'goodwill missions' and the players, sporting ambassadors.

Princess Chichibu relates in her memoirs that she and her husband came up from the country and spent a fortnight in Tokyo so that '. . . the Prince (by this time an ill man) could attend the team's matches against Japanese Universities'. He hosted a party for the Oxford team to which Crown Prince Akihito, who was about to start at Oxford University, was invited.[28] Having the support of Prince Chichibu, and receiving much interest from the press and general public, Oxford's tour was said to have started the rehabilitation of Japanese rugby.

After Oxford had led the way, Cambridge University followed in 1953, and a combined side from Oxford and Cambridge Universities visited in 1959. Ian Beer, the Cambridge captain on the 1953 tour reported the team's arrival in Japan and the celebrity welcome they received:

> The Pressmen descended on us as we left the aircraft, and the first flash-bulbs dazzled our eyes, unaccustomed as we were to public acclaim, and to the attention of so many people. Rapidly we realized the atmosphere was not only friendly, but homely; and to meet the Captains of the rugby teams of Tokyo at the airport made us realize that the spirit of a great game had extended right round the world. Lost in gossip about rugby we forgot our tiredness, and found ourselves laughing with our new friends when the Pressmen insisted on asking us our impressions of Japan: we were, I believe, still in the Customs shed!![29]

The sportsmanship of the Japanese players was remarked upon by Beer:

> Throughout our tour, their sportsmanship and manners

were of the highest level expected of rugby players. Fitness of their players was excellent, and every one of them was so keen to learn that I felt very sorry that we could spend only one morning coaching in Tokyo. We left behind some books on rugby and hope that they may help to stimulate further the enthusiasm of the game in Japan.[30]

After the success of these first post-war tours, the JRFU gained the confidence to issue invitations to other overseas sides, and Japan became established as a popular destination for visiting rugby teams. Regular touring also helped improve the JRFU's bank balance. Visiting sides tended to play matches against the national team, top universities such as Dōshisha, Waseda, Keiō and Meiji, and representative sides from Kyūshū, Kansai and Kantō.

Turning to international teams, England went on a tour of the Far East during the Rugby Football Union's centenary year in 1971. By accepting the JRFU's invitation, England showed its recognition of Japanese rugby. Japan was said to be an unknown quantity at that time, and England achieved only the narrowest of victories in the international in Tokyo by winning a 'hard-fought game' 6-3. Japan reciprocated with its first ever tour to Europe, and visited England, Wales and France in 1973, which was seen by rugby writers as 'Japan's biggest challenge yet'. There were further tours to Japan by Wales and Scotland in 1977, England and France, all in 1979, by Ireland in 1985 and Scotland in 1989. In 1973 Japan went to England, Wales and France, England and Scotland in 1976, Wales in 1983, and in 1986, tours to England and Scotland.

As the quality of rugby improved in the southern hemisphere, visits to and from Australia, New Zealand, Fiji and other British Commonwealth countries became more frequent. The relative proximity of Japan to these Pacific-rim countries made the cost of such visits more acceptable as compared with the UK. Japan has moreover put in regular appearances at the annual Hong Kong Sevens Tournament.

Another important feature in Japanese rugby's post-war development has been the recruitment of foreign rugby players as company employees since the 1970s. Employed on different terms from normal workers, they train almost every day and represent the company teams at the weekend. It would be fair to say that these foreign players have improved the standard of Japanese rugby. Related to that, many Japanese players have come to Britain either for university studies or for business and have played at a high enough standard to qualify for major British teams. Indeed within the large Japanese community in London a Japanese rugby team has been established. As for expatriates in Japan, the influence of the foreigners' clubs, KRAC and YCAC has continued and the Interport contests between them have continued to be an annual fixture.

As for the future of rugby in Japan, it is hard to forecast the popularity of the game. Soccer has grown since the creation of the J League, and with Japan and Korea jointly hosting the World Cup in 2002, it is likely to a create huge interest in football, probably at the expense of rugby. Rugby is still, however, strongly supported by bodies of enthusiasts and matches continue to be well attended whether at school, university or company level. Rugby in Japan seems to have a hard core of players who are extremely loyal and strive to promote the game, despite the fact that pitches and facilities remain poor. Family and company traditions ensure that great enthusiasm for the game will persist.

The seeds of rugby – a distinctly British sport – were planted in Japan a century ago. It caught the eye of *ryugakusei* like Tanaka, even Prince Chichibu, who thought they saw its relevance for Japan. It never became a majority sport but it survived in different conditions because of the dedication of local enthusiasts linked with ambassadors from abroad.

NOTES

Chapter 1 J.E. HOARE *Captain Broughton. HMS* Providence *(and her tender) and Japan 1794-98.*

A NOTE ON SOURCES

Much of the above account is based on Broughton's published journal, which appeared in 1804. Broughton may well have begun work on this fairly early on in his voyage, and sent back material to Britain as he went along. The drafts of at least part of the manuscript make up the Broughton papers which were formerly in the Royal United Services Institute but are now in the National Maritime Museum at Greenwich, and which have been examined. The papers add little to what is in the printed account, although they do show some interesting variations in spelling – 'Tartareau' for 'Tartary', for example. Broughton certainly sent back a copy of his log, which is now in the Office of the Hydrographer in Taunton. His official letters and his main log are in the Admiralty Papers at the Public Record Office, Kew. The published account and the two versions of the log are essentially the same.

The following have also proved useful:
Unpublished note, 'South Pacific: Captain William Broughton RN', 9 February 1996, by Dr D. Howlett, South and South East Asian Research Group, Research Analysts, Foreign and Commonwealth.
Aliens in the East: A New History of Japan's Foreign Intercourse, by Harry Emerson Wildes, (Philadelphia: University of Pennsylvania Press; Olondon: Oxford University Press, 1937). Wildes' gives an accurate account of Broughton's visit to Japan, except that he appears to date the first visit to 1795 instead of 1796.
'William Robert Broughton' *Dictionary of National Biography.*
'Broughton's schooner and the Bounty Mutineers', by Andrew C F David, *Mariner's Mirror,* vol. 63, no. 3, (August 1977), pp. 207-213.
Lord Minto in India: Life and Letters of Gilbert Elliot First Earl of Minto from 1807 to 1814, edited by his great-niece, the Countess of Mayo, (London: Longman, Green and Co., 1880).
The Gentleman's Magazine, vol. XCI (1824) vol. l, p.376, 648.
The Royal Navy: A History from the earliest times to the present, by William L Clowes, (7 vols. London: Sampson, Low, Master and Co., l900), vols. IV and V.
'Beloved, respected and lamented', *A story of the Mutiny on the Bounty,* by J. E. Chandler, (London: Tradescant Trust, 1987 – originally published 1973).
Mr Bligh's Bad Language: Passion, Power and Theatre on the Bounty, by Greg Dening, (Cambridge: Cambridge University Press, 1992).
'Early Korean-British relations', by Dr Kim Hong Ki, in *Korea and Britain Tomorrow: Towards a Broader Relationship,* edited by Chong-wha Chung and Boyd McLeary, (Seoul: Korean-British Association, Anglo-American Studies Institute, 1986), pp. 30-36.
'The centenary of Korean-British diplomatic relations: aspects of British interest and involvement in Korea 1600-1983', by J. E. Hoare, *Transactions of the Royal Asiatic Society Korea Branch,* vol. 58, (1983), pp. l-34.
The Northern Territories of Japan, by the Japan Society for Research on the Northern Territories, (Tokyo: Japan Society for Research on the Northern Territories, 1971), has a very brief account of Broughton's visit to Hokkaido and the Kuriles, and reproduces part of his charts relating to these areas.
Royal Chronicle of the Chosun Dynasty (in Korean), vol. 47, 20th. Year of King Jungjo, 6 September 1797, lunar calendar, (25 October 1797), reference kindly supplied by Mr H. Guack, Hyopsung Shipping Co., Pusan.
Letters from the British embassies in Tokyo and Seoul, 1995-1997.

Chapter 2 ANDREW COBBING *Itō Hirobumi in Britain.*

1. Erwin O. E. Von Baelz, *Awakening Japan: The Diary of a German Doctor*, trans. Eden and Cedar Paul (New York, 1932), p.312
2. Shunpō Kō Tsuikō Kai, *Itō Hirobumi Den*, vol.1 (Tokyo, 1940), p.28.
3. Itō did not receive full samurai status until early 1863, shortly before his departure for Britain.
4. *Itō Hirobumi Den*, pp.30-2
5. *Ibid.*, pp.39-42
6. *Ibid.*, p.35
7. *Ibid.*, pp.70-1, 73. This was the second attack on the legation, not to be confused with the first attack on the British Legation at Tōzenji on 5 July 1861 in which Laurence Oliphant was wounded.
8. Subu Kōhei (ed.), *Subu Masanosuke Den*, vol. 2 (Tokyo, 1977), pp.722-3
9. Details of Chōshū's preparations for this expedition can be found in *Itō Hirobumi Den*, *Subu Masanosuke Den*, *Bōchō Kaiten Shi*, *Segai Inoue Kō Den* and *Ōmura Masujiro Den*.
10. Komatsu Midori (ed.), *Itō Kō jikiwa* (Tokyo, 1936) p.123. *Itō Hirobumi Den*, pp.84-6
11. *Yoshida Shōin Zenshu* vol.10 (Tokyo, 1938), pp.435-6. Sakuma Shōzan's intervention perhaps saved Yoshida from death in 1854, but his crime in attempting to escape was later cited among the charges Yoshida faced before his execution in 1859.
12. Suematsu Kenchō *Bōchō Kaiten Shi*, vol.1 (Tokyo, 1967), p.426
13. *Itō Hirobumi Den*, p.88. *Subu Masanosuke Den*, pp.722-3
14. *Itō Ko Jikiwa*, p.126. In June 1869, after visiting Gower in Yokohama with Inoue Kaoru, Kido Takayoshi recalled: 'At the time that the policy of expulsion of the barbarians prevailed, Inoue, Itō, Yamao and I consulted him in secret about going abroad. He readily consented to help us; and we entrusted the arrangements to him.' Sidney Devere Brown and Akiko Hirota (trans.), *The Diary of Kido Takayoshi*, vol.1 (Tokyo, 1983), p.233
15. Shidō's report is reproduced in *Bōchō Kaiten Shi*, vol.1, pp.427-8, and *Itō Hirobumi Den*, pp.99-104. According to Itō's dictated memoirs, Gower gave them English words to repeat on a given cue as they passed the customs house so as to dispel any suspicions among the bakufu guards inside. Itō did not even know what these words meant. *Itō Kō Jikiwa*, pp.127-8
16. *Itō Hirobumi Den*, p.106. In order to protect their families, Shidō and Nomura both took the name of Inoue before they left, although it was as 'Shide' and 'Nomuran' that they were known in Britain.
17. This Keswick, described in Japanese records as the brother of (William) Keswick in Yokohama, may have been one of William's two younger brothers, J. J. J. or James Johnstone, who was based in Hong Kong. Maggie Keswick, *The Thistle and the Jade* (London, 1982), pp.38, 262
18. *Itō Kō Jikiwa*, p.125. *Itō Hirobumi Den*, pp.106-11
19. Inoue Kaoru Kō Denki Hensankai, *Segai Inoue Kō Den*, vol. 1 (Tokyo, 1968), pp.96-8
20. Matheson's recollections are reproduced in *Itō Hirobumi Den*, vol. 1, pp.979-82. The Williamsons lived at 16 Provost Road, Haverstock Hill in Belsize Park and were 'very poor' according to their daughter, Mrs Alice Maud Fison, but moved to 12 Fellows Road, Hampstead 'in 1864 or 1865'. Yumio Yamamoto, 'Inoue Masaru – 'Father' of the Japanese Railways', Ian Nish (ed.), *Britain & Japan: Biographical Portraits*, vol.2 (Richmond, 1997), p.342. College records indicate that Inoue Kaoru did not enrol, but a certain 'Ito Shunski' (No.372) is listed with the three others as having registered and paid on 22 July 1864. By this time, however, Itō was already back in Japan, suggesting that his companions paid his tuition fees for him in absentia. *Faculty of Arts Register*, University College London. There are very few records relating to Itō's time in Britain. Itō's biography records that he was on close terms with Algernon Bertram Mitford, an Oxford student, but Mitford left Oxford in 1857 and he was in St. Petersburg at this time. Similarly, I have seen no evidence for a more recent story that Itō and Inoue visited Aberdeen.
21. Yamamoto, 'Inoue Masaru', p.343. Asahina Chisen, *Meiji Kōshin Roku*, vol.1 (Tokyo, 1925), p.301
22. *Itō Kō Jikiwa*, p.209
23. *Itō Hirobumi Den*, pp.119-20, p.981
24. *Itō Kō Jikiwa*, p.131.
25. Memorandum by Reginald Russell, 1 July 1864, FO 46/49. Inuzuka Takaaki, *Nihon Gaku* July 1988, No.11, pp.48-9. Endō returned due to a pulmonary complaint recalled Matheson, but according to Takasugi Shinsaku, because he had fallen behind with his studies. *Itō Hirobumi Den*, pp.259, 991
26. *Itō Hirobumi Den*, p.121. *Itō Kō Jikiwa*, pp.132-3. Grace Fox, Britain and Japan, 1858-1883 (Oxford, 1969), p.132.
27. Ernest Mason Satow, *A Diplomat in Japan: An Inner History of the Japanese Reformation* (Tokyo,

1983), p.96

28. *Ibid.*, p.97

29. *Ibid.*, p.99. Itō and Inoue told Satow that they had handed Alcock's memorandum to Mōri 'in person', but in fact they did not deliver it at all, fearing this could only prejudice their cause. *Itō Hirobumi Den*, p.127

30. Satow, *A Diplomat in Japan*, p.131.

31. Edward Harrison, one of Glover's partners, perhaps helped Itō and Inoue during their stay in Yokohama in July 1864 (according to Itō's memoirs, Glover himself was there), and it was Harrison who took Itō to see Glover at his office in Nagasaki in April 1865. *Itō Hirobumi Den*, pp.120-1, 198. *Itō Kō Jikiwa*, p.132.

The story that Glover engineered the escape of the 'Chōshū Five' in 1863 appears to be based on hearsay first circulated in the 1900s. He did arrange the escape of three other Chōshū men in 1865, and the names of Glover and Gower were similar enough to invite confusion. An adaptation in which a Mr. Weigal of Glover & Co. appears putting the Chōshū students aboard 'a reluctant Captain J.S. Gower's vessel' is also incompatible with historical records. Cobbing, *The Japanese Discovery of Victorian Britain* (Richmond, 1998), p.225. Sidney Devere Brown, 'Nagasaki in the Meiji Restoration: Chōshū Loyalists and British Arms Merchants', *Crossroads*, No.1, 1993, (Nagasaki), p.16

32. *Itō Hirobumi Den*, pp.333-6

33. Satow, *A Diplomat in Japan*, p.327

34. *Ibid.*

35. Silvana De Maio, 'Engineering Education in Japan after the Iwakura Mission', Ian Nish (ed.), *The Iwakura Mission in America and Europe* (London, 1998), p.166. On the results of Itō's arrangements, see also Olive Checkland's portrait of Henry Dyer in this volume.

36. *The Diary of Kido Takayoshi*, p.233

Many thanks to J.E. Hoare and Olive Checkland for their kind help in preparing this paper.

Chapter 3 KOYAMA NOBURU *James Summers, 1828-91: Early Sinologist and Pioneer of Japanese Newspapers in London and English Literature in Japan*

1. For an example, Kindai bungaku *Kenkyū Sōsho* Vol.2, (Tokyo: Shōwa Joshi Daigaku Kindai Bunka Kenkyūjo, 1959) which includes 'James Summers'. Two items are listed as Summers' achievements (*gyōseki*). The first is *Taisei shimbun* and the second is the lectures of English literature. The authors of 'James Summers' part in *Kindai bungaku kenkyū sōsho* Vol.2 are Adachi Shizue and Sasaki Mitsuko. Almost identical articles by them as that of *Kindai bungaku kenkyū sōsho* Vol.2 also appeared as Adachi Shizue, 'Saō kenkyū no senkakusha, Samāzu', *Gakuen*, December 1940 and Sasaki Mitsuko, *Eigaku no reimei*, (Tokyo: Shōwa Joshi Daigaku Kindai Bunka Kenkyūjo, 1975). So, I have used the individual items of both authors for this article rather than that of *Kindai bungaku kenkyū sōsho* Vol.2.

2. Adachi Shizue, 'Saō kenkyū no senkakusha, Samāzu' *Gakuen*, December 1940.

3. Joseph Foster, *Alumni Oxonienses: the members of the University of Oxford 1715-1886: their parentage, birthplace, and year of birth, with a record of their degrees*, (Oxford: Parker and Co., 1888). p.1371.

4. Kamei Hideo and Matsuki Hiroshi, *Chōten niji wo haku*, (Sapporo: Hokkaidō Daigaku Tosho Kankōkai, 1998). p.442.

5. Tezuka Tatsumaro, *Eigakushi no shūhen*, (Tokyo: Azuma Shobō, 1968). p.193.

6. Lily Summers, 'Impressions of Japan in 1873 : Told by Old Foreign Resident', *Nippon Times*, 11, 18, 25 June, 1951.

7. James William Norton-Kyshe, *The history of the laws and courts of Hongkong*, Vol.1, (London: T. Fisher Unwin, Hong Kong: Noronha and Company, 1889). pp.244-245.; 'Journal of Occurrences', pp.669-670, *Chinese Repository*, Vol.18, December 1849.

8. Norton-Kyshe, *The history of the laws and courts of Hongkong*, Vol.1. p.248.

9. Norton-Kyshe, *The history of the laws and courts of Hongkong*, Vol.1. p.348.

10. Adachi Shizue, 'Saō kenkyū no senkakusha, Samāzu'; Sasaki Mitsuko, *Eigaku no reimei*, (Tokyo: Shōwa Joshi Daigaku Kindai Bunka Kenkyūjo, 1975). p.76.; *Crockford's clerical directory for 1865*, (London: Horace Cox, 1865). p.604.

11. James Summers, *A handbook of the Chinese language, part I and II grammar and chrestomathy*, (Oxford: Oxford University Press, 1863). title page.

12. Denis Twitchett, *Land tenure and the social order in T'ang and Sung China*, (London: School of Oriental and African Studies, University of London, 1962). pp.3-4.

13. George Thomas Staunton, *Memoirs of the chief incidents of the public life of Sir George Thomas Staunton, Bart*, (London: L. Booth, 1856) ; King's College, *Calendar*, 1865-66, (London: King's

355

College, 1865). p.99.
14. Twitchett, *Land tenure and the social order in T'ang and Sung China*. p.6.
15. Twitchett, *Land tenure and the social order in T'ang and Sung China*. p.6.
16. F.J.C. Hearnshaw, *The centenary history of King's College London 1828-1928*, (London: George G. Harrap & Company, 1929). p.250.
17. Hearnshaw, *The centenary history of King's College London 1828-1928*. p.250.
18. Twitchett, *Land tenure and the social order in T'ang and Sung China*. p.7.
19. *Report of the Committee appointed by the Lords Commissioners of His Majesty's Treasury to consider the Organisation of Oriental Studies in London*, (London: H.M.S.O., 1909) (Cd. 4560). Minutes of Evidence, Nos. 1995-96, p.74, evidence of Sir Ernest Satow.
20. Adachi Shizue, 'Saō kenkyū no senkakusha, Samāzu'; Sasaki Mitsuko, *Eigaku no reimei*. p.78.
21. Lily Summers, 'Impressions of Japan in 1873: Told by Old Foreign Resident'.
22. Shigehisa Tokutarō, 'Jēmuzu Samāzu', *Oyatoi gaikokujin*, Vol.5, (Tokyo: Shōgakukan, 1975). pp.160–161.
23. Suzuki Hidesaburō, *Hompō shimbun no kigen*, (Kyoto: Kuriosha, 1959). p.360.
24. *Meiji zenki zaisei keizai shiryō shūsei*, vol.10, (Tokyo: Kaizōsha, 1935). pp.350-351.
25. Minami Teisuke, *Kōtokuin goryakureki*, (mimeograph), (Tokyo, 1915). p.14.
26. F.V. Dickens, *Hyak nin is'shiu, or stanzas by a century of poets, being Japanese lyrical odes*, (London: Smith, Elder, & Co., 1866). ix.
27. James Summers, 'English in Japan', *Leisure Hours*, No. 1159, 14 March 1874.
28. James Summers, 'Practical lessons in Japanese', *Phoenix*, Nos. 26–29, July–October 1872.
29. Adachi Shizue, 'Saō kenkyū no senkakusha, Samāzu'.
30. Adachi Shizue, 'Saō kenkyū no senkakusha, Samāzu'.
31. Shiga Shigetaka, 'Chōrō Jēmusu Samumāsu sensei wo kokusu', *Kokkai shimbun*, No.283, 28th October 1891.
32. Kamei Hideo and Matsuki Hiroshi, *Chōten niji wo haku*. pp.212-213.
33. Kamei Hideo and Matsuki Hiroshi, *Chōten niji wo haku*. p.442.
34. Shigehisa Tokutarō, 'Jēmuzu Samāzu', *Oyatoi gaikokujin*, Vol.5. pp.160-167.
35. Tezuka Tatsumaro, *Eigakushi no shūhen*. p.177.
36. Tezuka Tatsumaro, *Eigakushi no shūhen*. p.180.
37. James Summers, 'On Chinese lexicography, with proposal for a new arrangement of the characters of that language', *Transactions of the Asiatic Society of Japan*, 1st series, Vol.12 (1883/84).
38. Harry Parkes Papers, Cambridge University Library. I am indebted for Mr. John Wells for finding this letter, the specimens of the dictionaries and the advertisement of subscription.
39. Adachi Shizue, 'Saō kenkyū no senkakusha, Samāzu; Sasaki Mitsuko, *Eigaku no reimei*. p.83.
40. 'Attacks on foreigners in Japan', *Times*, 27 June 1890; *Meiji nyūsu jiten*, Vol.4, (Tokyo: Mainichi Komyunikēshonzu, 1984). pp.648-649.
41. Adachi Shizue, 'Saō kenkyū no senkakusha, Samāzu; Sasaki Mitsuko, *Eigaku no reimei*. pp.82-83.

Chapter 4 TAMAKI NORIO *Fukuzawa Yukichi (1835-1901) the Finances of a Japanese Modernizer*

1. The list *Eiyo Kagami*, or List of Wealthy Men in Tokyo, was prepared in 1890 by Suzuki Sakae who provided us with detailed figures, the earliest and rarest personal information on incomes. Suzuki did not disclose his sources, but he drew on the official figures collected by the City Corporation of Tokyo. Suzuki's list is included in Shibuya Ryuichi (1988/97) ed. *Todōfukenbetsu shisanka jinushi sōran* (Prefectural lists of capitalists and landlords), vol. 1, Tokyo, Nihon Tosho Centre. For the income tax legislation, see S. Yukioka, *Shotokuzei hōjinzeiseidōshi sōkō* (History of income tax and corporate tax [draft], 2 vols, (Tokyo: Okurasho, 1955).
2. Moriyama, Nagasaki local samurai and an interpreter of Dutch for the bakufu, started learning English in the 1840s. His skill in spoken English was much appreciated by both the Americans and the British. The British consul general, Rutherford Alcock, was no exception. For more details, see Norio Tamaki, 'Yukichi Fukuzawa, the English speaking educator and businessman', prepared for the Anglo-Japanese History Workshops at Sheffield, 29 August to 1 September 1998.
3. *The Times*, 3 May 1862.
4. *The Times*, 26 May 1862.
5. Dr Chambers could be Robert Chambers of W. & R. Chambers, publishers in Edinburgh. Robert Chambers was appointed a judge in one of the sections of the International Exhibition in 1862. He was conferred the honorary degree of LL.D. from the University of St Andrews. See William Chambers (1879), *Memoir of William and Robert Chambers* (Edinburgh & London, W. & R. Chambers), pp.307, 325.

6. *The Times*, 3, 6, 8, 9, 12, 14, 19, 20, 21 May 1862.
7. Fukuzawa Yukichi, *Fukuzawa Yukichi zenshu* (Collected Works of Fukuzawa Yukichi, hereafter abbreviated as *CWYF*) (Tokyo: Iwanami Shoten, 1958-71) vol.17, pp.7-8.
8. The wrapping paper of the book, on which Fukuzawa wrote with India ink that he bought it in London in 1862, is the evidence.
9. More details will be discussed in the next section.
10. First published in 1864 by the Publishers Circular, London, and reprinted in 1963 by Kraus Reprint Corporation, New York.
11. 1 ryo=4s 8d.
12. *CWYF*, vol.1, p.29.
13. Ibid., p.26.
14. *CWYF*, vol.17, p.51.
15. *Keiō Gijyuku zōhanmokuroku* (n.d.) (Catalogue of Keiō publication), (Tokyo: Keiō Gijuku), contains the prices of the books published before February 1872.
16. *CWYF*, vol.17, p.52.
17. Ibid., p.55.
18. *Autobiography*, *CWYF*, vol.7, pp.112-4, 129.
19. *CWYF*, vol.17, p.56.
20. Ono Takeo, *Edo bukkajiten* (Dictionary of prices in Edo period), (Tokyo: Tenbosha, 1979) pp.115-6.
21. *CWYF*, vol.21, pp.279-80.
22. Imaizumi Mine, *Nagori no yume* (Lingering dream), (Tokyo: Tōyōbunko, 1963), p.37.
23. The site was Shinsenza, near the Shogun's Detached Villa. In 1871, the College eventually moved to Mita where Keiō University remains.
24. *CWYF*, vol.17, p.328.
25. Ibid., pp.341-2.
26. Ibid., pp.345-6.
27. Ibid., p354.
28. Ibid., p355.
29. Tamaki Norio, *Japanese Banking*, (Cambridge: Cambridge University Press, 1995), p.47.
30. Yokohama Shōkinginkō rep. 1976, *Yokohama Shōkinginkō shiryō* (Historical materials of Yokohama Specie Bank), vol.1, pp.33-55.
31. Onishi Rihei, *Asabuki Eiji kun denki* (Biography of Asabuki Eiji), (Tokyo: Tōshōshuppan, 1990), pp.80-4. Iwasakikedenki Kankōkai ed. *Iwasaki Yatarō den* (Biography of Iwasaki Yatarō), (Tokyo: Tokyo Daigaku Shuppankai, rep. 1979), vol.2, pp.334-5.
32. *CWYF*, vol.17, p.198.
33. Ōhashi Akio, *Gōtō Shōjirō to kindai Nihon* (Gōtō Shojiro and modern Japan), (Tokyo: Sanichishobo, 1993).
34. *CWYF*, vol.17, pp.347-8. Shoda's wife was Iwasaki Yataro's niece.
35. Ibid., p.447.
36. Both Nakamigawa and Koizumi had worked hard under the supervision of Professor Leone Levi (1821-1888), at King's College, London.
37. *CWYF*, vol.17, pp.347-8.
38. *CWYF*, vol.21, pp.6-12.
39. Maruzen, *Maruzen hyakunenshi* (Hundred year history of Maruzen), (Tokyo: Maruzen, 1980-81).
40. *CWYF*, vol.21, p.33.

Chapter 5 SIR HUGH CORTAZZI *Thomas Wright Blakiston (1832-91)*

1. 'Zoological Indications of Ancient Connection of the Japan Islands with the Continent' paper read to the Asiatic Society of Japan on 14 February 1883.
2. See the entry for Blakiston in the *Dictionary of National Biography* and Grace Fox *Britain and Japan 1858-1883*, (Oxford: Oxford University Press, 1969) pp. 348-350.
3. Major John Blakiston served in the Madras Engineers and the 27th Regiment (the Enniskillens). He was present at the battle of Assaye and took part in the Peninsular war.
4. Blakiston had been recommended to Palliser by the noted physicist and astronomer General Sir Edward Sabine. In 1858 a tiny settlement known as Red River, now Winnipeg, was the only habitation in central Canada except for a string of fur trading posts along the main rivers. Settlements to the east were cut off by the granite and swamp of the Canadian shield and to the west towards the Crown Colony of British Columbia by the Rocky Mountains. Palliser who came from Dublin was a man of rank and wealth. He enjoyed travel and hunting. He had spent two years in the American prairies in the late 1840s and was aware of the United States interest in

developing railway routes to the west. He feared that the United States might make claims to Canadian territory.

5.   Comment in the article on Blakiston in the *Dictionary of National Biography*.

6.   See *Japan in Yezo, a series of papers descriptive of journeys undertaken in the island of Yezo, at intervals between 1862 and 1882* by T.W.B. published in 1883 at Yokohama by the *Japan Gazette* and originally pulished in the *Japan Gazette* between February and October 1883. I am grateful to the Yokohama Archives of History for access to this work a photocopy of which Miss Ito, their archivist, kindly sent me as I could not discover a copy in Britain. I have sent photocopies to the British Library and the library of the Royal Geographical Society.

7.   According to Dr J.E.Hoare's lecture to the Japan Society on 17 December 1975 'Mr Enslie's Grievances: The Consul, the Ainu and the Bones'; (*Japan Society Bulletin* No 78, March 1976). Marr was one of the two assessors from the small British community in Hakodate in the consular court which was convened in December 1865 to try three British men

8.   Grace Fox: *Britain and Japan 1858-1883*, pp. 348-350.

9.   L.K.Herbert-Gustar and P.A.Nott: John Milne: *Father of Modern Seismology*, (Tenterden, Kent: Paul Norbury Publications, 1980).

10. *Japan in Yezo* Section X)

11. *Japan in Yezo* especially sections VIII, X, XVII, and XX. In section XVII he records his meeting with Penri, the old Ainu 'chief' who was well known to John Batchelor and who met Isabella Bird. Blakiston was scathing about some of Isabella Bird's observations.

12. *Japan in Yezo* section VII.

13. *Japan in Yezo* section XX.

14. *Japan in Yezo* section III.

15. I am indebted to Dr J.E.Hoare for information about this case details of which he came across in the records of the Shanghai Supreme Court (FO656) and in FO262 for 1873 and 1874.

16. Grace Fox *Britain and Japan 1858-1883*, p. 351.

17. *Dictionary of National Biography*.

18. On 8 September Sir Harry Parkes, the British Minister to Japan, at that time at Yokohama instructed Mr F.O.Adams, the Secretary to the Legation, accompanied by Ernest Satow, to embark on HMS *Rattler* and proceed to Hakodate. The purpose of their mission was to find out about Russian activities. Had they established hemselves in Kunashiri, Etorofu (referred to by Parkes as Iturup, or any part of Hokkaido (Parkes called the island Yesso)? Adams was to seek information in the first instance from Inouye Iwami, the senior Japanese government official at Hakodate. Parkes also wanted to know whether Shibetsu might 'possess commercial capabilities of some importance'. After investigating the position he was to go on to Niigata to find out what was happening there and then to Nanao. According to a despatch from Mr Eusden, British consul at Hakodate, dated 22 September 1868 a young Japanese official who had taken over at Hakodate, Shimizu Dani, had received a call from Mr Adams and had been gratified by the way in which he had been received when he paid his return call to HMS *Rattler*.

HMS *Rattler* sailed from Hakodate round the northern coast of Japan and foundered off Cape Soya on 24 September. The news appears to have reached Mr Eusden on 7 October 1868 by a message sent overland. Mr Eusden requested the help of the commander of the French corvette *Dupleix* which was then at Hakodate. Its commander Bergasse du Petit-Thouars had become friendly earlier that year with A.B.Mitford while the latter was representing Sir Harry Parkes at Osaka. After having obtained some coal from a British vessel du Petit-Thouars set forth with a Japanese pilot around the north western coast of the island. (See *Le Vice-Amiral Bergasse du Petit-Thouars D'Apres Ses Notes et Sa Corresponence 1832-1890*, (Paris: 1906) pp. 240-246).

At Cape Soya he made contact with Commander Stephenson, the Captain of HMS *Rattler* and with Mr Adams who had requested Stephenson to stop at Cape Soya so that he could call on the local officials there. At first Stephenson proposed to du Petit-Thouars that he should remain at Cape Soya with half the crew to look after the equipment, but du Petit-Thouars told him that the *Dupleix* would gladly take the whole crew of some 100 men and that the equipment could be safely left protected from the elements. The *Dupleix* made a quick get away as the winds were rising. Du Petit-Thouars praised the way in which Stephenson had maintained discipline in difficult circumstances although he seems to have had some doubts about the wisdom of bringing the *Rattler* so close to the shore. Commander Stephenson was the nephew of Admiral Sir Henry Keppel. As Stephenson also became an Admiral his loss of the *Rattler* does not seem to have affected his future career. Du Petit-Thouars and the French legation were generally suspicious of British motives and activities in Japan during 1868: the British were equally suspicious of the French. These suspicions did not prevent the two helping one another in times of difficulty.

19. According to *The Birds of the Japanese Empire* by Henry Seebohm, (London: Porter 1890), the results of Blakiston's observations were recorded in the ornithological journal *Ibis* in 1862. Some corrections and additions were published in the same journal in 1863. Blakiston sent from Hakodate at various times four boxes of birds which he had collected to Robert Swinhoe who

contributed papers to *Ibis* in 1874,1875,1876 and 1877. (According to the *History of the collections in the Natural History Museum in London* (London: 1906), Blakiston sent 59 birds from Japan which have been preserved in the Museum.) In 1878 Blakiston and Mr Harry Pryer of Yokohama contributed 'A Catalogue of the Birds of Japan'. They had 'visited the various museums in Japan' and compared their collections. After eliminating doubtful species the number of known species of Japanese birds was raised to 295. In January 1880 Blakiston and Pryer read a paper to the Asiatic Society of Japan based on their catalogue for *Ibis*. This was revised and published in the Transaction of the Asiatic Society in 1882 under the title 'Birds of Japan',adding 22 further species to those previously listed. An amended list was published in 1884. Blakiston also contributed various ornithological notes to *The Chrysanthemum*, another [natural history] journal in 1882 and 1883. Seebohm with whom Blakiston had been in touch produced papers for *Ibis* and *The Proceedings of the Zoological Society* in 1883 about Pied Wagtials of Japan and a new species of owl sent by Blakiston which was given the name *bubo blakistoni*. In 1886 Blakiston wrote a paper for *The Proceedings of the United States National Museum* on the 'Water-birds of Japan'.
20. Letter to Hugh Cortazzi dated 2 June 1996 from Dr Yokoyama Toshio of Kyoto University.

Chapter 6 PETER FRANCIS KORNICKI *Frederick Victor Dickins (1838-1915)*

Bibliographical note

In addition to the items mentioned in these notes there is a study in Japanese of Dickins' translations of Japanese literature by Kawamura Hatsue: *F.V. Dikkinzu: nihon bungaku eiyaku no senkusha* (Shichigatsudō, 1997). Of his letters, those to Satow are in the PRO, some to Karl Pearson are among the Pearson Manuscripts at University College, London, and some of his correspondence with Minakata Kumagusu is said to be at the Minakata Kumagusu Kinenkan at Shirahama in Wakayama prefecture. The Special Collections of the University of London Library contain many papers relating to his work as Registrar. On Dickins' early collection of Japanese books, now in the John Rylands University Library of Manchester, see note 11, below; his later collection of Japanese books, formerly held at Bristol University Library, has recently been sold by auction.

1. This is a shortened version of my introduction to the *Collected works of Frederick Victor Dickins*, which is to be published by Ganesha Publishing Ltd of Bristol in 1999; it appears here with the kind permission of Ganesha Publishing. For full documentation see the footnotes to the complete version.
2. 'Address delivered by Sir George Sansom at the Annual Ceremony 1956', *Journal of Asian studies* 24 (1964-5), pp. 563-7.
3. For the details of Dickins' life, see the obituaries in *The Lancet*, 2 Sep. 1915, p. 580, *Nature* 26 Aug. 1915, p. 708, and *The Wiltshire archaeological and natural history magazine* 39 (1915-17), pp. 273-7; for details of his career see his naval record at the Public Record Office (hereafter PRO): ADM 196/9, p. 296.
4. PRO: ADM 101/178, Medical and Surgical Journal of HMS *Coromandel*, 1 Jan. 1864 to 30 Sept. 1864.
5. PRO: ADM 125/119, p. 675.
6. PRO: PRO 30/33/11/4; Dickins to Satow 28 March 1905, 30 August 1905, 11 February 1909; Mary Dickins to Satow, 11 Sept. [1915].
7. [Dickins], 'Hints to students of the Japanese language', *Chinese and Japanese Repository* 17 (12 Dec. 1864), p. 216, and 'The temples of Kamakura near Yokohama in Japan', *ibid.*, 20 (1 March 1865), pp. 97-102; the author of these pieces is identified only as 'a Medical Officer of the Royal Navy', but since this is the same formula as that used by Dickins for his translations from *Hyakunin isshu*, which were published in the same journal (see below), it is clear that he was the author.
8. 'Hints to students of the Japanese language', *Chinese and Japanese Repository* 17 (12 Dec. 1864), p. 222; Dickins' translations, both literal and metrical, were first published as 'Translations of Japanese odes, from the *H'yak nin iss'shiu* (Stanzas from a hundred poets), by a Medical Officer of the Royal Navy', in the same journal, issues 20 (1 March 1865) to 28 (1 Nov. 1865).
9. *The Lancet*, 4 Sep. 1915, p. 580.
10. Letter from Dickins to Durnford dated April 1867 and pasted into vol. 1 of the copy of *Sōmoku zusetsu* that later entered Cambridge University Library (FJ.992.1); *Dictionary of National Biography*, First supplement, vol. 2, p. 171.
11. See P.F. Kornicki, 'The Japanese collection in the Bibliotheca Lindesiana', *Bulletin of the John Rylands University Library of Manchester* 75 (1993), pp. 209-300 (the Dickins books are described on pp. 231-42). Dickins, *Chiushingura; or the loyal league* (London: Allen & Co., 1880), translator's note, p. 7; *Westminster review*, July & October 1870, pp. 321-40.
12. PRO: FO 656/22: Dickins to Goodwin, 28 Oct. 1871. *Japan Weekly Mail*, 25 Nov. 1871, p. 655, 20 July 1878, p. 681; *Japan Mail* (fortnightly), 11 Jan. 1879.

13. *Japan Weekly Mail*, 16 Dec. 1871, p. 699, 25 March 1875, p. 183, 2 March 1878, p. 207, 4 May 1878, p. 417, & 11 May 1878, p. 444-6; Dickins and Stanley Lane Pool, *The life of Sir Harry Parkes*, vol. 2, p. 321, note.
14. *Japan Weekly Mail*, 10 Aug. 1872, p. 497.
15. *Japan Weekly Mail*, 17 Aug. 1872; 24 Aug. 1872, pp. 527-8, 532.
16. *Japan Weekly Mail*, 21 Sept. 1872; 28 Sept. 1872, p. 629.
17. Ishii Ryōsuke, ed., *Dajōkan nisshi*, 8 vols (Tokyo: Tōkyōdō Shuppan, 1980-2), 6, p. 200; *Meiji bunka zenshū* 11 (Tokyo: Nihon Hyōron Shinsha, 1956) pp. 9, 25-60; *Dainihon gaikō monjo* vol. 5, pp. 412-540.
18. *Japan Mail* (fortnightly edition), 23 Jan. 1875, pp. 61 & 71; *Japan Weekly Mail*, 20 July 1877, p. 681; Ebihara Hachirō, *Nihon ōji shinbun zasshi shi* (facsimile of 1934 edition; Tokyo: Meicho Fukyūkai, 1980), pp. 86, 92-3.
19. Douglas Moore Kenrick, 'A century of Western studies of Japan', *Transactions of the Asiatic Society of Japan* 14 (1978) pp. 101-5, 353, 359-61. Satow Papers, Public Record Office: PRO 30/33/11/5, Satow to Dickins, 4 Feb. 1880.
20. Satow Papers: PRO 30/33/11/5, Satow to Dickins, 25 July 1879, 4 Feb. 1880, 22 August 1880. *The Lancet*, 4 Sep. 1915, p. 580.
21. *Chiushingura; or the loyal league*, xiii, 148 (asterisk note).
22. Satow Papers: PRO 30/33/11/4, Dickins to Satow, 14 April 1908.
23. *Minakata Kumagusu zenshū*, vol. 7, pp. 16-19, 12: 102, 129; Minakata and Dickins, 'A Japanese Thoreau of the twelfth century', *Journal of the Royal Asiatic Society* (1905), 237; Satow Papers: PRO 30/33/11/4, Dickins to Satow, 9 Oct. 1904.
24. Dickins to Parkes, 21 Nov. 1880; *Japan Mail*, 23 Jan. 1882, pp. 527.
25. Satow Papers: PRO 30/33/11/4, Dickins to Satow, 30 August 1905; PRO 30/33/11/4, Dickins to Satow, 9 Oct. 1904.
26. *Transactions of the ninth international congress of orientalists* [London, 1892] (London: 1893), vol. 2, p. 667.
27. Sir Hugh Cortazzi, 'The Japan Society: a hundred-year history', in Hugh Cortazzi and Gordon Daniels, eds. *Britain and Japan 1859-1991: themes and personalities* (London: Routledge, 1991), pp. 1-53.

Chapter 7 OLIVE CHECKLAND *Kawanabe Kyōsai (1831-89), the Painter and the British*

1. With thanks to Kawanabi Kusumi for her help in 1997 at Warabe.
2. See T. Clark, *Demon of Painting, the Art of Kawanabe Kyōsai*, London: British Museum, 1993.
3. With thanks to Brenda Jordan, see also B. Jordan, 'Strange Fancies and Fresh Conceptions: Kyosai in an age of conflict' unpublished doctoral dissertation, University of Kansas, 1993.
4. See J. Conder, *Paintings and Studies by Kawanabe Kyōsai*, (Tokyo: Maruzen, 1911; reprinted Saitama: Kawanabe Kyōsai Memorial Museum, 1993), pp.1-14
5. See *Kyōsai Gadan, the life in art of Kyōsai Kawanabe Torku*, compiled by Baitei Gaso, translated from the Japanese by Scott Johnson and reprinted in 1983. It is not always easy to quote from *Kyōsai Gadan*, as it is not clear whether some direct speech was by Kyōsai, or not.
6. See *Kyōsai Gadan*, p. 36.
7. See *Kyōsai Gadan*, p. 36.
8. J. Conder, *Paintings and Studies by Kawanabe Kyōsai*, p. 18.
9. J. Conder, *Paintings and Studies by Kawanabe Kyōsai*, p. 19.
10. J. Conder, *Paintings and Studies by Kawanabe Kyōsai*, p. 20.
11. J. Conder, *Paintings and Studies by Kawanabe Kyōsai*, pp. 21-22.
12. See O. Checkland, *Britain's Encounter with Meiji Japan, 1868-1912*, (Basingstoke: Macmillan, 1989) p. 274, Note 58.
13. W. Anderson, 'A Japanese Artist, Kawanabe Kyōsai', *The Studio*, Vol XV, (1898) p. 32.
14. W. Anderson, 'A Japanese Artist, Kawanabe Kyōsai', *The Studio*, Vol XV, (1898) p. 35.
15. W. Anderson, 'A Japanese Artist, Kawanabe Kyōsai', *The Studio*, Vol XV, (1898) p. 38.
16. Copy of Will of William Anderson, No 1 Harley Street, London, died 27 October 1900.
17. M. Menpes, *Whistler As I Knew Him*, London: A and C Black, 1904, p. 39.
18. E. Evett, *The Critical Reception of Japanese Art in late nineteenth-century Europe*, Ann Arbor: UMI Research Press, 1982, p.16.
19. M. Menpes, *Magazine of Art*, 1888, p.195.
20. M. Menpes, *Whistler as I knew him*, 1904, pp.40-41.
21. E. Evett, *Critical Reception of Japanese Art*, p.16.
22. B. Jordan, 'Strange Fancies', p.339.
23. L.Smith, Foreword to Clark, *Demon of Painting*, p.7.

Chapter 8 NEIL PEDLAR *James Alfred Ewing and his Circle of Pioneering Physicists in Meiji Tokyo*

References

The Man of Room 40: The Life of Sir Alfred Ewing by A.W. Ewing. (London: Hutchison, 1939) Chapter 5: passim.

'Science and Society in Modern Japan: Selected Historical Sources'. Ed. Nakayama Shigeru, (Tokyo: University of Tokyo, 1974), pp.24–38 and passim.

1. 'The Development of Physics in Meiji Japan 1868-1912' (DPMJ) by Kenkichirō Koizumi. University of Pennsylvania, Ph.D. Dissertation 1973 (unpub.) p.206.
2. Ibid. p.206.
3. Ibid. p.199. (From *Tanakadate Aikitsu sensei* by Nakamura Seiji, Tokyo 1946.)
4. *Obituary Notices of Fellows of the Royal Society*, Volume 1 (1932-35) p.475/6.
5. *Dictionary of National Biography* (DNB) 1931-40. p.264.
6. *An Engineer's Outlook (AEO)* by Sir Alfred Ewing, (London: Mehtuen 1933) Preface p.xv.
7. *AEO* p.xiii.
8. *AEO* p.274.
9. *AEO* p.xiii.
10. *Science, Technology and Everyday Life 1870-1950* Ed. Colin Chant (London; New York: Routledge and Open University 1989) p.70.
11. *The Role of Foreign Employees in the Meiji Era in Japan* by Noboru Umetani, (Tokyo: Institute of Developing Economies 1971), p.59. (RFEMEJ).
12. John Perry, *Central*, vol. 7 (1910), 708. Quoted in *Britain's Encounters with Meiji Japan, 1868-1912* by Olive Checkland (Basingstoke: Macmillan 1989), p.85.
13. *RFEMEJ*, Umetani 1971. p.60.
14. *A Social History of Engineering* by W.H.G. Armytage. (London: Faber 1976), 4th Edn. p.233/4.
15. See DNB.
16. *Dictionary of Science and Technology* (London: Academic Press 1992).
17. *Made in Japan: Akio Morita and Sony* by Aki Morita, with E.M. Reingold and Mitsuko Shimomura. (London: Fontana/Collins 1987), p.56.
18. *AEO* p.xiv.
19. *Tokio Times*, 30 Nov. 1878.
20. Kew PRO: FO 345-34.
21. *Transactions of the Asiatic Society of Japan*. 3rd Series. Vol. 14. 1978. p.94.
22. DNB 1931-1940. p.265.
23. Internet www.dundee.ac.uk/physicsenginering/histry.htm
24. DNB 1931-1940. p.265.
25. DPMJ. p.208.

Chapter 9 J.E. HOARE *Captain Francis Brinkley, 1841-1912: Yatoi, Scholar and Apologist*

1. *Annual Registrar* vol. CLIV (1912), p. 122.
2. *Japan Punch*, June 1883.
3. See *Japan Weekly Mail* (cited as *JWM*), 5 April 1882 and 'Strange misrepresentations in connection with missionary work', *JWM*, 22 Dec. 1888.
4. *Colonial Office List*, 1868, 'Hong Kong'; for MacDonnel, see *Dictionary of National Biography*, and Frank Welsh, *A history of Hong Kong* (London: HarperCollins, 1993), pp. 237-8, 252-3.
5. Foreign Office records, embassy and consular records, Japan (FO262)/220, no. R.207, Major General Whitfield, Hong Kong to Adams, 5 December 1871.
6. FO262/207, F. O. Adams, chargé d'affaires, to Lord Granville, draft no, 11, 12 June 1871. Grace Fox, *Britain and Japan, 1859-1883*, (Oxford: Oxford University Press, 1969), p. 263 says that he learnt Japanese in order to teach better, but Adams wrote that his Japanese was already fluent by 1871.
7. FO262/205, Odo Russell to Adams, no. 16, 1 Sept. 1871; FO 262/220, no. R.207, Whitfield to Adams, 5 December 1871.
8. H. J. Jones, *Live machines: hired foreigners and Meiji Japan* (Tenterden, Kent: Paul Norbury Publications, 1980), p. 179, note 8. This incorrectly states that Brinkley was employed by the Fukui *han* from 1867 to 1871.
9. For the general history of foreign employees, or *o-yatoi gaikokujin*, see Jones, *Live Machines*, and Umetani Noburo, *Oyatoi gaikokujin: Meiji Nihon no wakiyakutachi* ('The Foreign Employees: Meiji Japan's Supporting Cast') (Tokyo: Nihon keizai shimbunsha, 1965).

10. Jones, *Live Machines*, p. 167n. For his salary, which fell from Mexican $500 to Mexican $350 between his first and last posts, see Neil Pedlar, *The Imported Pioneers: Westerners who helped build Modern Japan* (Folkestone: Japan Library, 1990), p. 145.

11. Public Record Office (PRO) Satow Papers (cited as PRO30/33)/11/2, Satow to W. G. Aston, 3 Sept. 1876.

12. *Tokio Times*, 4 August 1877. He lost his library in a second fire in May 1900. See A. D'Anethan, *Fourteen Years of Diplomatic Life in Japan* (London: Stanley, Paul and Co., 1912), p. 232.

13. Douglas Moore Kenrick, 'A century of Western Studies of Japan: The first hundred years of the Asiatic Society of Japan 1872-1972', *Transactions of the Asiatic Society of Japan*, Third Series, vol. 14 (1978), pp. 55, 82, 118, 268, 353, 401.

14. Koyama Noboru, *Kokusai kekkon daiichi-go: Meiji hitotachi no zakkon jishi*, ('The first international weddings: Racial intermarriage among people in the Meiji period'), (Tokyo: Kodansha, 1995), pp. 163-165. See also FO 881/8211, *Correspondence respecting the Law of Marriage in Japan, 1895-1899*.

15. *JWM* 7 April 1883.

16. FO262/364, Lord Tenterden (Foreign Office) to J. G. Kennedy, chargé d'affaires, Tokyo, no. 88, 16 December 1881, and enclosures, including Brinkley to the Deputy Adjutant General, Royal Artillery 26 Sept. 1881; FO262/392, no. 12, Brinkley to Sir Harry Parkes, 18 Jan. 1882, in which Brinkley claimed that he had applied for permission to retire in April 1881. For his formal departure, see *London Gazette* 24 November 1882, quoted in the *London and China Express*, 1 December 1882.

17. This account of Brinkley and the *Japan Mail* is largely based on J. E. Hoare, *Japan's Treaty Ports and Foreign Settlements: The Uninvited Guests 1858-1899* (Folkestone: Japan Library, 1994), Chapter 7, 'The Foreign Press'; and James Hoare , 'British Journalists in Meiji Japan', in *Britain and Japan: Biographical Portraits*, edited by Ian Nish, (Folkestone: Japan Library, 1994), pp. 20-32.

18. Debates about Reuters' telegrams occupied many pages of the treaty port press. See, for example, *JWM*, 6, 13 Sept. 1884, 11 Oct. 1890 and 8 Feb. 1896. See also James L. Huffman, *Creating a Public: People and Press in Meiji Japan* (Honolulu: University of Hawai'i Press, 1997), pp. 182, 455n.

19. Foreign Office records embassy and consular records Japan, records of the Tokyo vice-consulate (cited as FO798)/51, J. H. Longford to R. A. Mowat, Shanghai, no. 5, 20 Feb. 1893; Brinkley subsequently did take out probate. See also Hoare, *Uninvited Guests*, p.154; 'Annual Review' from the British ambassador in Tokyo for 1906, reprinted in Archive Research Ltd., editors, *Japan and Dependencies: Political and Economic Reports 1906-1960* (Farnham Common Slough: Archive Research Ltd., 1994), I, 31.

20. *London and China Express*, 9 Sept. 1887. Palmer is now better remembered as the architect of Yokohama's waterworks than as the *Times* correspondent – see *Yokohama shiryōkaikan, Yokohama kaikō shiryōkan: sōgō annai* ('Yokohama Archives of History: A complete guide'), (Yokohama: Yokohama shiryōkaikan, 4th. Edition, 1988), pp. 116-17.

21. Ian H. Nish, *The Anglo-Japanese Alliance: The Diplomacy of two Island Empires 1894-1907* (London: Athlone Press, 1966), p. 10; *History of The Times: The Twentieth Century Test 1884-1912*, written, edited and published by The Times of London (London: The Times, 1947). The only reference to Brinkley is on page 194.

22. *JWM*, 31 Jan. 1891. For earlier charges of isolation, see *JWM*, 21 May 1887.

23. Hoare, 'British journalists in Meiji Japan', pp. 21, 26; *Japan Times*, 29 October 1912; *Times*, 29 October 1912.

24. *Japan Punch* March 1885. *Punch*'s most famous comment on Brinkley dated from 1882: 'Left his Queen and Country to become a Japanese flunkey', *Japan Punch*, Oct. 1882. Punch regularly showed Brinkley dressed as a samurai.

25. E. B. Greene, *A New Englander in Japan* (Boston, Mass: Houghton, Mifflin and Co., 1927), pp. 284, 318-319; Nish, *The Anglo-Japanese Alliance*, p. 368.

26. William D. Wray, *Mitsubishi and the N.Y.K 1870-1914: Business Strategy in the Japanese Shipping Industry* (Cambridge, Mass., and London: Council on East Asian Studies, Harvard University, 1984), p. 443-44. *Who's Who in the Far East*, 1906-1907, noted Brinkley as a 'Foreign Adviser to Nippon Yusen Kisha'.

27. Sir Alfred East, *A British Artist in Meiji Japan*, edited by Sir Hugh Cortazzi (Brighton: In Print, 1991), pp. 64-65.

28. D'Anethan, *Fourteen Years of Diplomatic Life* pp. 411-412; Dallas Finn, 'Brinkley, Frank (1841-1912)', *Encyclopaedia of Japan* (Tokyo: Kodansha, 1982), I, 170-171.

29. Originally published in Tokyo by Sanseidō; reprinted as *Brinkley's Japanese Dictionary* (Cambridge: Heffer, 2 volumes 1963).

30. F. Brinkley, editor, *Japan described and illustrated by the Japanese* (Boston: J. B. Millet, 10 vols., 1897-1898).

NOTES

31. F. Brinkley, *Japan and China: their history, arts and literature* (London and Edinburgh: T. C. And E. C. Jack, 12 volumes, 1903-1904); the Japan section may have been issued as a separate set in the United States: F. Brinkley, *Japan: its history, arts and literature* (Boston: J. B. Miller Company, 8 volumes, 1901-1902); Capt. F. Brinkley, with the collaboration of Baron Kikuchi Dairoku, *A history of the Japanese people from the earliest times to the end of the Meiji era* (New York, London: Encyclopaedia Britannica Co., 1915).

32. Basil Hall Chamberlain, *Things Japanese: Being Notes on Various Subjects Connected with Japan* (London: John Murray; Yokohama: Kelly and Walsh, 5th. edition, 1905), pp. 67, 243. In this edition, there are numerous references to Brinkley's works under 'Books recommended'. In the edition entitled *Japanese Things* (Rutland, Vermont and Tokyo: Charles E. Tuttle Company, 1971), Brinkley's name lingers in the index, but the books referred to have all disappeared from the 'Books recommended' sections.

33. For the 1897 *Japan Times*, see M. Endo and F. Shimomura, editors, *Kokushi bunken kaisetsu: zoku* ('A collection of materials for national history: second series'), (Tokyo: Asakura shoten, 1965), pp. 437-438.

34. Yuzo Ota, *Basil Hall Chamberlain: Portrait of a Japanologist* (Richmond: Japan Library, 1998), p. 7; PRO30/33/11/7, Satow to F. V. Dickens.

Chapter 10 HAMISH ION *The Archdeacon and the Bishop: Alexander Croft Shaw, Edward Bickersteth, and Meiji Japan*

1. Reade to Truro, 6 October 1886. Archbishop Benson Papers, Lambeth Palace Library, volume 31 [hereafter cited as Benson Papers].
2. The vast majority of British Anglican missionaries working in Meiji Japan belonged to either the Church Missionary Society (CMS, Low Church) which had sent its first missionary to Nagasaki in 1869 or the Society for the Propagation of the Gospel in Foreign Parts (SPG, High Church) which started work in 1873. For a general historical survey of the British Protestant missionary movement in Japan, Korea, and Taiwan see A. H. Ion, *The Cross and the Rising Sun: Volume 2: The British Protestant Missionary Movement in Japan, Korea and Taiwan, 1865-1945* (Waterloo: Wilfrid Laurier University Press, 1993). Of very considerable value in terms of British Anglican missionary activity in Tokyo during the Meiji period is Cyril Hamilton Powles, *Victorian Missionaries in Meiji Japan: The Shiba Sect: 1873-1900* (Toronto: University of Toronto-York University Joint Centre on Modern East Asia, 1987). Helpful in revealing the differences between British Anglicans and other Christian missionary groups in Japan is Cyril Hamilton Powles, 'Foreign Missionaries and Japanese Culture in Late Nineteenth Century: Four Patterns of Approach', *The Northeast Asia Journal of Theology* (1969), pp. 14-28. A short but very useful overview is Helen Ballhatchet, 'British Missionaries in Meiji Japan', in Ian Nish, ed., *Britain & Japan: Biographical Portraits* (London: Japan Library, 1994), pp. 33-44. A brief account of British Protestant missionaries in Japan up to 1883 can be found in Grace Fox, *Britain and Japan 1858-1883* (Oxford: Clarendon Press, 1969), pp. 502-531. The standard Japanese language history of the Anglican Church in Japan remains Nippon Seikokai rekishi hensan iinkai, *Nippon Seikokai hyakunen shi* (Tokyo: Nippon Seikokai Kyomuin Bunsho Kyoku, 1959). A useful recent survey is the chapter by Ōe Mitsuro, 'Nippon Seikokai shi' in Dōshisha Daigaku Jinbun Kagaku Kenkyū Jo Hen, *Nihon Purotesutanto shokyoha shi no kenkyū* (Tokyo: Kyōbunkan, 1997), pp.17-73. Also highly useful are Tsukada Osamu, *Nippon Seikokai no keisei to kadai* (Tokyo: Seikokai Shuppan, 1979), and also by the same author, *Shoki Nippon Seikokai no keisei to Imai Judō* (Tokyo: Seikokai Shuppan, 1992).
3. For a brief biographical note about A. C. Shaw see Nihon Kirisutokyō rekishi Dai Jiten Henshū Iinkai. *Nihon Kirisutokō Rekishi Dai Jiten.* Tokyo: Kyōbunkan, 1988 [hereafter cited *NKRDJ*], p. 669. See also Cyril Hamilton Powles, 'Trinity's First Man to Japan', *Trinity* 9, no. 2 (1971), pp. 6-7. Of interest because of Shaw's key role in the establishment of St Andrew's Church is C. Kenneth Sansbury, *A History of St Andrew's Church, Tokyo (English Congregation) 1879-1939* (Tokyo: Sei Andorū Kyokai, 1940).
4. The other was William Ball Wright (1843-1912). Wright left Japan in 1882.
5. Charles F. Sweet, *New Life in the Oldest Empire* (London: SPCK, 1920), p. 107. See also Sansbury, p. 17.
6. For a short biographical note see *NKRDJ*, pp. 1154-1155. See also Gerald H. Anderson, *Biographical Dictionary of Christian Missions* (New York: Simon and Schuster Macmillan, 1998), p. 61; Samuel Bickersteth, *Life and Letters of Edward Bickersteth: Bishop of South Tokyo* (London: Sampson Low, Marston), 1899. See also May Bickersteth, *Japan As We Saw It* (London: Sampson Low, 1893). A. F. King and J. T. Imai, eds., *Edward Bickersteth, Missionary Bishop in Japan* (Tokyo: Kyobunkan, 1914).
7. For C. M. Williams see *NKRDJ*, p. 155. For a study of the American Church Mission in

Japan, see Henry St George Tucker, *The History of the Episcopal Church in Japan* (New York: Charles Scribner's Sons, 1938).

8. For a brief biographical note about Arthur Lloyd, see *NKRDJ*, p. 1521.

9. For Imai Judō (Toshimichi) see *NKRDJ*, pp.132B133. See also Tsukada Osamu, *Shoki Nippon Seikokai no keisei to Imai Judō* (Tokyuo: Seikokai Shuppan, 1992).

10. After his retirement from the University of Toronto, Professor Cyril Powles gave the author his file card collection of research notes on Japanese Christianity.This information is contained on a file card entitled 'The Shiba Sect: Victorian Missionaries in Meiji Japan 1870–1900: My Thesis (Conclusions).'

11. Tsukada Osamu, *Shoki Nippon Seikokai no keisei to Imai Judō*, p.84.

12. Among Lloyd's studies are *The Creed of Half Japan: Historical Sketches of Japanese Buddhism* (London: Smith Elder, 1911) and *The Wheat among the Tares: Studies of Buddhism in Japan* (London: Macmillan, 1908). Even though Lloyd's views of Buddhism must now be considered flawed, his books and also his many articles in the *Transactions of the Asiatic Society of Japan* (of which society he was an officer and active member) must be regarded as a significant pioneering effort However, Lloyd's most satisfactory book was his observations on Japanese society, chiefly that of Tokyo, entitled *Every-day Japan. Written after Twenty-five Years' Residence and Work in the Country* (London: Cassell, 1909).

13. See Toshio Yokoyama, *Japan in the Victorian Mind: A Study of Stereotyped Images of a Nation 1850-1880* (Basingstoke: The Macmillan Press, 1987). For a recent critical examination of the views of Lafcadio Hearn toward the Japanese especially in comparison with those of Basil Hall Chamberlain, see Yuzo Ota, *Basil Hall Chamberlain: Portrait of a Japanologist* (London: Japan Library, 1998), especially pp. 127-201.

14. For a discussion of this issue and its implications in regards to Japanese Anglican views of *tennosei*, see Tsukada Osamu, 'Nippon Seikokai kitōsho ni "Tennō no tame" no shō kitō no keifu,' *Kirisutokyo*, 25 (December 1983), pp. 69-92.

15. See Powles, *Victorian Missionaries in Meiji Japan*, pp. 99-103.

16. Sansbury, p. 5. The Church was destroyed in an earthquake on June 20 1894 and replaced by a wooden structure.

17. A. F. King, 'The New Temporary Church at Sakae Chō, Shiba,' *South Tokyo Diocesan Magazine*, VIII, 23 (April, 1904), pp. 14-15, p.15.

18. In an article written in 1891 dealing with summer climate of Karuizawa, C. G. Knott states that Karuizawa's history as a place where foreigners went 'dates from the year 1886, when the Venerable Archdeacon Shaw and Professor J. M. Dixon discovered its pecular merits.' See Cargill G. Knott, 'Notes on the Summer Climate of Karuizawa,' *Transactions of the Asiatic Society of Japan*, Series I, XIX (1891), pp. 565-577, p. 565. Shaw is buried in the cemetery of Karuizawa Nippon Seikokai Church.

19. Powles, *Victorian Missionaries in Meiji Japan*, p.62.

20. Sansbury, p. 2.

21. Shaw to Bullock, May 14 1874. Letters and Papers Bombay, Colombo, Labuan, North China, Victoria 1868-1874. United Society for the Propagation of the Gospel Archives. These archives were housed in Tufton Street, Westminster when they were consulted but have now moved to the Rhodes Library, Oxford.

22. *Nippon Seikokai hyakunen shi*, p.60. It can be assumed that it was more good manners in not wanting to disappoint Shaw rather than actual lasting Christian conviction which was the reason why Ozaki allowed him to be baptized.

23. Takako Shirai, 'Yukichi Fukuzawa and Early Missionaries in Japan,' *Japanese Friends of the Bodleian Newsletter*, Vol. 7 (Winter 1993/94), p. 4.

24. When Lloyd arrived in Japan, he had heavy debts in England to pay off. To teach at Keiō obviously helped him financially. In 1893 when he succeeded Walter Dening as the head of the English Department at Keiō, he apparently received a salary of ¥250 a month.

25. Shirai, 'Yukichi Fukuzawa and Early Missionaries in Japan,' p. 4.

26. The author wishes to thank Professor Cyril Powles for this information.

27. J. S. Motoda, *Nippon Seikokai shi* (Tokyo: Fukosha, 1910), p. 31.

28. Wright was responsible for opening Anglican work in Chiba Prefecture, see *Hyakunenshi*, p. 86.

29. Poole, who had been a Church Missionary Society missionary in India, was consecrated as the first British Anglican missionary bishop of Japan in 1883. Perhaps an unwise choice for he was already ill when he was consecrated, Poole died within two years. See *NKRDJ*, p. 1243.

30. Tsukada Osamu, *Shoki Nippon Seikokai no keisei to Imai Judō*, pp. 2-7.

31. For a biography of the Bishop E. H. Bickersteth see, Francis Keyes Aglionby, *The Life of Edward Henry Bickersteth: Bishop and Poet* (London: Longmans, Green, 1907).

32. Exeter to Benson, 23 September 1885. Benson Papers, volume 31.

33. S. A. Poole [Mrs. Bishop Poole] to Bishop Bickersteth [Exeter] 7 July 1885. Benson Papers,

volume 31. Mrs. Poole had written simply because one of Exeter's Epworth Tracts, AThe Master's Lesson' had been a great comfort to her terminally ill husband.
34. Exeter to Benson, 10 July 1885. Benson Papers, volume 31.
35. Edward Bickersteth to Exeter, 3 October 1885. Benson Papers volume 31.
36. Ibid.
37. Tucker to Benson, 2 November 1885. Benson Papers volume 31.
38. Exeter to Benson, 19 April 1883. Benson Papers volume 10.
39. Reade to Truro, 6 October 1885. Benson Papers volume 31.
40. Benson to Bickersteth. 20 October 1885. Benson Papers volume 31. For his acceptance, see Bickersteth to Benson, 21 October 1885.
41. Bickersteth to Benson, 21 June 1886. Benson Papers volume 41. The Presbyterian union that Bickersteth was referring to was that of the American and Scottish Presbyterian missions leading to the formation of the Nippon Kirisuto Kyokai.
42. Ibid.
43. Bickersteth to Benson, 21 September 1886. Benson Papers volume 41.
44. Ibid.
45. Henry St George Tucker, *The History of the Episcopal Church in Japan* (New York: Charles Scribner's Sons, 1938), p. 139.
46. Westcott to Benson, December 1886. Benson Papers volume 41.
47. Fenn to Benson, 6 December 1886. Benson Papers volume 41.
48. Extract of letter from A. B. Hutchinson dated 22 February 1887. Benson Papers volume 52.
49. Bickersteth to Fenn, 11 March 1887. Benson Papers volume 52. Bickersteth was aware that there might be difficulties in the future concerning the Japanese Prayer Book for he pointed out to Benson in August that the CMS Committee was opposed to the insertion of the American Consecration Prayer in the Communion office into the Prayer Book as an alternative form. See Bickersteth to Benson, 26 August 1887. Benson Papers volume 65.
50. Bickersteth to Fenn, 11 March 1887. Benson Papers volume 52.
51. Ibid.
52. Bickersteth to Benson, 26 August 1887. Memorandum on the formation of an Ecclesiastical Province in China and Japan. Benson Papers volume 65.
53. Westcott to Benson, May 28 1888. Benson Papers volume 52.
54. Bickersteth to Fenn, 11 March 1887. Benson Papers volume 52.
55. Ibid.
56. Bickersteth to Benson, 10 March 1887. Benson Papers volume 52.
57. From 1900 these two missions were formally associated with the SPG.
58. Alfreda Arnold, compiler, *Church Work in Japan* (London: Society for the Propagation of the Gospel in Foreign Parts, 1905), p. 62.
59. For the names of those who joined St Andrew's, see Arnold, *Church Work in Japan*, pp. 64-65.
60. For his part Bickersteth believed that his marriage would not cause any problems for St Andrew's for his many absences from Tokyo had meant that his headship was only nominal. See Bickersteth to Benson, 14 July 1893. Benson Papers volume 125.
61. Bickersteth to Benson, 26 August 1887. Benson Papers volume 65.
62. Cyril Hamilton Powles, *Victorian Missionaries in Meiji Japan*, p. 79.
63. *The Canadian Church Magazine and Mission News*, Vol. 8 (November 1894), p. 242.
64. Bickersteth to Benson, 28 November 1892. Benson Papers volume 113.
65. Ibid. Enclosure: Memorandum on the increase of the Missionary Episcopate in Japan.
66. Shaw to Benson, 11 October 1895. Benson Papers volume 141.
67. York to Benson, 4 January 1896. Benson Papers volume 141.
68. Ibid.

Chapter 11 OLIVE CHECKLAND *Henry Dyer of The Imperial College of Engineering, Tokyo, and afterwards, in Glasgow*

1. For a broader treatment and more detail see O.Checkland, *Britain's Encounter with Meiji Japan 1868-1912*, (Basingstoke and London: Macmillan 1989). This book is also available in Japanese from Hōsei University Press, Tokyo. See also the University of Strathclyde Website, http://www.cs.strath.ac.uk/rbh/hd/index.html
2. With thanks to Brian Lambie, Biggar, Lanarkshire.
3. Anon, *Appointment of Professor Lewis D.B.Gordon*, (Glasgow: University of Glasgow, Faculty of Engineering, no date). Hugh B.Sutherland, *Rankine, his life and times*, (London: Institution of Civil Engineers, 1973).
4. D.A.Low, *The Whitworth Book*, (London, New York: Longmans Green & Co, 1926), p.34.

5. The University of Glasgow introduced the Bachelor of Science degree in 1873, Henry Dyer (and Thomas Urquhart) were the first graduates of the University to obtain this degree.
6. With thanks to Yamao Shin'ichi, Roppongi, Tokyo, for his help.
7. Papers relating to the Imperial College of Engineering, Tokyo, are held in the University of Tokyo; in the Dyer Collection at the Mitchell Library, Glasgow; the library of the University of Glasgow, and the archives of the University of Glasgow.
8. Copy of Marriage Certification, 23 May 1874, with thanks to Robin Hunter.
9. See the *Japan Weekly Mail*, 16 July 1882, with thanks to Katoh Shoji.
10. *Introduction of Western Culture into Japan in the Age of her Modernisation*, supplement to *Tokyo Municipal News*, 1967, p.7.
11. W. Ayrton, Report in H. Dyer, *General Report on Imperial College of Engineering by the Principal*, (Tokyo: Imperial College of Engineering, 1877).
12. E. Divers, Report in H. Dyer, *General Report on Imperial College of Engineering by the Principal*, (Tokyo: Imperial College of Engineering, 1877).
13. J. Perry, *Central*, Vol.7, (1910), p.708.
14. H. Dyer, *General Report on Imperial College of Engineering by the Principal*, (Tokyo: Imperial College of Engineering, 1877), section on Akabane Engineering Works, p.39.
15. Akabane Engineering Works, copy in the Cabinet Library, Tokyo.
16. C. Whitney, *Clara's Diary*, (Tokyo and New York: Kodansha,1981), p.184.
17. See B.Baker, *The Forth Bridge*, London, 1882.
18. Shida's Correspondence with Kelvin, Kelvin's papers, S126-S130, University of Cambridge Library.
19. J.F.C.Conn, *Department of Naval Architecture and Ocean Engineering, the University of Glasgow, 1883-1983*, (Glasgow: Marine Publications International Ltd., 1983). And see H.Dyer, *Testimonials*, Court Papers, University of Glasgow Archives.
20. See H.Dyer, *Testimonials*, pp.31-32 and *Glasgow Herald*, 15May 1886.
21. See A.R.Buchan (ed.), *A Goodly Heritage, A Hundred Years of Civil Engineering at Strathclyde University, 1887-1987*, (Glasgow: Dept. of Civil Engineering, University of Strathclyde, 1987).
22. For details of Henry Dyer's publications see Select Bibliography in O.Checkland, *Britain's Encounter with Meiji Japan*, (1989) and the University of Strathclyde, Henry Dyer Website, http://www.cs.strath.ac.uk/obh/hd/index.html
23. H.Dyer, *The Evolution of Industry*, pp.274-275.
24. H.Dyer, *The Evolution of Industry*, Chapter 6, pp.110-123.
25. Glasgow University Archives, Court Minutes, 1901.
26. See Andrew Cobbing, 'Itō Hirubumi in Britain' in this volume.
27. H.M. Matheson, *Memorials of Hugh M. Matheson* (London, 1899).

Chapter 12 IAN NISH *Aōki Shūzō (1844-1914)*

1. Sakane Yoshihisa, *Aōki Shūzō jiden* (Tokyo: Tōyō Bunko, 1970), pp. 117-227 .
2. S.D. Brown and Akiko Hirota, *The Diary of Kido Takayoshi*, 2 vols. (Tokyo: Tokyo University Press, 1985), vol. 2, pp. 199, 301, 317
3. Ulrich Wattenberg in Ian Nish (ed.), *The Iwakura Mission* (Folkestone: Japan Library, 1998), p. 120
4. Sakane, *Aōki Shūzō jiden*, p. 73ff; *Gaimushō no 100 nen*, 2 vols (Tokyo : Hara Shobo, 1969), vol. 1, p. 335
5. Sakane, *Aōki Shūzō jiden*, p. 111ff
6. Andrew Fraser et al. (ed.), *Japan's Early Parliaments, 1890-1905* (London : Routledge, 1995), pp. 1, 7; Sakane, *Aōki Shūzō jiden*, ch. 23; Ian Nish, 'The Japanese Constitution of 1889' in *International Studies* (STICERD, LSE), 208(1989), pp. 1-11
7. Ian Nish (ed.), *Asia, 1860-1914*, vol. 3 Japanese Treaty Revision, 1878-94 in the series *British Documents on Foreign Affairs*, (Maryland: University Publications of America, 1989), (hereafter cited as 'BDOFA'); Sakane, *Aōki Shūzō jiden*, p. 172ff
8. Sakane, *Aōki Shūzō jiden*, chs. 17-19, indicates how seriously Aoki took this incident
9. *BDOFA*, vol. 3, no. 111
10. Hugh Cortazzi and Gordon Daniels (eds), *Great Britain and Japan: Themes and Personalities* (London : Routledge, 1991), p. 10
11. *BDOFA*, vol. 3, nos 127, 132-6; Ian Nish, 'J.H. Gubbins' in Nish (ed.), *Britain and Japan : Biographical Portraits*, vol. 2, (Folkestone: Japan Library, 1997), pp. 108-12; Sakane, p. 201ff
12. On Aoki's reluctance, see Sakane, *Aōki Shūzō jiden*, pp. 218-19. *BDOFA*, vol. 3, nos 150-2
13. Ikei Masaru (ed.), *Uchida Yasuya* (Tokyo: Kajima, 1969), pp. 17-20
14. Ian Nish, 'Japan Reverses the Unequal Treaties' in *Journal of Oriental Studies* (Hongkong), 13(1975), 137-45; *BDOFA*, vol. 3, nos 185, 256, 259

15. Mutsu Munemitsu, *Kenkenroku*, trans. Gordon Berger (Tokyo: Tokyo University Press, 1982), pp. 238-40
16. *Meiji 'news' jiten, 1893-97* (Tokyo: Mainichi Communications, 1985), p. 276
17. *Nihon gaikō bunsho, 1894*, no. 720. I am grateful to Dr Janet Hunter for elucidating the financial equivalent of the publicity budget.
18. Sakane, *Aōki Shūzō jiden*, p. 238; Mutsu, *Kenkenroku*, p. 283
19. *Gaimushō no 100-nen*, vol. 1, pp. 340-7 deals with the exchange of Aōki-Mutsu messages in great detail
20. Sakane, *Aōki Shūzō jiden*, ch. 21
21. Tokutomi Iichirō, *Kōshaku Yamagata Aritomo-den*, 3 vols (Tokyo: Minyusha, 1933), vol. 3, pp. 342-3
22. George Lensen, *Korea and Manchuria between Russia and Japan, 1895-1904: Observations of Sir Ernest Satow*, (Tallahassee: Diplomatic Press, 1966).
23. Sakane, *Aōki Shūzō jiden*, p. 330. Aōki refers to 'sengo shōri', thereby implying that he saw it as a war. *Meiji 'news' jiten, 1898-1902*, pp. 348-51; *Yamagata-den*, vol. 3, pp. 413-14
24. *Nihon gaikō bunsho, 1900*, pp. 51-4
25. F.S.G. Piggott, *Broken Thread* (Aldershot : Gale and Polden, 1950), p. 30
26. MacDonald to Grey, 9 Jan. 1906 in (British) Foreign Office 371/85 (Public Record Office, Kew)
27. Akira Iriye, *Pacific Estrangement: Japanese and American Expansionism, 1897-1911* (Cambridge: Harvard UP, 1972); and R.A. Esthus, *Theodore Roosevelt and Japan* (Seattle: Washington UP, 1966), p. 145, 178
28. Esthus, pp. 205-8
29. Tokyo embassy report for the year 1907 in Foreign Office 371/472
30. Sakane, *Aōki Shūzō jiden*, ch. 27 and appendix
31. *Gaimushō no 100-nen*, vol. 1, p. 335
32. BDOFA, vol. 9, p. 172
33. R.H.P. Mason, 'Foreign Affairs Debates, 1890-1' in Fraser, *op. cit.*, p. 180

Chapter 13 IAN GOW *The Douglas Mission (1873-79) and Meiji Naval Education*

1. The best treatment in English of Bakumatsu naval training is Cornwall, Peter G, *The Meiji Navy: Training in an Age of Change* Ph.D., (University of Michigan, 1970) pp. 58-74.
2. Perry, John C, 'Great Britain and the Emergence of Japan as a Naval Power' *Monumenta Nipponica*, Vol. 21, (1966), pp 305-322. p317
3. *op.cit.* p309. The most important work on the IJN in English is D.C. Evans and Mark R. Peattie *Kaigun: Strategy, Tactics and Technology in the Imperial Japanese Navy* (Annapolis, Md: Naval Institute Press, 1997), p.12 erroneously refers to the Tracey mission as a 'two man mission' in fact there were 17.
4. Shinohara, Hiroshi, *Nihon Kaigun Oyatoi Gaijin*, (Tokyo: 1988) p.94.
5. *Ibid.*, p.101.
6. Jones, Hilary *Live Machines: Hired Foreigners and Meiji Japan* (Tenterden, Kent: Paul Norbury Publications 1980) p.2.
7. Shinohara, *op.cit.* devotes 6 pages to Hawes (pp. 121-127) and 3 for James (pp. 156-158).
8. Shinohara, *op.cit.* pp. 114-116.
9. Boeicho Boei Kenshujo Senshishitsu *Daihonei Kaigunbu: Rengo Kantai* I, (Tokyo, 1975). p.6 and Ikeda Kiyoshi *Kaigun to Nihon* (Tokyo: Chuo Koronsha, 1983) p.148.
10. Shinohara, *op.cit.* pp. 119-120.
11. Chamberlain, Basil Hall *Things Japanese* (London: Kegan, Paul and Trench, 1890) p.349.
12. Shinohara, *op.cit.* pp. 149-150.
13. Shinohara, *op.cit.* pp. 164-165 .
14. On Douglas see his son Archibald C, 'The Genesis of Japan's Navy', *Japan Society of London: Transactions and Proceedings*, Vol. 36, (1938, pp. 19-28, and also his *Life of Admiral Sir Archibald Lucius Douglas RN GCB* (Totnes, Devon: Mortimer Brothers, 1938) See also his granddaughter Elizabeth Kellock 'The Douglas Mission and the making of the Japanese Navy' *Japan Digest*, Oct. 1990 pp 38-42. I am also deeply grateful to Mrs Kellock supplying me with personal letters as well as her unpublished manuscript on Douglas (Hereafter the Kellock papers). The best treatments in Japanese are Ikeda *Kaigun to Nihon* pp. 149-156 and his revised Ikeda *Nihon no Kaigun* Vol 1 Tokyo: 1987 pp. 110-120 and Shinohara *op.cit.* pp. 163-188.
15. *Ibid.*, Shinohara p.181
16. Ikeda (1987) *op.cit.* p.156
17. *Ibid.*, p149.

18. *Ibid.*, p.149.
19. *Ibid.*, p.149
20. Ikeda (1987) *op.cit.* p.114.
21. *Ibid.*, p.114.
22. Ikeda (1983) *op.cit.* p.149.
23. *Ibid.*, p.150.
24. Jones, *op.cit.* pp. 85-86.
25. Douglas, *op.cit. A Life of*. . . p.76.
26. Kellock, *op.cit.* p.42.
27. Douglas, *op.cit. A Life of* . . . p.79.
28. I am indebted to Dr Gordon Daniels, the authority on Sir Harry Parkes for this insight.
29. Douglas, *op.cit. A Life of* . . . pp. 73-74.
30. Ikeda, *op.cit.* p.148.
31. Shinohara, *op.cit.* p.86 and Evans and Peattie, *op.cit.* p.12 and p.33 .
32. John C. Perry *Great Britain and the Imperial Japanese Navy 1858-1905* Ph.D. Harvard 1963 makes extensive use of the Ingles papers.
33. Perry (1966), *op.cit.* p.315
34. Evans and Peattie, *op.cit.* p.12.
35. Shinohara, *op.cit.* pp. 155-156. Interestingly a number of British recipients appear including some who worked for the Navy Ministry as well as those who worked in the Naval educational establishments. Douglas received, however, a higher award than any except for the Frenchman Emile Bertin, who also received the Order of the Rising Sun First Class. Ingles received the Order of the Sacred Treasure Second Class and John Matthew James the Order of the Rising Sun Second Class.
36. *Ibid.*, p.163.
37. Kellock Papers, *op.cit.*
38. Cited in Perry (1966), *op.cit.* p.305.
39. *Ibid.*, p.305.

Chapter 14 PHILIP TOWLE *British Naval and Military Observers of the Russo-Japanese War*

1. Foreign Office papers, Public Record Office, London, FO/46/578, Pakenham letter to MacDonald, 16 April 1904.
2. For a recent analysis of the Geoben and Breslau incident see Geoffrey Miller, *Superior Force: The Conspiracy behind the Escape of Geoben and Breslau*, Hull: University of Hull Press, 1996.
3. A complete list of attachés and language officers up to 1924 is contained in M.D. Kennedy, *The Military Side of Japanese Life*, (London: Constable, 1924), Appendix, p.357 passim.
4. Noel papers, National Maritime Museum, NOE/4-5b , Lord Selborne to Admiral Noel, 13 April 1904 and Troubridge to Noel, 14 April 1904.
5. War Office papers, Public Record Office, WO/106/38, Gerard report of 30 March 1905.
6. Ian Hamilton, *The Happy Warrior: A Life of General Sir Ian Hamilton*, (London: Cassell, 1966).
7. Kitchener papers, HH 30, Hamilton to Kitchener, 20 September 1904.
8. Aylmer Haldane Papers, National Library of Scotland, 2070/2/Box 2, Volume l, Haldane to his mother, 29 March and 27 April 1904. For Haldane see also General Sir Aylmer Haldane, *A Soldier's Saga*, (Edinburgh and London: William Blackwood, 1948).
9. FO/46 582 MacDonald to the Foreign Office, 1 and 15 February 1904; FO/46/578 MacDonald to the Foreign Office, 8 May 1904.
10. G. Ogawa, *Expenditures of the Russo-Japanese War*, (New York: Oxford University Press, 1923), p. 94.
11. Kitchener papers, H 23, Hamilton to Kitchener, 22 July 1904 and H 32 Hamilton to Kitchener 15 October 1904.
12. Haldane papers, 2070/1 Box la/ Volume 1, diary entry for 15 June 1904.
13. Loc cit, diary entry for 6 July 1904 and FO/46/582, MacDonald to the Foreign Office; Lionel James, *Times of Stress*, (London: John Murray, 1929), pp. 6 and 7.
14. Roberts papers, 7101/23/52, Nicholson to Roberts, 20 August 1904; Kitchener papers, HH 30, Hamilton to Kitchener, 20 September 1904.
15. Kitchener papers, HH 27, Hamilton to Rawlinson, 25 August 1904.
16. Hamilton papers, 25/12 Hamilton to his wife, 31 December 1904; Max Hoffmann, *War Diaries and Others Papers*, (London: Martin Secker, 1929), p.13.
17. On Thacker see the Wilkinson papers, Nicholson to Wilkinson, 22 September 1904;J.M. Hitsman and M. Morton, "Canada's first Military Attaché", *Military Affairs*, October 1970; Kitchener papers, HH 30, Hamilton to Kitchener 23 September and 5 October 1904. On Hoad

see FO/46/579, MacDonald to the Foreign Office, 22 September 1904.
18. *The Army and Navy Gazette*, 16 March and 25 March 1905. Hutton papers, 50082, Hutton letter of 19 April 1904; Balfour papers, 4970, Brodrick to Balfour, 14 February and 17 June 1903.
19. General Sir Montagu Gerard, *Leaves from the Diary of a Sportsman and Soldier*, (London: John Murray, 1903).
20. W.H.H.Waters, *Secret and Confidential*, (London: John Murray, 1926), pp. 28-29.
21. Roberts papers 7101/23/53. Probyn to Roberts, 18 July 1904; Waters, *Russia Then and Now*, (London: John Murray, 1935), p.188.
22. Kitchener papers, HH16 Gerard to Kitchener, 1 June 1904; see also G.H.G. Mockler and H.C.Holman, *Confidential Report on the Russo-Japanese War*, War Office Library; WO/106/38, Gerard report of 13 August 1904.
23. WO/106/38, Home's letters of 3,7 and 9 August 1904. Holman was to achieve great distinction during the British intervention in south Russia during the 1920s.
24. Waters, *Secret and Confidential*, p.279 passim.
25. For Gerard's reports see WO/106/38 and WO/106/39. For praise for him from the correspondents and the other attachés see F. McCormick, *The Tragedy of Russia in Pacific Asia*, (London: Grant Richards, 1909), Volume, 2, p.298. McCormick greatly admired Gerard's courage and kindness.
26. Sir Julian Corbett's best known work is *Some Principles of Maritime Strategy* which was edited by Dr E.J. Grove and reissued by Brasseys, London in 1988 and *England in the Seven Years War*, which was reissued by Greenwood Press, London and California in 1992.
27. See the report by Birkbeck in *British Officers Reports on the Russo-Japanese War*, Volume 2, pp. 233 and 256 passim; WO/33/337 report by Home.
28. *British Officers Reports*, Volume 2, p.177.
29. Mockler and Holman, *Confidential Report*. WO/33/337 reports by Home and Waters; WO/ 106/38 , report by Gerard, 9 September 1904; Kitchener papers, HH 42, undated letter from Hamilton to Kitchener.
30. Jon Tetsuro Sumida, *In Defence of Naval Supremacy: Finance, Technology and British Naval Policy 1889-1914*, (London and New York: Routledge, 1993).
31. *Naval Necessities*, Admiralty Library, Volume 2.
32. Noel papers, NOE/8/b Troubridge report of 20 February 1904.
33. ADM/1/7775, Pakenham report on the battle of 10 August 1904.
34. *Half Yearly Report on Progress in Naval Gunnery* Number 9, Admiralty Library, July 1907.
35. ADM/1/7775, Pakenham report on the battle of 10 August; *Printed Attachés' Reports*, Volume 3, Jackson report of 6 May 1905.
36. A.T.Mahan, 'Reflections Historic and Other Suggested by the Battle of the Sea of Japan', *United States Naval Institute Proceedings*, June 1906. See also W.D.Pulleston, *Mahan; His Life and Works*, (London: Jonathan Cape, 1939).
37. Angus Hamilton, *Korea*, (London: William Heinemann, 1904), p.130 passim.
38. Quoted in Philip Towle, 'The debate on wartime censorship in Britain 1902-1914' in B.Bond and J. Roy (Eds.), *War and Society*, Volume 1, (London: Croom Helm, 1976).
39. Sir Ian Hamilton, *A Staff-Officer's Scrapbook During the Russo-Japanese War*, (London: Edward Arnold, 1906), p.10 passim.
40. Hamilton papers, King's College, London, 7/3/17/2 and 7/3/17/3, Hamilton to L.S.Amery, 20 July 1905. See also FO/371/179, report by Sir Claude MacDonald on a public speech he gave in Japan in March 1906. See also FO/181/823 for reports on Japanese behaviour during and after the Russo-Japanese War.
41. Kennedy, *The Military Side of Japanese Life*.
42. F.S.G.Piggott, *Broken Thread, An Autobiography*, (Aldershot: Gale and Polden, 1950).
43. CAB/38/26/3, 'The Historical Section' by the Secretary of the Committee of Imperial Defence, 30 January 1914.

Chapter 15 SAMMY I. TSUNEMATSU *Natsume Sōseki and the Pre-Raphaelites — The depiction of Ophelia in Sōseki's The Three-Cornered World—*

This chapter is revised and expanded version of my 'Natsume Sōseki and Pre-Raphaelites', Sōseki Museum News Letter Spring 1994 issue. I am grateful to those who made various comments, especially Dr Ingar Sigrun Brodey, co-translator of Natsume Sōseki *Travels in Manchuria and Korea*, (Folkestone: Global Books, forthcoming).
1. Sammy Tsunematsu, 'Kochira Rondon Sōseki Kinenkan' (Sōseki Museum Calling), *Chukō Bunko*, 1998, p.104.
2. Natsume Sōseki, 'Bungakuron' Preface to *The Criticism of Literature* 1907
3. Yoko Matsuoka McClellan, *Magomusume kara mita Sōseki* ('Sōseki seen by his grand-

daughter'), (Tokyo: Shincho-Sha, 1995), p.19.
4.   Natsume Sōseki, *Botchan*, 1906 p.69 translated by Umeji Sasaki, 1968
5.   Nstsume Sōseki, *Meian* (1917), p.94 *Light and Darkness* translated by V.H.Viglielmo, (New York: Putnam 1971).
6.   Natsume Sōseki, Letter 1901
7.   Natsume Sōseki, *Watashino Kojinshuji*, 1914 'My Individualism', translated by Jay Rubin, *Monumenta Nipponica* Vol. XXXIV, I (Spring), p.32
8.   Beongcheon Yu, Preface to *Natsume Sōseki* New York: Twayne Publisher 1969
9.   Kyoko Natsume, *Sōseki no Omoide* 1928, Recollections of Sōseki
10. Natsume Sōsekii|i|i|i|i|i|i|i|i|i|i|i|i|i|i|i|ƙ, vol.16, 1967 p.544 'Yoga Kusamakura'
11. Natsume Sōseki, Kusamakura, *Sōseki Zenshu* vol.2 1966 p.406 *The Three-Cornered World*, translated by Alan Turney, (New York: Putnam, 1965).
12. Natsume Sōseki, *Sōseki Zenshu* vol.2 p.173
13. Natsume Sōseki, *Sōseki Zenshu*, 1966, vol.2
14. Eto Jun, *Sōseki to Sono Jidai*, Tokyo: Shinchosha, 1970 vol.2 p.9
15. W. Holman Hunt, *Pre-Raphaelitism and the Pre-Raphaelite Brotherhood*, p.262, vol.I, 1967
16. John Guille Millais, *The Life and Letters of Sir Everett Millais*, vol.1, p.30, (London: Methuen, 1899).
17. W.Holman Hunt, *Pre-Raphaelitism and the Pre-Raphaelite Brotherhood*, vol.I, p.72, 1967
18. W.Holman Hunt, *Pre-Raphaelitism and the Pre-Raphaelite Brotherhood*, vol.I, p.263, 1967
19. John Guille Millais, *The Life and Letters of Sir Everett Millais*, vol.1, p.119, 1899
20. Henry Stapylton manuscripts Ref.2473/14/12 at Surrey Record Office
21. Henry Stapylton manuscripts Ref.2508/5/1 at Surrey Record Office

Further readings
Toshiyuki Takamiya and Andrew Armour, *Kairoko: A Dirge* 1985
Takehisa Iijima and James M. Vardaman, Jr. *The World of Natsume Sōseki* 1987
Peter Milward and Kii Nakano, trans. and edit. *The Tower of London* (Brighton: In Print, 1992).
Van C. Gessel, *Three Modern Novelists – Sōseki, Tanizaki, Kawabata* (New York, Tokyo: Kodansha, 1993).
Angela Yu, *Chaos and Order in the Works of Natsume Sōseki*, 1998

Chapter 16 TADASHI KURAMATSU *A Great Ordinary Man: Saitō Makoto (1858-1936) and Anglo-Japanese Relations*

1.   The author would like to thank Professor Ian Nish who kindly read an earlier version of this paper, for his valuable comments and generous encouragement. The author is also grateful to Anne Hemingway, Madeleine Neave and Dr Thomas Otte for their help with this essay. Unless otherwise noted, this article is based on a four-volume (just under 3,500 pages) official biography of Saitō, *Shishaku Saitō Makoto-den*, published posthumously in 1941. Though it is not unlike other official biographies in Japan, in that it is devoid of anything critical or negative about the subject, it makes full use of Saitō's diary (which he probably started as a student at the Naval Academy and sometimes kept in English) and his papers (he kept almost all correspondence), thus adding more credibility. Most of his papers and diary are deposited at the National Diet Library, Tokyo. For those who are under time-constraint, there is S. Aritake, *Saitō Makoto* (Tokyo, 1958), which summarizes the official biography in less than 300 pages.
2.   Mr George Caiger who, we understand, taught English to Saitō at one point regarded him 'one of the most pro-British Japanese in the 1930s'. The author is indebted to Professor Nish for this information.
3.   Takano (1804-51) who was a student at P.F. von Siebold's Narutaki-juku in Nagasaki was prosecuted for writing *Yume-monogatari* (The Story of a Dream) in 1838, arguing against the Edo government's decision to fire at an American ship *Morrison*, which the Dutch mistakenly communicated to the Japanese as a British ship. See W.G. Beasley, *Great Britain and the Opening of Japan 1834-1858* pbk edition (Folkestone: Japan Library 1995), pp.25-8, 34-5.
4.   Gotō (1857-1929) was a doctor by training, having studied for two years in Germany. He was the first President of the Manchurian Railway (1905), the first President of the Railway Agency (1908). He also served as Communication, Home and Foreign Minister. In 1924 he became again the first President of the forerunner of NHK and is called 'father of railway and broadcasting in Japan'.
5.   It was renamed *kaigun heigakkō* in 1876.
6.   The author would like to thank Mr Kiyoshi Kikuchi, the Director of the Saitō Makoto Memorial Museum, for the help given during his visit to the museum, which is located at Saitō's birthplace.

7. An all-steel ship built in Britain in 1878 with 3,777-ton displacement.
8. At the time there were only two naval attaché posts in existence, one to Britain and the other to Russia, both being established in 1880. Thereafter, China (1887), Korea (1887), France (1888), Italy (1889) and Germany (1890). Naval attachés in London usually held the rank of Captain.
9. After enjoying Niagara Falls with the Prince and others, on its way to New York, the train collided with another and Saitō was trapped in his compartment and barely escaped. Saitō started to celebrate the day – 22 May – as his second birthday thereafter.
10. He became Prime Minister in 1888.
11. In October 1887 Vice-Admiral Kabayama Sukenori, the Vice-Minister of the Navy, came to the United States on another learning tour to Western countries. Once again Saitō acted as a guide and took the party to the navy yard, ammunition factories, etc. Most importantly, among the party was Lieutenant-Commander Yamamoto Gonbei who would later be the major influence in Saitō's career.
12. It consisted of six cruisers: *Takachiho*, *Fuso*, *Yamato*, *Katsuragi*, *Musashi* and *Naniwa*. In January 1890 *Musashi* was replaced by *Takao*.
13. On 5 February 1892 Saitō married Nire Haruko, a daughter of Vice-Admiral Nire Kagenori through the good offices of Captain Yamamoto Gonbei.
14. Subsequently on 8 July 1895 the House of Lords ruled in favour of the Japanese and ordered that all the costs be paid by P & O. The matter was eventually settled out of court and P & O agreed to pay £10,000 compensation. It should be noted, though, that the ruling was only on the technical issue of whether P & O could counter-sue or not and it had already taken nearly three years.
15. For the incident see Kiyoshi Ikeda, 'The Silent Admiral: Tōgō Heihachirō (1848-1934) and Britain' in I. Nish (ed.), *Britain and Japan: Biographical Portraits*, (Folkestone: Japan Library, 1994), pp.111-2.
16. He had been educated at Cambridge and was regarded as 'pro-British'. I. Nish, *The Anglo-Japanese Alliance: The Diplomacy of Two Island Empires 1894-1907* 2nd Ed. (London: Athlone Press, 1985), p.13 n.2. He was later sent to Britain during the period of the Russo-Japanese War to cultivate good feelings towards Japan. See *Ibid.*, pp.284-6, 304 and Appendix F.
17. Asked by Saigō, Saitō visited Mutsu for a briefing. The latter was ill-disposed and lying in his bed: 'Since I was close to him I spoke to him rather unreservedly, saying "I don't have to go, do I?" to which he replied, "since this was decided at a Cabinet meeting you have no alternative but to go"... Then Vice-Minister Hayashi Tadasu came. He came to discuss [with Mutsu] how to declare war against China and he seemed puzzled by the outspoken way I was talking to the Minister, not knowing the Minister and I were intimate.' Japan and China both declared war on 1 August.
18. The resignation was, though, mainly to take responsibility for its Home Minister's having heavily interfered with the election.
19. Cf. I. Gow, 'Admiral Katō Kanji: Heretic, Hero, or the Unorthodox in Pursuit of an Orthodox Naval Policy' in B. McKercher & A.H. Ion (eds), *Military Heretics: The Unorthodox in Policy and Strategy* (Westport, 1994), pp.143-64.
20. For a description of annual dinners in its early days see H. Cortazzi, 'The Japan Society: A Hundred-Year History' in H. Cortazzi & G. Daniels (eds), *Britain and Japan 859-1991: Themes and Personalities* (London: Routledge, 1991), pp.8-13.
21. See Cortazzi, pp.11-2; S. Lee (ed.), *Dictionary of National Biography* Second Supplement Vol.I (London, 1912), pp.58-60.
22. Saitō was given a Jubilee Memorial Medal.
23. The maximum drought of a ship allowed by the regulation was twenty-five feet and seven inches, while *Fuji* drew over twenty-six feet when it was loaded with a thousand-ton coal.
24. The three cruisers of the same class, *Matsushima*, *Hashidate* and *Itsukushima* were named after the famous *sankei* (three scenic spots) in Japan. The design was done by a Frenchman Emile Bertin.
25. Admiral Nomura Kichisaburō, who at one time served as Saitō's secretary, later reminisced that Saitō's policy statements often 'left unsaid 20% of the statements prepared for him'. Ikeda Kiyoshi, *Nihon no kaigun* Vol.2 (Tokyo, 1993), p.35.
26. See Nish, *The Anglo-Japanese Alliance*, pp.251-3.
27. Renamed as *Kasuga* and *Nisshin*, respectively.
28. The effort to keep it secret was such that Saitō with his wife went to a dinner held by the US Military Attaché on 4 February so as not to give a clue to foreign representatives.
29. See, for example, Ikeda, 'Tōgō Heihachirō', pp.115-9. Also see J.S. Corbett, *Maritime Operations in the Russo-Japanese War, 1904-1905* 2 Vols (Annapolis, 1994).
30. For example, see Captain Jackson's note of his conversation with Saitō, n.d.[1905], ADM1/7840, PRO, Kew. Also see P. Towle, 'British Observers of the Russo-Japanese War', *Aspects of the Russo-Japanese War* LSE: STICERD International Studies Discussion Paper, No.IS/98/351 (July

1998), pp.23–34, and the revised and expanded version in this volume.
31. The date became his 'third birthday'.
32. For the Conference and background of Saitō's appointment see T. Kuramatsu, 'Japan and the Geneva Naval Conference of 1927: Preparations for the Conference, December 1926 to June 1927', *The Navy in Interwar Japan* LSE: STICERD International Studies Discussion Paper, No.IS/96/311 (July 1996), pp.11–42; S. Asada, 'From Washington to London: The Imperial Japanese Navy and the Politics of Naval Limitation, 1921-1930', E. Goldstein & J. Maurer (eds), *The Washington Conference, 1921-22: Naval Rivalry, East Asian Stability and the Road to Pearl Harbor* (London, 1994), pp.162-9.
33. When first asked by the Prime Minister Hara to go to Washington, Katō recommended Saitō instead. Entries of 24 & 25 Aug. 1921, Hara Keiichirō (ed.), *Hara Kei Nikki* Vol.5 (Tokyo, 1965), p.428.
34. Tilley to FO, 7 Apr. 1927, W4032/61/98, FO371/12667, PRO Kew. Frank Ashton-Gwatkin of the Far Eastern department also commented that it was 'a well-chosen delegation'. Note by Ashton-Gwatkin, 6 May 1927, W4032/61/98, FO371/12667. Their American counterparts agreed: 'There is probably no more highly respected man in Japanese public life today than Viscount Saito, and his attitude has, in the past, been friendly towards the United States.' Memorandum, unsigned [Western European Affairs Division], 31 Mar. 1927, 500.A15a1/163, RG59, National Archives, Washington, DC.
35. According to Ashton-Gwatkin, 'The Japanese believe in big battalions at Conferences. It gives them confidence; it is good training for their younger diplomats etc.; and they like a joy ride at Government expense.' Note by Ashton-Gwatkin, 2 June 1927, W4735/61/98, FO371/12667
36. She was Ineko, a daughter of Yamamoto Gombei.
37. *Nihon gaikō bunsho: Junevu kaigun gunbi seigen kaigi*, (Tokyo: Ministry of Foreign Affairs, 1982), pp.54-5. One of the chief delegates, Ishii, was critical of the Navy's pro-British stance and ordered strict neutrality. Ishii Kikujirō, *Gaikō zuiso*, (Tokyo, 1967), pp.42-3.
38. Sir Austen Chamberlain was the Foreign Secretary.
39. Caroline Bridgeman to Maurice Bridgeman, 20 June 1937, 4629/1/1927/47, Bridgeman Papers, Shropshire Records & Research Centre, Shrewsbury.
40. P. Williamson, *The Modernisation of Conservative Politics: The Diaries and Letters of William Bridgeman, 1904-1935* (London, 1989), P.206.
41. Asada, p.164.
42. L.G. Wickham (ed.), *Dictionary of National Biography* 1931-1940 (London, 1949), p.670.
43. Both served as C-in-C, China Station: Admiral Sir Arthur Moore, 1906-8 and Admiral of the Fleet Sir Hedworth Meux, 1908-10.
44. Lindley to Simon, 26 May 1932, F5011/40/23, FO371/16243.
45. Shigemitsu Mamoru, *Showa no Dōran* Vol.1 (Tokyo, 1952), p.75. It is interesting to note, however, that Captain John Vivian, the British naval attaché in Tokyo, thought that Shigemitsu 'must be a super-optimist' when the latter '. . . deplored the fact that the navy had become extremely vocal in political matters. . . [and said] "this has got to be changed in the army and the navy, and the new Government intends to alter the psychology of the services, and very quickly, too"'. Minutes by Vivian, 13 Feb., 1936, F1487/204/23, FO371/20282.
46. Clive to FO, 31 Dec. 1935, F891/204/23, FO371/20282. Regarding Saitō himself, he continued that 'I cannot but admire his dignity and his devotion to the public service of his country in consenting to emerge once more, at the age of 78, to assume the important duties of Lord Keeper of the Privy Seal.'
47. J. Grew, *Ten Years in Japan* (New York: Simon and Schuster, 1944), pp.171–4. The film was 'Naughty Marietta' by Victor Herbert.

Chapter 18 KEIKO ITOH *Hisaakira Kanō (1886-1963): International Banker from a Daimyo Family*

1. The names of Japanese persons in this article will be the first name followed by family name for those who were known as such internationally, but for those who were known only in a Japanese context are mentioned with family name first, in the Japanese manner.
2. Kano Hisaakira, 'Memories of Assignments Abroad', Shokin-jin (internal YSB newsletter), last edition 1947
3. *Nichiei Shinshi*, December 1922.
4. *Nichiei Shinshi*, June 1923.
5. Sheldon Garon, *The State and Labor in Modern Japan*, (Berkeley and Los Angeles: University of California Press, 1987).
6. 'Tales from My Life in London', an interview with Kano Hisaakira in *Shokin-jin*, 1947.
7. Ibid.

8.   Osono Junya *Kagoshima no Kangyō Chiji: Kanō Hisayoshi Shōden* (Kagoshima's Industrial Governor: A Short Biography of Kanō Hisayoshi), (Kagoshima: Shunendō Shōten, 1979).
9.   Hisaakira's younger son, Hisanori, recalls in his autobiography (see footnote below) that the family '. . . move from Tokyo to Kagoshima was rather grand, just by the number of people travelling: apart from my parents, there were grandmother, two older sisters, my brother, four younger sisters, two wet nurses, one babysitter, and a male helper'.
10.   Kanō Hisanori, '*Zaibei Doho no Hitori toshite*' (As a Member of Japanese Compatriots in America), unpublished autobiography, 1976.
11.   Gotō Masao, *Gotō Haruko* (Haruko was one of Hisaakira's younger sisters who married Gotō Fumio, Minister of Agriculture and Home Minister in the 1930s), unpublished memoirs, 1984.
12.   The four younger Kanō daughters were made to wear the 'Kanō improved dress' not only to school, but on other occasions as well, and according to family stories, they absolutely hated it.
13.   Sheldon Garon, *Molding Japanese Minds: The State in Everyday Life*, (Princeton: Princeton University Press, 1997), pp.98–100.
14.   Interview with Nakamura Hisatsugu, second son of Hisaakira and Tatsuko. August 1998.
15.   Robert N. Bellah, *Tokugawa Religion: The Values of Pre-Industrial Japan*, (Boston: Beacon Press, 1957).
16.   In the event, before reaching Alcock's bedroom (Alcock, in fact, was not even there as he was in Britain on home leave), Gunbei was discovered by two British sailors on guard, and after a scuffle, killed both of them with his sword and fled. The *jōi* movement, although in itself was limited to a segment of the samurai and other classes and was based ultimately on unrealistic beliefs, was nevertheless one of the major strands of thought and action that led eventually to the Meiji Restoration of 1868. Its advocates were against the Tokugawa Bakufu for opening up Japan's trade to Western powers under unequal treaties that gave them extra-territoriality and the right to set their own tariffs. The foreign merchants who came to the treaty ports moreover, behaved badly and arrogantly. Their commercial methods and their lifestyle were reprehensible to many of the Japanese who had any contact with them and added to the anti-foreign sentiment held by the *jōi* advocates. (Source: Itō Tadao, *Bakusei, Matsumoto Han to Sonjō no Ugoki* (Bakufu Policy, Matsumoto Han and the Sonjo Movement), private print,1990)
17.   Hisanori Kanō, 'Zaibei Doho'.
18.   Interview with Rosa Hideko Itoh, née Kanō, May 1995.
19.   Interview with Mr. Shigeo Horie, 1991.
20.   *Transactions and Proceedings of the Japan Society*, London. Vol.XXXIV, 1936-7.
21.   Anthony Best, 'Can Anything be Done?: The Role of Private Initiatives in Anglo-Japanese Relations 1939-1941', *Japan Society Proceedings* 122, Autumn 1993.
22.   Horie Shigeo, 'Yoshida-san no Omoide' in *Ningen: Yoshida Shigeru*, ed. Yoshida Shigeru Kinen Jigyo-dan, (Tokyo: Chūōkorōn, 1991).
23.   Hisaakira Kano, *My London Records*, private print, Tokyo 1956.
24.   Hisaakira Kano, *My London Records*, private print, Tokyo 1956.
25.   Home Office records. Still classified when I was given access in spring 1998, but were due to become public in the PRO.

Chapter 19 ANTONY BEST *'That Loyal British Subject'?: Arthur Edwardes and Anglo-Japanese Relations, 1932-41*

The author would like to acknowledge the kindness of the Master and Fellows of Trinity College, Cambridge for permission to quote from the Butler Papers, and the Foreign and Commonwealth Office for permission to quote from Cadogan diaries.

1.   PRO FO371/13904 F910/52/10 Wellesley minute 11 March 1929.
2.   M. Atkins, *Informal Empire in Crisis: British Diplomacy and the Chinese Customs Succession, 1927-1929*, (Ithaca: Cornell East Asia Series, 1995) p.43.
3.   Atkins, op.cit. pp.34-7.
4.   On Edwardes's resignation see Atkins, op.cit. pp.73-91.
5.   PRO FO371/14744 F5750/4256/10 Lampson (Nanking) to Henderson 19 September 1930 no. 139, and F6328/4256/10 Edwardes to Wellesley 5 November 1930. The eventual outcome of this edifying contest of wills is unclear as the file for 1931 has been destroyed.
6.   For Japanese support of Edwardes see Atkins, op.cit. p.38 and p.63.
7.   Y. Watanabe & T. Itō (eds.), *Shigemitsu Mamoru Shuki* [Shigemitsu Memoirs] Vol.1 (Tokyo: Chūō Korōnsha, 1993) pp.22-3.
8.   PRO FO371/17140 F5534/5125/10 Gascoigne (Tokyo) memorandum 20 May 1933.
9.   PRO FO371/17085 F1038/52/10 Maze (CMC) to Ingram (Peking) 7 December 1932.
10.   R. Street diary entry 17 March 1933 in M. Dupree (ed.), *Lancashire and Whitehall: The Diary*

of Sir Raymond Street, Vol.1, 1931-39, (Manchester: Manchester University Press, 1987) pp.221-2.
11. For Maze see PRO FO371/17085 F1038/52/10 Ingram to Wellesley (FO) 28 December 1932, for Crowe see PRO FO371/17111 F1997/445/10 Crowe (DOT) minute 24 March 1933.
12. PRO FO371/17112 F4531/445/10 Lampson (Peking) to Crowe 15 May 1933.
13. PRO FO371/17112 F5850/445/10 Lampson to Crowe 7 November 1933.
14. For the intelligence material see, for example, PRO HW12/165 BJ.051580 Tokyo to Hsinking 1 March decrypted 4 March 1933. On the press coverage see FO371/17140 F5125/5125/10 Snow (Tokyo) to Simon 2 August 1933 tel.219.
15. PRO FO371/17140 F5534/5125/10 Gascoigne (Tokyo) memorandum 14 July 1933.
16. PRO FO371/17112 F5850/445/10 Randall (FE Dept) to Crowe 7 September 1933.
17. Gwynne to Edwardes 26 February 1934, and Gwynne to Edwardes 20 March 1934 in Gwynne Papers, Bodleian Library, Oxford, MS Gwynne 18.
18. N. Chamberlain diary entry 20 April 1934 in Chamberlain Papers, Birmingham University Library, NC2/23a.
19. Saionji/Harada diary, entry for 15 October 1934 (State Department, Washington, 1977) pp.1025-6. See also S. Hatano, 'Yoshida junetsushi no shuhen' [Ambassador Yoshida's Tour of the Periphery] *Ningen Yoshida Shigeru* [Yoshida Shigeru: The Man] (Tokyo: Chūō Korōnsha, 1991) pp.318-9.
20. PRO T172/1831 Edwardes to Fisher 26 November 1934.
21. See G. Bennett, 'British Policy in the Far East 1933-1936: Treasury and Foreign Office', *Modern Asian Studies,* 1992, Vol.26, No.3, pp.556-60.
22. Hatano, op.cit. pp.321-2.
23. PRO T172/1831 Edwardes memorandum 14 January 1935.
24. Y Watanabe & T. Itō, op.cit. p.26.
25. See I. Nish, 'Anglo-Japanese Alienation Revisited', in S. Dockrill (ed.), *From Pearl Harbor to Hiroshima: The Second World War in Asia and the South Pacific, 1941-45,* (Basingstoke: Macmillan, 1994) pp.19-22.
26. C. Hosoya, 'Britain and the United States in Japan's View of the International System, 1919-1937' in I. Nish (ed.), *Anglo-Japanese Alienation, 1919-1952,* (Cambridge: Cambridge University Press, 1982) p.22.
27. PRO T160/1198 F15140/1 Leith-Ross to Waley 14 May 1937.
28. M. Kennedy diary entries for 21 January and 3 March 1936 in Malcolm Kennedy Papers, Sheffield University Library, Diary 4/30.
29. Edwardes to Amau 10 January 1938 in Amau Papers, National Diet Library, Tokyo, Letter no.850.
30. Edwardes to Amau 29 December 1937, Amau Papers, Letter no.848.
31. PRO FO371/23424 F0862/24/10 Bernard (Jardine Matheson) to Howe (FE Dept) 26 July 1939, and Dening (FE Dept) minute 3 August 1939.
32. Y Watanabe & T. Itō, op.cit. p.27.
33. PRO FO371/23532 F9583/6457/10 Butler minute 26 August 1939.
34. PRO FO371/23536 F9061/176/23 Halifax/Shigemitsu talk 28 August 1939, and PRO FO371/23532 F9630/6457/10 Butler/Shigemitsu talk 29 August 1939.
35. PRO FO371/23556 F10459/176/23 'General Attitude Towards Anglo-Japanese Relations' Edwardes memorandum 22 September 1939.
36. Ibid, Dening minute 28 September 1939.
37. Edwardes to Butler 4 July and 24 July 1940, in Butler Papers, Trinity College Library, Cambridge, RAB E3/5[33] and RAB E3/5[36].
38. Edwardes to Butler 31 July 1940, Butler Papers, RAB E3/5[39].
39. Edwardes to Piggott 17 June 1940, in Piggott Papers, Imperial War Museum, London.
40. Edwardes to Butler 2 September 1940, Butler Papers, RAB E3/5[42].
41. PRO FO371/24725 F3592/23/23 Dening minute 8 August 1940.
42. Butler minute for Sterndale Bennett 6 September 1940, Butler Papers, RAB E3/5[46].
43. Cadogan diary entry 22 February 1941, in Cadogan Papers, Churchill College, Cambridge, ACAD1/10.
44. Cadogan diary entry 8 October 1941, Cadogan Papers, ACAD1/10.
45. Churchill to Eden 13 September 1941, in Avon Papers, Birmingham University Library, AP20/8/548.
46. PRO PREM3 252/5 Eden to Churchill 17 September 1941 PM/41/110, and Swinton to Churchill 24 September 1941.
47. PRO PREM3 252/5 Swinton to Churchill 24 September 1941. On the Sempill case see *The Independent* 24 August 1998 p.6.
48. Record Management Services, Home Office to the author 3 August 1998.
49. M.Shigemitsu, *Gaikō Kaisoroku* [Diplomatic Memoirs] (Tokyo: Mainichi Shimbun, 1978) pp.190-3.

Chapter 20 EDNA READ NEAL *Takayuki Eguchi*

Further reading

Connery Chappell	*Island of Barbed Wire* (London: Robert Hale, 1984)
Sadao Oba	*The Japanese Community in Britain 1870-1945*
Richard Storry	*A History of Modern Japan* (Harmondsworth: Penguin Books, 1960, 1990)
Mine Toshirō	*Indo no Koku-netsu Sabaku ni Nipponjin Shuyojo ga atta*

Winifred Thompson Eguchi

Her life was a switchback of wealth and poverty. Winifred struggled through the war without an income, raising rabbits, chickens and vegetables and sewing to earn money. Her endurance and achievements earned the greatest respect and affection from her many friends. She enjoyed gardening, reading and travelling, and in her seventies wrote her autobiography, 180 pages of closely typed foolscap. Winifred lived a full life for ninety-two years and died in 1994.

Edna Read Neal

Well known for her work over twenty years, promoting the work of artists in the new city of Milton Keynes. Fellow of The Royal Society of Arts, member of the Board of the Milton Keynes Theatre and Gallery and director of the art consultancy, Edna Read and Associates, Edna has two artist daughters and three grandchildren. In 1992, she married Dr David Neal, an archaeologist specializing in villa excavation and Roman mosaics.

She has spent the last three years researching the lives of her parents and the resulting text entitled 'Loving and Loathing' has just been completed.

Most rewarding for her has been the reunion and reconciliation of the English and Japanese members of the family. The close relationship which has developed with her stepsister, Takako, and her family being a great mutual happiness.

Chapter 21 NEIL PEDLAR *John Morris, George Orwell, the BBC and Wartime Japan*

1. *The Phoenix Cup: Some notes on Japan in 1946* (London: Cresset Press 1947) (TPC) p.21.
2. *Traveller from Tokyo*, (London: Cresset Press 1943) (*TFT*) p.12.
3. *Who's Who* 1984.
4. *TFT* p.10.
5. Quoted in Morris' *TFT*. p.20. Source not quoted.
6. *TFT* p.22
7. *TFT* p.51
8. *TFT* p.53 – Morris' source of information not quoted. Possibly from unrecorded accurate hearsay, for Americans used to swear 'allegiance to the flag' daily in every school, and Britons sing the National anthem frequently. But no minions are reported to have 'topped' themselves for a failure in performing such mythical ceremonies.
9. *TFT* p.42
10. A. Howard & E. Newman *The Menacing Rise of Japan – Ninety Years of Crafty Statesmanship In Pictures* (London: Harrap, 1943). Picture 163.
11. This writer's conversation with Japanese friends in 1975 who were attending school then.
12. *TFT* pp. 121 & 122.
13. *TFT* pp.102-106.
14. *TFT* p.125.
15. *TFT* pp.126-130.
16. *TFT* p.136.
17. *TFT* p151.
18. John Morris, *Hired to Kill* (London: Rupert Hart-Davis & the Cresset Press 1960) p.11.
19. Bernard Crick, *George Orwell – A Life* (London: Secker & Warburg 1980) p.285.
20. *The World of George Orwell*, ed. by Miriam Gross, (London: Wiedenfeld and Nicholson, 1971), 'Orwell at the BBC' by William Empson, p.95.
21. *Penguin New Writing* No. 40, Sept. 1950. 'Some Are More Equal Than Others' by John Morris.
22. J.R. Hammond, *A George Orwell Companion: A guide to the novels, documentaries and essays* (London: Macmillan, 1982), p.169.
23. George Orwell, *Ninety Eighty-Four* (1949) The Authoritative Text, (Harmondsworth: Penguin, 1987), p.34. Hereafter '1984'.
24. '1984' pp.221-222.
25. *TFT* p.160.
26. B.H. Chamberlain *The Invention of a New Religion* (London: Issued for the Rationalist Press Association), Watts & Co. 1912. (*INR*.)

27. Yuzo Ota, *Basil Hall Chamberlain – Portrait of a Japanologist* (Richmond, Surrey: Japan Library 1998), pp.67-68.
28. *INR*. p.9.
29. *INR*. p.13.
30. *INR*. p.17.
31. '1984' p.47.
32. '1984' p.38.
33. '1984' pp.26-27.
34. '1984' p.63.
35. '1984' p.311.
36. *INR* pp.26-27.
37. Satoshi Kamata, *Japan in the Passing Lane* (JPL) (New York: Pantheon Books, 1982), p.9.
38. *JPL* p.87.
39. *JPL* pp.xi-xii.
40. *TPC* p.ix.
41. *TPC* p.59.
42. *TPC* pp.140-143.
43. *TPC* pp.146-157.
44. *TPC* p.185.
45. Written Autumn 1942: *The Collected Essays, Journalism & Letters of George Orwell*, (Harmondsworth: Penguin, 1970) II p.305.

Chapter 23 PHILLIDA PURVIS *Kazuko Aso, DBE, 1915-96*

1. Yuki Yoshida, *Whispering Leaves in Grosvenor Square, 1936-1937*, (London: Longmans, Green and Co., 1938 and Folkestone, Kent: Oriental Global, 1997).
2. Masako Shirasu, *Yuugawo*, Chapter entitled 'Yoshida Kenichi no koto'
3. Shigeru Yoshida, *Memoirs*, (London: Heinemann, 1962).
4. Yoshida, *Memoirs*
5. Kazuko Yoshida, 'The Japanese Woman' in Japan Society of London, *Transactions and Proceedings*, XXXV (1937-8)
6-11. *Whispering Leaves*
12. Kazuko Yoshida, 'The Japanese Woman'
13. Introduction to *Whispering Leaves*, 'Historical Setting: The Yoshidas in Grosvenor Square' by Ian Nish
14. Kazuko Aso, *Chichi: Yoshida Shigeru*, (Tokyo: Kobunsha, 1993)
15. Yoshida, *Memoirs*
16. Yoshida, *Memoirs*
17-20. Kazuko Aso, *Chichi, Yoshida Shigeru*
21. Yoshida, *Memoirs*

Chapter 24 SIR HUGH CORTAZZI *Sir John Pilcher GCMG (1912-90)*

Note: I am indebted to Delia Pilcher and other friends for information about John Pilcher. I am also grateful to the Foreign Office for allowing me to see some of his despatches and to quote from them.

Chapter 25 SIR HUGH CORTAZZI *Ariyoshi Yoshiya, KBE (Hon) (1901-82)*

Note: The quotations from Ariyoshi are selected from his book *Half a century of Shipping*, (Tokyo: Tokyo News Service Ltd., 1977), from his little collection of essays entitled *Kangaroo, Crocodile and Rabbit Hutch* (undated and privately printed) and from the essays which he contributed from time to time To *Shipping and Trade News* under the general title of 'My Eyes, Ears and Pen'. I have not found space to quote from his interesting essay (undated and privately printed), entitled 'The Historical Position of Women in Japanese Society' Nor have I been able to include any extracts from his speech to the Tokyo Club on 23 March 1970 entitled 'The Shipping and the Kenban' which covers aspects of the entertainment trade in Japan. Quotations from Sir John Nicholson and Sir Kerry St Johnston are takem from their contributions to Ariyoshi's official obituary published by NYK and from comments made to me by Sir Kerry St Johnston.

Chapter 26 DANIEL GALLIMORE *Ninagawa Yukio (b 1935)*

I would like to record my special thanks to Yukio Ninagawa for my interview with him, to Thelma Holt for the original inspiration, and to Misa Hayashi of Point Tokyo for assistance with research materials. Thanks are also due to Sweetpea Slight, Holly Kendrick, Brian Powell and to my wife Misako.

BIBLIOGRAPHY

Barnes, Peter, 'Working with Yukio Ninagawa', *New Theatre Quarterly*, 8: 32 (November 1992), pp. 389-91
Billington, Michael, 'Noh Way', *The Guardian*, 28.11.92, pp. 25-7
Cook, Christopher, 'Oedipal odyssey to the house that Ninagawa built', *Insight Japan*, pp. 42-3
Goodman, David G, *Japanese Drama and Culture in the 1960s: The Return of the Gods* (Armonk, N.Y: ME Sharpe Inc, 1988)
In Contact With the Gods? Directors talk theatre, ed Maria M Delgado & Paul Heritage (Manchester: Manchester University Press, 1996)
Japan Information and Cultural Centre (Embassy of Japan, London), 'Directing a Dream', *Japan*, 1.10.96, p. 3
Japan Information and Cultural Centre, *Japan*, 'Rehearsing with Ninagawa', 4.3.97, p. 2
King, Robert L, 'Edinburgh and the Idea of a Festival', *Massachusetts Review*, 33: 2 (Summer 1992), pp. 305-12
Miyashita Nobuo, 'Yukio Ninagawa, Theatrical Pacesetter', *Japan Quarterly*, 34: 4 (October-December 1987), pp. 400-4
Nihon no Sheikusupia 100-nen ('A hundred years of Shakespeare in Japan'), ed Anzai Tetsuo (Tokyo: Aratake Shuppan, 1989)
Ninagawa Yukio, *BGM anata wa makase* ('You take care of the background music') (Tokyo: Sankei Shuppan, 1982)
Ninagawa Yukio, *Ninagawa Yukio no kozure ookami densetsu* ('Yukio Ninagawa's tale of the wolf and the child') (Tokyo: Koike Shōin, 1998)
Ninagawa Yukio, *Note 1969-1988* (Tokyo: Kawade Shōbo, 1989)
Ninagawa Yukio, *Sen no naifu, sen no me* ('A thousand knives, a thousand eyes eyes') (Tokyo: Kinokuniya Shōten, 1993)
Richie, Donald, *The Films of Akira Kurosawa* (Berkeley, Calif: University of California Press, 1965)
Senda Akihiko, *The Voyage of Contemporary Japanese Theatre*, tr J Thomas Rimer (Honolulu: University of Hawai'i Press, 1997)
Shakespeare East and West, ed Minoru Fujita & Leonard Pronko (Folkestone, Kent: Japan Library, 1996)
Takahashi Yasunari, '*Hamlet* and the Anxiety of Modern Japan', *Shakespeare Survey 48: Shakespeare and Cultural Exchange* (Cambridge University Press, 1995), pp. 99-111
Theater Japan (Tokyo: The Japan Foundation, 1993)

1.   *Nihon no Sheikusupia 100-nen*, pp. 7-9. Fukuda was also the first major translator of Shakespeare to use contemporary Japanese.
2.   Stated in an interview with the present writer held at the Barbican on 29 August, 1998.
3.   Ninagawa (1993), pp. 202-4.
4.   In an interview with Nobuo Miyashita, Ninagawa said of his birthplace: 'The laborers came from all over Japan; the town of Kawaguchi itself gave the impression of a sort of human slag heap. Scenes of masses of people were burned into my memory from childhood. Maybe what I'm trying to do on the stage is recreate those images.'
5.   Ninagawa (1993), pp. 195-6. Kaisei was then and is still now one of the most prestigious public high schools in Japan, with several students passing each year on to the top universities in Japan. The education there can be expected to have given Ninagawa a thorough grounding in the reading of both English and classical Japanese.
6.   Ibid, p. 147.
7.   Ibid, p. 13.
8.   Ibid, p. 14.
9.   'Rehearsing with Ninagawa', *Japan*, 4.3.97. The two interns were named Sean Jones and David Royland.
10. See the Introduction to Goodman and the Translator's Introduction and Prologue for discussions of this period. Ninagawa and his peers were reacting as much against the hierarchy of the *shingeki* companies as against their comfortable ideologies. These companies had become like the classical theatre in promoting those with seniority and connections above the young and

inexperienced. It was difficult for the latter to get anything but small parts.

11. For Ninagawa, nihilistic feelings may have been as much personal as political. The death of his elder brother definitely led him to ask the question why. Ninagawa (1993), p. 198.

12. One of Ninagawa's first productions with the Ninagawa Studio (1984) was a *shingeki* favourite, Chekhov's *The Three Sisters*.

13. Even today, there is no kind of government subsidy in Japan for either the commercial, the small theatre nor any of the other specialist theatres.

14. They appeared in the foyer as the audience were coming out after the performance.

15. See Ninagawa (1989), pp. 10-23, for blocking plans, photographs and production notes of *Shinjo ni afururu keihakusa*.

16. Ironically, the only actor with any hint of classical training was a Japanese-Korean *kyōgen* actor called Haruhiko Jo who played . . . Malvolio.

17. See the essay by Robert L King for a full review of this production.

18. This production also went to Plymouth and Newcastle.

19. Ninagawa's British tours are produced in cooperation with Thelma Holt Limited.

20. Stated in interview with present writer.

21. Quoted in recent newspaper interview. Source unidentified.

22. In an interview with Michael Billington in 1992, Ninagawa said that 'Whether I was doing classics or new plays, I felt I wasn't catching the mood of the present. My talent was diminishing, I was copying myself, repeating old models. If *The Tempest* hadn't worked, I would simply have stopped directing. Perhaps the reason that it came off is that I put myself with Prospero.' Billington, p. 25.

23. 'Directing a Dream', *Japan*, 1.10.96.

24. *Theater Japan*, pp. 84-5 & 276-7.

25. See Richie, pp. 115-24, for a full analysis of this film.

26. *Macbeth*, V.v.28.

27. Just as Shimizu and Kara (not to mention his youthful actors) connect Ninagawa with contemporary culture, the Meiji-born Akimoto connects him with the classics. She is one of the few living playwrights capable of writing in the classical style and yet also received a thorough grounding in the *shingeki*.

28. They might also be said to exude a dim but distinctive warmth since for the last fifteen minutes of the Ninagawa production, the stage was overcome by an artificial snowstorm and the two lovers killed themselves in the snow.

29. *In Contact With The Gods?*, p. 197.

30. In Act I of the Ninagawa production, all references to Athens were in fact cut.

31. See Senda for reviews by a Japanese drama critic of this and most of Ninagawa's other other major productions over the last thirty years.

32. In *Sen no naifu, sen no me*, Ninagawa comes out with the very Tokyoite remark that 'I really feel as if everything [in my career] has begun and ended in a coffee shop.' Ninagawa (1993), p. 220.

33. Miyashita, p. 404.

34. See, for example, his story 'Patriotism' in *Death in Midsummer and Other Stories* (Tokyo and Rutland Vt: Tuttle, 1987). Ninagawa himself is not immune to the Mishima phenomenon since in 1975 he directed two of Mishima's modern noh dramas, *Sotoba komachi* ('The Beautiful Lady of Stupa') and *Yoroboshi* ('Yoroboshi'). The production was revived in 1990. Michael Billingon has called Ninagawa 'an artist with a poetic sensitivity towards change and decay' (Billington, p 27) although it has to be added that Ninagawa's productions seldom indulge in decay for its own sake. I believe his vision to be ultimately an optimistic one.

35. From Director's Note to Programme for his production of *Twelfth Night* at the Sai no kuni Saitama Arts Theatre (October 1998). After *Romeo and Juliet*, this is the second in the series of the Complete Works to be directed there.

Chapter 27 ALISON NISH *Britain's Contribution to the Development of Rugby Football in Japan 1874-1998*

1. *Japan Yearbook 1933*

2. Kayama and Ikeguchi, *Kindai Ragubi 100 nen* (Tokyo: 1960), pp. 132-3

3. S. Kayama, *Nihon Ragubi Shi* (Tokyo: Ragubi Kyokai, 1966), pp. 1-13

4. Letter written by Clarke to Keiō University in 1931, *Nihon Ragubi Shi* p.6

5. E.B. Clarke, *Stray Leaves: Essays and Sketches* (Tokyo: Kenkyusha, 1936)

6. Ibid

7. Ibid

8. Kayama and Ikeguchi, op. cit., p.14

9. Kayama and Ikeguchi, op. cit., p.8
10. *Diaries of Lord Davies of Llandinam*, quoted in a lecture to Japan Society by David Steeds to whom I am grateful.
11. Kayama and Ikeguchi, op. cit, p.144
12. Ibid, p.215 Kayama, who was an official at the games, was in charge of explaining rugby to the Prince who often asked Kayama to accompany him to rugby thereafter
13. A.C. Douglas, *Life of Admiral Sir A.L. Douglas* (Totnes: Mortimer, 1938), pp. 58, 65
14. E M Kellock, 'Admiral Sir A Douglas – His Naval and Diplomatic Career', MSS
15. C. Bullock, *Etajima. The Dartmouth of Japan* (London: Sampson Lowe (1942), pp. 32–4
16. Ibid, p.33
17. Kayama and Ikeguchi, op. cit. Poem entitled 'Up,up' by Edmund Blunden
18. Ibid, p.216
19. Ibid, p.217
20. Princess Chichibu, *The Silver Drum* (Folkestone: Global Oriental, 1996), p.131
21. Manshu Ragubi, *Ragubi benran* (Dairen: Manshu ragubi Kyokai 1935)
22. *Keiō Gijuku taiiku nempyo*
23. Shukyu Kyokai, eds., *Kindai Nihon ragubi*
24. Ikeguchi and Kayama, op. cit., pp. 206-7
25. *Bulletin of the Japan Society of London*, (June 1953) No 10, pp. 17-20
26. *Bulletin of the Japan Society of London* (February 1953) No 9, p.5
27. *Bulletin of the Japan Society of London* (June 1953) No 10, p.19
28. Princess Chichibu, op. cit., p.183
29. *Bulletin of the Japan Society of London* (1954) No. 13, p.12
30. Ibid, p.13

Index